DIARIES OF THE
CHINESE MARTYRS

DIARIES
OF THE
CHINESE
MARTYRS

Stories of Heroic Catholics
Living in Mao's China

Edited by Gerolamo Fazzini

Preface by Bernardo Cervellera

Translated by Charlotte J. Fasi

SOPHIA INSTITUTE PRESS
Manchester, New Hampshire

Sophia Institute Press
Box 5284, Manchester, NH 03108
1-800-888-9344

www.SophiaInstitute.com

Sophia Institute Press® is a registered trademark of Sophia Institute.

Library of Congress Cataloging-in-Publication Data

Names: Fazzini, Gerolamo, editor. | Cervellera, Bernardo, writer of
    preface. | Fasi, Charlotte J., translator.
Title: Diaries of the Chinese martyrs : stories of heroic Catholics living in
    Mao's China / edited by Gerolamo Fazzini ; preface by Bernardo Cervellera
    ; translated by Charlotte J. Fasi.
Other titles: In catene per Cristo. English
Description: Manchester, New Hampshire : Sophia Institute Press, 2016. |
    "Published in 2015 by Editrice Missionaria Italiana (EMI), Bologna, Italy,
    under the title In Catene per Cristo." | Includes bibliographical
    references.
Identifiers: LCCN 2016000044 | ISBN 9781622823215 (pbk. : alk. paper)
Subjects: LCSH: Christian martyrs—China—Biography.
Classification: LCC BR1608.C6 I613 2016 | DDC 272/.90951—dc23 LC record available at
http://lccn.loc.gov/2016000044

First printing

To
the Holy Guardian Angels
and to
my brother, Joseph Paul Fasi

– C.J.F

I want you to know, brethren, that what has happened to me has really served to advance the gospel, so that it has become known throughout the whole praetorian guard and to all the rest that my imprisonment is for Christ; and most of the brethren have been made confident in the Lord because of my imprisonment, and are much more bold to speak the word of God without fear.

Some indeed preach Christ from envy and rivalry, but others from good will. The latter do it out of love, knowing that I am put here for the defense of the gospel; the former proclaim Christ out of partisanship, not sincerely but thinking to afflict me in my imprisonment. What then? Only that in every way, whether in pretense or in truth, Christ is proclaimed; and in that I rejoice.... For to me to live is Christ, and to die is gain.

—Philippians 1:12–18, 21

CONTENTS

PREFACE

Never, as in these times, as Pope Francis has often emphasized, have so many martyrs been "killed throughout the world solely because they are Christians."

During Holy Week of 2015 the pope did not miss an opportunity to recall this drama, which is linked to Jesus Christ under the Cross. He began Palm Sunday recalling "Christ's way": the humiliation of the Passion as lived by all those who are persecuted because of their faith. "Let us also think of those who through their faithful adherence to the Gospel are paying personally for their beliefs. And let us think of our brothers and sisters who are persecuted because they are Christian; they are today's martyrs. They do not deny Jesus; rather, they bear insults and outrages with dignity, following him on his way: 'We can speak of clouds [multitudes] of witnesses'" (cf. Heb. 12:1).

Francis concluded his Easter Monday Regina Caeli address—after five other appeals to catechesis, Masses, and messages—with a decisive jolt to the international community: that it "not remain mute and inert" before all the "unacceptable crimes" toward "our brothers and sisters, persecuted, exiled, killed and decapitated solely because they are Christian." Such a crime, he continued, "constitutes a worrisome disappearance of the most elementary human rights." Departing from his prepared remarks, he then repeated: "I truly wish that the international community will not turn away from this problem."

On March 15, giving precedence to the topic after the attack on two churches in Lahore, in Pakistan, Francis had said: "Christians are being persecuted. Our brothers and sisters are spilling blood solely because they are Christian." And he invited all the faithful to pray so that "this persecution against Christians, which the world is ignoring, will end."

There is, then, a diffuse Christian persecution that the world is trying to hide and will not look in the face.

In the days approaching Easter, only a few press organizations reported some evidence of this evil abyss with all its horror. There were also reports of massacres of Christians in Kenya, Syria, Iraq, and Libya, where our brothers and sisters are killed by haughty Islamist militiamen for their adherence to the faith. But the majority of the reporting does not go beyond the persecutions in the Muslim world. No one has ever cited the persecutions of the Chinese Catholics and Protestants.

Just one week before Easter, two priests of Harbin (a province of Heilongjiang) were abducted by the police. Father Quan Shaoyun, forty-one years old, and Father Cao Jianyou, forty-three years old, had just celebrated Mass when a group of police arrested them and carried them away to an unknown place. Both were part of a Catholic "underground" community not recognized by the government. Their crime was having celebrated Mass in a place not registered with the Ministry of Religious Affairs. For this they were treated like dangerous criminals. Sometime before, at the end of January 2015, a notice circulated reporting the death of the bishop Cosma Shi Enxiangdi Yixian (Hebei) at the age of ninety-four. He had spent fifty of those ninety-four years in prison for not wishing to break his ties with the pope. The Chinese government refused to give the body or his ashes to his family and even claimed publicly that the cause of the bishop's death was probably drunkenness.

In March 2015, Huang Yizi, a Protestant pastor of Wenzhou (Zhejiang) was condemned for having attempted to stop the demolition of a church. For months in the province of Zhejiang there was an active campaign to destroy crosses and sacred buildings, guilty of "ruining views of the skyline." Thus, some four hundred crosses and the same number of bell towers, along with a number of churches, were destroyed. The Protestant and the Catholic faithful accused the local government of wishing to suffocate the growth of the Christian communities that were so vibrant in that region.

Preface

Unfortunately, few in the mass media truly wish to report this news. Rather, they gag themselves, preferring to burn incense to the giant Chinese economy, so useful in times of crisis.

In the Western mentality there exists a false impression: since China changed her economic system (from communist to liberal to anarchy), everything changed. As a result, currently, China is a place of splendid well-being and tranquil religious liberty.

But it is not. Besides the misery of the countryside and their migrant enslaved workers, there are also in China those who suffer and those who are imprisoned because of their faith. The most glaring example is that of Monsignor Thaddeus Ma Daqin, auxiliary bishop of Shanghai. During the celebration of his episcopal consecration, July 7, 2012, Monsignor Ma expressed his desire to resign from his duties carried out up to then for the Patriotic Catholic Association (the party organism that controls the life of the Christian communities) so that he might dedicate all his energies to pastoral activities and evangelization. The afternoon of that same day, he was taken away. He disappeared for some time, and later it was confirmed that he was under house arrest, with limited movement, at the seminary of Sheshan in Shanghai. From the beginning of March 2013, Bishop Ma has been confined to the seminary, deprived of his personal liberty and prevented from exercising his episcopal functions.

Why this emphasis in the preface of a book that speaks of persecutions in the time of Mao Zedong? Above all, it demonstrates that the facts narrated in this book do not belong to the distant past; indeed, they are continuous. Perhaps, at times, they are less cruel, but there is always the same absolute control exercised over the lives of Christians.

The second motive for the publication of these diaries is to overcome the silence of the persecutions in the period of Mao, which have been treated by too few specialists and historians. I think that speaking of such dramatic events in the relatively recent past will help stimulate discussion on the current persecutions. It is worth repeating the adage that those who do not remember history are condemned to repeat it. Therefore, those who hide the persecutions of the past also hide those of the present.

DIARIES OF THE CHINESE MARTYRS

China has great need of facing her past. She must avoid exalting an apparent economic progress while simultaneously refusing to face the human failure of her leaders and their insane ideology.

Diaries of the Chinese Martyrs can give a hand to the truth and to China. Because—and it is also the opinion of diverse historians—if China does not succeed in basing her progress on great spiritual ideals, all her richness risks crumbling. We are not alone in saying it. This has been repeated by authoritative Chinese intellectuals, as, for example, Liu Ping, an academic of the social sciences at Peking, who has analyzed the "Achilles' heel of Chinese strength" in a series of articles published in *AsiaNews* in 2012.

There is, also, a parallel between the sufferings of the martyrs and the vivacity of the Chinese Christian community today: among Catholics there are 150,000 adults baptized each year. Therefore, one cannot be anything but grateful to the testimonies gathered in this book. The blood poured out in beatings, in prisons, and in labor camps has borne witness to a love toward God and toward the Chinese that perhaps no party leader has ever manifested. Furthermore, the tranquil joy of these abridged testimonies has produced an increase in the number of new Christians. Publishing their stories is our expression of gratitude to them and to God.

—Bernardo Cervellera
Missionary of Pime
Director of *AsiaNews*

INTRODUCTION

In the span of half a century, so many books, testimonies, and films have been published on the Shoah, that tragic symbol of the 1900s, that it is difficult, if not impossible, to quantify. Yet, even now—more than seventy years after the Holocaust—new documentaries and unpublished histories are appearing on this topic. Is it something to marvel at? No, not at all: in each story persons of flesh and blood emerge from oblivion to add a detail or nuance to the great fresco of that tragedy.

Something of the kind also serves the Catholic victims of the Maoist revolution, the topic of this book. It is not the first time that diaries and stories have been published to cast light on this immense tragedy. But as we confront the dramatic events that have marked the twentieth century, we must conclude that the story of the Chinese Revolution (and that of the Church in China between the forties and fifties) is nearly unknown in the West. And the little that is known, except for rare exceptions, is confined to the academic and missionary environments. Public opinion, including the most acculturated sectors in the Catholic world, more or less, totally ignores the course of this drama, particularly the extraordinary number of heroic stories that were lived in the course of that long period.

In the case of the Chinese, there is no doubt that there has been a serious problem in accessing sources. The historian Andrea Riccardi who has worked in the archives of the Commission of New Martyrs, has observed that "the number of reports regarding this sorrowful Church history, presented to the Commission, does not approach the sum of those who have lived it." Of the many Chinese Christians we know of, there is scarce news; often there is only a name and a date (at times not even that) or some testimony or imprecise information. Many, of whom there is no trace, have disappeared in the concentration camps from overwork, fatigue, or deportation. Many have died of hunger and exhaustion and in obscure ways through illnesses contracted in the hardest of conditions. Others were dispersed throughout the enormous Chinese territory.

As shall be seen, however, testimonies of intense and dramatic persecutions are not lacking. And it is worth the effort to become familiar with them.

Much Too Long Hidden in Drawers

Among the numerous Catholics who have been imprisoned in China for thirty years or more, there are quite a few who have left their memoirs. Many of these diaries have been kept in drawers for a long period. There were valid motivations: they did not wish to collide with the political authorities, thereby placing our brothers and sisters in the faith in even more danger. However, it is necessary to admit that there was also a kind of reluctance, even on the part of the members of the Church, in pointedly denouncing the persecutions sustained under the Mao regime.... But to continue on this path of silence today would be unpardonable and incomprehensible.... We have a duty to remember, and in particular to remember the martyrs of the twentieth century, all the martyrs, under any regime, and to speak out.

These courageous words written by Cardinal Joseph Zen Zekiun in the preface of *The Red Book of Chinese Martyrs*[1] resound even today. It also condenses the essential motives that are the basis of this present book; perhaps it is even more interesting than its precedent. In fact, *Diaries of the Chinese Martyrs* is a rich collection of autobiographical testimonies from persons

[1] G. Fazzini, *Il libro rosso dei martiri cinesi* (Cinisello, Balsamo: Edizioni San Paolo, 2007), 5–6.

who experienced unspeakable sufferings for their faith by a regime that wished to create a "new man" by blotting out every trace of God.

Strictly speaking, none of the protagonists of what is narrated here could be called a martyr according to the canonical acceptance of the term, since, fortunately, it concerns persons who survived the long and incredible tortures to which they were subjected. But because of the extreme severity of their sufferings and the spiritual intensity that flourishes in their writings, we do not hesitate to call them martyrs, or "witnesses," in reference to the original meaning of the word.

These testimonies that have long been kept in drawers, and, when diffused, have known a very limited circulation, are, for the first time, revealed to all in this current publication. We take the case of the memoirs of Bishop Dominic Tang, pastor of Canton, presented in the pages that follow this introduction. Even an expert such as the Jesuit historian Michel Masson, in a study on Jesuit missionaries in China, writes that Tang and his confreres "after 1949 found themselves immersed to the extreme in the Communist Chinese world, imprisoned elbow to elbow with all the outcasts of the socialist society. During all these years in the laogai [gulag], they wrote nothing."[2]

Many years later these same authors self-censored their own books, having been convinced that the "new times" appeared to be so promising for the Catholic Church that it would have served no purpose to speak of that dark period. In the early sixties, a Chinese Catholic, the brother of a bishop (whose name we do not know), sent to Hong Kong the detailed story of the persecution undergone by the Catholic Church. It was translated into Italian at the beginning of the eighties but never published. Father Piero Gheddo tells us that none of the publishing houses consulted had shown any interest. But what is even more surprising is that, after having learned the news, the author was not at all sorry about it. In fact, he wrote: "Currently, the Chinese society is rapidly changing and the events of the 1950s

---

[2] A. Paolucci and G. Morello, *Ai crinali della storia, Padre Matteo Ricci fra Roma e Pechino* (Torino: Umberto Allemandi, 2009), 47.

have been tossed into the trash can of history.... Therefore, my book, *The True Face of the Church in China* ... is better left unpublished!"[3]

Not in agreement with him was Cardinal Joseph Zen:

> The victims—or perhaps better, the protagonists—of that season of persecution are by now disappearing. Truly there is no motive for continuing to be silent. Indeed, I wish that the young priests and the Chinese faithful would gather from the mouths of the elderly the stories of suffering and martyrdom that have not been recorded and which risk being lost from memory forever. This "gathering from memory," I believe, is one of the services that the young Chinese Catholics can render to our Church in China, to our nation and to all the Church.

In fact, at a distance of more than half a century the observation made by Gaetano Pollio, the author of the first memorial in this volume, a missionary of Pime and bishop of Kaifeng remains true: "Too little is known of the sad martyrdom of the oppressed peoples and that of persecuted Catholics (and not only for China)."

A Simple but Granite Faith

The first fundamental reason for this new editorial initiative is exquisitely spiritual. These pages are of the highest valor, presented as inspiration for meditation and prayer, the fruit of lives lived according to the extreme radicality of the gospel. In their simplicity, and at times in a very dry style, these pages exude faith—a faith put to the test of humiliation, blind violence, and hunger and torture; a faith tempered by the most terrible adversities, but which survives and still shines today, more luminous than ever. Remember the martyrs, their perseverance and their courage; it is a way of strengthening *our* faith, especially in the contemporary cultural context that is marked by what sociologists call a "weak adherence or belonging."

---

[3] See P. Gheddo, *Lettere di cristiani dalla Cina* (Bologna: EMI, 1980), 50-51.

From the beginning of his pontificate, Pope Francis has called on the Church to struggle against the temptation of mediocrity, of a "negotiated" faith. On April 6, 2013, during his customary daily Mass at St. Martha's House, he said: "How goes the Faith? Is it strong? Or is it at times a bit like rose water? Are we courageous like Peter or a little bit tepid?" Peter—the pope observed—does not suppress the Faith; he does not descend into compromises, because "the Faith is nonnegotiable." "There has been in the history of the people of God, this temptation: to cut off a piece of the Faith." But—Francis added—"when we begin to cut the Faith, to negotiate the Faith, selling a little to the one making the best offer, we begin to travel the path of apostasy, of unfaithfulness to the Lord." The pope then continued: "In order to find martyrs it is not necessary to go to the catacombs or to the Coliseum: the martyrs are now living, in so many countries. Today, in the twenty-first century, our Church is a Church of martyrs." And this "gives strength to us, to those of us, who at times, have a faith that is weak."[4]

Celebrating the martyrs keeps us attentive to their memory. Even more, it is a gesture of profound ecclesial solidarity with the churches—particularly, the Chinese Church—that are "sisters in torment" because they are tested by persecution and martyrdom. A Church that wishes to call itself truly Catholic cannot ignore the joys and sorrows of the diverse local churches. It is difficult for us to imagine it, but even today priests and bishops continue to be held in detention in China. For them it is essential to know that, in the spirit of the communion that characterizes the Church, they are not alone, that there are people who pray for them, who know their sufferings, and who are united to the Lord in prayer with them.

In his diary, Monsignor Dominic Tang clearly states that it was precisely this sense of communion that supported him in the long years of forced solitude: "Although I was removed from the external world, I knew that

---

[4] Pope Francis, *La verità è un incontro. Omelie da Santa Marta* (Milano: Rizzoli, 2015), 61.

the Catholics of all the Church, together with the Jesuits, were sustaining me: that my priests and my faithful were praying for me, and that I was not being rejected by the people. And this gave me great spiritual strength."

Unfortunately, today, in spite of living in a "global village" in which technologies permit the speediest global communications, at home in our Western Christian communities, we frequently close ourselves off from the rest of the world, concentrating solely on our own pastoral problems. But Cardinal Zen reminds us that the "confessors and the martyrs of the Church in China belong to the entire Christian community and that it is not only our right but also our duty to publicize their testimonies so that they may nourish the faith of Christians throughout the world."[5]

The system of the Chinese gulag, the *laogai* (reform through labor), has been described in copious detail by Harry Wu, the celebrated activist who since 1995 has found refuge and freedom in the United States and is the author of a successful book [with Carolyn Wakeman] entitled *Bitter Winds, My Years in the Chinese Gulag*. In his text, which is written from the point of view of a Christian who was taught by missionaries, the declaration of horror that prevails in his story is largely that of his own personal Calvary; something that characterizes and unites his story to those you will find in the following pages.[6]

It was faith—a simple, but granite faith—that permitted a generation of Chinese Christians to remain faithful to the gospel and to the Church during those terrible decades of ideological fury, and this simple faith is the basis of the stories presented here. For example, John Liao Shouji writes in *My Life in the Laogai, Diary of a Chinese Catholic*, one of the texts that is part of our book:

[5] Fazzini, *Il libro rosso dei martiri cinesi*, 6.

[6] In 1992 Harry Wu founded and continues to direct the Laogai Research Foundation, which is engaged in monitoring and making known the reality of the laogai, the forced-labor camps in China. Wu was condemned in 1960 to forced labor and, after passing through twelve of the camps, was liberated in 1979. In 1985 he succeeded in reaching the United States, where he continues to live and work.

At the time of my return, in the spring of 1952, there remained to our home only a vegetable garden, which had belonged to my parents (and which was taken away two years later) so that they were literally left with nothing, not even a pair of shoes or other kinds of primary necessities. From then on my family and the entire class of ex-property owners were subjected to every type of privation and mistreatment. My mother told me that both she and my father had often thought of committing suicide, ... but fortunately their Christian faith and their trust in God impeded them from completing such an action.

It is faith — a strong faith in Christ crucified, died, and risen — that motivated Monsignor Tang, bishop of Canton, who spent twenty-two years in prison (and whose memoirs are presented in the second chapter) to write of his own experience of persecution:

> I decided to tell the ... story of all that occurred in the Archdiocese of Canton [Guangzhou] from 1951 to 1981, so that everyone may know ... what happened to me in these years and to take into account the various and difficult situations they stirred up. But the most important thing is to understand and to appreciate how our Heavenly Father has preserved our diocese throughout thousands of dangers and how he affably treated his servant, showering many special graces on him. The understanding of such concepts will certainly be difficult for those who have not had a way of personally experiencing "the depth of the riches and wisdom and knowledge of God!" (Rom. 11:33).

Of course, it is only in the view of the Cross that one can make sense of such extreme and inhuman experiences. Faith generates obedience, and obedience patience, together with the extraordinary willingness to put oneself on the "way of the Cross," exactly like the Master two thousand years ago. Again Bishop Tang: "One day would pass, another begin, and the new day was exactly like the preceding day. Each day and each year were the same as the preceding day and the preceding year. One could say that life was joyless. The only thing that one could truly do was to become intimately united to God, to become inebriated with love for God."

The Objective of the Persecution

The principal reason for the Communist fury toward the Catholic Church's hierarchy and many of the faithful (beginning with the adherents to the Legion of Mary) is to break, at all costs, the ties between the Chinese Catholic Church and the universal Church; the tie that is represented in its supreme form by the pope. This was easier said than done. This attempt to separate the Chinese Catholic Church from the Mother Church also explains the attitude of the different Christian denominations with regard to the Chinese power.

In his diary, Monsignor Pollio very clearly explains that:

The true motive of the persecution was the "reform" that the government wished to impose on us Catholics. In September of 1950 this reform was imposed on all the Protestants of China. There were at the time 162 Protestant denominations sowing their doctrinal errors and generating a true confusion of ideas and obstructing our apostolic work. Solely in my city of Kaifeng there were thirteen Protestant sects. Although the number of foreign Protestant pastors was superior to that of the Catholic missionaries and their financial power a hundred times superior to that of the Catholic Church, Protestantism in China had fewer than two million followers. Then, all the Protestants of China collapsed at the feet of the government, accepting that reform that would have led them to the apostasy of their faith.

According to Pollio:

How could we have adhered to a similar reform, which not only would have rendered us schismatic and heretical, but which would have also brought us a renunciation by Christ [apostasy]? We could not. It was my duty to write to the priests and to all Christians, explaining and preaching, in public and in private, the extremely grave obligation for us to energetically reject the reform and the ecclesiastical jurisdiction. [Fortunately,] no one compromised or wavered over the threefold independence or the reform.

Also, for Monsignor Tang the choice of remaining tied to Rome, to the pope, and to the universal Church was irrevocable: it did not concern a formal question, nor did it go to the essence of the Faith; cost what it cost. Thus, after a good twenty-two years in jail, Tang was called to the last interrogation. Here is how he recalls it:

> "For what regards the Vatican, how do you see it? What do you know of it? What are your sentiments?"
>
> In the depth of my heart I knew that if I did not respond according to their ideas I would not have been able to imagine the consequences. However, I firmly declared: "There is a dogmatic, inseparable tie between the Vatican and us. If we separate from the Vatican, we would no longer be part of the Catholic Church. Without the pope there is no Catholic Church. For the Protestants it is different, because they do not have a pope."
>
> On hearing that, the judge became very stern and replied angrily: "You are not the least bit changed; return to your cell and try to reeducate yourself!"

The Courage of the Laity

Of the four testimonies presented in this volume, only one is the work of a faithful layman. This is due to the fact that, for motives easily perceived, the writings of the priests and bishops had greater possibilities of circulating, both in China and abroad. But it would be a mistake to think that the laity had a marginal part in the battle for the defense of the autonomy of the Catholic Church. Therefore, at this point, it seems opportune that we offer a meritorious homage to all the Catholics and in particular those of

China who distinguished themselves in such a way. Reported here is a most interesting passage from *They Fled from Red China* by Father Leon Chan:

> In jail, at the beginning, they would say to us that only the best among us would be permitted to join the associations of the Christian patriots. Then the insistence became stronger, until, after 1958, there were true moral and physical pressures attempting to force us to declare our separation from Rome.
>
> During the first few years there were many Christians, especially young people, who truly had the courage of lions: They said clearly and firmly that they would have never condemned the pope and the bishops. As a result many of them were incarcerated. When it concerned eliminating foreign missionaries (1951 and 1954) they tried to find Christians among their members who would be disposed to accuse them of imaginary crimes. But although there were many incarcerated and beaten for this reason, rarely did anyone give in, rarely was anyone conquered by his sufferings. At times a written document was already prepared with the accusations. Signing it would liberate the prisoner from all his misery. Yet, also in this, only a very few gave in; the majority ended up with forced labor as a result, or they were dismissed when they had already ruined their health. Only in heaven will we be able to admire the heroism of the many Chinese Christians who were true martyrs for their faith.

In the final story, *My Life in the Laogai*, we have a clear and splendid confirmation of Chinese Christian sacrifice. John Liao Shouji writes:

> Considering my slight health at the beginning of my sentence of some twenty years; the lack of food, the heavy work and the wounds suffered (from which many lost their life), simply being alive and being able to tell my story is, in itself, an extraordinary fact.... But even more miraculous is the fact that I exited such an experience of physical, mental, and moral pressures with my faith intact. Indeed, it was even more deeply rooted in God because of the dangers from

which he preserved me, especially from ceding to the Communists out of weakness or fear. It was not unusual for Catholics to succumb to pressures imposed on them during a succession of purges and persecutions.... I thank God that he did not ever permit me to betray him; I fought the good battle and I maintained the faith.

The Ecumenism of Blood

From the testimonies gathered here there appears to be a clear difference between the attitude of the Catholic Church and the Chinese Protestants toward the so-called liberation. The first (the Catholic Church) substantially maintained her fidelity to the pope, repeatedly opposing the attempts to subject her to the Chinese political power through the Patriotic Association.[7] But the Protestant churches made a different choice, taking a common position that since then has been called the Movement of the Three Autonomies. That takes nothing away from the diverse pastors and the simple faithful who have shared the fate of many Catholics, imprisoned, tried, and, if not put to death, detained for many years. We have a precious example of this "ecumenism of blood" in the diary of Bishop Tang: "Besides prayers and meditations, each day, in a low voice, I sang some hymns: 'Jesus, I live for you; Jesus, I die for you; Jesus, I belong to you. Whether I live or whether I die, I am for Jesus!' This hymn was taught to me by a Protestant detainee who was in the cell with me."

Forgiveness, the Trademark of the Christian Martyr

Faith stirs up the extraordinary capacity to forgive one's own persecutors, which is the authentic "trademark" of Christian martyrdom. It is the

---

[7] The Patriotic Association of Chinese Catholics is the structure placed in action by the authorities to "liberate" the Church from the temptations of the elements considered contrary to the cause of revolution. Reactivated after the Cultural Revolution, even today it enjoys support of the public authority, which makes use of it to control the activities of Catholics.

standard of the Master who on the Cross prayed for the pardon of his executioners "because they did not know what they were doing" (see Luke 23:34). The authors—protagonists—of these diaries also manifest this inclination to forgive. A passage, among so many, from the hand of Monsignor Pollio, affirms it: "In that sorrow, in the midst of so much desperation, I felt closer to God, who instilled in me the strength to bear everything. The words of the Master echoed in my mind: 'If the world hates you, know that it has hated me before it hated you' [John 15:18]. Also: "Pray for those who persecute you." And as I prayed for my persecutors, I felt myself loving them: 'Love your enemies' [Matt. 5:44]."

A Forgotten Story

Besides the spiritual nature of the stories that you have in your hands, there is also a historical character that obliges us to pay particular attention to the testimonies gathered in this book.

For example, there is the contribution offered by Father Leon Chan in his I Fled from Red China, which appeared in the Notebook of the Catholic Missions in 1963. Father Chan, a diocesan priest in Hong Kong, had fled from China in May 1962, after having been imprisoned thirteen years under the Communist regime. In presenting his story to us, Father Gheddi affirms that, at the time, Father Chan's was the first direct witness of the events of that period. Seven years prior to his flight (around 1956), when the last foreign missionary was expelled from China—there was not a single Chinese priest who could testify abroad of the drama of the Church in Chinese at that period. In recognition of the historical value of that text, "an Italian editor" asked Father Chan[8] to write about his experiences so that "his story might be published in a book that would then be presented to the international market." That project was never carried out. Only

---

[8]   As has already been said, it originally concerned an interview that here, for the purpose of uniformity with the other texts, we have transformed into a testimony in the first person.

now, through this work, has that text been brought to the attention of the general public.

Not less interesting is the story related by Monsignor Pollio that opens this volume. As Father Gheddo explained, the expulsion of the Italian bishop from China in 1951 and the subsequent publication of his diary, *Cross of God among the Crossbars: The Story of the Detainee in Cell No. 4*, marked an authentic turn in the perception in Italy (but not only Italy) of the drama of the Church in China of that time:

> From 1949 to 1954, the expulsion of missionaries and missionary nuns from China occurred nearly on a daily basis.... Given the repetition of these happenings the Italian press no longer reacted to them. However, among those four who were expelled October 8, 1951, was a well-known personality, the archbishop of Kaifeng, Monsignor Gaetano Pollio, who in the preceding years had taken a courageous position against the advance of the Communist army in China.... Thus, his expulsion did not pass unnoticed and in the days following his release Italian radio and newspapers reported the news accompanied by photographs and interviews with the archbishop, which were diffused by news agencies that had correspondents in Hong Kong.

In addition: upon Pollio's reentry into Italy—notes Gheddo—Pope Pius XII entrusted him with the mandate to speak of "the Church of silence" in China and, more generally, the Church in all the countries with Communist regimes.

We are, therefore, in the presence of an authoritative witness. One who will change the perception of the real situation of the Church in China. Again Father Gheddo: "Up until 1951 the news of the persecution of the 'Middle Country' was accepted with some indifference by public opinion in Italy and in the West. Even among Catholics there were many voices sympathetic to the Chinese and critical of the missionaries." Burdening the Chinese Catholics was the offensive label "Christians of rice," those who were accused of having bartered faith in exchange for material advantages.

But then, thanks to testimonies like those gathered in this book, those critics were informed that "'the Christians of rice' were the same who were then killed for not renouncing their Faith." Addressing that point Father Gheddo—who had toured around eighty countries and interviewed thousands of bishops and men and women of the Church in every part of the world—was able to write: "I believe that in these modern times no country has had so many authentic Christian martyrs as China!"

A Revisitation (and Demythologization) of Maoism

In brief, the texts we are proposing offer a precious contribution to whoever wishes to know, in deeds, the Chinese business between the forties and the sixties of the last century: those years in which the myth of Mao was established. A myth that, as it happens in these cases has its priests and its liturgies—among which is the principle of self-criticism in public[9]—their established texts, and so on. And precisely because the dominant opinion obscured the critical voices, the critical voices no longer spoke out, or they resorted to self-censure. Once again we cite Cardinal Zen: "For many years Maoism has been exalted beyond the limits of rationality. And those who were not in agreement have not had the courage, or the interior liberty, to speak beyond that ideological chorus, perhaps in order not to be numbered among the reactionaries."

It is only in relatively recent times that, in the West, the figure of Mao[10] and the history of the Chinese Revolution have begun to be reread critically,

---

[9]   It seems that self-criticism has not gone out of fashion. Recently, we learned from *Repubblica* (newspaper) the disturbing news according to which the transmission of the State TV most followed by the Chinese is "Session of Criticism and Self-Criticism."

[10] In 2005 the appearance of the book *Mao, The Unknown Story*—a monumental biography signed by Jung Chang together with her husband, John Halliday, a historian—has thrown a stone in the pond. And Li Zhisui, the personal medical doctor of Mao Ze-dong, published his *Memoirs: The Private Life of Chairman Mao, The Memoirs of Mao's Personal Physician* (New York: Random House, 1994), the most critical book regarding Mao.

thus restoring value to the eyewitness testimony of those missionaries who were consciously silenced for so long.

Stefano Cammelli—in *When the Orient Was Tinted Red*,[11] a dense collection of essays on the Chinese Revolution—goes over the violent historical period from the massacre of the Communists worked by Chiang Kai-shek in 1927 to the foundation of the Chinese Republic in 1949. The thesis of his book, the fruit of twelve years' work, is that the history of the Chinese Revolution, an ideological and mythical adventure that the European left has followed with admiration, had been substantially rewritten. The *j'accuse* of Cammelli resounds unequivocally: the Western historians have ignored the missionary sources, thus depriving themselves of a precious and irreplaceable component.[12] Cammelli affirms, for example, that

> many tortures that the missionary literature has related (the days in prison without anyone explaining what is happening, being forced to sit on the ground for days without being able to lean against a wall, without getting up or lying down, the lack of water, being forced to dispatch one's bodily needs exactly where one is seated and to remain there without the right to get up, et cetera) are the same tortures submitted to by the Communist leaders who survived the purges in Jangxi and Yan'an before the arrival of Mao.[13]

Cammelli then accuses "the community of experts" of having raised a "wall of such high dimensions that even today in many university ambiences" it weighs heavily on "two extremely refined intellectuals," one of

---

[11] Cammelli's work was published by a Polonews paper (Bologna 2013), with the support of the cultural Ticino-Cina Association.

[12] "Deciding to renounce these sources was the most incomprehensible and false choice of all the historiography on the Chinese revolution from the 1950s on," Cammelli writes.

[13] The author cites several passages from an autobiography, *In the Land of Mao Tse'Tung*, by a missionary of Pime, Carlo Suigo, published in 1961; in part it coincides with what was written in Edgar Snow's *Red Star Over China* (Random House, 1944), which contributed to the building of the myth that Chinese Communism was different from that of Russia.

which was the Hungarian Jesuit Laszlo Ladany; for decades Ladany was the soul of the celebrated newsletter *China News Analysis*.[14] The China reality was denounced by Ladany and many others. Father Li Chang, a Chinese priest and author of an interesting autobiographical memoir writes: "The Cultural Revolution had hurled the entire country into total chaos. No one worked anymore. Young and old, without distinction, spent all their time at the 'mass meetings' [sessions of struggle].... One is not straying too far from the truth when one affirms that, in those years, the country had become a giant madhouse."[15] These words that weigh like boulders, are abysmally distant from the enthusiastic description of the Chinese situation offered, for years, by the *maîtres à penser* (masters of thought) at home in the West, still fascinated and infatuated with the Great Helmsman (Mao) and his appalling and risky social experiments.[16]

Also John Liao Shouji, in *My Life in the Laogai*, describes the reduction of emotions and sentiments that life prolonged in prison imposed on the detainees. We have reached a scientific annihilation perversely inflicted on man. It is quite different from the liberation depicted by the Maoist propaganda!

The myth of Mao, it is noted, had begun to take form at the end of the 1930s, thanks to *The Red Star Over China*, a book with strong propagandist tones by the American journalist Edgar Snow, author of a memorable interview with the future Chinese leader. In the 1950s and the 1960s numerous western intellectuals rendered the figure of Mao so popular that

[14] He was ostracized by the experts because he was one of the first to denounce the massive campaign of purgation at the beginning of the 1950s; the first to delineate the political project the Great Leap Forward; the first to understand the immense human tragedy it provoked. Moreover, the Hungarian Jesuit "gathered the dimensions of the vastness of the tragedy of the Cultural Revolution and was among the first to present it as a pure political purgation of the old guard that was no longer faithful to Mao," unpardonable sins in the eyes of those blinded by ideology.

[15] Fazzini, *Il libro rosso dei martiri cinesi*, 151.

[16] G. Fazzini, "For the Maoists of Italy It Is Time for the *Mea Culpa*" (in Italian), in *Vita e Pensiero*, no. 1 (2007).

it verged on idolatry. Leading the way was Simone de Beauvoir, a French author whose journey to China gave way to *The Long March: An Account of Modern China* (1955), and became a best seller. Many other enthusiastic writers followed (in Italy Moravia, la Macciocchi, Parise . . .). The height of success for Maoism beyond the bamboo curtain will reach its peak with the social revolution known as Sixty-Eight.

There were also criticisms in the years leading to 1968: denunciations and testimonies of the horrors of the Red Guards, the techniques of brain-washing, the mass deportation to the laogai (and there still are today) in conditions not dissimilar to those of the Soviet gulags. But the critical voices were stamped counterrevolutionary and, in the last analysis, judged unreliable. In 1973 the Italian edition of *Prisoner of Mao* by Jean Pasqualini was published. After growing up in China, Pasqualini was imprisoned "for counterrevolutionary crimes." Then in 1964 the author found refuge in France, where he began to write about his experiences in a Chinese labor camp. But he was not believed. In the preface of the Italian edition Renata Pisu[17] writes: "Intellectuals and French Sinologists coalesced against him, maintaining that he was being paid by the American secret service as an agent of the CIA."

Recent historical acquisitions are presenting a more objective way of judging the figure of Mao and his time, beginning from the very well-documented volume by Jasper Becker, *The Revolution of Hunger, China 1958–62: The Secret Famine.*[18] In light of these and other recent works, it is possible to affirm that the "Red Sun" is responsible—directly or slightly less—for

---

[17] The case of Pisu is interesting. Fascinated by Mao, as were many others of her generation, the journalist, a key correspondent for *Repubblica*, a major Italian newspaper, then disassociated herself from the veneration of the *Little Red Book* and Maoist mythology. She relates it herself, with great courage, in the preface of another book—*L'allodola e il drago* di Wang Xiaoling (Casale Monferrato: Pimme, 1993), autobiography of a believer who survived the laogai—that contributed to the umpteenth blow with the pickax to Mao's totem.

[18] *Il Saggiatore* (Milano, 1998).

crimes on a par or even superior to the cruelty, intensity, and duration of those imposed by Stalin and Hitler. It is not an affirmation for effect: a former member of the National Fascist Party abroad, Chen Yizi, affirmed seeing an internal Communist Party document quantifying eighty million deaths "by natural causes" in the period of the "Great Leap Forward (1958-1961)."[19]

Let us leave to historians the task of judging Mao's legacy. Here it will be enough to point out that only in recent years has the unauthorized public been able to access autobiographical testimonies on the laogai, that is, the Chinese forced-labor camps.[20] What's more, anyone who wished information on the laogai was able to attain it. As already stated, years ago, Harry Wu, one of the most famous Chinese dissidents, documented the number, the characteristics, and the operation of the labor camps. Even if we are a long way from knowing the details of life in these camps—as happened, for example, with the Soviet gulags thanks to the writings of Solzhenitsyn—what matters to us here and what we must emphasize is that, concerning China, the ideological slant in Western historiography and journalism has limited the possibility of knowing and of making known the stories of Christian persecution and martyrdom.

In China, during the sixties, while the cult of the Great Helmsman was imposed with force—distorting consciences and subjecting the masses—in Europe, Maoism was propagandized as the "good face" of Communism, enlisting sympathizers even in Catholic homes.

---

[19] "Today the judgment of historians is more or less unanimous in considering Mao responsible for the appalling number of victims, perhaps up to 70 million dead," writes Federico Rampini, then correspondent to Peking for *Repubblica*, in *L'ombra di Mao: Sulle trace del Grande Timoniere per capire il presente di Cina, Tibet, Corea del Nord e il futuro del mondo* (Milano: Mondadori, 2007). Rampini writes: "The real knowledge of Mao is still extremely limited, both among his fellow countrymen and foreign public opinion. In the West, apart from a restricted number of specialists and enthusiasts, information on him is vague, obsolete, and often incorrect.

[20] See, for example, Chen Ming, *Dark Clouds Gathering*, published in Italy in 2006 by Marsilio (but to the present forbidden in China).

Introduction

The Reality behind the Veil of Propaganda

Those reading *Diaries of the Chinese Martyrs* will find numerous facts and episodes that eloquently demonstrate the true and intrinsically violent nature of Maoism. In John Liao Shouji's *My Life in the Laogai*, for example, we come across the story of Dr. Mo, "who exercised his practice as a consultant at a large hospital at Peking and at an orphanage managed by nuns."[21] He was very courageous and incorruptible—the author writes—but he paid a high price. Two or three years later, after returning from a trip to Hong Kong, as soon as the train reached its destination, he was arrested without warning. His family did not receive any explanation or information until five or six months later, when he wrote to them from prison: he had been condemned to fifteen years for having collaborated with the religious imperialists. A few months before the end of his sentence, when the Cultural Revolution was at its height,[22] at a gathering of prisoners he was accused publicly and ordered to bow his head in recognition of his crimes. He refused to admit any wrongdoing, and, as a consequence, a large stone was tied at his neck in order to force him to lower his head. He died several days later as a result of this torture.

The same John Liao Shouji documents the progressive deterioration of the prisoners assigned to forced-labor according to the most chilling logic—man is a wolf to his fellow man (*homo homini lupus*): "More oppressive than the physical misery were the inhumane psychological difficulties." In the prisons and in the forced labor camps every type of prisoner and convict was mixed together: men guilty of the most unthinkable crimes lived, worked, and studied with others accused solely of political offenses. A detainee could trust none of them. The prisoners were encouraged to

[21] It concerns Mo Xingling, one of the brothers of Teresa Mo of whom much is spoken of in the book.
[22] The "Great Cultural Revolution" was launched by Mao in the summer of 1966 and lasted ten years, with phases more or less acute. Praised in the preamble of the Constitution of 1975 and still more in that of 1978, it is today officially detested and condemned as the most grave disaster of the founding of the popular Republic of China.

foment disorder, to spy, to lie, and to do whatever they could to gain benefits. A person might appear very sincere and open, but in reality he would not hesitate to betray someone in order to obtain an advantage. Similarly, one could not form alliances with anyone; consciences were corrupted. The bad became even worse, and prisoners looked for any opportunity to create disorder through deceptions and strategies.

In the labor camps, hunger pangs reigned, along with—often—a polar cold. In *My Life in the Laogai* we read: "Our meals were miserable: even the peanut shells were ground up and offered as food. Moreover, I soon became aware that that food was the cause of internal hemorrhaging, and so, notwithstanding our diet was at a level of starvation, I no longer ate the peanut shells. Wild herbs and a scant quantity of rice were all the food that we had; with that nourishment we had to work ten hours a day. "

On his part, Monsignor Tang confirms: "Given that there was no seasoning in the boiled rice, we would buy salt for ten cents a packet. We would add a little salt to the boiled rice in order to give it a little flavor. Nevertheless, many prisoners suffered from beriberi because of the malnutrition." As a result, we could not even buy salt. It was very difficult to tolerate all this. But this was the life of a detainee!

"Persecution Will Bear Fruit for the Church"

In concluding, we wish to reemphasize that although these texts are to be read as historical documents, their principal value is spiritual. The same protagonists of this business, even being at arms' length from Communism, would never venture into the art of anti-Communist propaganda, out of either hostility or vengeance. Nor do we intend to. We prefer to assume the authentically evangelical style of these martyrs, who are always convinced of one thing: that the sufferings they have lived and accepted in the name of faith have spoken more than words could possibly speak, even to the point of finding their way into the hearts of their persecutors. Particularly eloquent is a passage from *I Fled from Red China*, where Father Chan—it was 1963—writes:

The admiration for the Church and for the Catholics came directly from this. The same Communist policemen, when they were in a mood for sharing, confessed to me several times, that they admired us and that they could not understand how we were able to suffer prison for an idea and for fidelity to the pope who lived so far away.... The patience and the calm of the Catholics and the priests condemned unjustly was something that the people, including the Communists, could not explain. The other prisoners would cry, would suffer desperation and at times would commit suicide. But we, generally, remained calm and tranquil. At various times I heard people who came to the prison praise the attitude of the Catholics and the priests, saying that they were helping everyone by giving good example and not cursing.

One day, when I was at forced labor, I was asked by another condemned man if I was Catholic.

"Why do you ask?" I replied.

"I don't know," he said to me. "You do everything differently from the rest of us."

Therefore, I think that the persecution will bear good fruit for the Church. I am truly convinced of it. By now in China everyone knows the Church for what it is; that is, a society formed, in general, by good people who help others, who are ready to die as witnesses to their Faith; everyone knows that the Church has been opposed to Communism from the beginning.... I think that when Communism will disappear, many will come to us to ask for the solution to the problems of life. Even now, in times of persecution, many have said to me that they would like to be able to become Catholics. It the sincere wish that we offer to the Chinese Church for decades to come.

BIBLIOGRAPHICAL NOTE

Gaetano Pollio, *Cross of Gold among the Crossbars*

Cross of Gold among the Crossbars: The Story of a Detainee in Cell No. 4 was originally published *pro manuscripto* (PDL) by Pime (Latin acronym for Pontifical Institute for Foreign Missions) of Naples in 1960, with a preface by Professor Gastone Lambertini and edited by Salvatore Menditti, a member of the Legion of Mary.

Before compiling his memoirs, Bishop Pollio had risked exposing his witness of the faith—which, without exaggeration can be considered heroic—in various public circumstances.

The footnotes in this chapter have been written by the editor and by Father Mario Marazzi, a missionary of Pime at Hong Kong.

Dominic Tang, *[My Story:] A Bishop in the Prisons of Mao*

The autobiography of Monsignor Dominic Tang—at the initiative of some of Pime's priests, Giacomo Girardi (deceased), Mario Marazzi, and Giancarlo Politi (a correspondent for AsiaNews)—appeared in Italian for the first time in 1990, by Emi Press of Bologna (*Casa Editrice Missionaria*), under the title *In Mao's Prisons, the Diary of a Bishop*.

In this current edition, the editors, in the interest of coherency, have made some modifications to the original text. In addition, the 2015 publication also presents two new brief chapters (24 and 25), translated by Father Marazzi, that make reference to the Chinese and English publications dated 1994.

Also, in this case, names of persons follow the Romanization (the phonetic transliteration) of the Cantonese (except for some known personalities, such as Mao Zedong), while those relative to a locality keep to the *pinyin*, the official Romanization adopted in the People's Republic of China.

John Liao Shouji, My *Life in the Laogai*

This text (translated by Mauro and Lucia Scalfi and revised by Roberto Beretta) was published in Italy in 1991 by Emi under the title *My Life in the Gulag: Diary of a Chinese Catholic*, at the initiative of two priests, Fathers Politi and Marazzi, who also edited the notes.

In the present title, the precise Chinese term *laogai*, which is by now diffuse in nonspecialized publications, is preferred over *gulag*. The gulag, used in the former Soviet Union, became a symbol of repression and was much in vogue at the time of the first Italian translation. The official term used in China is *laogai*, "reeducation through work."

As to the Romanization of the Chinese terms: all the names (of persons and places) are in *pinyin*.

In the 1991 text, some names of persons and places were changed out of fear of retaliation. In the current edition, at the request of the wife of the author, Teresa Mo Liao, we have restored the original and authentic terms. In addition, the 2015 edition is equipped with a brief testimony by Mrs. Teresa Mo Liao, requested by the publisher and sent directly from Australia, where she lives.

Leon Chan, *I Fled Red China*

This text revisits the interview of the Chinese priest Leon Chan, of the Diocese of Hong Kong, who fled China in May of 1962, after having lived under the Communist regime for thirteen years. We made the editorial choice of eliminating Father Piero Gheddo's questions in order to adapt the style of his story to that of the others, which were written in the first person.

Bibliographical Note

After it initially appeared on the pages of *The Catholic Missions* in 1962, the interview of Father Chan was published the following year in the *Quaderni* (Notebooks) of the magazine and enjoyed immediate success. Consequently, it was translated into Spanish, French, and German. At the first session of Vatican Council II (October–December 1962), at the request of ten bishops (some of whom had been expelled by China), it was read and commented on at a meeting of exiled Chinese bishops, who praised it as one of the most authoritative documents of recent times on the situation of the Church in China.

Following his liberation, Father Chan was received in a private audience by Pope St. John XXIII, to whom he gave a broad account of the situation of the Catholic Church in China and of his personal experiences as a priest who had experienced persecution. The interview was published in the weeks immediately following.

From the introduction written by Father Gheddo in 1963 we learn that "an Italian publisher" was brought forward in an attempt to try to "convince Father Chan to write a memoir of his personal experiences in China to be published in Italy and then launched on the international market." The project, however, was never realized.

Lastly, with respect to the first version, it was now possible to mention the name of the locality where the protagonist lived, Huiyang, which it was thought advisable to omit at the time of the interview.

DIARIES OF THE
CHINESE MARTYRS

GAETANO POLLIO

INTRODUCTION

"The cross that I wear on my chest is the cross of a martyr. It is my most precious possession, because it is the only object that I was able to salvage from the fury of persecution in China.... It calls to mind the holocaust of a martyr; and it reminds me of the personal Calvary inflicted on me by those who wished to cut down and destroy the Cross of Christ. But His Cross has always triumphed and always will triumph." In these words, taken from the opening chapter, lies the deep meaning of the autobiographical story of Monsignor Gaetano Pollio, missionary of the Pontifical Institute of Foreign Missions (Pime) and archbishop of Kaifeng, China, until his expulsion in 1951.[23]

The "cross of gold" of the title had belonged to Monsignor Antonio Barosi, also a missionary of Pime, which Pollio was miraculously given after all had been convinced that it was lost. This, thanks to an elderly Chinese who, after having retrieved it from some soldiers, jealously guarded it until he had an opportunity to hand it over to the archbishop.

The Odyssey of the Catholic Church in China

The symbolic episode cited above summarizes the difficult season lived by the Chinese Catholic Church beginning from the Institution of the

[23] Monsignor Pollio edited another diary, relative to the period from 1935 to 1943: 420 pages that were the testimony of Father Crotti and represented a "mine of information." See Amelio Crotti, *Gaetano Pollio (1911–1991): Archivescovo of Kaifeng (China)* (Bologna: Emi, 2002).

People's Republic of China (1949) to the death of Mao Zedong (1976). Like Barosi's gold cross, the Chinese Catholic church was not heard from for a long time and was even feared to have definitively disappeared.

In fact, during the fifties and the sixties, the Chinese Church was struck down with a violence rarely verifiable in other historical epochs and in other countries. That brutal persecution caused thousands of deaths, the imprisonment and forced labor of hundreds of thousands of persons, and the expulsion of all the missionaries. As a result, inside and outside China, the overwhelming majority was convinced that the "evil tree of Christianity" had been totally uprooted. Father Piero Gheddi wrote: "When I went to China for the first time in 1973, we would often tell the Chinese guides that we wished to see a church and the response was always the same: 'The new China has learned to do without God.' "[24]

It is precisely Father Gheddo who effectively testifies how the matter of Monsignor Pollio opened the eyes of Italian public opinion that, up to that moment, had lived with substantial disinterest the drama of the Catholic Church in China. "With the expulsion of Pollio and many other witnesses," he wrote, "one began to understand that the anti-religious persecution was not in any way the fault of the missionaries; rather it was a strategic decision of the Chinese Communist Party; not only against the Catholic Church (struck first), but against all religions."[25]

The Singular Experience of Pollio at Kaifeng

Monsignor Pollio's missionary and personal experience is placed at the beginning of the most dramatic period ever lived by the Chinese Catholic Church. Born at Meta di Sorrento in 1911, he was ordained a priest in 1934 and was sent the following year on a mission to Kaifeng, in the province of Henan. After the martyrdom of Bishop Barosi, Pollio was appointed to take over the mission, which was located in territories that had been

[24] Gheddo, *Lettere di cristiani dalla Cina*, April 22, 2012.
[25] Ibid., p. 8.

occupied by the Japanese during the Second World War. The day after the Japanese were expelled from that territory, December 12, 1946, he was nominated archbishop of Kaifeng. In June 1948 the area where he worked was shaken by the civil war between the Nationalists and the Communists. Knowing full well that he was risking his life—only a few months before one of his confreres was consumed by martyrdom—Monsignor Pollio decided to remain; and he did not turn back.

After taking the city of Kaifeng, the Communists arrested Bishop Pollio and, subjecting him to an extremely harsh prison regime, tried to force him to detach himself from Rome and embrace the "reformed church." It did not succeed. Then, in the summer of 1951 they decided to expel him from the country, together with other Pime missionaries.[26]

The years lived by Pollio—and narrated here—represent a crucial chapter in recent Chinese history. As he observes: "Kaifeng was the first provincial capital to fall under the domination of Red China.... The fall of Kaifeng was not only an episode of the civil war that Chiang Kai-shek and Mao Zedong were fighting; it was the beginning of the end for Nationalist China. We foreigners in China understood it clearly, and we anxiously followed these events."

"We All Remained at Our Posts"

What sense does rereading these pages have at a distance of more than half a century? Beyond the historical value, it is worth the effort to emphasize the profound spiritual significance of the *Cross of Gold among the Crossbars.* Pollio explains it in this testament: "I thank God for giving me the grace to witness him in the religious persecution in China and in the prisons,

---

[26] After spending some time in Hong Kong, in October Pollio returned to Italy. He worked for Pime until September 8, 1960, when he was nominated archbishop of Otranto. Then, on February 5, 1969, he was nominated archbishop of Salerno. After he was struck by a serious illness, he resigned his office on October 20, 1984. He passed away on March 13, 1991, at the age of seventy-nine.

where I experienced the greatest joy of my life: to suffer for Christ and to forgive [my persecutors]." This fidelity to the gospel distinguishes each story of martyrdom, and in the martyrdom of Monsignor Pollio there is a specific nuance, as appropriately observed by his confrere and prison companion Father Amelio Crotti: "His sanctity is not that of a mystic, a founder of congregations or a cloistered monk; rather it is that of a bishop, a pastor of a diocese, and of his awareness of being everything for Christ."[27] It is the sanctity of the pastor who does not abandon his flock when he sees the wolf coming.

Therefore, it does not surprise the reader that the witness of Chinese Catholics begins with the autobiographical text of an Italian bishop. The choice is also motivated by chronological reasons (the diary of Pollio begins halfway through the forties) and is supported by others not less important. Like St. Joseph Freinademetz—a Ladin (from northern Italy) missionary active in China for many years (author of *I Love China and the Chinese: I Would Be Ready to Die a Thousand Times for Them*)—Monsignor Pollio also felt a very strong affection for the Chinese people, and he willingly submitted to incredible sufferings, humiliations, and privations. Not only that: if he had been able, he would have remained in "his" China even to his last breath. As he writes in the conclusion of this book: I am now in the fatherland (Italy), and, although I am surrounded by affection and esteem, my heart remains down there; it remains in Kaifeng." This is why we include the very Italian Gaetano Pollio in the list of the "Chinese martyrs" of the 1900s.

The Accusation of Imperialism

In light of what has been said, it is not difficult to understand how the Communists' slanderous charge of "imperialist" was offensive to him and to all the European missionaries. In his case the Communist propaganda was ruthless in its aggression, insulting one who so loved his people, so

---

[27] See Crotti, *Gaetano Pollio*, 1.

"enculturated" we would say today. But in the eyes of the Communists his enculturation became synonymous with betrayal.

The catalogue of lies strung together against Pollio synthesized the gamut of the worst anti-Christian prejudices dumped on the foreign missionaries, their favorite target. A newspaper of that era, cited by the bishop, provides an example: "These people wrap themselves in the mantle of religion and, with a face suffused with the light of philanthropy, pretend that the Gospel opens the kingdom of heaven to everyone. Thus, they narcotize the Chinese people with this shameful propaganda and enslave them with their deceit."

The truth—which we know today—was very different: throughout their life the missionaries were the ones who in reality bathed the sweat and dried the tears, which in time would become their fortunate motto: "servant of the people."

Grace Finds Its Way into Prison

Among the various interests in the diary of Monsignor Pollio, there is, of course, its documentary value. He tells of the terrible sufferings of the detainees; of listening to the thuds of their tortured bodies falling to the floor after being tied to the beams by their thumbs. Each abuse wounded his spirit: "The blows of the fallen victims reverberated in my heart, and I was saddened by so many injustices and tortures."

Yet, even in a context of such extreme degradation, God made Himself present. Truly touching—for example—are the holy Masses celebrated clandestinely behind the bars.[28]

Persecution challenges faith. And, as it happened to Jesus, it becomes a sign of contradiction (see Luke 2:34). Pollio relates his story like a Via

---

[28] As also in the example of the Vietnamese cardinal François-Xavier Nguyên Van Thuân (1928–2002), president of the Pontifical Council on Justice and Peace, who spent three years in prison and wrote of it in *Five Loaves and Two Fishes: From the Suffering in Prison to Joyful Witness of Faith* (Cinisello Balsamo: Edizioni San Paolo, 1997). In 2013 the diocesan phase of his beatification was completed.

Crucis, and in the midst of it emerges a new Judas, the figure of a seminarian traitor, who uses a four-year-old companion by the name of Siao Mei (Little Beauty) like an ornament.

Pollio's words of faith, as simple as they are profound, "moved the heart of the Holy Father Pius XII."

This story—as I was saying—is constructed like a Via Crucis. The passage in which Pollio recalls the trial of a Protestant pastor brings to mind Pilate's judgment; also the last episode of Pollio's imprisonment is presented like a convincing analogy of Christ's road to Calvary. But it would be a mistake to read the comparison with the Passion of Christ as arrogance. Rather, throughout his entire persecution, Monsignor Pollio wished to walk the same path as the Master, even to offering the supreme gift of his life. Therefore, he declared himself "happy to offer my life for my friends and to declare to all the pagan masses that the Catholic missionaries are truly the good pastors of whom Jesus speaks, ready to give their lives for their sheep, not like the hirelings that abandon the flock at the approach of the wolf."

Here is a love that knows no half measures—precisely like that of Christ on the Cross.

CROSS OF GOLD
AMONG THE BARS

The Story of a Detainee in Cell No. 4

The Sweetest Memory

The cross that I wear on my chest is the cross of a martyr. And it represents my most treasured possession, because it was the only object that I could save from the storm of persecution in China. It has a story that must be told. When the mission of Kaifeng was vacated for matters related to the health of its founder, Monsignor Noé, Father Antonio Barosi, a missionary of Nanyang, was appointed the apostolic administrator. Having heard of the gifts of our new leader—at Nanyang he had left a profound imprint—we received him with much affection and enthusiasm. But unfortunately, the times at Kaifeng were very sad for the apostolic vicariate.

The terrible Yellow River, which had been diverted by the Nationalists in June 1938 (in order to stop the advancement of the Japanese toward the West), had dragged thousands of villages into its vertiginous course and its muddy waters covered more than half of our vast missionary territories: the East was controlled by the Japanese and the West by the Nationalist regime. This painful situation lasted a good nine years.

The flooded areas, called wastelands ("land of no one"), were occupied by the first arrivals, but, with the same facility with which they were occupied, they were also abandoned: first by a succession of Japanese troops, then by the armed Nationalists, the Communist hordes, bandits, and snipers, one following the other.

In the mere fourteen months he remained in our midst, Monsignor Barosi visited all the districts, bringing his word of encouragement and comfort to the faithful missionaries at their posts and supporting the Christians in their difficulties. During the same period he administered more than two thousand baptisms.

In November of 1941, one last district remained to be visited, the most distant from the center, placed right in the wastelands, that of Ting-t'suen. Monsignor Barosi arrived there November 19, celebrated Mass, and exhorted his sons and daughters to "be ready to die for Christ." With him were three other missionaries: Fathers Mario Zanardi, Bruno Zanella, and Gerolamo Lazzaroni. While the four were having a modest dinner, the soldier-brigands, who then became Communists, placed Ting-t'suen under attack. Entering the residence, they slaughtered the four apostles of Christ—[tossing] their bodies into a well—and then they left the village.

After the brigands left, an elderly catechist by the name of John Ts'uei, having been gagged and tied together with other local residents, managed to untie himself and free the others. He then found Monsignor Barosi's cross on the ground. Picking it up, he kissed it and brought it to his village, where he hid it under a tree without saying anything to anyone, not even his family. The old man had intended to restore it to the mission's superiors as soon as the storm passed. For many years we at Kaifeng believed that Monsignor Barosi had been robbed of his cross by the soldier-brigands.

On April 12, 1947, the city of Kaifeng was festively awaiting the arrival of Monsignor Riberi, the apostolic internuncio, who on the following day was coming to consecrate the archbishop. All the bishops of the province had gathered there for the occasion.

In the afternoon of that day, while we held an episcopal conference presided over by Riberi, John Ts'uei arrived at Kaifeng. He was, by then, eighty years old and he had walked nearly two hundred kilometers [about 124 miles]. "I wish to speak to our archbishop," he told a missionary.

"Impossible; the archbishop is in a meeting with the Pope's representative," the missionary responded.

"I have a gift to give him that will give him much pleasure; I have come a long way precisely for this, from Ting-t'suen."

"Then give it to me."

"I cannot. I shall wait here," and he sat outside the bishop's residence and waited for hours. Then, as I was leaving the residence to go to the refectory, John, the trusted catechist, with a cry of joy, prostrated himself at my feet and making a triple Sign of the Cross, got up and. taking a small package from his pocket, gave it to me, saying: "I have jealously guarded it for more than five years," and he burst into tears. Poor John: from the day that the four victims were immolated, his district had remained without a missionary.

I opened the little package. A tremor of emotion ran through my veins; I fixed my eyes on John, but my feelings impeded me from speaking. I recognized the cross of the martyred Barosi and kissed it devoutly. The cross of Kaifeng's first martyr was saved.

In 1948 we fell under the red regime of Mao Zedong; the following year we noticed the warning signs of the persecution. In January of 1951 I found myself under house arrest in my bishop's residence for not having wished to adhere to the new national schismatic church, and in that same month I received orders from the police to make a detailed inventory of all the furniture, all the objects in the residence, and even my own personal effects. One cannot resist with impunity the police of an oppressive and terroristic government. And we obeyed them in everything, but not in what went against the faith. I had to register even the cross, which I had lovingly worn on my breast since the day of my consecration. I listed it like this: "a copper cross of the same metal." The cross was gold, but many considered our gold copper or something of little value.

On April 1, 1951, I was arrested and led to prison, charged with obstructing the establishment of the new national church. The rooms I occupied in the episcopal residence were sealed. During my detention in the prisons, the police often went to the residence and, removing the seals, stole archives, correspondence, and various objects, including the gold cross and a ring.

In the course of my ninth trial, as I was entering the courtroom in the midst of the usual platoon of torturers, I saw the cross on the judges' table, which one of them immediately covered with a newspaper.

On October 1 of the same year I was removed from the prison and handed over to the military that was to lead me to the frontier: I had been sentenced to exile. For four days I was guarded by soldiers in a room with two other missionaries who were also being expelled from China.

I did not regret losing my books, my clothing, and the other objects I possessed; however I was sad to lose the cross. Gathering my courage, I called to the colonel, the same police officer who had imprisoned me, and I said to him: "Every condemned man is granted a last request—and for me exile is like a death sentence—so I have called you because I have a favor to ask."

"What do you want?" the colonel responded with his usual hostility.

"That copper cross, the souvenir of my mamma," I said in *mou-ts'in*, which in the mandarin dialect is used commonly to indicate a natural mamma, our Mother Mary, and the Mother Church.

"Where is that copper cross?"

"When I was imprisoned, I left it on the table of my study; where it is now I have no idea." I could not say that I had seen it in court, or I would have compromised the result of my request.

The colonel went away without showing any concern for my request. I did not despair; I would have tried again.

The following day he returned and, throwing down the cross on the table, said: "Is this it?" I did not immediately respond, nor did I reveal my joy in seeing it again. In the cross there is a precious relic: a piece of the sacred wood on which our Redeemer died. In order to ascertain that the dear treasure had not been removed, I pretended not to recognize the cross and examined it; and when I was sure that it had not been opened, I responded: "Yes." I kissed it and was about to put it around my neck when the colonel thundered: "Give it back to me." For a moment I felt lost and

I doubted that I would be able to get it back again. I handed it back to the colonel. Fixing his feline eyes on me, he said: "You must die with it and all your followers with you," and, cursing, he flung the cross on the floor and trampled it with his foot.

I judged well in deciding not to respond, and I picked up the cross and, kissing it again, put it around my neck. The cross once again was saved from the hands of its enemies.

On October 5 I left Kaifeng; on the 8th, I crossed the frontier and entered Hong Kong, holding tightly that sign of redemption around my neck.

For me, this episcopal cross represents the most precious memory and the most precious relic. I wear it daily on my breast. I look at it, I squeeze it in my hands, and I kiss it. It reminds me of a martyr's sacrifice; of the Calvary of pains inflicted on me by those who wish to beat and destroy the Cross of Christ. But His Cross has always triumphed and always will triumph.

Dark Clouds over Kaifeng

It would be impossible to narrate the entire story of the painful prison experience I suffered under the Chinese Communist regime; but what is possible is to bear witness to the truth, that is, the true situation of the Catholic Church in China.

My seventeen years spent in China at Kaifeng passed from one painful experience to another: banditry, war, floods, Communism, persecution, and finally exile.

After the bloody storm of the Nippon-Chinese war, which ended in 1945; and after the flooding of the Yellow River, which for nine years (1938–1947), with devastating fury, caused the disappearance of thousands of villages, we fell into the red torment of Communism. We knew no peace in China.

In 1947 I wrote the following to the Superior General:

The entire Archdiocese of Kaifeng is in the hands of the Communists, with the exception of the city of Kaifeng and two small districts nearby. It is a true desolation. The heart cries to see our best districts go to ruin. Several districts have expelled their priests. The Church's residences are occupied by the Communists; in the churches themselves they hold town meetings and issue judgments against the rich, the government employees, the Christians, et cetera. Altars, sacred objects, images, and statues have been smashed to pieces and burned. It is a storm that is worse than all that has been lived up to this day. How shall we exit from it all? Only God knows; we abandon ourselves completely to his hands. It is the hour of blood! Is our blood also necessary . . . ? We have lived the tragedy of the Yellow River for nine years; we have seen the waters whirling in a vortex over the vast expanses of our missions, sweeping away everything in its fury: villages, homes, men, women, and livestock. And now the Communists are advancing; they are like the yellow waters: nothing can resist their fury, everything is destroyed. The tragedy of the yellow waters lasted nine years; how long will this Communist hurricane last?"

And the hour also came for Kaifeng. On May 30, 1948, the first religious festival celebrated in the streets of our city was greeted by the respectful admiration of the mostly pagan crowd. It was the extremely successful procession of Corpus Domini: it was the first time that Christ passed triumphantly through those streets accompanied by the songs of Catholics and catechumens, to which the two thousand students of our primary and middle schools united their voices. Christ wanted that triumph before the dolorous days of our persecution.

On June 17 of the same year Kaifeng was already surrounded by Communist troops. There were six days of bloody combat, outside and inside the walls of our city, between the twenty thousand Nationalist soldiers and the four hundred thousand red Communists. Kaifeng fell piece by piece into the hands of the Communists. The suburbs were reduced to a heap of smoking ruins. More than thirty thousand houses were destroyed by bombs and gunfire; more than twenty thousand of the civilians and regular soldiers were killed (it was impossible to know the end of six thousand Nationalist soldiers taken prisoner); the suicide of the Nationalist general, the head of the defense, and the sacking on the part of the Reds and the rabble were the principal happenings of those sad days of steel and fire. Our bell tower received two shots of cannon. A young girl of our Holy Infancy Club (orphanage) was found dead in a well. The body of their leader was riddled with projectiles and died immediately.

After 1942 (when Kaifeng had been destroyed by the waters of the Yellow River, which had been diverted in order to drown the Japanese) the city lived through their second greatest calamity. I witnessed all of it; I had wished to stay in the residence together with some priests and the red horde whom the general command had put up at my episcopal residence for some days.

Kaifeng was the first provincial capital to fall under the domination of Reds in China. With three hundred thousand inhabitants, it is the capital of Honan, the ecclesial province of which I was the metropolitan (archbishop). The provinces in China are extremely vast: for example, Honan has more than thirty million inhabitants and covers a territory larger than half of Italy.

The fall of Kaifeng was a grave blow to the prestige of the government of Nanking. Was this fall a betrayal? Exactly a week before, the minister of war, General Ho Ying-chin, had assured the population of Honan that the Communists would not attack Kaifeng, and many citizens were deluded by his words. The fall of Kaifeng was not only an episode of the civil war being fought between Chiang Kai-shek[29] and Mao Zedong; it was the beginning of the end for Nationalist China. We foreigners in China clearly understood it, and we followed the events with concern. Some months later Tsinan fell. With the exception of the capitals of the province, nearly all the other cities, the mandarin seats, fell into the hands of the Reds; very often they were retaken by the Nationalists, massacred, looted, and sacked. Such was

[29] Together with Mao Zedong, Chiang Kai-shek was one of the protagonists of the Chinese political life of the last century.

the fate of all the cities of my archdiocese. That civil-war plan caused the ruin of entire cities and the extreme misery of their inhabitants.

In April of 1949 the Communist army was on the banks of the Blue River, which divides Central China from the south; it had already conquered all the vast territory that goes from the Yellow River to the Blue River and that constitutes Central China. In April of the same year, the Reds, because of the betrayals of the Nationalist generals, passed the Blue River at more points: Nanking, the capital of the nation, fell immediately, and at the end of 1949, the red avalanche was at Canton, the extreme south of China. In two years the armies of Mao Zedong occupied all of China, from Manchuria and lower Mongolia to Canton. And so this is how China, today, is Communist—not through political elections and not through the will of the people; it is Communist through military occupation. On October 1, 1949, the Republic of China was solemnly proclaimed.

From the first days of the occupation we repeatedly heard hard and injurious phrases from the soldiers: "What are you foreigners doing here? We do not need you. What you teach under the name of religion is all superstition and the opium of the people.... God does not exist," et cetera. Those soldiers did not know how to hide the true face of Communism and all that they had learned during their indoctrinations.

We missionaries, comforted by the words of the Holy Father, remained at our posts, so that we could demonstrate to the Catholics and to the pagans that we were the good pastors of whom Jesus speaks, and that we had gone to China not for political or financial ends, but in order to spread the gospel and to establish the Church.

The China that had been "liberated" that day lost the joy of living.

The First Signs of the Persecution

In the first months of the occupation, the Communist government's tactic toward the Catholic Church was to pretend to ignore her existence. Among the various factors influencing this ploy was, for example: the number of Catholics (two thousand in Kaifeng City), the vitality of the Church in her multiple works, and the Christian life lived in all its sincerity. In every corner of the city, liberty of religion was proclaimed. On the walls of the cathedral and on our residences, we read in very large letters: "*Sin Kiao Tze You*" (liberty of religion), and, I must say, truthfully, that in those first months we were nearly unaware of a change in regimes; our works went forward regularly.

It was especially through our work in education, assistance, and charity that we had been able to penetrate the mass of infidels: works that cost us sacrifice and tears. In the city of Kaifeng we had a regional seminary where seminarians came from the entire province to study philosophy and theology, a minor seminary, a high school, and a middle school for boys with 550 students, a high school and a middle school for girls with 990 students, ten elementary schools, a hospital with sixty beds, eleven dispensaries (clinics), a Holy Infancy Orphanage, and a rest home under construction for the elderly.

Even while enjoying a limited liberty of religion, our Christians were often forced to listen to false doctrines on materialism, evolution, divorce, and the origin of man from the monkey. On our part, we tried to refute these errors using modern books on apology and gathering the youth together to offer courses in religious culture.

At the beginning of 1949 the Chinese government changed its modus operandi toward the Catholic Church and showed us its true face. In January a pamphlet was published promoting religious liberty, and then in February another followed entitled: "*Fang Pei Mi Sin*" (looking at super-stitions). An insistent propaganda had begun to be employed to convince the people that man does not have an immortal soul, that religions are superstitions and therefore useless, and that Catholic priests are parasites.

The propaganda passed from words to deeds: in that year nearly all the churches and chapels, the residences of the missionaries, the schools and the dispensaries in the district of my mission were occupied or confiscated. Restrictions were placed on worship, and liberty of movement was taken away. Throughout Kaifeng Catholic charities and residences were taken over by the government.

DIARIES OF THE CHINESE MARTYRS

On July 7 numerous government emissaries came to my office demanding a friendly cession of the ecclesiastical properties: the cathedral, the episcopal residence, the schools, and the hospitals. "When you occupied the churches, the chapels, and the residences of the districts, to whom did you ask permission? Today you come to ask my consent? I know where you are going with this. You have the power, you are the government, and you have soldiers and arms. Go occupy what you please, but I will never give you my consent. As long as I am free I will defend the rights of God and the Church. All that remains to me is to tell you the truth and to defend justice."

Beginning on that day, there was a progressive occupation of the mission's local schools, the missionaries' residences, and the convents. When in August of the same year (1949) the government wished to occupy the space housing the Holy Infancy, I strongly protested. We had no other shelter for those sixty poor babies. I then received a written order demanding that the babies leave the orphanage within five days, under pain of my arrest. Those innocent babies, thrown out on the street with only their rags, crying and clinging to the nuns, was such an inhuman spectacle that even the souls of some of the honest pagans were affected. I had to shelter them in damp shanties, where they remained until the next peremptory government decree ordering the complete dissolution of the Holy Infancy.

After the proclamation of the government of the People's Republic of China, attacks against the Church, the Vatican, and the pope increased. Religion was called the "opium of the people," and the pope was proclaimed "the enemy of humankind." The missionaries were charged with being "spies of the imperialist governments, emissaries of the Vatican, the center of worldly imperialism, and parasites and oppressors of the Chinese."

In that same October, I received an arrest warrant placing me and all my missionaries under semi-house arrest. I could not leave the city of Kaifeng. If I went out, I was followed by the police. In the episcopal residence we were subjected to continual visits day and night (even two or three times in the same night) on the part of the police, who were armed to the teeth. My opposition to the lack of freedom to worship and to all the outrages and injustices toward the Church and our mission attracted the hatred of the government, of the party, and all its multiple sectors.

In 1950 there was another slanderous campaign against the Church and the missionaries on the part of the propagandists and the Communist press (the only press in China). According to these people, our schools were "bulwarks of imperialism that deprived the students [male and female] of their liberty" And so the end of 1950 also marked the sunset of our schools, from which so many fruits had been attained, and at the cost of immense sacrifices. In May of that year they desired at all costs to occupy my cathedral, the only church that was still free in the entire, vast ecclesiastical province. I cried out: "I will protest with the central government of Peking [Beijing] and make them aware of the forced occupation of all 170,000 Catholics of the province." Thus, I succeeded to keep it free.

Then the government came for the hospital, which it appropriated toward the end of that year. The regional seminary, still existing as a moral entity, had three-quarters of their building occupied. The minor seminary had to be dissolved by order of the police. With tears in my eyes I assisted at the dismantling of our works. I saw our churches and chapels reduced to stalls, magazines, barracks, and public offices. At the end of 1950 all the works of our mission were either dissolved or closed up. There was nothing left free for worship except the cathedral and some chapels. All the residences of the missionaries were occupied. In a few districts there were some rooms used by the foreign missionaries and the remaining local priests, who had no possibility of moving. The Christians, by now abandoned and deprived of spiritual assistance, were left to themselves. It was a sorrowful vision that, unfortunately, only got worse.

During the summer and autumn, the government looked for many and various ways of finding me in "error" in order to get their hands on me. But the hour of the true sacrifice had not yet come. For several months various agents of the government came each day to the episcopal residence and subjected me to nerve-racking interrogations. They obliged me to make a complete inventory of all the existing objects in the residence, in the cathedral, and even among my personal effects and to fill a large notebook with all the information. It was a tedious and annoying task because I knew that so much of the Lord's goods would end up in their jaws.

Yet during all this struggle and potential danger, we were joyful, truly happy being faithful to the pope's exhortation to remain at our post; and this peace and serenity in suffering hardships and injustice irritated our Communist companions.

Someone has called what we were experiencing in 1949 and 1950 a persecution. But I wish to be precise toward the atheistic Chinese government. I do not wish to call persecution the confiscation of goods, the occupation of our churches, of our residences, and of our works; or the restrictions on worship, the semi-house arrest, et cetera: I wish only to call them warning signs of the persecution. At this point, the persecution was at the door, and it burst in on us like a hurricane.

From "Reform" to Hostility

The true motive of the persecution was the "reform" that the government wished to impose on us Catholics. In September of 1950 this reform was imposed on all Protestants of China. There were [then] in China 162 Protestant denominations that, sowing their erroneous doctrines and generating a true confusion of ideas, hindered our apostolic work. In Kaifeng alone, my city, there were thirteen Protestant sects. Although the number of foreign pastors was superior to that of the Catholic missionaries and their financial power was a hundred times superior to that of the Catholic Church, Protestantism in China claimed only about two million adherents. Yet all the Protestants in China shamefully collapsed at the feet of the government, accepting the reform, which led them to abandon the principles of their faith.

After this collapse, I went out one afternoon and ran into the so-called bishop of the Canadian Anglican Church. He was of Chinese origins but was educated in Canada. I asked him: "Did you sign the reform?"

He responded: "I put my name to a movement of patriotic love, because up to this date the foreigners have oppressed us." (While he was speaking like this, he was still receiving his generous stipend from Canada.)

And I said to him, "You signed a proclamation opposing Christ," and I explained the content of the reform.

That false bishop, fixing his eyes on me, said: "We are not like you Catholic priests: we have wives and children."

"For the love of Christ," I replied, "it is necessary to renounce wife and children."

He was afraid and went away, and I never saw him again.

I began to raise my voice against the reform even before it was proposed to Catholics. Three months after the collapse of the Protestants in November of 1950, the government unleashed a powerful propaganda campaign through the media. Employing the standard calumnies, lies, and intimidations, they attempted to make our Catholics give in to the reform in the same way that it had happened with the Protestants.

This reform was also presented to the Catholics with the title the "Movement of the Triple Independence," which is economic independence, independence from propaganda, and independence from the hierarchy.[30] In substance it includes the following points: (1) economic independence from abroad; (2) permission to propagate only the Chinese religion; (3) separation from the pope; (4) denial or reform of some dogmas of the Church; (5) transformation of Catholicism into a political instrument in the hands of the government; (6) liberation of the Church from the imperialists (that is, foreign missionaries); (7) foundation of the national (state-controlled) Catholic Chinese church; (8) "purification" of the Gospel in order to adapt it to the Marxist-Leninist doctrines.

We could not have adhered to a single reform; each one would have made us schismatic and heretical and would have brought us to apostasy. It was my duty to write to the priests and to the Christians, to explain and to preach, in public and in private, our very serious obligation to reject the reform energetically.

---

[30] This movement was begun among the Protestants in 1893 at Shanghai and re-elaborated in 1951 by Wu Yaozong, upon the request of Premier Zhou Enlai.

Why such a rigid position? In the city of Kaifeng there was a Catholic from Peking who was an old Communist, with more than twenty years of militancy in the party; he was a smoker of opium and heroin. Everyone in China knows that when a rabid smoker of such drugs has no money, he sells wife and children to buy a little of the putrid stuff. And so he discovered that he could profit from my domicile conditions of semi–house arrest, and he would come to take away from the episcopal residence any objects that he could sell for money. One day I detained him: "Do you trust a Catholic bishop?" I said to him.

"Yes, especially if he is European."

"Well, then," I continued, "out of respect for your old papa, catechist, why not tell me which decrees from Peking or Moscow concern the Catholic Church?"

He promised to bring me some secret memorandums; in fact, on various occasions he brought me several circulars (a good seventeen) that came from Moscow, translated in Chinese and given only to the old party members or issued by the central government of Peking. From those memorandums I learned of the genuine diabolical content of the reform, presented with the bland name of Movement of the Triple Independence.

The struggle had begun: on one side was the government with all its powers and means, and on the other side, those of us who, even in the state of semi-liberty, opposed them with a strong resistance.

At the beginning of 1951 hatred of the Catholic Church spread like wildfire, and January of that year marked the true beginning of the religious persecution in all of China, although for some missions in the interior of China the persecution began with Christmas of 1950. The vigil of that Christmas was a day of orders and counter-orders on the part of the local government and the police. They forced us to destroy the Nativity already set up, to rip up the large murals illustrating the mystery of Christ's birth, and to remove every decoration in the cathedral.

Because we had expected some harassment on the part of the local government, we had asked [the Vatican] and obtained in advance from the Holy Father the option of celebrating a valid vigil Mass in the afternoon or in the evening with the effect of fulfilling our Christmas duty. While I was at the foot of the altar, selecting the sacred vestments for the Mass, a police platoon entered the cathedral and forced me to follow them to the police station. I had just a moment to tell a missionary to celebrate the Mass. In his office the police chief asked me in a surly manner: "Who gave you permission to celebrate Christmas?"

I responded: "For Catholics it is a holy day of obligation, and as such it is marked in red on the calendar printed for Christians with the permission of the government."

And the chief: "Higher orders have been issued forbidding the celebration of Christmas this year; the transgressors will be severely punished."

I asked to be able to celebrate Christmas as a regular Sunday in ordinary time, but he refused me. Then I asked if I could celebrate a weekday Mass and was prohibited from doing so. On that day of universal joy our churches remained closed, and our residences put under guard. For us it was a Christmas in mourning; it was more like Good Friday, because that Christmas day was the day that began the Church's "Via Crucis" in China: the long and exhausting martyrdom of a glorious Church in chains.

The Accusation of "Imperialist"

On January 8, 1951, ten officials came to the episcopal residence to give me an ultimatum: "Clearly explain to the government your position regarding the reform." I was happy to respond. I explained the triple independence or reform, and the reasons we Catholics could not accept it. They, not content, wished to have a more explicit declaration, and then articulating my words, I said: "Whether as a private individual or as the archbishop and metropolitan, I cannot ever accept the reform; my priests and nuns, whether foreigners or Chinese, and my Christians cannot accept the reform. If a priest, a nun, or a Christian adheres to it, I shall punish them with canonical sanctions. As long as I have a crumb of liberty, I shall apply all the means at my disposition to obstruct the rising and forming of the independent, schismatic national Chinese church in my ecclesiastical province and in my archdiocese."

After this frank declaration, the chief of the expedition, companion Kuo, and I looked at each other in silence. Then, pale and astonished, he gave the order to leave, and the officials silently left the episcopal residence.

Two days after, in a public assembly, crowded with students and members of the red associations, the authorities of the government and the party, said, "The head of the Catholic Church of Kaifeng not only has explicitly declared a wish to punish those who adhere to the independent national church but has dared to obstruct its rise and formation; well, we today declare him an imperialist." To be declared an imperialist in a Communist regime means to be declared an enemy of the government, an enemy of the people, a reactionary, and a subversive. That was the day of my condemnation, January 10, 1951.

That evening my missionaries expressed their solidarity with their presence and with their words of support and asked me for my blessing, which they thought would be my last: it was a very moving scene. I was ready for any event; I was already prepared for everything. In adherence to the norms received by the Holy See, I even nominated a delegate vicar, a Chinese priest, Father Steven Ho, who would succeed me as head of the mission in case of my imprisonment or exile.

On January 17, the Catholics of Kaifeng were forced to participate, in procession, in an anti-American, pro-Korean War demonstration. On their part, the Catholics informed the authorities that they would take part only as a demonstration of patriotic love and never as an anti-Christian demonstration. They were reassured and that morning, many, having decided to defend their Faith, approached the altar to receive the Eucharist.

When the procession of four hundred Catholic participants was leaving the residence, students from the boys' middle school Hua Yang joined the group with two large posters depicting pictures offensive to our religion; the Christians managed to rip the posters from the students' hands and tear them to shreds. An elderly Churchwarden cried out: "This is today's first victory: everyone on their knees. As we stand before our bishop, who represents the pope, let us profess our faith, which, perhaps today, we will have to defend. Let us sing the Our Father, the Hail Mary, and the Creed!" And they sang their profession of faith accompanied by the notes of a pathetic melodia (similar to a harmonica). It was a moving moment: many were teary-eyed.

I did my best to encourage those dear children: "Today we must be ready to manifest our love for our Faith and for our country. Be courageous, and remember how I have always repeated in the last months: "Show your strength." Deeply moved, I blessed them.

Along the streets and in the public square the young people were expected, as a sign of approval, to respond to the acclamations by raising clenched fists. But when the cries were in praise of the Chinese national church or the triple reform or in condemnation of the pope, our young people, notwithstanding the threats of the Reds, did not raise their fists nor did they accept the fliers expressing antireligious propaganda.

My arrest, feared by the missionaries, did not happen immediately; the Lord wished me to remain semiliberated for the rest of January and all of February and March; and I continued to struggle. It was, however, possible for me to strengthen many Christians in faith and to prepare everyone for the persecution. During those three months, the press spewed calumnies and lies on me and on the Church. In an attempt to catch me red-handed and, therefore, to be able to arrest me, nothing was left untried; for entire days I was subjected to unnerving interrogations, while, on the walls of the episcopal residence and on the building itself, posters appeared with inscriptions and drawings of individuals opposed to me. In an attempt to provoke me, the Popular Front mobilized young people who, each day, staged a racket under my windows and covered the walls with vulgar insults. Sometimes they broke the windows of our rooms, but it was all useless. There was no reaction on my part except for dutiful protests.

The day of my imprisonment came on April 1, 1951, a Sunday in Albis (low Mass). On that day the Christians were celebrating the fourth anniversary of my episcopal consecration and the twenty-fifth anniversary of one of the missionary priests. From the first hours of the morning I noted an unusual coming and going in the area of the residence; I told my people to be vigilant, prudent, and calm. During the sacred functions we heard sounds of gongs, horns, and tambourines mixed with shouts. They wished to disturb our functions and provoke our reaction. I gave orders to the Christians not to move.

Just as the sacred functions were finished, there appeared at the door of the cathedral a gathering of young people from the Popular Front, all of them students, male and female, with their fists held up against me shouting: "Down with the imperialist Pollio! Death to you! Leave China!" At the same time I saw all the walls of the cathedral and the residence and the town wall literally full of offensive and obscene figures. That tumultuous crowd was waiting for a rude gesture from me, a hard word to lead me to their ends. Very slowly I managed to arrive at the episcopal residence (a distance of about fifteen meters from the cathedral) without offering anything and with a smile on my lips.

They were also shouting, "Down with the Christians, followers of European dogs," when suddenly a cry was heard from a missionary, Father Edoardo Piccinini: "Long live the pope, long live our archbishop!" For the Catholics it was the sign for the counterattack. One side was shouting, "Down with ..." and the other side, the Christians, were shouting at the top of their voices, "Long live ..." The police who had already encircled the residence immediately entered the courtyard, and the colonel, accompanied by four armed policemen, went straight into my office.

"What is going on in the courtyard?" he asked me.

And I: "I'm asking you, Colonel, what is happening?"

"This is how you respond to your government?"

And I: "Today it is my turn to respond like this." (I knew in fact that it was the government inciting what was happening.)

"Put handcuffs on him," he shouted to the police officers; then in a threatening and excited tone he fixed his feline eyes on me and said: "Imperialist, you are responsible for the tumult that occurred today in the courtyards of this residence."

Decisively and calmly fixing my eyes on him, I said: "Colonel, I say to you that you alone and the young people from the Popular Front are responsible for the tumult."

He, with an imperious manner and voice, responded: "Silence, imperialist, you are not permitted to speak. I declare you under arrest."

The Courage of the Faith

I was declared under arrest by the one responsible for the tumult that occurred at my residence. I was now in the hands of the government; the desired prey of the last two years was finally taken, and not for purposes of expulsion. The police scattered the crowd and stood guard over me. After a brief time they brought me to the police headquarters. While I was in the middle of a platoon of police officers descending the stairs of my episcopal residence, a group of young Catholic girls and boys, all members of the Legion of Mary,[31] courageously stopped that armed procession and said to the colonel: "You wish to bring our bishop to jail not because he is an imperialist but because he is against the schism [reform]; well, you know that not even we will sign the reform; we will never detach ourselves from the pope, and we will never betray that Faith that the missionaries, with their sacrifices and efforts, have brought us from Rome."

The colonel tried to convince those young people of my imperialism in China, but he did not succeed. Then he began threatening them and took their names and addresses. Those courageous young people, having seen that there was nothing to do, said: "Colonel, you wish at all costs to imprison our archbishop; well, you, he, and your police officers will have to pass over our heads"; and they sat down on the stoop in front of the episcopal residence. They were then forced out of the residence and the house was put under guard.

Toward evening, some police officers, furnished with a written warrant, led me and Father Piccinini away. Brother Francesco Quartieri also wished

---

[31] The Legion of Mary was founded in Dublin 1921 by Frank Duff.

to follow me; as always, he was close to me in the moments of major difficulties. We were conducted to the office of the police, where that same evening, we submitted to the first interrogation. I defended the rights of the Church, and I accused the young people of the Popular Front of having invaded the courtyards of the episcopal residence and having staged a demonstration of hate against religion and Europeans. The judge jumped to his feet and, cursing me, said: "Only you imperialists are invaders and not the young people of the Popular Front or the Communists. The government protects religion and Europeans. This evening, in this courtroom, you have added a serious charge to your already serious crimes: that of calling young Communists invaders. You are an imperialist, an enemy of the people; therefore, the young people, coming into the residence to do what they did, have demonstrated their love for their country."

He forbade me to speak. I was declared guilty, and at midnight sharp I was enclosed in a prison cell annexed to the police office; Father Piccinini and Brother Francesco were put into another cell.

While in prison that first night, I was thinking over the events of the day, when suddenly I heard voices of young girls outside my door. They seemed to be voices I knew. Perhaps they were the voices of my Christians, my catechumens, or students at our high school and girls' middle school. Were they already, at that young age, confined by the government? I cupped my hand to my ear, but I could not hear clearly. Suddenly I heard the desperate cry of a little girl about four years old: "Mamma, mamma, let's go home," and the mamma said: "Baby doll, don't cry, the police brought us here; [but] they will not kill us, we shall return home in a few days, you shall see." From the desperate cry of that innocent baby, and from the voice of that mamma, twenty-eight years old, I understood that they were the same young people and girls who, on the preceding day, had wished to defend the innocence of their archbishop and thus attest to their total adherence to the pope and to the Catholic Faith. On that same night, the police had arrested them and conducted them to that prison with chains on their hands.

Eight of the girls, among whom were the mamma and baby, were shut up in a cell next to mine; one of them was conducted into the harsh prison, where I would then be passed and where I had the consolation of seeing one day through the bars; another young woman, because of her strength and courage, was put in a cell by herself. The young men were locked up in the area solely for men.

The morning of the second day, Father Amelio Crotti, pastor of the cathedral, joined us in prison. That night, while our first trial was beginning, our residence was surrounded by soldiers and policemen who were carrying out an extremely thorough search that lasted until morning and concluded with the arrest of Father Crotti. Father Piccinini was transferred to my cell, while Father Crotti and Brother Francesco ended up in another cell. All four of us remained in this prison for 129 days, from April 1 to August 7.

From the first days in the cell I felt an extraordinary peace, that of witnessing Christ through the sufferings of a spiteful persecution. I went over the cause of my imprisonment, that of remaining in communion with Rome, and I felt an unspeakable joy. Moreover, with my arrest, I had been considered worthy of opening the legal proceedings of the bishops and the missionaries.

This thought, although it caused me so much joy, also came with a veil of sadness. For nearly six months we had fought bitterly with the atheistic Communist government that had tempted us with every type of allurement and deceit in order to make us separate from Rome and fell the Christians. To this end they unleashed a massive journalistic propaganda campaign, but the Christians solidly resisted, following their pastor. They heard the cries: "The Chinese for China, and the Chinese for the liberty of their popular institutions. Let the Christians have their faith, but they must adhere to the Three Autonomies; they must be free from doctrinal formalism and free from hierarchical dependence on the Vatican." But the Christians held firm; even in public demonstrations they energetically rejected the reform.

Only one fell: a youth, eighteen years old. And since I have promised to speak keeping to the truth, I must mention that this fellow was a seminarian, a student at the junior-high level of the minor seminary: educated and helped by the missionaries, he had been sent to the seminary in order to become one of tomorrow's apostles on earth. These boys had to attend the missionary middle school (even after it was guided by the Communists), and in this school Ly Mao Te—the student in question—had drunk the Communists' antireligious and xenophobic poison. Our exhortations were wasted on him, as were those of his classmates. Several times he led groups of young Communists and students of the Popular Front into my office in order to insult and provoke me. But I treated them with sincere charity, so that they might come to their senses. One day, among the other insults, he said to me: "Either you resign as archbishop and leave China, or the government and the progressive party will deport you."

I replied to him: "Neither the government nor you progressives have any power to dismiss me." He reported each word and exhortation to the police, adding false statements and calumnies. He went so far as to sign the reform. I gave him the opportunity of a retraction, even sending friends and relatives to persuade him, but he reacted angrily, preferring to persist in his error. I had to excommunicate him. From the day that the canonical sanction fell on him, Ly Mao Te was like one possessed by the devil. And it was precisely this seminarian traitor who most often presented himself at my trials, repeating his false testimony; it was he who in the famous popular judgment, of which I shall speak in its time, slapped me publicly.

While heroic young boys and girls, in chains in that prison, gave heroic example for their Faith, Ly Mao Te came into that same prison to betray other Christians. Those were the joys and sorrows of the first days in my dark, but beloved cell.

Six Months of Trials

My detention, like that of the other three missionaries, lasted exactly six months, during which I was subjected to a good thirty-two penal trials.

I remained in the first prison, next to the police headquarters, from the night of April 1 to August 7, 1951. During this period, I was put on trial a good twenty-two times. A special tribunal, composed of civil judges and representatives of the Communist governmental organizations, was instituted to judge me. At times the number of presiding judges reached fifteen.

The trials under the Communist regime are nerve-racking. Their form of justice is absurd: they invent inaccurate and improbable charges, read the most repugnant depositions, and present numerous false witnesses; and the detainee is always under an increasingly threatening pressure until he confesses the crimes ascribed to him.

What were the charges against me? At first, only eight charges regarded the Faith, and I promptly signed them during the second trial, happy to offer my life for my Faith and to demonstrate to the masses of pagans that the Catholic missionaries are truly the good pastors of which Jesus speaks, ready to give their lives for their sheep, and not mercenaries who abandon the flock at the approach of the wolf, as some in China have demonstrated.

These eight charges that bring me honor and that appear in the definitive sentence were the following:

1. having written to the bishops and the missionaries against the reform

2. having sent circulars to the Christians

3. having excommunicated the seminarian traitor Ly Mao Te

4. having instituted the Legion of Mary in my mission

5. having maintained that the Legion of Mary was not a subversive organization aimed at the defeat of the regime of the people of China in coordination with the interests of the imperialists

6. having exhorted the faithful not to adhere to the schism

7. having obstructed our Catholic youth from enrolling in the Popular Front

8. having suspended the members of the Chinese national church from the sacraments, declaring them faithless

But these eight accusations were not enough for the condemnation desired by those bringing the charges; so they took up another seventy-two charges unrelated to the Faith, some of which were extremely grave and regarded betrayal, espionage, conspiracies, and collaboration with America.

DIARIES OF THE CHINESE MARTYRS

I wish briefly to bring up one of the most serious charges. I was accused of being an American spy in China, ably covering up the espionage with the mantle of missionary work. I was accused of annually receiving from the American government the sum of $300,000 in order to sustain my imperialist activity and to organize within the Chinese territory an espionage service favoring the Nationalists against Red China. I was accused of having corrupted two officers of the Chinese army, offering each one three and a half million dollars and sending them to Formosa (Taiwan) to collaborate with Chiang Kai-shek against Mao Zedong. I was accused of having called the Japanese airplanes into the refugee camps that we missionaries had built in the enormous inundation of the Yellow River (diverted by the Nationalists in June of 1938 near Kaifeng in order to stop the Japanese advance toward the west, which had transformed my vast archdiocese into a great yellow sea). In a Catholic weekly that I founded at Kaifeng, which lasted only two months, I was charged with having printed signs accusing Russia of religious persecution and massacres of priests. Finally, I was charged with possessing a clandestine radio-transmission apparatus and of transmitting calumnies against Communist China.

Many other imputations were heaped upon me in the name of the people and their government.

The Dynamics of the Trials

The trials were dramatic. I was placed in the accuser's box surrounded by police officers who were armed with submachine guns, rifles, pistols, and with chains and irons. The trials almost always took place at night and lasted from three to eight hours. There was no defense, outside of my firm will to resist the absurd and false charges. Often I was not even permitted to defend myself in order to demonstrate the falsity of the accusations. The presiding judge used every means to cause me to contradict myself so that he could accuse me of being a liar. In order to force me to confess my crimes, false witnesses were introduced into the trial and forced to recite their part against me.

In the procedural debates, much time was occupied by the account of the charges, the deposition of the false witnesses, and the reading of records from past trials. They were meticulously, minutely written, often with ambiguous phrases, with the objective of finding some minor disagreement. The judges would repeat the same presumed crimes against the "people" and against the "government of the people"; no defense assisted me, and at times I was authorized to respond only yes or no and nothing else. When I was permitted to defend myself, and my arguments threatened to make their fragile and inconsistent castle of charges collapse, an angry voice would thunder: "Quiet, imperialist, you are prohibited from speaking." I would then be led out of the room and placed against a wall; and after a half-hour break I would be led back into the room in order to listen to the new charges against me.

Very often, during the trials, the judges tried to convince me that America, in its intrusive imperialist action, was completely at the service of the pope, which—for them—represented the most terrible warmongering in the world, and that the war was made by imperialist nations in the name of the people. When I was permitted to speak, I defended to the last the innocence of the pope; I demonstrated the paternal work of the supreme pontiff for all the people, without distinction of race and religion. But some voices would silence me, and it was necessary to obey.

I was serene. I was always held up by the Faith and by the awareness of my duty. I did not wish to admit to anything, not even a minimal charge, nor did I wish to put my signature to any of the ambiguous charges that were imposed on me, not even the slightest. I signed none of them; I always signed my firm and decisive no to all the judges' absurdities.

The mental stress imposed on the person subjected to this process tends to weaken his reflexes and willpower, making him the easy prey of the interrogators. I have seen several incarcerated, who were malnourished and exhausted by a long period of detention, often with chains at their feet and irons at their wrists, admitting to faults, after having insistently sustained their innocence. Their hope of living had failed, and the tortures bowed them physically.

DIARIES OF THE CHINESE MARTYRS

The Chinese tortures are terrible; confessions are the only means of putting an end to an impossible situation. Then come the harsh sentences, forced labor, or even death as their result. The judges were weakening me physically.

Once during a trial that lasted eight hours, I fell down in a faint. After a five-minute break the judge ordered the trial to proceed: "Let the trial continue!" And I responded resolutely, "Yes, continue"; and although soaked with a cold sweat and with a droning in my ears and my vision blurred, I held firm another two hours. My will had not slackened.

I wish to describe briefly a scene from a criminal trial, which reveals the machinations of some of the Communist officials. The judge read long depositions that I resolutely denied.

"We have witnesses!" the judge shouted.

"Let them appear," I replied.

An officer, a youth wearing a Russian uniform and carrying arms, was led into the courtroom.

"Do you know me?" he said to me. "I am Hoang T'ao."

"I have never heard this name, nor do I know if such a person exists."

"The day of August 13, 1948," continued the officer, "I came to your episcopal residence in your office, and you exhorted me to betray the party, to go to that brigand Chiang Kai-shek, in order to cooperate with him against our leader Mao Zedong."

"I firmly deny having ever seen this officer. May I ask a question?"

And after receiving an affirmative response from the head judge, I asked that faux officer: "Were you in my office?"

"Yes, twice."

"Is my office situated west or east of the episcopal residence?"

"Who doesn't know it?" he responded coldly and embarrassed.

"Pray, please tell me."

"Your office is to the east of the episcopal residence," he said cynically.

"Honorable judges, I decisively reject his false testimony; he has been to my office twice for long interrogations, and he does not know that it is west of the episcopal residence."

The judges jumped up on their feet, shouting and threatening me; the police, meanwhile, were making noise with their arms and their chains attempting to frighten me.

An order was imposed on the guards to lead me out of the courtroom. I was led to a courtyard and placed with my shoulders against the wall, with a guard standing over me. I started to recite some prayers. A guard asked me: "Why are you moving your lips?"

"I am praying to my God."

"I forbid you to pray to God with your lips."

"Then I shall pray with my heart," I responded.

And the guard: "Not even with your heart can you pray."

About a half hour later I was led back into the courtroom; the officer who claimed to have visited me in my office was no longer there, and the judges passed on to other charges.

Life in Prison

For the first two months of my detention, in the local prison next to the police station, I was put in the same cell with Father Piccinini, while Father Crotti and Brother Francesco were placed in another cell. During the first week of June all three of them were transferred to a large room, where there were already dozens of detainees; and so I remained alone until August 7.

In that damp and dark cell, of just a few square feet, the time was spent between interrogations and trials, between prayers and the desire to know what was being said beyond the prison cells. The passing days were long and monotonous. Each religious object that I had was confiscated, and so were my eyeglasses, which were given back to me so that I could read the trial record. I did not have a single book to read: I dared to ask someone for one, but it was not granted to me. My confreres were living under the same conditions.

Often outside the door of my cell some guards would read aloud various articles from the newspapers, with the intention of making me hear the latest news and intimidate me. In these articles it was said that all the

people of the province (thirty million) were deeply offended by my imperialist activity and had staged public demonstrations in many cities, asking
the government for my punishment. After my expulsion from China I
found a way of consulting some of those newspapers, and therefore I was
able to copy some of the articles that I had already listened to from the
prison guards:

> People of Honan, let us wake up to the crimes of the imperialists,
> who have drugged the Chinese youth and children.... Since the
> Opium War the imperialists have been invading and sacking our
> China; besides using every form of economic, political, and military
> aggression, they have made use of the missionaries, who in their
> own country were put under serious espionage training. These
> same missionaries wrap themselves in the mantle of religion, and
> with a face suffused with philanthropy and with the pretext that the
> Gospel opens the kingdom of heaven, come to China to carry out
> their shameful mission of deceit, narcotizing the Chinese people
> and subjugating them. These people employ every type of method
> to deceive the Chinese people; from their infancy they make them
> forget their mother country. The imperialists Pollio and Crotti have
> made use of schools, orphanages, and hospitals like an insignia for
> secretly organizing reactionary associations: the Legion of Mary,
> the Eucharistic Crusade, the Daughters of Mary, et cetera. They
> have assaulted the Chinese people, helping themselves to every
> antirevolutionary cultural means and activity to diffuse the poison
> and damage the youth and the Chinese children.... They [mis-
> sionaries], with their compulsion, have not permitted their young
> scholars to join the New Democratic Youth organization. Of the
> hundred or more Christian students who were under the control
> of the so-called spiritual authority of the imperialist Pollio, not one
> has dared to join the New Democratic Youth. Chinese people, it
> is time to wake up; we cannot support this criminal activity.... Let
> us ask that Pollio and Crotti be severely punished.

On April 24, I heard clamors and shouts coming from the large theater located a few hundred meters from the prison. It was a meeting organized by the police in opposition to the imperialist nations, a so-called reunion, which the seminarians, the missionaries, and the Chinese priests were obligated to attend. The seminarians testified:

> From the first discourse, it was evident that the gathering was against archbishop Pollio and the missionaries of the Catholic Church. At the end of the discourse one of the accusers was shouting invectives against the archbishop and the Church, and all the people had to repeat the same phrases with a raised fist. The vast theater, which held four thousand spectators, resounded with cries and raised fists against the archbishop and the missionaries imprisoned with him. But in the midst of that crowd there was a small group of about thirty-eight courageous seminarians and Christians, who did not cry out or raise their fists. Seven of those young men, imprisoned from the night of April 1 to April 2, were led from the prison to that theater in order to listen for seven hours to those horrible crimes falsely attributed to their archbishop, so that they also could denounce him. From the stage, the accusers, one after the other, spewed calumnies against Monsignor Pollio and the missionary detainees, and the people responded in chorus hurling curses against them.

To describe my feelings about what I saw and heard during my imprisonment is impossible. Even now, I can think of it only with horror. Each day, new chained prisoners arrived at the prison, and that was just one of the many prisons in Kaifeng. The same scene and the same rotations were repeated in all the prisons. After a certain period of detention, the detainees were passed on to tougher prisons or to forced labor, or death. Those who were considered "progressive," or who had a bit of land, or who had done military service, suffered terribly: after having been falsely accused, they were required to submit to reeducation in dark, gloomy prison cells, even though many of them had already been marked for execution. I saw people stretched to the limits by spurious accusations and who in the end felt compelled to accept them. I read the desperation in the faces of the many who had fallen into the hands of a government that would exhaust them, crush them, and then end their lives with the slightest nod from a judge. I heard the shouts and the cries of people subjected to unjust trials, being forced to admit to nonexistent crimes, and to testify against other victims who were already doomed by the government.

I heard the screams of the prisoners subjected to torture, and I know well the horror of Chinese torture. The thud of the victims falling to the floor after having been tied to the beams by their thumbs pierced my soul.

I saw detainees reduced to rags, desperately admitting their own guilt, although they were innocent, just to put an end to the torment.

On June 13 the police called another meeting, this time against Monsignor Antonio Riberi, the apostolic internuncio (papal representative) in China; and on that day, as on April 24, I heard the cries of anger and hatred toward the pope's representative. An article in the *Honan Journal*, read to me by a judge, referred, among other charges, to the following: "The people will not tolerate the fact that an immigrant from Monaco, Antonio Riberi, [would] openly interfere in the Christian movement of patriotic love [the movement of the reform of the Catholic Church] and asks the government for his expulsion. The imperialist Riberi has always been and continues to be an enemy of the Chinese people and the new liberated China. He is a dog that runs behind American imperialism and a criminal cooperator of Chiang Kai-shek," et cetera.

The police chief wanted me to denounce Monsignor Riberi, who was my superior, but I defended the internuncio's innocence and affirmed my devotion to him, saying that I was delighted to be his friend.

In court on the following day, I was ordered to translate into Chinese the correspondence between Monsignor Riberi and me, correspondence that I had not had time to burn and that the police had sequestered on April 2. I responded: "I will never do it. I have no intention of doing it. You cannot obligate me to do it. You translate it." With a kick I was put out of the courtroom and led back to my cell.

The morning of June 20, all the Italian missionary residents were brought to the office of the police for interrogation. All the priests passed by my cell: from the small window, across the grate, I was able to see them, and they were able to see my head. They tried to hide their deep emotion on seeing me again after nearly two months. They spoke Italian among themselves loudly enough for me to hear, and so I was able to learn a few things regarding the priests, the Christians, and the missionary districts.

In July three priests of the regional seminary were expelled and had to pick up the documents for their trip at the police station. Once more they passed by my cell, and Father Giovanni Galmarini, tearfully, brushing against my window, humbly asked me: "Monsignor, bless us," and he burst into tears. I blessed him and the other two who were expelled with him.

"Blessed are those who are persecuted for righteousness' sake," our Lord proclaimed (Matt. 5:10); and in that cell I felt truly blessed to suffer for truth and justice and to bear witness to Jesus in my faith.

Praying in the Catacombs

During that sorrowful first period in that prison annexed to the police station, where privileged Christians were praying, suffering, and sacrificing themselves, day by day, for the triumph of the Faith, I had the consolation of reliving the scenes of the catacombs. I had, above all, the comfort of being able to celebrate clandestinely the holy Mass a good fifty-nine times. In my cell there was a footstool, and I thought: this will be my altar. I had a bowl for the boiled water that is given to the prisoners twice a day, and I said: this shall be my chalice. Since in those days the charges against me were of a political nature, the Communist leaders feared that I would become ill and die in prison and thus be deprived of the joy of seeing me shot; therefore, they permitted a catechist from the episcopal residence to bring me some wheat bread; and so a mouthful of this bread became my host.

What was still lacking for the celebration of the Mass was wine, but by resorting to a trick I also succeeded in getting wine. In China wine or vinegar from grapes did not exist; both were made from grains. I asked the head jailer for a bottle of grape vinegar for medicinal purposes because, I said, a little vinegar taken on an empty stomach would give me strength. The chief asked someone at the episcopal residence for some grape vinegar; the missionaries understood that I did not want grape vinegar, but wine from grapes, and they gave me a bottle of wine for the Mass. The little bottle was examined by the judges, who declared that it truly contained vinegar. And so a good four times I managed to have the wine brought to me.

Dressed like a convict, lacking priestly vestments, altar cloths, and candles; and either standing or seated on the floor before that footstool, I offered, on a piece of paper or in the palm of my hand some bread; and I offered in that cup a little wine, and I continued the Mass, from the Preface to the Communion. I also managed to say the Mass in honor of the Virgin Mary and to have the Canon—the words of the consecration—printed on some strips of paper, in which the missionaries had wrapped the bread; and so I was able to celebrate many times the entire sacrifice from the beginning to the end. Unfortunately, one day, a guard, while making a thorough search of the cell, discovered those strips of paper and ripped them up, ignoring, however, the contents.

I celebrated Mass fifty-nine times, always eluding the attention of the guards, who often would glance unexpectedly in my cell while I was celebrating. But they were never aware that I was carrying out the most sacred act that exists; to them I was always in complete observance of the police regulations. That Mass celebrated under those conditions, in that Communist prison was being blessed from heaven.

The Story of Siao Mei

Eight of the girls who heroically defended their Faith and my innocence were imprisoned and enclosed in a cell next to mine: among these was a mamma of a nearly four-year-old girl by the name of Siao Mei (Little Beauty). Those heroic women wished to communicate with me but did not know how to do it. Then they thought of the little girl. They asked the head jailer for permission, solely for the little one, to be able to leave the cell for a few hours each day in order to breathe better air. Given the narrowness of the cell and the frailty of the little girl, the permission was granted. And Siao Mei, while in the courtyard when the guards were at a little distance from my door, would say to me: "Our bishop, how are you? Mamma and the aunts send you their greetings. [The aunts were actually friends of her mother.] What should I say to them?"

And I: "Little one, tell your mamma and the aunts not to fear, not to sign the reform, but to be strong and to recite many Rosaries."

When those Christian women were incarcerated, they were not required to hand over the religious objects that they had had on their persons. So in the semi-obscurity of the cell and in the silence ... the prayer of those women, repeated hundreds of times, rose up to heaven: "Hail Mary," so that all were strong in their faith; "Hail Mary," for the triumph of religion and of Christ; "Hail Mary," for the persecuted and the persecutors. And in the course of three months, through that innocent little girl, nearly each day it was possible for me to communicate with my Christians.

If the jailer was approaching my door while Siao Mei was speaking with me, the child would not run away: she would distance herself with indifference a few steps, crouch down to the ground, and play with the dust and little stones, singing softly to herself, and in this way she always eluded the attention of the bullies.

One day I said to Siao Mei: "Bring me a rosary, the smallest that you have in the cell." The following day, the little one came and tried to pass a rosary through the crack in the door, but she did not succeed; the beads of the rosary were too big. "Hide it," I suggested to her, "tell your mamma to make me a rosary with some twine, if you have any" (it was forbidden to have any rope, twine, belts, or anything similar in the prison). A few days later Siao Mei returned and passed me something through the crack: it was some thin twine about 20 centimeters long. I examined it: that twine had been braided with threads taken from their dresses and bore twenty little knots: for two decades of the Rosary. For various months I recited my Rosaries on that little cord, while my thoughts were drawn toward the endless territories where the persecution was raging and is raging still today, and where millions of our brothers and sisters were resisting and are still resisting, every type of sufferance and violence.

"To whom do you wish the greater good, to the Lord or to the president, Mao Zedong?" It was a question asked each day of Siao Mei by a thug, and she was always ready: "To Jesus," and she turned her back and walked toward the cell where her mamma was waiting for her.

Another day the same colonel of the police force and director of the prison said to her: "Your archbishop has committed many crimes; he is bad" and then he shouted: "Down with Yang Lin [my Chinese name]!"

And the little one said: "No, he is good." At other times, when the gendarme were cursing or laughing at our holy religion, when it was threatened or attacked, the little one preferred to cry loudly and, with tears, to liberate herself from those wolves in police uniforms.

The imprisoned Christian women, wishing to make a brief course of spiritual exercises in that narrow and damp little cell, desired some themes from me for their meditations, and it was again through Siao Mei that I was able to provide them with the subjects for their meditation. Seated on the ground those young women, witnesses of God and the Church, spent five days in meditation and prayer, tasting the joy of the spirit and strengthening their purpose of suffering for the Church and the pope. Siao Mei, sitting silently near her mamma and raising her little hands, joined the innocent prayer that was reaching heaven.

Because of the scarce food and the foul air, the little one's delicate limbs did not resist the discomforts, and twice Siao Mei became ill. On the hard mat the little angel, because of the high fever and some stomach pains and headaches, was crying and calling ardently for her maternal grandmother (an elderly woman who was ill and remained at home alone after the arrest of her daughter and little granddaughter), and often she would be delirious. Only the exhortations of her mamma and her "aunts" to suffer for Jesus could calm the little girl, happy to offer her contribution for the triumph of Christ.

The Eucharist behind the Bars

The cell next to mine, with the eight young women of whom I spoke, together with Siao Mei, had become a sanctuary: in it the daily sufferance was sanctified, and many times the consecrated host was able clandestinely to penetrate that enclosure. Since they were not on trial, but only under the interrogators, whose goal was to extort charges against us, the girls were able to receive food from relatives, through the jailers. My missionaries thought of giving them the Eucharist, as comfort and strength in our daily earthly pilgrimage.

The breads in China are small, formed like a cone and steamed rather than baked. They are completely soft—there is no crust—so by making a small incision, it was easy to hide something small and subtle. The missionaries would hide little particles of consecrated hosts in these breads; the breads were then brought to the jail by the relatives of the young women and consigned to the jailers, who then brought them to the cell. The heroic detainees would break the breads and find the consecrated hosts and then with their own hands receive Communion.

Certainly, those were the happiest days of our detainment, when Jesus penetrated that cell in order to sanctify it and to give those prisoners renewed strength. We spent many feast days in that gloomy prison: they were days of sweet religious memories, of hope in the victory of the Church, of joy in offering to Jesus our own sufferings. Such were the days of the Ascension, Pentecost, Corpus Christi, and the first Fridays and first Saturdays of the months from May to August and of the other Sundays. In my cell Jesus came down and changed a most precious piece of bread into his Body and Blood, placed in a bowl, while in the other cell He entered, through the hands of the very people who hated him, in order to find Himself in friendly and faithful hands.

Each time those witnesses of the Faith received the Eucharist, they would leave a particle of the bread, and sit there on the stools making adoration all day in silence. Praying aloud was prohibited in the prison, but from those warm hearts, prayers [like incense] were raised up to and penetrated the heavens. Sometimes I thought: that lurid cell that was hiding

45

the King of kings was more precious than our churches, too often deserted. In their passionate and total dedication, those young women manifested their fidelity and love for Jesus: to die rather than bow to an atheistic government and to die rather than abandon their allegiance to the Faith. In the evening, the last particle that was not received in Communion during the morning was consumed. The adoration ceased, the shadows of night fell, new cries and tears would be listened to, but the fervor of our souls continued, and the intention of offering ourselves up for Jesus increased.

In the wall that divided our cells there was a hole stopped up with paper and covered from my side with a paper stuck to the wall; the guards did not understand the importance of that hole. And it was through that hole that a good three times I let descend on the heads of my faithful ones sacramental absolution. They felt the need of purifying themselves ever more, in order to be more worthy of Jesus, their only treasure and for some, their spouse. "I absolve you," I repeated with emotion from my cell, and a soft cry echoed my sacramental words. Was it a cry over physical pains, mistreatment, or torture? No, they were tears of joy for having been chosen to suffer false accusations in the name of Jesus, tears of those who understood the value of the sacraments in those circumstances.

It was not easy for me—nor for the young women—to stay at that hole in the wall, even briefly, because the guards watched us continuously from the window of the door, and it was necessary to take advantage of the occasions in which their vigilance was less severe and the guarding of the cells was left to only one sentry.

On three occasions a general meeting of the police was called in order to hatch new plots against the innocent Christians and to invent new crimes committed by the missionary "imperialists." A public assembly was called against some who were guilty of possessing lands: after they were dragged with their hands tied before the people's court, they were then sent to their execution. Lastly, an expedition of well-nourished police squadrons would go out to stir up fear in the population and return with a large group of the arrested, one tied to the other and each one bearing a look of panic and death on his face or a sense of that desperation or regret for not having first ended his existence. These were the situations I observed looking through the hole, and raising my hand, I absolved them.

On June 30, feast of St. Paul, in the early hours of the afternoon a young Christian was in front of my cell; he was tightly tied to a rope and had irons at his wrists. Two sentries stood guard over him. I saw him and I fixed my eyes on him through the crack in my door. From time to time, without stirring up suspicions, he would look at my cell, which he appeared to know, with a glance that seemed to say, "You see, I did not betray my Faith. They wanted me to adhere to the reform, but I preferred this rope and these irons."

What a difference between his comportment and that of the pagans arrested with him; he had no sense of sorrow on his face; indeed, his look reflected the pride of showing himself Christian. On his nude and dirty chest there appeared an old crucifix. When he was moved in order to go into the courtroom, this prayer came to me spontaneously: "St. Paul, you who experienced chains and prisons, loosen the ropes and the irons and restore him to his poor family."

The Christian women languishing in the cell near mine, in a magnificent display of fraternal understanding, were living deeds worthy of their sisters of the first centuries of the Church. In the third courtyard of the prison, their friend Josephine Ly, whom I have mentioned, because of her faith and her courage, was relegated to a damp, dark cell. The women thought: we can see our archbishop through a small grate, when he is led to the trials; we can communicate with him through Siao Mei; we are able to receive the comfort of the Eucharist. But in her prison, Josephine Ly has none of these consolations: we need to send her the Eucharist. But how do we do it? They thought again of Siao Mei. For several days they instructed her well. On June 8, the time approached in which the sentry got up to open the door to allow Siao Mei to leave the cell. The Christians took a consecrated particle, folded it in a clean tissue and put it in the pocket of the little one's dress, next to her heart. The mother of the little girl was nervous and unsure of the plan. Through the hole in that cell she asked me if she should allow her to go on that dangerous errand.

The young mother feared that the guards would discover the Eucharist, in which case the Host would be profaned and other missionaries, together with the bearers of the precious Bread, would be imprisoned.... After considering the responsibility and the gravity of the plan, I responded with a monosyllable: "Yes," and I traced a Sign of the Cross toward the nearby cell, imploring the protection of heaven on dear little Siao Mei. But that mamma, not yet content, took the hands of her little creature, raised them to the level of her face and asked her: "Tell me, Siao Mei, if the guard finds the Host on you, what will you do?" And the little one calmly said: "If one of the sentries finds this host on me, be certain, mamma, I would eat it and I would not give it to the jailer." These words moved the paternal heart of the Holy Father Pius XII, when I told him the story in a private audience that I had with him on my return from China, and they caused him to exclaim: "A dogmatic response."

Dear Siao Mei had understood that if a sacrilegious (wicked) hand had attempted to profane the holy Host, although she had not made her first Communion, she would have been able to receive Jesus, because she could not have given the particle of the Eucharist to a Communist guard, a pagan enemy of God.

The padlock creaked, and the door was opened. Siao Mei, smiling and indifferent, left the cell and stayed in the first courtyard playing by herself; and then she moved to the second courtyard without any difficulty. In that courtyard the guard wished to send her away; it was a guard with a haughty expression, one who had given proof of his loyalty and his capacity to tighten the chains of many innocent victims.

"I wish to see my aunt Josephine Ly," Siao Mei said.

"You cannot," the guard responded roughly.

"Why can't I? She is my aunt." And she began to shout: "Aunt Josephine, Aunt Josephine!"

The guard yelled harshly and wished to push the child out of the courtyard, but Saio Mei purposely began to cry and sob loudly. The guard, fearing he would be accused of having hit the little girl, swiftly opened Josephine Ly's cell and let the little angel inside. And innocent

Siao Mei gave Josephine the precious little tissue.... She remained there in the cell for a little while and then gave out another cry, and the guard opened the door again. Thus, with tears and some little tricks, Siao Mei succeeded in bringing Communion to the faux aunt. In that dark prison, criminal sentences were being issued against the innocent or against the followers of Christ, and while scenes of terror and horror were being renewed, we were living scenes of piety and love, scenes of the first centuries of the Church.

Before the persecution broke out, one evening in March 1951, kneeling before the image of the Sacred Heart of Jesus, Siao Mei repeated together with her mamma this prayer: "O Jesus, the storm rails against the Church, but we do not want to go to Hell. We wish to be always with you, we promise you that we shall remain faithful to your vicar, the pope, to our archbishop, and to our missionary priests."

This prayer flowed spontaneously from the heart of the young Christian mamma, who truly felt her faith. But then the hour of darkness came. The young mamma, in a moment of weakness and confusion, was led to sign the "triple independence," which was equivalent to an act of adhesion to the schism. As a consequence of this action, she was invited to appear on the stage of the people's theater, where thousands of schoolchildren and authorities of the province were gathered to speak against the Church and the missionaries.

"You see," she said, "I have a very intelligent and pious little girl who could become like St. Thérèse of the Child Jesus, but perhaps she will never have this honor, because we are poor! It is time to distance the imperialists from China."

While the mamma was reciting this part, Siao Mei was also on the stage, and the agents of the police were offering her candy in order to keep her tranquil. When her mamma said that also the archbishop was an imperialist, the little girl promptly let the candies fall and ran to her mother, tugging at her dress, saying while sobbing: "Mamma, let's go home."

After they returned home, for many days Siao Mei did nothing other than repeat: "Mamma, did we not promise the Sacred Heart of Jesus that we wished always to remain united to the pope, to the archbishop, and to the missionaries? Mamma, we must not go to hell."

Moved by these words and overcome by remorse for having renounced her Faith, that brave woman went back to the missionary and confessed her sin; she decided to bear everything, even prison, in order to remain faithful to the promises she made to the Sacred Heart of Jesus. And for Jesus she became imprisoned and remained there with Siao Mei for three months.

When she was granted provisional liberty and could return home, all the Christians wished to see her and to question her child prodigy.

"Siao Mei, what would you like to do?"

"My great desire is to unite myself to Jesus in Holy Communion."

And the missionaries who remained free wished to satisfy that ardent desire. They questioned her on the catechism and were surprised at the precise responses she gave to all the questions. They did not think that they could deny Communion to that angel of strength, who had suffered prison out of love for Jesus; and thus at the age of three years and nine months they admitted her to the Eucharistic table. Sometime later the vicar general also gave her the sacrament of Confirmation.

The greatness of spirit of this marvelous child appears evident also in other particulars of her life. One day a Mr. Kao, the director of the former Catholic girls' school, a faithless progressive, went to Siao Mei's mamma. As soon as the little one saw him enter the house, she planted herself in front of him and asked: "What have you come here to do?"

"I must speak with your mamma," the gentleman Mr. Kao responded.

The little one turned to her mamma: "Do not go out of the house," and turning toward the visitor said: "You have betrayed the Faith; if you wish to go to hell, go there, but do not come here looking for us. Here you are not welcome. Go away." I do not know what went through the soul of that Christian traitor, but having been addressed in that manner; he bowed his head before the authority of that little child and went away without a word.

One morning, after the functions in the cathedral, Siao Mei was approached by Mr. Mong, another Christian progressive, who, smiling, offered her compliments and candy.

The little one took two steps back and said: "I know that you are a member of the reform church. Therefore, I do not accept your candies."

The mamma, having heard this, in a tone of disapproval said to her: "My daughter, do not be rude."

"But mamma, do you believe that we have to be afraid? I have received Confirmation, and I am a soldier of Jesus Christ."

Late one evening little Siao Mei was in bed while her mother was finishing some tasks. Before going to sleep she wished to put the bedsheets in order. Her daughter had put them in disarray, but to her surprise she noted here and there some pieces of brick.

"What imagination this child has! Amusing herself playing with pieces of bricks." She threw them away but did not make a fuss over it. In the heart of the night, Siao Mei woke up and called: "Mamma, mamma."

"What do you want? Go to sleep, my little one."

"I cannot find the bricks."

"What are you looking for? It is late, go to sleep."

"No, find me the bricks. I do not wish to sleep comfortably in my bed, while so many other Christians are suffering in prison for Jesus." And she would not quiet down until her mamma gave back to her those pieces of brick.

Ferocity against the Legion of Mary

On July 28, Saturday, I was led back to court, where I immediately submitted to the last of the twenty trials to which I was subjected during the four months of my detention in the first prison (April through July). Four judges were present; some were writing, and then there were the usual thugs. The chief of police, who was presiding over the session, began:

"Does there exist in the city of Kaifeng the Legion of Mary?"

I: "Yes."

"Who instituted the Legion of Mary at Kaifeng?"

"I did."

"When?"

DIARIES OF THE CHINESE MARTYRS

"On December 8, 1947."

"We are tired of you. You do not wish to confess to anyone the crimes you have committed, yet they are numerous. Today's sessions will concern solely the Legion of Mary. I am hoping that four months of detention has done you good. We have made you reflect much on the sincerity and the kindness of the government, which wishes to pardon you. Respond therefore, by confessing your crimes."

After pausing for several minutes, a second judge asked me: "Is not the Legion of Mary a reactionary organization, an instrument of imperialism in the hands of you missionaries who cover yourselves with the mantle of a lamb in order to propagate the gospel, but within you are wolves that undermine the foundations of the democratic-progressive State of China? Admit it."

"I certainly cannot admit it. The Legion is an association of fervent Christians that, under the auspices of the most holy Virgin, is dedicated to a more profound personal spirituality and apostolate. We missionaries feel that we are truly good pastors and not wolves; we do not put on any mantle, but we present ourselves to the people with the truth of the gospel."

I wished to proceed in order to explain the scope of the Legion, but the imperious voice of the chief ordered me to be silent.

"In the North, where the weed of the Legion is flourishing and already counts several hundred leaders, the government has dug up many crimes. At Tientsin the leaders of the Legion receive forty-five American dollars a month for their espionage against China. You do not need these few dollars; you receive $300,000 each year, and you use that money from America for espionage in your province and for the terrorist organization. We have discovered secret conspiracies against the Christian progressives, who have awakened from your narcotization and have adhered to the reform. You call them apostates and you try to kill them. Can you deny this?"

I: "I do not deny having called 'apostate' those who have adhered to the movement for the independence of the Church, like the progressive seminarian Ly Mao Te [smiles of scorn on the lips of those present], but I firmly deny the conspiracies and the crimes charged to the Legion of Mary."

The judge stood up: "You deny? Even the press has spoken of it."

The police chief intervened: "This is a serious insult toward the government. We represent the government, and today with this insult you have been saddled with a new offense, and it will weigh heavily on you."

I: "I do not believe in your press when it concerns things regarding the Church, because I have found it untruthful. When it speaks of politics I do not give my opinion; politics does not interest me."

The chief shouted: "Demonstrate that the government-supported press is untruthful."

I: "Do you recall last January 17? On that day the Catholics of Kaifeng, by order of the police, had to take part in an anti-American demonstration, and they participated solely after having obtained assurance on the part of the government that they would not have to accept or sign the triple independence by the church. The anti-American parade was then transformed also into an anti-Christian parade. No one of my Christians accepted the reform, you know it, yet the following day what did the *Journal of Honan* write falsely in very large letters? It wrote that all the Catholics of Kaifeng had been awakened and had approved the triple independence enthusiastically."

The colonel said, "Quiet. The antirevolutionary elements of the Legion will be punished in accordance with the regulations. You also are one of these elements, and you shall be punished most severely, given your stubbornness in denying everything."

A minute of silence followed from both sides.

The judge began again: "Do you confess that Riberi, that citizen of Monaco, your so-called apostolic internuncio, a Vatican spy in our nation, has toured many provinces of China in order to plot, in collaboration with the brigand Chiang Kai-shek, a plan of war against the government of the Chinese people? Do you confess that in view of this plan, he has placed you, his faithful dog, here at Kaifeng as archbishop, so that you may organize the Catholics of this city and all the provinces against the Communists?

I: "Monsignor Riberi, apostolic internuncio, is not a Vatican spy. Before your rise to power, and before the installment of the government of the people at Peking [October 1, 1949], he visited some provinces of China solely for ecclesiastical business. He has not plotted any war plan. It was not he who nominated me archbishop of Kaifeng, but the pope, because only the pope can nominate bishops and archbishops."

The judge continued to insist: "Following Riberi's directives, you have instituted the Legion of Mary at Kaifeng, you are surrounded by a group of counterrevolutionaries, and you are conspiring against the new China and the Chinese."

I: "Neither I, nor the missionaries, nor the Christians are hatching plots; our action is in the light of the sun, as is the work of the Legion; you can still ask its members. During the interrogations at the episcopal residence, when I was being held under semi-house arrest, I often explained the goal of the Legion, and I also put it in writing."

The judge again: "Then you do not admit that you distributed knives to the Fathers Crotti, Châtel, and Salvi and to some faithful Christians—traitors of the fatherland and true criminals—threatening with death those Christians who would have signed for the independence of the church?"

I: "I resolutely reject this calumny; I deny having distributed knives to the Fathers Crotti, Châtel, and Salvi and to some of the faithful Christians who you say are traitors."

It was the chief's turn: "It is not necessary; the police have gathered some of them, they are in our hands."

Actually, in this trial they did not bring forward the false witnesses, nor did they present the presumed knives in evidence.

After another hour of similar martyrdom, the voice of the chief thundered: "Lead him back to his cell." Then turning to me: "Four months in prison has not been long enough for you to recover your senses? The law will punish you severely. Only with your blood will we be able to vindicate the blood of so many Chinese, victims of your espionage and crimes."

I said nothing. I was led back to the cell.

That evening, stretched out on my mat, I was not able to close my eyes; not out of fear of the threat, but for the joy of feeling myself destined for the firing squad. I repeated without tiring myself: "Queen of martyrs, pray for us now and at the hour of our death. Behold your victim, O Lord, make him pure, make him holy, so that he may be worthy of being sacrificed for you."

Some days before this trial, a proclamation of the government of Kaifeng had prohibited the existence of "the secret association of the Legion of Mary under the guidance of the imperialists and foreign reactionaries Pollio and Crotti." It ordered all the leaders and members of the Legion "to report to the police in order to identify the imperialists; to resign from the Legion; to declare the organization reactionary; to make a record of all the activities carried out by the Legion: the consignment of books, registers, prayer manuals, and banners; and to confess to its imperialistic aims and perverse nature." As a result: "All those that will accept the above-mentioned regulations will obtain a pardon from the government of the people; but those who remain obstinate in their own errors will be preparing their own ruin."

The Arrest and the Prison

Under the totalitarian regime Red China was populated with prisons: each village of a certain importance, each mandarin seat, and each capital of a province had its prison. The civil community, which had by now become familiar with the methods and severity of the Communist court, did not marvel at it.

In Kaifeng, the capital city of Honan, there were in 1950 to 1951 a good forty-two prisons, two of which were the most severe. Here heaps of the so-called major delinquents of the province, persons who, in the judgment of the leaders, represented an obstacle to the good of the society, would have to submit to the most serious punishment. And we were an obstacle: we did not wish to give in to the will of the government to subjugate the Church; therefore, we expected to be severely punished. In fact the hardest prison was awaiting us. We foresaw unheard-of atrocities by the Godless; however, we knew that it was a privilege to suffer for Jesus and for the cause of the Church: we will suffer, we said, but we will never cede.

DIARIES OF THE CHINESE MARTYRS

On July 29 some imprisoned Christians were liberated. However, they did not reacquire their true liberty: once at home, they had to live under house arrest, always ready to be called to testify against us.

Meanwhile, those who were liberated were waiting for orders in the courtyard in front of my cell, and I was able to observe what was happening from the small opening in the door. In the hands of a heroic little teacher, Ly Ming We Gertrude, I saw a crucifix and I recognized it. Gertrude was turned toward my door and was moving the crucifix in her hands in the hope of making me furtively see it. I did see it. There is a story behind that sacred object.

When the persecution began to rage in Kaifeng, the zealous Father Crotti formed and prepared a group of thirteen "volunteers" — teachers and students from the girls' high school — who would continue to sustain the weakest Christians throughout the struggle. On March 14, 1951, this group of heroines of the Faith promised solemnly before me to be God's apostles during the time of this persecution. They were perhaps conscious of its tragic future significance, but they did not go back on it, as was wished by those who aimed to separate the Catholics from Rome. I blessed each one of them and handed them a crucifix. Being aware of the painful moments that those heroic women would have to encounter, I exhorted them to take strength and comfort in that crucifix and always to carry it on them, above all, when they would be left without pastors and deprived of the Eucharist.

"Perhaps," I added, "it is my last gift." It was so. I was no longer able to speak with them, and two weeks later I was already among the criminals.

On August 7, 1951, in the early hours of the morning, the colonel, head of the police (the one who had arrested me on April 1) came into my cell and said: "Since you did not wish to confess your crimes, today you shall go on to the military tribunal of the province. Three other crooks, your companions in imperialism, will follow you." (He was referring to Father Piccinini, Father Crotti and Brother Francesco.)

He slammed the door in anger and went out. After a few hours, they led the "three bad crooks" into the courtyard outside my cell; my door was thrown open, and I joined my dear confreres. I looked at their pale and thin faces that revealed the signs of their suffering; they opened their eyes, fixing them on me. We exchanged a few words of fraternal encouragement, while a fearsome platoon of policemen and jailers surrounded us. The cavernous voice of the leader repeated: "You are assigned to the military tribunal, and you will change prisons."

We had to cross a good part of the city in the summer heat of August, so in order to avoid sunstroke, we asked for a straw hat, which we bought with the money sequestered from us.

While we were waiting in silence, Josephine Ly was led into the same courtyard. The heroic girl bore the signs of irons having bound her wrists for two months; her face had become delicate and transparent. She looked at the missionaries, then at me, bowing her head, and tears fell from her eyes; she did not know how to resist the sorrowful sight of her archbishop and the priests in that state surrounded by thugs.

We were put in a line, single file, flanked by two wings of well-armed police: with me were Father Crotti, Father Piccinini, Brother Francesco, and Josephine. And thus, in short sleeves, they made us walk across some principal streets of the city among a crowd that mutely assisted at that rather dismal procession.

Could the dates April 1 and August 7 have been purely coincidental? Not at all. April 1 was the Sunday in Albis (*Domenica in Albis depositis*) and the feast of the anniversary of my episcopal consecration; August 7 fell on my name day. Since on both dates numerous Christians wished to offer their best wishes and celebrate [with me], those same days were chosen by the police to inflict gross humiliations on me: and with my arrest and the sight of that funereal procession through the city streets, [they believed that they had succeeded].

After arriving at the seat of the tribunal, while officials were standing guard over me, we stopped briefly in the atrium, where Father Crotti managed to say to the heroic twenty-year-old Josephine: "Great, now you have known how to suffer; you can say you are totally of Jesus." Did she shed tears of pity and commiseration for herself? No, she shed tears of sorrow for having to detach herself from her spiritual guides whom perhaps she would never see again.

We were divided and led to separate small cells, where we submitted singly to an interrogation. The judge told me: "You shall go into one of our cells, where you shall have time to reflect. You have been manipulated by American imperialism; you have sabotaged the patriotic movement's reform of the Chinese church; you are a spy and a traitor; you have established the Legion of Mary at Kaifeng; you have plotted with the reactionary and secret organizations; and you have discredited the government. In brief, you are an imperialist under orders of the Vatican and America. Reflect and confess your crimes."

In the afternoon of that day, while the scorching heat was burning us, the two priests and I, under military guard, were led like evildoers to a harsh prison. The following day Brother Francesco and Josephine followed us to a vast, isolated, squalid building. Before entering this prison I was subjected to a thorough search: according to the prison rules, I had to hand over my shoelaces, suspenders, and other things.

After passing through the massive steel door, we found ourselves in the prison's long, dark corridors, which gave off a stench like the sepulchral fetor of decaying corpses; on either side of the hallway the cells' massive doors were fortified with heavy locks and chains. We immediately encountered some of the faces brutalized by suffering—the poor beings who preceded us in that place. "Will we also become so spectral?" I thought, while each one was being assigned a cell. In that place of supreme humiliation and scorn every type of pain awaited me. "Remain with me, Lord," I repeated, while the cell door was closing behind me. "Let us suffer together, and let us die together."

In the Midst of Delinquents

The prison of the military tribunal, intended for the worst delinquents, was situated northeast of Kaifeng, inside the walls of the city. All around one felt the immense solitude and the sense of desperation pervading it. The savagery that I experienced in this horrendous place still stirs up tremors of emotion.

I was enclosed in cell number 4, on the north side. It measured 4 by 2.1 meters; within languished eight inmates. I was the ninth.

This prison—under the Nationalists—held 200 to 250 inmates. During the Japanese occupation it was used as a stable, but with the advent of Mao it reverted to a place of detention and through the tortures imposed on us became a place of sorrow.

When I entered that horrible prison, on August 7, there were already 600 inmates crowded together. The majority were innocent victims whose number soon rose to more than 900. The prison comprised 104 cells; each cell, having been intended for two or three detainees, held eight, ten, or at times twelve; for some weeks there were nine in my cell, then ten, and for half of September there were eleven of us.

On the outside of the door of each cell were small wooden tablets, 15 by 5 centimeters, one for each occupant; on these were written the occupant's name, surname, age, and reason for incarceration. On my tablet the Chinese characters were larger and more pronounced: "YANG LIN (my name in Chinese), Italian, fifty years old, false archbishop of the Catholic Church, antirevolutionary, enemy of the people and of the government, transferred here from the police prison, August 7."

In the cell we were forced to be seated on the floor the entire day, from 5 a.m. to 10 p.m., without being able to get up and move; because the floor was damp, after a brief time my body was covered with sores.

It was, moreover, prohibited to lean your back against the wall, and we had to be seated 15 to 20 centimeters away from it. We waited for the change of the guards, which occurred every two hours, in the hope that someone more human would be tolerant in permitting us to lean a bit against the wall, lightening the pain of immobility that tormented us.

But it was difficult to meet up with humane guards: my presence in that place, the fear of being accused of having pity on an "imperialist" like me, rendered the jailers even harder toward us and more loyal to the harsh overseers.

DIARIES OF THE CHINESE MARTYRS

Mice of every dimension, but especially the gross sewer rats, had free entrance; they went from cell to cell, nearly like residents and not intruders. Scorpions of the tropical climates, always ready to defend themselves with their sharp, poisonous sting, causing enormous pain and sometimes death, kept us on our guard. Bedbugs, lice, and other insects flourished and multiplied. My cell companions dedicated hours each day chasing these bothersome and dangerous insects.

At 10 p.m., at the hissing sound of the whistle and a shout from the guard, we would promptly lie down on the floor and rest until the following morning, when another whistle and another shout obliged us to take up the usual painful and uncomfortable posture. During the brief repose the rats circled around us, and often I awoke from their running on my legs or pulling at my hair and my beard, which had become long and unkempt.

In order to be able to rest more tranquilly, we tried to make friends with the rats, tossing pieces of bread on the floor, which they would devour while we observed close up their lucid red-gray skin.

To inflict greater suffering (something worthy of barbarous cruelty), in the space of twenty-four hours, the heavy iron doors were opened only twice; fifteen armed thugs led us to a canopy, a very brief distance from my cell, in order to satisfy our natural necessities. Under this roof there were fifteen small pits in the ground: the break could not exceed two or three minutes.

The loathsome meals that were brought to us twice a day consisted of a piece of black bread, not of wheat, but of melick or sorghum, with beans; all of it contained in a pot of hot, often evil-smelling, water with some ginger seeds or garlic, and, at times, a small amount of vegetables or broth of an indefinable composition. These were our daily provisions, morning and evening. At mealtime the cell occupants were very solicitous of one another, serving one another from the bowl, solely to be able to get up for a brief instant from the floor and to be able to make those few movements that were denied us throughout the long day. Because of the scarcity of that wretched food, we all became walking skeletons.

Some of the nine hundred detainees were forced to drag iron chains tied to their feet and wear irons at their wrists tied behind their backs. The chains were applied solely with a ruling handed down by the tribunal and only the tribunal could remove them. The wrist irons were not like handcuffs that permitted a certain agility of movements; they tightly squeezed the wrists and, unlike the leg chains, could be imposed by the head jailer or simply any guard and at times for frivolous motives.

Both the chains and the irons were carried day and night.

The chains were one of the major torments; they were all the same length, about forty-five centimeters, but of various weights, from two to ten kilos [about four to twenty-two pounds]. They comprised two rough circles that surrounded the leg above the instep of the foot and locked, each one, with a pin also of iron. From each circle a pin of eight centimeters was placed from one of the circles to the other, forcing the prisoner to walk with his legs open. When the chain was too heavy and the prisoner, because of the long, extenuating detention or for the other tortures sustained, could no longer drag the weight, he was then given an iron rod with a hook at one end, so that he could lift the chain at the center and thus be able to walk, but very slowly. I have watched these poor wretches engage hours just to cover the three kilometers from the prison to the tribunal.

One might ask me how those who carried the chains at their feet and irons at their hands tied behind their backs were able to eat that crust of black bread and drink water. Like dogs! They had to push the bread against the wall with their heads in order to bite it, and then they would immerse their tongue in the water and sip it one drop at a time.

For two weeks I sat next to one of these misfortunates who wore chains weighing eight kilos [about seventeen pounds] and with his hands tied behind his back. At mealtime he refused at least twice to take a bite, in order not to subject himself to such humiliation, eating like a beast. He was a young officer of the Nationalist Army, thirty-two years old. The second day I took his piece of bread, broke it, and put it into his mouth. The guard saw me from the crack in the door and yelled: "Imperialist Pollio, you are going against the rules of the prison, even here you wish to oppress the Chinese. Get on your feet, four hours with your hands up." I was in the fifth month of my prison term, and, after so many trials and sufferings, I could not hold myself up on my feet. But I soon got into the position of the ordered punishment. Because of my weak condition my arms fell down without my even being aware of it, but a few kicks or shoves or fists from the guard obliged me to raise them again. As God wished, the four hours passed, and I fell, deprived of my senses, to the floor.

But the third day human pity conquered me again, and I broke the crust of bread and put the pieces on the floor in front of my companion in pain with the objective of facilitating his eating them.

The same guard saw the pieces of bread and asked who broke them up. I confessed to him. "Today's infraction is less serious than yesterday; you shall stand at attention for two hours." And I had to submit to the punishment.

About every ten days the inmates changed cells. I remained in cell 4, north side, until the end of my detention. The change of prisons had its purposes. A monstrous thing, and feared by everyone, was the presence of spies in the cells; everyone ignored who they were. In many cells there was a spy who was always substituted with the change of the occupants of the cell, chosen especially among those who wore the chains and the irons. It was indeed for the most part those unfortunates who, in the hope of having their punishment lightened at the time of their sentence, promised to report the complaints and deeds of their misfortunate companions. I saw someone tortured after false accusations were made against him by this type of spying.

A worsening of the punishment or a lengthening of the sentence could also have happened to me. I was ready for everything, all the subtle tortures they could apply to bow my body and to break my will. Therefore I never tired of saying: "Into your hands, Lord, I commend my spirit and entrust my body."

The Elimination of the "Reactionaries"

During the period of detention in the harsh prison, I was subjected to further military tribunals, which were under the authority of that prison.

And thus, with the twenty-two tribunals already sustained in the police prison, the number of my trials rose to thirty-two.

Although this military tribunal was more severe and more feared than the others, these trials were carried out with less bellicose apparatus and were staged with a more refined strategy.

The last ten trials found me physically extremely weak (I had lost thirty kilos—more than sixty-six pounds!), but the strength of my spirits was undiminished. None of the persecutors succeeded to bow my will or the ardor of my faith, not even with a weapon in their fist. I recall it, not out of vanity, but in order to render my gratitude publicly to the Holy Spirit for the assistance granted to me. Did not Jesus say to the apostles: "[Y]ou will be dragged before governors and kings for my sake, to bear testimony before them and the Gentiles. When they deliver you up, do not be anxious how you are to speak or what you are to say; for what you are to say will be given to you in that hour" (Matt. 10:18–19).

The same presumed crimes against the "people" and against the "popular government" were repeated against me with the same nerve-racking monotony. I was accused of connivance with the Americans in order to organize a progressive espionage service in China favoring the Nationalists, and numerous other crimes. I owe to the assistance promised by the Redeemer that I did not fall into contradictions, so that I could always deny the false accusations and so that I always had the physical strength to make them correct the ambiguous forms of the trial record at the end of each session.

The military tribunal was three kilometers from the prison. I was escorted by two to four guards into the court and back to my cell. Given the weakness of my body, the journey seemed interminable to me. The people were advised of my passage and were obliged to appear at this dismal spectacle in order to inflict greater humiliations on me. And indeed the streets were always crowded with students and people enrolled in the red associations, and they launched the filthiest abuses and the most vulgar curses, with cries of "down" or "death."

Once, in an effort to intimidate me, I was forced to attend the trials of two inmates. I was placed in an immense space at the entrance of the harsh prison. In the room I made out the defendant with his feet chained and covered with blood, standing upright before a commissioner and three agents of the military tribunal. A guard (the one who had picked me up from my cell), with a revolver in his fist, pointed me to the corner of the room, where I promptly moved, while the guard followed me, always remaining at my side, with the pistol pointed against me.

The commissioner said to the accused: "You have betrayed three companions, handing them over to the Nationalist brigands in the village of She-Liou; it has been two months since you have denied the charges. Is it not time to conclude the affair?"

"I do not have anything to add," the defendant responded. "I did not commit this crime."

"You still deny it!" the commissioner shouted. "Take him away; send him to the furnaces to work with chains on his feet." Then the commissioner's threatening glance turned toward me.

Another defendant entered. The commissioner began: "You, officer of the false Nationalist Army, with your troops you ambushed a small squadron of our liberators of the new great and free China: relate how this happened." The ex-officer had irons at his wrists behind his back; he was a colonel in the Nationalist Army, and he related how, on the outskirts of Lo Yang, he had surrounded a hundred Communist soldiers, capturing twelve of them and wounding ten.

"And the prisoners?" the commissioner screamed, while two were writing the colonel's confessions.

"I handed them over to the division's command," the officer responded.

"Chains at his feet!" the commissioner shouted, rising. "Announce the sentence. The traitors must be punished." The ex-colonel was led out.

It was then my turn. After I approached the commissioner's bench, he immediately said to me with a grim look: "All those who have attempted to ruin the new and free China will receive what they deserve. The current government, at the directives of the great leader, Mao Zedong, who is kind, is willing to pardon certain categories of reactionaries as long as they confess their crimes. You are part of this bunch; therefore respond with sincerity, confessing everything. Have you obstructed the movement of the reform and the rising of the Nationalist church, liberated from the slavery of the Vatican?"

"Yes."

"Do you repent this sabotage?"

"No," I responded.

"Don't you know that in this way you have attempted to destroy the new China, that it has cost the blood of hundreds of thousands of our companions?"

"I have not attacked the State; it is my duty as the Catholic archbishop to oppose any movement that is against the principles of the Faith. On the other hand, from the first days of the occupation you have written in very large letters on the very walls of my residence "freedom of religion." Therefore, I have the right to defend my religion, a right given to me by the State."

"You do not have this right. The freedom of religion is understood in the sense that we, the government, have the power to grant freedom of worship or obstruct it, while you imperialists cannot obstruct any movement desired or not desired by the State, even if it goes against your Faith, as you say." Then he added scornfully: "Your religion is superstition."

"No, absolutely not; religion is love toward God, men, and nature; it is a need of the soul that tends to looks toward its Creator."

"What Creator? Work created the world. You narcotize our people in order to make them easier prey for your imperialist governments and the Vatican, the servant of America."

"The Catholic Church is universal. It is not at the service of any government, nor are we emissaries or spies for our governments."

"You can say this," the commissioner continued, getting more surly, "hiding under the mantle of the lamb that hides the claws of the lion. Your time in China is finished."

There was a brief pause. We looked in each other's faces for a few moments, silently. I was about to respond, when the commissioner began again in a hostile tone: "How many Catholics are there in the world?"

"More than four hundred million."

"It is the greatest moral damage ever imposed on humanity. How is it possible that so many nations, throughout so many centuries, have not tried, first with conviction and then with force, to destroy this disgrace that is your religion?"

"Yes, many governments have attempted, but they did not succeed." And I had begun to speak of the persecutions of the first three centuries of the Church, of the barbarians and the other persecutions, of the French Revolution, when the commissioner banged a fist on the table, and interrupting me said with force: "We will succeed. It cannot be permitted that you Catholics force four hundred million persons to go to Mass each Sunday, taking from the State four hundred million hours of work each week. It is a loss of twenty billion working hours a year."

"Even non-Catholics," I responded, "at least the majority, rest one day a week."

"Error: people are for the State and not for God, who does not exist. Only the State exists. It is necessary to work much for the emancipation of the world."

At the end the commissioner asked me: "If we give you liberty, will you sign the reform and support the national church?"

"No," I responded.

And the judge: "Then your bones will continue to rot until you change your mind and you are stripped of every imperialist sentiment."

Clandestine Absolution

Two young women were in the harsh prison, which had a female division; both were arrested at night between the first and the second of April 1951, a little after my imprisonment. The first, Catherine Ho Yu Fen, was brought there the same day as my arrest; the second was the heroic Josephine Ly.[32]

---

[32] The arrest of Monsignor Pollio and of some Chinese laymen was described, with particular devotion, by one of the protagonists: Gertrude Li Min-wen,

In Catherine's cell, among the other fifty detainees, there was a seller of opium and heroin. Catherine, with prayer and love, with patience and example, succeeded in converting her to our Faith. "Agatha, I baptize you in the name of the Father, the Son, and the Holy Spirit," and at the same time the water bathed the forehead of that woman, who in that place of torments was regenerated by grace.

Catherine knew that I was in that place of sorrow, on the north side, but she did not know the number of my cell. But what could she do in order to see me? The inmates who were given jobs were able to circulate in determined areas of the courtyards assigned to them, and often they could even push themselves under the cells. Catherine and the newly baptized asked to be admitted to work: only this way, they were thinking, could they manage to go out of the cell and have some chance of seeing the archbishop. Their application was accepted: Catherine and Agatha were employed to work with the sacks, which they had to wash and lay out in the sun and sew.

The women who were employed or forced to work were able to circulate solely in the courtyard adjacent to the north side; but Catherine and Agatha did not know whether I was among the cells facing the north or the south. It was the doubt that tormented the ardent Catherine, because she knew that the north wing of the prison had a double row of cells with a corridor in the center.

They initiated their search. For several days they laid out their sacks under some cells; they spoke to each other in the hope that if they were near my cell, I would hear them. But it was useless. With only five cells remaining for them to stretch out the sacks, they nearly lost hope. Then, toward eleven on August 30, while I was in the painful immobility of the cell, thinking about the indoctrination lesson just imparted to me, I

---

who was affiliated with the Legion of Mary and for this was imprisoned. Gertrude miraculously managed to send her diary abroad, thanks to a missionary of Pime, Giovanni Carbone, who cut the pages and sewed them between the soles of his shoes at the moment of his expulsion from China in 1952. See Fazzini, *Il libro rosso dei martiri cinesi*, 178ff.

heard a very distant voice from the window that I knew very well: "It is all useless, he is not here; he must be in a cell on the south side." Each cell had, at the height of about eighty centimeters, a space in the wall with an iron grating, from which a bit of light and air entered. The place assigned to me was near the little window, and, although I was seated on the floor, given my height I could look out from time to time at what was happening in the courtyard.

On hearing that voice I turned my head immediately, and I saw Catherine Ho and the neophyte (novice). She was thin, and her face had a bluish tinge. I gave a sudden cough, Catherine promptly turned, and a smile of joy illuminated her face. Finally she had found me. Pretending to work and changing the place of the sacks, she said: "Archbishop, I always pray for you. I have been accused of being an accomplice with some spies and of being reactionary because I was the head of the local Legion of Mary. The Virgin will win. And you, when will you leave this place?"

"I do not know," I responded.

"I pray that you will be liberated soon." Then she said: "Give me absolution."

While I was seated at my place I recited the sacramental formula, and I traced the Sign of the Cross. Catherine was blessed and joyfully went away. I never saw her again. Did she see me in the semi-darkness of the cell? I could not say. My companions in the cell heard the response and were aware of the Sign of the Cross, and they knew that the girl was Catholic. Fortunately, during that period there was not a single spy, because nothing happened to me.

I knew then that Catherine after some months of detention was liberated and condemned to house arrest in her own home. Love for Christ and faith in Him made her overcome every obstacle.

Next to me in cell 4, a detainee sat with his legs crossed, and blood flowed from them because of the chains he had been wearing for a long time at his feet. Now and then I would clean those sores with a piece of a rag, because that unhappy soul also had his hands enclosed in irons. On September 3, while I was carrying out that charitable operation, I was seen by the guard. With a cry and a bang on the padlock the jailer ran toward me, cursing, and then he enclosed my wrists between two tight circles of iron.

The irons were squeezing me, impeding the circulation of the blood. I did not know how much time I would have to wear them; a cell companion said not more than ten to twenty hours. While still moaning from the painful sores, my cell companion, a poor pagan, expressed delicate words of gratitude and solidarity to me, and of dismay for the injustices and cruelty of the torturers.

After a few hours of that torment, my hands were livid and cold. As I had already offered all of myself to God, happy to witness, with the sacrifice of my life, to the Faith I preached, also in that moment I offered my hands to God, because I thought that ten to twenty hours later that torture would have ended with their amputation. Once again the Lord met me.

Rarely did the head jailer enter our cells, but that day he came. Perhaps he was advised of the pain that was inflicted on me. I plucked up my courage and, showing him my hands, I said: "Are the irons put on like this?"

"Why did they put them on you?"

"For having performed an act of charity toward this poor detainee."

The word *charity* infuriated him; his face became livid, and staring at me with two small eyes, he cried out sternly: "Charity does not exist. You are delinquents who have assailed the new China of Mao, and we hate you. The government could order your death from one moment to another, but does not wish it because it desires to torment you with pinpricks and enjoy your slow and desperate death." He left the cell, leaving the door ajar. He returned, changed the irons for larger ones, ordered me to sit down on the floor, and locked the heavy door with a chain. I felt the blood reflowing in my hands as life returned to them.

Another detainee was reduced to the end of his life by the bestial hate that the emissaries of the party nurtured against him. He was innocent: the only crime of which he was accused was that of possessing about sixty hectares (six thousand acres) of land, part sandy, part productive. Everyone at Kaifeng knew him: young and poor, he had begun a very modest business selling cigarettes and peanuts with his own savings. Little by little he managed to buy some land, which he cultivated with his brothers. The family was numerous, more than thirty persons. In forty years of work and sweat, that family succeeded in creating a comfortable life for themselves, living, however, very soberly.

Kuo Chen Han, the young man, languished for over four months in prison with eight kilos [about seventeen pounds] of chains at his feet and with his wrists in irons. He had submitted to only one trial, the one in which the chains had been applied. In the cell he cursed us, and he cursed the government; he wished to die. He was often suspended from the beams, beaten to near death so that he would confess the harsh demands that he had made against the poor and reveal where the family's gold and silver was hidden, and finally declare himself culpable of being a landowner, therefore an extortioner of the people.

Repeatedly I exhorted him to be trusting, and very often he would calm down. But the tortures of every type reduced him to a skeleton. When he was restored to his family, he was a wrecked human being. After a brief time he died.

I recall with sorrow the sarcasm and the invectives against that poor innocent, when his body was taken out of the cell by the torturers: that body, already nearly a cadaver, was not spared kicks and blows. It was the hatred of the supposed rich.

And hate is taught to today's generations in China; it is the same hate that is taught in the satellite nations: hate toward religion, hate for capitalists, hate for imperialists, hate for those who are not Communists. The school of hate begins soon. All the efforts are concentrated particularly on the young, on the adolescents and even infants, the easy prey. And the majority of the agents of the police, the public employees, and the leaders of the various red associations are the young who are brought from those areas that, at one time, had felt the red oppression.

I had known pagan egoism. But now I was discovering the death of liberty, and in a period of persecutions, I assisted at these distressing tragedies: when the light of the gospel does not shine, there is only darkness. The followers of Mao Zedong, who were enthralled with Moscow, wished to destroy love and to live in the hate and desolation of death. Only God is charity.

Among the Tortures and Temptations of Suicide

One morning in early September the terrible and painful sound of chains, mixed with savage shouts and desperate cries, reached our ears. We cell companions looked at each other, stunned. What could be happening in that place? It could not have been an insurrection, because there were well-armed guards everywhere; and so our thoughts leaned toward the unspeakable torture inflicted on the new arrivals. In fact, each day there was someone crossing the threshold in order to join our sufferings.

The cries came nearer; we clearly perceived the imprecations against heaven and earth, against Stalin and Mao Zedong, insults against the so-called government of the people. The noise of the chains also became stronger. Curiosity, mixed with panic, came over my cell companions.

Still remaining seated on the floor at my post, I managed to look out of the grate into the courtyard and see what was happening; and I saw passing under our cell about two hundred prisoners, loaded with construction material, curved under the weight of beams, sacks of cement, bricks, and stones. They were in single file and were arduously dragging the chains at their feet. But why? By now our prison could no longer host the "worst delinquents" of the entire vast province: it was necessary to enlarge it, and the tribunal had ordered the majority of the inmates who wore chains to forced labor. The irons were taken from their wrists, while the chains were left at their feet.

I looked at that caravan of sorrow: they pierced my soul with feelings of profound commiseration and suffering.

Now and then someone fell to the ground under the weight. I did not pay attention to the curses that came from the lips of those desperate souls; I did not notice their skeletal bodies. Rather, my glance remained fixed on their legs, on the point where they were enclosed in the circles of iron. I saw the squirting of blood, the streaming of a putrid liquid and the pus; I saw pieces of skin or scraps of rotted flesh fall, I saw the circles of iron beating against the uncovered bones, causing unheard-of pain. I understood why they cried out against the government and the leaders: they preferred to be shot immediately, cut off from their existence, rather than to live a life worse than that of beasts.

I did not know how to resist that spectacle, as the tears fell from my eyes. I had never cried in prison for myself: I was happy to suffer for Christ, and I desired to seal with my blood the Faith that I preached. But that excruciating scene moved me deeply.

Among those condemned, curved under heavy weights, I glimpsed at two with serene faces; these also had their feet bound with chains; these also were forced to work; but they were not cursing. Why were they serene? I fixed my glance on them because it seemed to me that I knew them: they were two of my Christians. They had not wished to adhere to the schismatic movement, and the government had imprisoned them with the accusation that they were enemies of the country. During their trial they were frank in their responses to the accusations and strong in rejecting the traps imposed on them to get them to adhere to the schismatic national church; their faith had given them energy. The false accusations that led to their arrest and condemnation did not eliminate the certainty of suffering for the Church: they knew how to love God and the country, and this awareness elevated them above their persecutors. The Faith and the eternal words of the Gospel: "[Y]our reward is great in heaven" (Matt. 5:12) gave them the moral strength to bear the bitterness of the prison and the tortures of those forced labors.

After the sentence was handed down by the tribunal, they were passed on to the forced labors, returned to prison, or transferred to other places. (But very often one passed from the prison to work without any sentence from the tribunal.) The hardest and most feared sentence was the work at the furnaces, where they baked the bricks, and from where they always returned with their health in worse condition.

I also knew the pain of work. I was assigned the most humble, disheartening, and repugnant jobs. Together with an ex-general of the Nationalist

Army, a professor from the university, and other detainees I had to mix excrement with soil, fill baskets with it, and then load them onto carts. I was assigned to this task for fifteen days. The guards, in seeing me intent on this type of labor, smiled and sneered; they were so pleased to see a Catholic bishop and European do this work.

Another extremely hard punishment of that prison was being forced to stare at a white wall that rose up to a meter and a half above us detainees, while powerful lights were lit behind it. This was a pain that was rarely inflicted; in my cell we experienced it only five times.

We could not resist that type of torture. We could not close our eyes, or we would suffer the pain of the irons. After ten to twenty minutes our eyes began to tear and our head ache, while our face was bathed with a cold sweat. A few minutes later, although we were already seated on the floor, we fell to the ground in a faint.

As one of us fell, prostrated, a guard promptly came and responded to the swoon with kicks. I also fell prostrate, all five times, and only once was I able to feel the kicks.

I recall hearing, late at night on three occasions, the noise of a truck breaking the silence of the tomb in which the prison and the surrounding area was wrapped. For some it aroused fear and dread; for others it brought hope of putting an end to the sufferings. The motor stopped, there were a few minutes of silence, and then we heard the clinking of chains of some of the cells. Then some of the inmates were selected and lifted up on the truck. Everything was carried out in silence; outside our doors we heard only the steps of the executioners and the victims.

Again the din of the motor, and the truck drove off.

A quarter of an hour later there were two hails of gunfire, and the lives of those unfortunates were truncated.

The third time we did not hear the barrage, only the prolonged and wrenching cries of the condemned being buried alive: a horrifying death. I remember not sleeping that night: the thought kept coming back to me of the description, from a fourteen-year-old boy, of the death of Father Carlo Osnaghi, a missionary of Kaifeng, who had been taken by brigands and buried alive on a chilly night between the first and second of February 1941. His cadaver was then stolen by an opium smoker.

Many of my incarcerated companions languished in prison, they rotted for months and months and some for years. They were overwhelmed by desperation, and it was so severe that many of them thought of suicide as liberation; but suicide was impossible.

From time to time someone, being overwhelmed by the sufferings and tortures, and not able to attempt suicide, would spew injurious words against the government and the authorities, in the hope of being condemned to death in order to abbreviate the days of his pain. But for this type of detainee the process never began; they were abandoned in the lurid prison to that craving and to going crazy and rotting. They asked for a quick death, and for this they had to taste a slow death.

Suicide was impossible because the guards removed every means that could serve that end: in the cell there was neither a pot, nor pieces of twine, nor straps, nor suspenders, nor toothpicks to eat; indeed we were obligated to watch out for each other, because the tribunal held us responsible for any one of the cellmates who voluntarily did himself harm or took his life.

A seller of heroin, a young man of twenty-eight, received notice on September 13 of his sentence of twenty years in prison; his days would be spent in forced labor, presumably at the furnaces. The following morning, while fifteen of us were led to the eaves, as usual, for nature's needs, that young man fled from the line, slipped through the door that was in the center of the courtyard, and headed to the well. A splash, and the young man was in the water. The guards caught up with him after he took off and extracted him from the water alive; he was immediately put on his feet and enclosed in heavy chains of eight kilos. He confessed that he had attempted suicide because he could no longer tolerate the tortures of prison life, and his entire being rebelled at the thought of spending twenty years in a similar state.

In that place of sorrow, in the midst of so much desperation, I felt closer to God, who instilled in me the strength to bear everything. The words of the Master resounded in my mind: "If the world hates you, know that it has hated me before it hated you" [John 15:18]. Also: "Pray for those who persecute you." And as I prayed for my persecutors, I felt myself loving them: "Love your enemies" [Matt. 5:44].

Purges and Massacres

In countries behind the iron curtain generations were educated at the school of hate. At this school the Bolshevik man of tomorrow was being formed.

Jesus had issued a command, a program for all his followers to the end of the world: "To love God above all things and to love your neighbor as yourself" (see Matt. 22:37, 39). After nineteen centuries, from Moscow came another command, an antithesis of Jesus: "Down with love of your neighbor. We have need of hate. Hate is holy." No civilization can remain indifferent before religion; men (and women) will be able to love or to hate. The Communists have chosen hate, because Communism is not civilization; it is barbarism, the greatest barbarism of history.

The goals that Communism aims for in the nations under the red yoke are principally to change man's mentality and personality, in order to then change the social structure of the country. Thus, it also happened in China, beginning with its "liberation."

The Communists knew well that it would not be easy to change the mentality and the traditions of the Chinese people, whose history goes back more than four thousand years; therefore, it was necessary, above all, to pressure the youth. Among the many means of cramming the young brains—radio, propaganda, press, school, et cetera—the principal method was and always remains indoctrination.

For the students of both sexes indoctrination begins from elementary school and continues in the junior and senior high schools, on up. The soldiers, the police, the prison guards, the government employees, the teachers, and each social class are subjected to a daily hour of indoctrination, which during certain periods of the year, or during extraordinary events, is prolonged for more hours of the day. Even the populous could not escape it.

DIARIES OF THE CHINESE MARTYRS

Little groups of eight to ten persons are consumed with thoroughly examining the doctrines of Marx, Engels, Lenin, and Stalin, their discourses and those of Mao Zedong; national and international events must be commented on in light of the orthodox thought of Moscow; suppressions imposed on China by the "imperialist" nations must be explained [through the same Marxist-Leninist prism].

Each one is required to take an active part: interrogating, responding, discussing, and annotating in suitable notebooks. Each week ten groups are gathered in an assembly, presided over by a leader, in order to communicate the results.

Some of the subtle methods inculcated in the indoctrinations are: hatred of religion, which for the Communists always remains the same "opium of the people," according to the principle and judgment of Marx; hatred toward the Vatican, which they define as the center of international espionage; and hatred for "imperialist" nations, those that are not based on the so-called popular democracies. Also inculcated are the children's distrust toward their parents, which sows discord and alienation in the family. Children are asked to inform on their parents, what they are doing, and who their friends are, if they love the State, or if they are in subversive relationships; they are also given leave to denounce them or even to report them to the government in order to punish them. Filial love and loyalty is transferred to the government; faith is inculcated in the infallibility of the party and in the omnipotence and invincibility of the Red Army, which together with the Chinese forces will "liberate the world" from slavery. It is necessary to arrive at the cult and deification of the red regime that is placed above all else.

When I was in the police prison, the indoctrination of a group of guards took place right outside the door of my cell; for four long months I had to hear every type of calumny and bestiality. When the discussions concerned religion, the Vatican, or Italy, my guards raised their voices to make me hear more clearly. I curled up in a corner of the cell, and I prayed to God to pardon them and to illuminate their blindness; I meditated on those lessons of hate that were penetrating the hearts of the young people and the children.

One of the many painful cases kept coming back to me, the fruit of an instilled hatred. One of my catechists had an eight-year-old son, a student in the second grade. One day the child did not wish to write his homework assignment and merited a slap from his father. The child got up, cursed at his father, and ran to the police.

"What do you want?" the police officer asked him.

"My father hit me."

"Why?"

"Because I spoke well of Mao Zedong and my father told me to stop, but I continued; then he hit me, because he is a reactionary."

That night the catechist was arrested. He had to spend three months in detention.

Other than the ordinary indoctrination, there are also schools run by the party with special courses in Marxist-Communist culture, where lessons are taught on the history of the Bolshevik party and Communism, on the political development of the nations guided by Communism, and on the means of attaining humanity's "liberation" from religion, from property, and from every kind of slavery still in force in the noncommunist world.

In the harsh prison a government activist often came to our cell to give lessons in indoctrination. I understood that he was sent to provoke a reaction from me. I knew that I must be silent, and I wished to be, because the activist did not ever directly attack the religion or the pope; he was only imparting lessons on Marxism. If he had blamed religion or spewed calumnies against the pope, I would have certainly taken up their defense, even at the cost of the irons or the chains at my feet.

Some books were placed in our cell that I wished to read. I shudder now, as I did then. In those books were the most absurd doctrines on the creation of the world and man, of the blackest calumnies against the pope and the clergy (especially the missionaries in China), as well as outrageous vignettes and completely distorted historical facts.

At times I even heard some inmates swear against their own children, cursing the day of their birth. They were in prison for having been accused by their children, simply because they did not share their ideas.

DIARIES OF THE CHINESE MARTYRS

The parents had wished to speak, and the children denounced them to the authorities.

The elimination of those who do not agree to change or to give in has always been, and still is, the way of the red government in China. Following the typical bloody systems of Communism throughout the world, China lived months and years of terror, during which there were great bloodbaths.

Three of the great slaughters are verified. I witnessed the first, the greatest of the three, nearly in its entirety: it is called the Purge of the Counter Revolutionaries. It began in December of 1950 and ended in June of 1952: there were eighteen months of massacres.

The blacklists of banishment were compiled in the offices of the police and the government. They represented the names of the ancient Nationalist Party, the landowners, those who had had relationships with the Japanese during the Nipponese military occupation, public officials of the past government, the bourgeois or middle class, many Catholics, and all those who did not nurture good sentiments toward the new regime. All of these were called "reactionaries" and "subversives."

It was necessary to purge China.

I remember that period with horror: of not spending a day or night without learning of the arrest and disappearance of known individuals. The captured were hauled in by the net-full, in each city and zone, without any formality or mandate. Every means was utilized: perfidy, espionage, betrayal, and slander. I heard police officers forcing people to accuse poor innocents, threatening prison in case of omitted charges; I've seen with my own eyes people arrested and put in prison only because they refused to make a false accusation. Because the existing prisons were already full, the houses of the deported, purged, or incarcerated were confiscated and transformed into places of detention.

During those eighteen months of terror in China, up to a thousand persons a day were shot; they were sentenced either by a tribunal or by the appearance of a trial, but a much greater number disappeared without notification or trial. The majority of the killings were verified in the first ten months of that bloody period, during which, in some villages of my archdiocese, the percentage reached three for each hundred inhabitants. Solely during that first purge in China, ten million people were massacred. Often in the cities the executions were carried out publicly in order to strike terror into the hearts of the people.

That terror brought mutual distrust: each one suspected the other. The husband suspected the wife, the wife, the husband; the parents feared their own children, but the children did not fear their parents; long-time friendships chilled; children were obligated to denounce their parents even if they spoke only one word that did not conform to Communist orthodoxy.

I wish to relate briefly an episode that horrified many and made them tremble with dismay. At Kaifeng there was a Protestant pastor, a Baptist, an honest man. His oldest son was eighteen and imbued with the indoctrination that he received at school; therefore, he was considered "advanced," and the leaders looked to this young man with hope.

The youngster, Luo Chen Han, began to hate religion, which he repudiated publicly; and then he joined the struggle against the members of that Baptist sect, including his own family. He heaped hatred on them, especially his father. The young man reported him very often to the police, accusing him of nonexisting crimes and of collaboration with the imperialist Americans, on whom, in the past, that sect at Kaifeng had depended. The accusations were so many and of such a nature that the young man obtained the effect he had desired: the arrest of his father. During three trials Luo Chen Han appeared before the tribunal to testify against his father, and each time he invented new crimes (in part suggested by the government) that weighed heavily on the parent's shoulders.

The day of the public trial arrived. On the stage, where the pastor was placed with his hands tied, in the midst of the guards, the son also came up; and after launching charges and calumnies, he asked the government for the death penalty for his father. The government authorities responded to that request with the false ambiguity of the Communist system: "The government cannot condemn, because today it is the people who command."

And turning toward the popular masses they said: "You have heard from the son all the crimes committed by this reactionary: what shall we do about it?" And the people, raising their fists on high, shouted: "Death, death!"

The leader who was orchestrating the popular judgment said to the Protestant pastor: "You see, we are not condemning you, the government is benign, but it must respect the will of the people, which has the right to purge the new China of those who obstruct its progress and its ascent."

The death sentence (already prepared in precedence) was read. The pastor was immediately led to the execution. A Communist soldier shot that innocent man, who fell exhaling his last breath. The son, the cruel and inhumane Luo Chen Han, assisted with satisfaction at the execution of the one who had given him life.

This news, which I learned while I found myself in the harsh prison, disturbed and upset me. China was submitting to a bloodbath stirred up by the Communist hatred of Christianity.

The Humiliation of the "Popular" Judgment

After so many trials and so many tortures a grave humiliation was awaiting me: to be exposed publicly on a stage, the object of calumny on the part of the accusers and jeering on the part of the spectators in the so-called people's judgment.

And I was not alone in submitting to it: with me were Father Crotti, Father Piccinini and Brother Francesco, to which was added a heroic Christian teacher, Josephine Ly, a woman we have already met.

Before I was imprisoned and then during my detention, many Christians from my archdiocese, from the cities and the villages, had climbed up on the stage of the people's court to be publicly condemned, and from there they were passed on to the prison or to forced labor or to death. As a pastor, I could not flee from this suffering; indeed it had to be more serious and more humiliating for the shepherd than for the lambs. [And so it was.]

The popular, or people's, judgment is a judicial system much in use in the Communist regimes. The accused is dragged onto a stage set up for a trial or to a public square, or to a large locale or to the periphery of a village, and before him is a sea of people forced to participate at the judgment. Very often the accused, who already is a prisoner, is put on his knees; other times he is on his feet or seated on a low stool, always with his head bowed and nearly always struck from time to time by the accusers or the bullies. The trial always lasts a long time, not less than four hours. In many cases the guilty (or presumed such) falls deprived of his senses; then he is taken back to prison in order to submit to another shorter trial, which ends with the sentence—for the most part, death.

On the stage, accusers and calumniators follow one after the other. They are poor unfortunates obligated by the police to give false evidence to the strangest accusations, without concern about the consequences for the defendant. Many times the government writes down the accusations and forces the "witness" to memorize them. The person forced to testify usually has his own case pending and therefore cannot refuse to cooperate.

To each charge the people shout, "Death, death!" Their condemnation concludes the people's trial. In the majority of the cases, the sentence is death.

September 21, 1951, was the day of my popular trial: it was scheduled to last eight hours, during which my companions and I had to kneel on the stage; but then the judges limited it to five hours.

On that day, at eight in the morning, we were picked up at our cells and brought to a room where a judge, who was awaiting us, got straight to the point: "Now you will be led to the people's trial. The people will judge you. Do not fear; no harm will be done to you. However, even if you do not approve of what will be said regarding you or what will be done, do not forget that you will not be able to defend yourselves in any way. Otherwise ..."

He signaled the guard, and we returned to the courtyard, where well-armed soldiers were lined up waiting for us.

We saw the head jailer arriving equipped with several pairs of handcuffs, and we knew the meaning of the threat "otherwise." When he was in front of me asking for my wrists, I said to him: "Why these irons? Have I not always observed the prison regulations? Why inflict another humiliation on me?" And he said to us: "I must put these handcuffs on you, but if you promise to behave, I shall spare you this shame."

From the iron gate we saw Josephine Ly, the twenty-year-old heroine, a teacher at our elementary school, walking between two guards. She then joined our group.

We set out, closely surrounded by fifteen soldiers: each of us, in single file, had two guards, each one armed with a pistol in his fist. Some soldiers were at the head of this strange procession, others behind us, and the last soldier carried a submachine gun on his shoulder.

We walked quickly, in marching step, crossing several city streets. Posters and paper banners of every kind covered the city's walls and homes, all of them filled with curses directed precisely against us, in particular, against me and Father Crotti. In addition, large strips of red cloth were placed across the streets with similar inscriptions. It was a procession of hate, of Communist hate against those who wished to defend the Faith and the Church.

At 10 a.m. we reached the great citizen theater, a place reserved exclusively for patriotic and civil demonstrations. Outside the theater hundreds and hundreds of students, having been incited by the leaders, greeted us with cries of "Down with them! Kill them!" A great number of curiosity seekers came just to look around.

I glanced around, but I saw very few Christians. I was glad: they preferred to vanish rather than assist at the unjust treatment and trial of their pastor and of being forced to raise their fist, shouting insults against him. While we paused outside the theater, an aspiring Chinese nun courageously crossed the lines of soldiers, looked at me attentively and with her head made a slight bow. Fortunately her gesture was unobserved.

Although only a few Christians were forced to assist at the spectacle, all twenty seminarians from the regional seminary received orders from the provincial government "to be present" at the trial of Pollio and companions. These seminarians, who had to put up with every type of oppression, were subjected to repeated indoctrinations and wrote memorable responses with heroic strength. In the long struggle with the Communists, not one of them gave in.

A group of them made their way into the theater without being recognized and remained until the end, using suitable precautions and attentively following every scene of the farce; another group of three remained outside. Profiting from the confusion and the rumpus going on around us, these three seminarians approached me and, pretending to speak among themselves, said aloud: "*Ecce sacerdos magnus,*"[33] so I could hear them. And I heard them and looked at them. This greeting in the midst of so much mockery gave me great comfort.

Our gloomy procession entered the theater, which was already filled. We passed through the general hostility, and then we were led into some adjacent hovels, well guarded by many arms. Father Crotti, passing next to Josephine and glancing at her proud face, pale from exhaustion, managed to speak softly to her: "Courage, today is Friday. Think of Jesus on the Cross." Prudently, she did not respond, but her eyes sparkled with the ardor and strength of martyrs.

Meanwhile in the theater, a leader harangued the crowd: "In a few minutes the five delinquents will come into your presence. By now you know their crimes and their imperialism, and you will know how to judge them with justice. You will cry out, 'Down with them! Death! Leave China!' so they will understand at last that the people of the new China of Mao Zedong have awakened; the new China of Mao Zedong knows them and is offended by them and wants justice." The harangue was protracted in this tone for a good ten minutes.

We were led into the theater and forced to walk a lap in the midst of the crowd, which was shouting and cursing as they held their fists up to our noses. We climbed onto the stage, where five tall stools, about twenty centimeters high, were lined up; and, once the roll was called, we sat down. Behind each of us there was a policeman.

On the stage, sitting behind us, were twenty bigwigs of the Communist Party; in front of us there was an audience of two to three thousand people. The theater could not have held any more. The authorities handed out

---

[33] Behold a great priest.

booklets and pamphlets filled with the usual indoctrination against our imperialism, and in particular my "crimes," along with instructions on how to respond during the trial: indeed, both the accusers and the listeners carried them out extremely well. Included among that massive audience were government employees, the police, and students and representatives of every social class. I cannot forget those grim and threatening faces bursting with hate, only hate; those ferocious expressions of anger and fury, and those harsh scowls filled with indignation.

After the crowd had been silenced, the ceremonial head of the event, the leader of the New Democratic Youth, or the Popular Front, a sly personality who did so much evil to my Christians, made the opening presentation. Then the mayor of the city, in representation of the people of Kaifeng, spoke, declaring to the assembly that he was no longer capable of considering these men anything but "ugly tools"; and, in fact, in his discourse he always referred to us with this derogatory expression. After the mayor, the event's promoter, the police commissioner, commander of the Provincial Police, would have come to the microphone, but because he was engaged elsewhere, the secretary general of the Office of the Provincial Police substituted for him. The secretary, having been poisoned with hate, exposed a long series of charges and crimes; some regarded the missionary priests, but the majority regarded me. Among the accusations, some concerned the Faith, and I was content with this. The others were false accusations and calumnies that I had resolutely rejected in the tribunals, where I had appeared so many times.

As it happened, ten unfortunate Christians, who were either blinded by lies and tricks or frightened by threatened punishments, gave in to pressures and vexations and dared to go up on that stage and relate improbable things. One of them did not hesitate to declare himself against his archbishop. But all were not true "progressives"; we were able to see and understand that their words were in contrast with their conscience: indeed, later, in private, they confessed their repentance to our missionaries. One of them said to our missionaries: "If only I could see my archbishop once again to ask for and to hear his words of pardon." But he was not able to see me again: I had been exiled from China.

One of the accusers, while speaking, no longer had the strength to proceed and had to leave the stage; then the master of ceremonies repeated those charges that they had forced the Christian to pronounce.

Three of those ten seemed convinced: they were all students, products of our schools, all of which had been expropriated. We know that students are always a useful instrument whenever they are in the hands of the "government of the people."

Also the seminarian traitor Ly Mao Te, of whom I have already spoken, a true son of the lie, got up on the stage, and as if possessed by the devil he recited his part for half an hour, testifying how he had been oppressed by the imperialist tyranny (perhaps because I had suspended him from the sacraments), launching insults and lies. Not content with all that and moved by an insane fury, he punched me and Father Crotti and spit in my face several times.

All those on the platform frenetically applauded that gesture; at the same time, they cried out with satanic pleasure: "Good. Let's send them to their death!" Ly Mao Te recited his part well! He had been seen preparing it for a week, assisted by an able red teacher.

Between one discourse and another, or interrupting a speaker, the people would raise their fists implacably against us, yet we remained tranquil, even serene. The trial lasted five hours, and through it all we were exposed to a public mockery, which we had to endure in the strictest silence.

Before that public furor, while listening to so many lies, and while observing those cowardly Christians, my soul's pardon prevailed over all of it. I pardoned everyone. But in a special way, while I received punches and spitting, I pardoned the ex-seminarian Ly Mao Te, as also I pardon him today. There is nothing more beautiful than a generous pardon, and nothing brings one closer to the Divine Redeemer.

Condemned to Exile

The torment of the people's trial was coming to an end. After five hours, a printed paper was distributed to each of the three thousand spectators and accusers. Everyone devoured it. We did not know what that paper contained; we did not immediately understand what was stirring up such interest and pleasure. I believed it was another infamous charge; it was, instead, our sentence.

I cannot hide, not even today, my surprise at the diffusion of my sentence. I knew that the tribunal usually drafted only five copies of any sentence: one for the condemned, the others for the various offices; why then were thousands of copies of our sentence printed and distributed to everyone? This action was also designed to strike us with a new humiliation.

A definitive order, accompanied by a fist in our backs by the guard, made us get up and stand at attention. Absolute silence was ordered during and after the reading of the sentence.

Before reading the sentence, the leader of the Military Commission of Control, who was also the chief judge of the military tribunal and who had presided over ten trials against me, announced: "For the ugly tools Pollio and Crotti it has been decreed by the people that, for the many crimes committed by these oppressors, they be condemned to the pain of twenty-four years of reclusion, which is equivalent to twelve years of forced labor. The government of the province and the military tribunal would, of course, have ratified the sentence, but for particular reasons the central government of Peking wished to become involved. This government wished to inflict a greater punishment: the pain of exile for the two aforementioned ugly tools, and for their companions, a punishment proportionate to their crimes."

During the trial there was an attempt to record the process in order to have a record of my presumed affirmations. The commissioner had requested that an audio recording be made available for all to hear. As for the results, the judge's questions were very clear, but my responses were so confused that not a word was perceptible. It was a true humiliation; so, in order to save face, one of them said: "This machine is not functioning well; therefore, you will not be able to perceive the responses."

Strange: why were the questions so clear and my responses so confused? Was it not the same machine?

The commissioner then read the sentence. It contained the accusations against Father Crotti and me for the following serious faults:

1. having carried out antirevolutionary work at Kaifeng by the creation in 1947 of the Legion of Mary, a reactionary organization, founded on the order of the imperialist Riberi (the apostolic internuncio in China)

2. having founded at Kaifeng the *Catholic Weekly* with the intention of obstructing the "liberation" of the people on the part of the red troops

3. having profited from our position as missionaries in order to prohibit the Christians, and especially the young, to take part in the organizations that were atheist and hostile to the religion: the New Democratic Youth, the Popular Front, the Pioneers of China, et cetera

4. having instigated the Christians, April 1, to rough up some students beloved of the country (those students who were crying out, "Down with the imperialists Pollio and Crotti" and "Leave China," as I have said)

5. having distributed reactionary books (books that rejected the Marxist-Leninist system and materialism, and apologetic books) and of having diffused subversive notices, ruining the work of the people of the new China

6. being opposed to the reform, called the Movement of the Three Autonomies, destined to found the national schismatic church, free from the imperialism of the missionaries and from the impression of the Vatican, and suitable to the principles of Marx and Lenin

Then he read the less serious crimes against Father Piccinini, Brother Francesco, and Josephine Ly.

These were the charges, but the real motive for our blame was our opposition to the schismatic movement. Together with the Catholic Church, we represented what the Communists called the "last bulwark of the imperialism of Kaifeng." Therefore, there was a true coalition of all the red forces of the city against us in order to deliver a strong offensive against the Church. Some leaders compared the struggle undertaken against the Church to that of the Chinese soldiers against the Americans in Korea.

The charge ended with our sentence: for me, Father Crotti, and Father Piccinini, after having served six months of prison, exile from China; for Brother Francesco, expulsion from China; for Josephine Ly, four months of prison and three years of deprivations of her civil rights. The sentences were received with clamorous cries, but we were tranquil; we did not feel defeated; we knew that we were closer to God.

I asked myself many times: Why was the sentence replete with charges regarding the faith—which to us were honorable—and not charges of a political character? The Lord blinded the enemies: this paper issued by the military tribunal that I keep today as a precious relic, represents the primary advantage of the Church.

In the early hours of the afternoon, we were made to descend the stage and return to the prison. At the door of the great theater, we were once again the target of vile insults on the part of students, male and female, who spitefully cried out: "Kill them; don't return them to the prison!" But here also, in the midst of the scorn and hate of so many people, there were some hearts that did not know how to detach themselves from us and who followed us with love. Those courageous seminarians were here again. Approaching me and pretending to speak English among themselves, they said, in a way for me to hear: "*Benedictus qui venit nomine Domini. Hosanna in excelsis.*"[34]

We returned to the prison in the same order and formation in which we had come; it was a real march. Josephine Ly, who was last in the line, was often pushed by the soldiers and forced to run in order to catch up with us; they would often shout at her, calling her a "European bitch, a follower of European dogs."

---

[34] Blessed is he who comes in the name of the Lord. Hosanna in the highest.

A dense crowd followed us to the prison, cursing at us and shouting insults.

The cell was a relief: my temples hammered me, I could not hold up, and I fell down completely deprived of my senses.

I had just revived when the chain rattled and a guard called: "Wiang Ti Yang, come out." Two soldiers were waiting at the door. Wiang Ti Yang was the inmate who sat next to me in the cell: his death sentence had arrived, and he was being led to his execution. I shall never forget his cry of desperation. A few hours later he was among the purged. He left behind a libretto given to him by the guards for his indoctrination; I took it and by chance read this phrase from Lenin: "Three-quarters of humanity will die, so that the remaining quarter can become Communist." The poor Chinese people, into what hands they have fallen ...

Those who are without God, who are the enemies of God and the Church, and the enemies of every liberty, were sowing the Chinese soil with ruins, bathing it with human blood, and paving it with human bodies in the millions. Too little is known of those men and women. Too little is known of the sad martyrdom of the oppressed peoples and the persecuted Catholics. Yet those tortures inflicted on us by the barbarity of the Communists were dear to us: through our sufferings we were able to testify to the Faith that we preached, and through our example as good pastors we were able to strengthen the faith of the weak.

The bitter sentence of exile resonated in my heart, and the thought of having to abandon China, our country of adoption, saddened me. The thought of having fulfilled my duty comforted me, and the sufferings of so many innocents persecuted for their faith gave me hope for the future rebirth of the Church in China.

My "Via Crucis" through the Streets of Kaifeng

By now only a few days separated me from release. Soon I would have to leave China. But also during those last days in prison I had to drink the last drop of the bitter chalice of sufferings.

DIARIES OF THE CHINESE MARTYRS

It was September 29, 1951: toward eight, two guards picked me up from my cell and led me into a room where a month before they had assisted me, in order to intimidate me, at the trial of two "reactionary" detainees.

In the courtyard two policemen approached me, one at each side; the head jailer ordered them to lead me to the tribunal.

At the military tribunal the usual judge said to me: "Now you shall go to your residence, where the representatives of the various government offices and the council of the reformed Church are waiting for you: you shall carry out the transfer." They were hard words for me: besides the pain they caused me, they were hiding some trap.

We left the tribunal, and the number of police increased to four. After arriving at the residence, I was kept under guard at the entrance. A strong emotion swept over me as I looked once again at the cathedral and the episcopal residence and thought that in a few days I would have to leave everything. I was then ordered to speak only in Chinese and led into the building.

In a room, there were about ten high government officials and some members of the new schismatic church waiting for me. They made me sit at a table, while opposite me sat Father Ho, the priest designated by me to run the mission in case of my imprisonment or expulsion, according to the directives of the Congregation for the Propagation of the Faith. I made the handover aloud, repeating what I had written in a document already in possession of Father Ho. The officials, not content, wished for a written document; I rewrote it immediately in Latin, and it was also translated into Chinese. I signed it and handed it over to Father Ho. The officials wished it to be signed by all the priests who were present; it was not necessary, but I contented them. But when they requested that the members of the schismatic church sign, I vigorously opposed it, notwithstanding the ire and the threats of the representatives of the Communist government.

After Father Ho read the act of the consignment, I said aloud, emphasizing each word: "Beginning this day you are responsible for the mission of Kaifeng in all things spiritual and material. But remember that you are not a bishop, and all those present here know this. Furthermore,

Father Ho, remember that you are not the archbishop; therefore, you have no authority over the other missions of the province of Honan, nor can you get involved in their affairs." A chorus of shouts and curses followed my words. After the tumult ceased, I continued unperturbed: "You have said that the consignment ought to be done according to the laws of the Catholic Church; well, it is the law of the Church that the archbishop and bishops can be nominated only from Rome. This is why I had to make this declaration to Father Ho."

I was constrained to open the two safes and to expose the contents. In the first part there were only the deeds of the residence; in the second there was some money, some gold, and some other objects. During this operation the police photographers continuously took photographs. They tried to catch on film the moment I opened a small packet of gold, but I resolutely opposed them and tossed it to one of the officials.

During the walk through the episcopal residence, some of my Italian missionaries followed me; I was forbidden to speak with them, however. At a moment when the police were distracted, I, being visibly moved, managed to say only two words of greeting.

I was feeling a loss of strength, so, in order that I not fall to the floor in a faint, they had to give me some stimulants and allow me to sit a few times. In a small sitting room I had something to eat, but immediately after that, the order arrived to return to the prison. I got up, took two steps, turned pale, tottered, and fell to the floor. They left me there for half an hour, but then a message arrived from the prison saying that I must return immediately. I asked for a cart or some other means to assist me, but it was not granted. Resolute, I got up, pale and wan, and with a supreme force of will I set out, always surrounded by the police.

After leaving the residence, I saw the street packed with people, with students and young people. It seemed to me that they were raising the usual cries of "down with," "death," and "traitor." Little by little as we proceeded, the mob grew from five hundred to a thousand persons. Then it became an immense, confused mass; even the number of guards gradually increased along the way. Walking from the residence to the prison, a distance of little more than three kilometers, became a procession of hate, a procession of stones, rotten fruit, spitting, and a continuous launch of curses and insults. The hate was the most prominent note of that tragic "Via Crucis."

I often swooned, and many times the extreme exhaustion threatened to collapse my resistance.

As God wished, I reached the prison and as soon as the chains clanged and the door creaked behind me, I fell on the floor, worn out.

During the entire sorrowful period I lived under the Communist government, that "Via Crucis," experienced publicly, was one of the things that pained me most.

Exile

On October 1, at the termination of the six-month prison sentence, we were led to the tribunal, where a judge told us that we were free, but under surveillance. In reality we did not obtain our liberty, because they led us to a type of hotel under military guard, without any of the missionaries or Christians able to approach us.

In the afternoon of October 5 an order of departure was given to us, and we were led by many guards to the railroad station, which for the occasion was surrounded by a hundred policemen and soldiers out of fear of demonstration on the part of the Catholics.

I cannot describe the emotion I felt when the train left Kaifeng. The guards that were watching us prohibited us from speaking among ourselves on the train, but Father Piccinini, pretending to pray, said to me, "Monsignor, raise your hand once to bless our city." I traced a small Sign of the Cross, reciting the formula with a strong sob at my throat that prevented me from speaking the words, while some tears fell from my eyes. *Adieu, Kaifeng. When will I see you again?*

The trip from Kaifeng to the frontier lasted three days and three nights. We were escorted by some soldiers that from time to time harassed us, while we, closed in the sorrow of exile and separation from our mission, thought and prayed.

October 8 we reached Canton; from this city, still on the train, we arrived at the frontier, where the famous bridge of Lo Wu divided the red continent from the small British colony of Hong Kong. There were other annoyances and nuisances before they permitted us to leave the bridge but by now we were accustomed to it. Then finally we were given the order to depart, and we crossed the bridge, leaving behind us the land our mission loved so much. We fell into the arms of the confreres who came to receive us. We were truly free in a free land: no more grim faces, no more bayonets and guards, no more prison and trials, no more tortures and forced labor; instead we felt surrounded by affection and joy. The brief distance from the frontier to Hong Kong was spent between questions and responses. At Hong Kong the apostolic internuncio and many priests and Christians were waiting for us.

We arrived at Hong Kong worn out and spectral, so much so that we were forced to recuperate for a certain period in the hospital.

I remained in the English colony for four months, during which I was able to receive news secretly from Kaifeng. There the struggle continued, and other Christians were imprisoned. I often prostrated myself in the silence of a chapel before the tabernacle, thinking: "How beautiful the Church is; this great family that once again has so many persecuted and suffering children, who are giving precious testimony of their love, even, at times, with the sacrifice of their blood!"

In February of 1952 I returned to Italy, where I arrived at the airport on the eleventh.

Now I am in my fatherland. And, although I am surrounded by affection and esteem, my heart has remained down there; it has remained at Kaifeng. Mine is a heart that cries over Kaifeng's destruction, over the profaned churches, and over the storm of blood that has swept away our missions, putting our Christians on trial. The only hope that sustains me in exile is the hope of taking up the same path, of crossing the seas again and returning to Kaifeng to live the rest of my life until my last breath, reconstructing the mission of Kaifeng and expanding the reign of Jesus.

DOMINIC
TANG, S.J.

INTRODUCTION

Although each of the four personal stories contained in this book is identical in the political context—there is always the Maoist revolution with its various campaigns—and although each is similar in background—the same events: the threats, the arrests, the detentions, and the indoctrinations that follow one after the other—and although the protagonists are very similar to each other, each story is an authentic microcosm, rich in its own details and nuances that make it different. Each person, even if subjected to the same brutality, reacts in a different way, and each one lives interiorly his own particular Calvary.

All this appears very clear in the chapter regarding Dominic Tang Yi-ming, the archbishop of Canton who was arrested in 1958, and then, without ever having been formally tried in a court of law,[35] spent twenty-two years in detention.

---

[35] Dominic Tang Yi-ming was born at Hong Kong in 1908. He entered the Society of Jesus in 1930 and continued his studies at Macao (then a Portuguese colony) and later in Europe. After his return to China, he studied theology at Shanghai, where he was ordained a priest in 1941. When the armed Communists took Canton, Father Tang was working as a missionary in a district outside Macao. In 1950 he was designated by Pope Pius XII to substitute, as apostolic administrator, for the outgoing French missionary, Bishop Gustave Deswaziere.

After being arrested on February 5, 1958, he spent twenty-two years in detention until he was liberated in 1980. He then went to Hong Kong for a delicate operation. After regaining his health he went to Rome where he received the title of archbishop of Guangzhou (even up to that moment he was still the apostolic administrator). The pope wished with this

DIARIES OF THE CHINESE MARTYRS

A Man of Exceptional Character and Stature

Today the name of Monsignor Tang does not say very much, but at the time, he held one of the most delicate positions in the Chinese church, and he distinguished himself as one of the most significant ecclesial personalities. It is worth citing here a brief summary of the concluding pages of the book, where Bishop Tang speaks of his liberation and his encounter with the Holy See:

> The journalists from all the important Hong Kong dailies arrived at the college of Wah Yan. Cardinal Casaroli [Vatican Secretary of State] and I each read a communiqué, after which, for more than an hour, we responded to the numerous questions put to us by the journalists. Most touched on the possibility of establishing a relationship with Peking. Cardinal Casaroli responded that from the Vatican's point of view, without a doubt, there were many diplomatic means available to resolve the problem of Taiwan. As for the Patriotic Association of Chinese Catholics, under certain conditions, their present status could change, from illegal to acceptability by the Church.[36] They asked me if I would be able to

---

appointment to honor a man who had suffered long for the Faith and also to express all his love and attention toward the Church in China and her people. But the Chinese government considered the deed an affront and denied Tang the possibility of returning to Canton. From then, Monsignor Tang lived in exile in Hong Kong. He then died in San Francisco in 1996.

The information reported here is taken from *Giovanni Paolo II e la Cina*, by Gianni Criveller (published in the paper edition of *AsiaNews*, June 2005, and from the chapter "Important figures of the Chinese Church," by Father Giancarlo Politi in the volume *Cattolici in Cina, Una storia di fedeltà, le sfide del futuro* (Cinisello Balsamo: Edizioni San Paolo, 1998), edited by Gerolamo Fazzini and Angelo S. Lazzarotto.

[36] We have presented the Patriotic Association of Chinese Catholics (PACC) in note 8 of the general introduction of this book. Here we recall that Benedict XVI, in his 2007 *Lettera ai cattolici cinesi*, defined the PACC "irreconcilable with Catholic doctrine."

function as a bridge. I said that I would do everything that was in my power to do. The following morning the cardinal asked me to stay in contact with the government of Peking and to act as an intermediary. Before leaving, he invited me to go to Rome. The Holy Father wished to see me.

The Jesuit Temperament

Listening to the voice of Monsignor Tang we hear a protagonist of the events speaking; no less interesting is the exquisite personal aspect of the pages that follow. But what strikes one the most in this account is his stubbornness, his capacity to resist outrages with a mixture of convinced faith and extraordinary human solidity: a combination he credits—and he does not ever make a mystery of it—to his membership in the Society of Jesus and the severe and rigorous training he received as a young man.

The Jesuit temperament, which is disposed to obedience, *perinde ac cadaver* (submission of a disciple to a spiritual leader in "the manner of a corpse"), emerges very limpidly in Tang, beginning with his tortured nomination as bishop of Canton. "I was reluctant to accept the nomination, because we Jesuits usually do not become bishops; but on the other hand," he observed, "I recalled the fact that many foreign bishops had been sent out of the country by the 'government of the people,' and as a result there was no Chinese bishop in southern China. If I also had refused to become bishop, there probably would not be a bishop in the entire region, and this would not have been a good thing for the Church."

Martyrdom: A Serene Vocation

We read in Monsignor Tang's diary: "From the moment [1951] I became the apostolic administrator in Canton, I bore the responsibility of the entire diocese. I had also foreseen, for some time, the possibility of being imprisoned. Sister Maria Lau Suet-fan always said to me: 'Your vocation as bishop is the vocation of incarceration.' And I have always prayed to God to obtain the grace of this vocation."

The willingness of Bishop Tang to make this extreme sacrifice moved and impressed the people. "During the three years of the natural calamities [1959–1962], for six months of the year we ate only spinach and for the remaining six months we ate only cabbage. The greens had already flowered; the stems were hard, and everything was cooked without oil. As a result, my head was always spinning. I would think: 'If the Lord makes me die, I shall be very content because it will mean that I shall die for the Church.' When I felt wretched, I tried to think of what martyrdom means: to sacrifice oneself for God."

The Secret Weapon: Interior Discipline

Jesuit spirituality has already been mentioned as one of Dominic Tang's personal traits. Some brief passages cited here will verify how this interior discipline, so dear to the sons of Ignatius (founder of the Jesuits), became the secret weapon that helped Monsignor Tang to bear the pressures of the hunger and cold and of all the various tortures and discomforts.... Monsignor Tang notes:

> Alongside the prison regulations and schedules, I followed my own program. Each morning, after getting up, I would recite the Apostles' Creed, offering the day to God. Then I would say the *Veni Creator* [Come, Holy Spirit], because each day so many things happened that gave me need of the light of the Holy Spirit to descend upon me. Then I would meditate for half an hour.... It pleased me, above all, to meditate on the Passion of Christ.... When I prayed I put my hands under the newspaper and pretended to read it.... I prayed before and after every meal. But before and after every meal the guards would come to spy on me. If they suspected that I was praying, they would reproach me.... Once a year I prayed the eight-day Spiritual Exercises [of St. Ignatius Loyola], with two meditations

each day. Further, I interrogated myself on my relationship with God, with others, and with myself and on the three vows [chastity, poverty, and obedience]. I did the Spiritual Exercises faithfully, even during difficult times. They were a central point in my life, and the source of my renewal and correction.

The Mysterious (yet Real) Closeness of God

The habit of discernment and the capacity to see God's will in events—even those totally adverse—make up part of the Jesuit DNA. Yet, Monsignor Tang's isolation was such that not even his relatives knew whether he was living. In 1969 his Jesuit confreres, not having received news of him for a long time, even listed him among the dead. Despite this enormously difficult situation, his awareness of being persecuted for his fidelity to the pope, and as a disciple of Christ, inspired the bishop to say astonishing things:

> God gave me the grace to be optimistic, which continuously encouraged me to look at the good side of things and only rarely the ugly side. I was incarcerated for God and for the Church; my conscience was at peace, because I had done my duty regarding God and the Church. If one day I died, I would die in peace. If one day I was released, I would have continued to serve God and the Church. These thoughts and happy sentiments, this peace that I had in the depth of my soul sustained me during those twenty-two long winters and summers that I lived in prison.

In spite of all the terrible sufferings, Monsignor Tang never felt abandoned by God. To the contrary, he felt a mysterious friendly presence in the most difficult moments, beginning with the interminable interrogations to which he was subjected. "When, in prison, everything became exhausting and difficult to bear, I thought of the sufferings that Jesus experienced, and then I was able to bear the weight of my situation. I am weak, and so I asked the Lord to help me, to teach me how to act, and then I felt reinvigorated."

DIARIES OF THE CHINESE MARTYRS

Persons Reduced to a Number

Like the other texts in this volume—besides its exquisitely spiritual aspect—the diary of Monsignor Tang proves interesting for its documentary value. We learn, for example, that—on a par with what happened in the Nazi lagers—the Chinese prisoners were reduced to numbers. Tang relates: "I was transferred to section 3 of the principal prison of Canton. There all the prisoners were called by numbers. Names were not permitted. My number was 2202."

Monsignor Tang's experience was unique in many ways. The bishop lived a very long period in total solitude: a condition that would have caused many, even the strongest, to capitulate. Yet he miraculously, resisted:

> During the twenty-two years I was imprisoned, I never received a letter from anyone in my family or from among my friends. Nor did I receive a single visitor, not even a few months before my release—with the exception of Chan Nai-choh [the caretaker at the episcopal residence].... For seventeen years I did not receive a piece of toilet paper or a bar of soap. I slept on a wooden bench, with a blanket I brought with me to the prison.... I did not receive letters from my relatives, nor did the prison authorities allow me to write. I did not know anything about the situation of the Church beyond the prison or about the condition of my relatives.

The Faith—a Duel of Ideologies

Some of the most interesting pages in his diary regard the duel between the Catholic bishop and his atheistic jailers and those indoctrinated with the communist and positivist ideologies. The latter tried in vain to eliminate the pastor's trust in God, which, although supported by faith, they believed, was being profoundly challenged by the Marxist system and by the scientific and technological successes that purported to prove the uselessness of the God of Jesus Christ. But the bishop's faith was, as usual, indestructible: "When I was attacked by materialism, by atheism, or by false scientific arguments, I immediately turned to God and asked him for the necessary grace to keep me firm in my faith."

PREFACE

The Lord's Boundless Grace

After I had confronted innumerable difficulties and obstacles, the Lord's boundless grace has finally led me in peace to Hong Kong, my native city. Certainly, pen and ink could not possibly express, not even minimally, the depth of my gratitude; this, notwithstanding, in order to respond to the requests of the faithful of my diocese, I have decided to narrate, systematically and in chronological order, the many things that occurred in the Archdiocese of Canton (Guangzhou) between 1951 and 1981, so that everyone may understand the changes that have taken place in the diocese as well as what happened to me during these years; and as a result they will be able to evaluate the various and difficult situations that have been created.

But the most important thing to understand is how our loving, heavenly Father has preserved our diocese through thousands of dangers, as, in the same way, he has preserved his servant, showering me with many special graces. The understanding of such concepts will certainly be difficult for those who have not had a way of personally experiencing "how inscrutable are his ways!" (cf. Rom. 11:33).

—Dominic Tang, S.J.

IN MAO'S PRISONS

The Diary of a Bishop

A Troubled Nomination

One day in November 1950, a registered letter arrived from Nanjing.... I opened the envelope. The letter came from the apostolic internuncio, Monsignor Antonio Riberi, who at that time was at Nanjing. The letter was stamped, "*Secretum Sancti Officii*" (Secret: the Holy See). The text said: "Pope Pius XII has decided to nominate Dominic Tang apostolic administrator of the Archdiocese of Canton (Guangzhou) with the rights and duties of a residential bishop. I hope that you wish to comply with the Holy Father's wish and accept, with generosity, the office being offered to you, particularly in consideration of the current, special circumstances in China created by the Communist occupation."

After reading the letter, I was not only surprised by its unexpected arrival but was also overcome by a feeling of fear: it was a very serious responsibility.

The next day I went to Macao to meet with my superior, the Jesuit Father Anacleto Dias. I explained to him the motive for my visit and showed him the letter. After he read it, he said to me: "The Holy See has knocked at your door only now. The pope had already made the same offer to some other priests, and they refused; now he is doing the same with you. You must reflect on it and make a decision!"

My thoughts on the proposal were conflicting: on the one hand, I was reluctant to accept the nomination, because we Jesuits usually do not become bishops; but on the other hand, I recalled the fact that many foreign bishops had been sent out of the country by the "government of the people" and as a result there was no Chinese bishop in southern China. If I also had refused to become bishop, there probably would not be a bishop in the entire region and this would not have been a good thing for the Church in southern China. For these reasons I found it difficult to make a decision, so I said that I wished first to see Father Elia Marcal, who was the Jesuit superior of Zhaoqing and also the vicar general for that part of the Diocese of Macao.

Furthermore, Father Dias added: "Before the Holy See asked for your consensus they made inquiries at Rome and obtained permission from the father general (Pedro Arrupe), who is aware of the business and in agreement with it." He continued: "Try, seriously, to make your choice, whatever it is, before God. Write a letter to Monsignor Riberi informing him that you intend to make a private retreat in order to reflect on the matter and that, after having dutifully reflected, you will send him an official response."

While leaving the office of Father Dias, I thought: "I must ask the advice of an elderly priest and hear his opinion on the matter before I decide." So I immediately went to see Father Vincent Leung Wai-to. After reading the letter, Father Leung said: "In the current situation, that presents so many difficulties, it will be hard to be a bishop of Canton. Monsignor Antoine Fourquet had tried to nominate Peter Chan, but then he changed his mind. In the end, he consecrated Bonaventure Yeung Fuk-tseuk, bishop, but he did not give him any power. At the death of Monsignor Yeung, the Holy See asked Father Tsoi and others to become bishop of Canton, but they did not wish to accept."

My heart was anxious. I returned to Shiqi for an eight-day spiritual retreat in order to understand the will of God. I had just gone on my knees before the Most Holy Sacrament when I felt myself fill up with emotion and tears. I thought that in that precise historical moment, under the government of the Communists, the situation was decidedly brutal and the circumstances extremely difficult. The diocese covered a vast area, comprising fifteen districts.

The relationships were tense: priests and nuns were not harmoniously integrated with the local population, and the diocese was poor. However, I thought, as a Jesuit, I would have to submit myself to the will of the pope. I also considered the needs of the Church at that time. After a violent interior conflict, I made a definite decision: to accept the papal nomination.

After I finished the retreat, I wrote the following response, in Latin, to Monsignor Riberi's letter:

> Dear Monsignor Riberi, I accept the decision of Pope Pius XII to nominate me apostolic administrator of the Archdiocese of Canton with respect and gratitude. However, seeing that the territory of that archdiocese is extensive and densely populated, and that I feel foreign in a diocese where the inhabitants are subjected to a Communist regime, it was very difficult for me to make this decision. But, as a Jesuit, I know that I must submit with pleasure to the will of the pope. For this reason I have decided to accept the papal nomination as apostolic administrator of the Diocese of Canton and titular bishop of Elatea. With complete sincerity I ask with all my heart that the Holy Spirit assist me to fulfill this office worthily. And I ask you to pray for me.

I returned to Macao and met with Father Dias. He asked me about the nomination as bishop, and I told him that I had decided to accept the pope's proposal.

Later, through Father Leung, I received a special-delivery letter from a visitor (envoy),[37] Father Paul O'Brien, a Jesuit, who asked me to come immediately to Macao for a meeting. At that time, he lived and worked at Hong Kong and had come to Macao precisely to speak with me. He said to me: "News has reached me that you are to become bishop of Canton. Is it true?"

I responded: "Yes."

---

[37] In the Society of Jesus the envoy in this situation, who is on a special mission for the Holy See or the supreme general of the Jesuits, is called the "visitor."

He continued: "It is better, for your own good, not to accept. The Diocese of Canton is very poor, and the situation is complicated: you will not be able to do anything. You should refuse the appointment."

I told him that by now I had accepted it, that I had given my consent and could not take it back.

"Why did you not speak to me first?" he asked me.

"Because it was a secret from the Holy See," I said.

He continued: "Ah, we are already at this level. I heard about this from Monsignor Riberi when I arrived at Nanjing, but I did not think that it was already established. Now, since it is all arranged, there is nothing more to say about it."

I asked him to pray for me, and I returned immediately to Shiqi.

I had become rather uneasy. After a few days, I received a letter from Monsignor Riberi in which he said: "I know that you have accepted the papal nomination. Leave immediately for Canton without saying anything to anyone. Establish yourself in the house of the Jesuits situated at 225 Yuet Sau Pak Street. If the superior asks you for the motive for your presence at Canton, simply respond that the highest authorities have asked you to carry out an assignment in the area. Wait on Yuet Sau Pak for the arrival of the papal bull."

I hurriedly finished all the diocesan business left in abeyance in the district of Zhongshan. At that time I was the vicar forane of the Diocese of Zhongshan, pastor of Shiqi, director of the elementary school Po Ling, and responsible for the nursery school Pui Ki.

I entrusted the parish of Shiqi to Father Matteo Tse Hau-pei, who, later, would die in a forced-labor camp in the province of Qinghai.

Tse Yu-choh became director of the elementary school Po Ling (he would then be beaten to death in prison), and Kwong Sz-ying took responsibility of the nursery school Pui Ki. It was during that period that Father Simone Wong lai-sau of the Xiaolin village was arrested.

Fearing it was my turn to be arrested, I thought up an excuse to go to Canton for a brief period and, without taking leave of anyone, reached my new residence in secret in order to attend to my nomination.

When I arrived at Canton, on the night of December 30, 1950, in the area of Yuet Sau Pak, it was totally without electricity. I took a rickshaw to my new post. The police stopped me and asked me why I was going to Canton. I deceived them with four fibs, saying that I was working in a school and that the books I had with me were only for private use.

When I reached Canton, I went immediately to Monsignor Gustave Deswaziere, who was already informed of everything. He said he knew of my arrival from the papal bull. Later, we discussed some of the problems concerning the priests of the diocese, as well as financial and business matters.

About a month after my arrival at Canton, Monsignor Deswaziere granted me the bull of my nomination. He told me to move immediately to my domicile from Yuet Sau Pak Street to the episcopal residence of Shek Shat.[38]

I carried out the change immediately and transferred to Shek Shat.

The Bishop's Consecration

At the beginning, we wished to celebrate the consecration ceremony at Shanghai, since a discreet number of bishops resided there, among them Monsignor Ignatius Gong Pinmei,[39] Monsignor Simone Kaimin, and

---

[38] The cathedral of Canton, dedicated to the Sacred Heart of Jesus, is commonly called Shek Shat (house of stone), because the walls and columns are of granite. It is a majestic structure in the neo-Gothic style and took twenty-five years to complete, in 1888.

[39] Ignazio Gong Pinmei was one of the principal ecclesial figures of the Chinese Church of the last century. He was born at Shanghai on August 2, 1900, of a Catholic family; he was ordained a priest in 1930 and nominated bishop of Shanghai in 1950. On September 8, 1955, he was arrested together with more than two hundred among the priests and the faithful of the diocese. Condemned by the Chinese government to life in prison for "counterrevolutionary activity," he remained in prison for thirty-three years. Thanks to pressure from diverse international personalities, he was released in July 1985 and placed under house arrest until 1987, when he was invited to the United States for medical attention. In 1979 he was proclaimed cardinal *in pectore* (unrevealed, known solely by the pope, who

Monsignor James Walsh.[40] But we feared that the Communist government would impede me from returning to Canton. For this reason, Father O'Meara wrote to the Jesuit superior of Hong Kong, requesting a dispensation from Rome, which would allow a single bishop to preside over the ceremony. We also sent an express letter to Monsignor Riberi at Nanjing, asking him for the same permission. The consensus from both arrived at Canton on the same day.

On February 15, 1951, the government closed the borders of the province of Guangdong. Those who intended to go to Hong Kong and to Macao would now have to apply for special permission. We feared that the Communist government was intending to expel or incarcerate Monsignor Deswaziere from the country. The priests of Canton exhorted me to have the consecration as soon as possible. Therefore, we quickly arranged the preparations and moved the date from the nineteenth of February to the thirteenth.

---

would communicate the appointment to the world, and to Gong himself, only in 1991). In 1998 he was officially exiled. He died on March 12, 2000, from stomach cancer.

Requests for the opening of the process for his beatification have come from many and various parts. See http://www.asianews.it/notizie-it/I-10anni-dalla-morte-del-card.-Gong-Pinmei:-si-at-tende-la-causa-di-beatifica-zione-17730.html.

[40] American bishop James Walsh arrived in China in 1918 with three Maryknoll companions. On May 22, 1927, at the age of thirty-six, he was ordained a bishop for the Diocese of Kongmoon (now Jiangmen) in China. The consecration was held at Shangchuan Island, in the South China Sea, on whose coast St. Francis Xavier, the apostle of the Indies, died in 1552.

In 1948, after a period in the United States as superior general of the missionaries of Maryknoll, upon the request of the Holy See, Walsh returned to Shanghai to coordinate the missionary activities of the place.

He was arrested by Communists in 1958 and condemned to twenty years in prison. After twelve years of detention in isolation, he was suddenly released in 1970. He was the last Western missionary to leave Communist China after the "liberation" of 1949. After returning definitively to the United States, he died at the age of ninety, on July 29, 1981, at Maryknoll, New York. See James T. Myers, *Nemici senza fucile* (Milan: Jaca Book, 1994), 225ff.

That day, the consecration ceremony was held in the chapel on the first floor of the episcopal residence by Monsignor Deswaziere. His concelebrants were the vicar general of the Diocese of Canton, Father Andrew Chan Yik-san, and Father Gioacchino Lau Him-sheung. Among the participants were the diocesan priests, some foreign Jesuits, some Maryknoll priests, the mother general of the Chinese sisters of the Immaculate Conception, Sister Rosa Chan Chi-to, the mother provincial of the Canadian sisters of Our Lady of the Angels, the mother provincial of the Canadian sisters of the Immaculate Conception of Montreal, and also the French consul ad interim and some others. The ceremony lasted an hour and a half; it was simple but solemn.

The same day, Monsignor Deswaziere served a banquet in my honor; all the priests of the area were invited and took part. During his discourse, spoken in Latin, Monsignor Deswaziere expressed his congratulations to me. He affirmed that the new bishop, accepting the nomination of the Holy See in such difficult times was demonstrating absolute obedience and a spirit of sacrifice. During my remarks, spoken in Latin, I expressed my gratitude:

> The missionaries of Paris have worked in the Diocese of Canton for more than one hundred years; they have shed blood and sweat in order to build many churches and convert many men and women to the Catholic Faith, even to making themselves living temples of God. I shall do my best to safeguard all of that. I agreed to become the bishop of Canton because I intend to prove my fidelity to God and to the Church. For this reason, I am acting in the pure spirit of sacrifice and not for any other goals.

The evening of February 18, 1951, in the parlor of the episcopal residence, the vicar general, Father Andrew Chan, announced to the representatives of the Faith: "The Holy See has nominated Dominic Tang bishop of Canton. From today he substitutes Monsignor Deswaziere and is officially installed as the pastoral guide of the diocese."

On Sunday, February 19, at nine in the morning, in the cathedral of Shek Shat, we held a solemn Mass. After the Mass I went out to meet the faithful who had come from the various parishes of the city (Canton) to congratulate their new bishop.

The next day I sent official letters announcing my nomination to the civic leaders of the province of Guangdong and of the city of Canton. Subsequently, I convened a meeting of all the diocesan priests at the episcopal residence in order to discuss with them some of the problems of the diocese.

Hard Times for the Church

In February of 1951 the "government of the people" of Canton decided to make an inventory of the land and buildings owned by foreigners. The government had declared that the right of property would not be recognized without the registration of all tangible assets. I entrusted the task to Father Andrew Lin, Father Louis Yip Seung, and Father Joachim Lau.

On the day preceding the "liberation" of 1949 (the assumption of power by the Communists)[41] all the deeds of the diocese were brought to the House of Nazareth for the Foreign Missions of Paris, on Pokfulam Street, at Hong Kong for safekeeping.

The registration process lasted more than two months. Each morning at eight, our priests went to the Office for the Management of Real Estate (near the government's city hall) and got in line. The officials[42] employed with this task treated the common people, even more so the clergy, with arrogance and scorn.

The deeds to the house and all the land belonging to the diocese were consigned to that office. Although the priests repeatedly asked for receipts, the Communist leaders always refused to release them.

Before the registration was concluded, the diocese unexpectedly received a communiqué from the Office for the Management of Real Estate,

---

[41] *Liberation* is the term commonly used in China to indicate the assumption of power by the Communists. In 1949 it became the normal point of reference, as in "before the liberation" and "after the liberation."

[42] These particular officials were State employees who were party members and worked in the public sector.

which imposed a tax relative to all the Church property, to be paid within an established date and which included: the buildings for the parochial schools, the Sacred Heart Cathedral, the Sacred Heart Middle School, the Ming Tak Nursery School, and all the other institutions. We were also required to pay taxes for all open spaces, gardens, paths, and sidewalks. Shek Shat was heavily taxed, as were the diocesan buildings in the center of the city. All together we had to pay 170 million yuan.[43] If the taxes were not paid within forty days, a fine of 2 million yuan would be added.

After the arrival of the communiqué, I met with all the priests of the city (at times until late at night) to discuss how to confront the situation. We all agreed that there was no escape from the way the government had begun to persecute the Church financially. Operatively, we decided to move in two directions. First, we would attempt to present a rendering of the Church's difficult financial situation. Not being a productive entity,[44] we were not able to pay such high taxes; for this reason we asked the government to reduce them. Second, we tried to increase our income as a way to resolve the case, at least for the moment, and also if, by chance, the government refused our petition.

I went often, in person, together with the priests, to the city's Office of Civil Administration and to the main branch of the Tax Department to speak with the officials and to explain our problems to them, but the Church's requests were never accepted. I also attempted to visit some of the faithful who were well off financially and well known, such as Fung Chuk-man—who had married Chan Tsz-pik, a devout Catholic—Kwan Pak-luk, and others, to ask for their help. They were delighted to receive a visit from the bishop but in order to avoid problems they declined.

At that time the government had asked the Church to hand over their schools (the Sacred Heart Middle School, the elementary schools, the

---

[43] The yuan is a unit of Chinese money, now called RMB (*renminbi*, that is "the money of the people").

[44] The "unity of work," the entity in which each urban inhabitant was employed. It could be a government office, a factory, a hospital or a school, etc.

girls' middle school, and all the others) and to unite with the Movement of Reform of the Three Autonomies.

The diocese was on the brink of bankruptcy. Very little money remained. There were then thirty-eight priests, some nuns, and some lay catechists and various employees. Our monthly expenses were more or less 10,000 Hong Kong dollars (about 1,700 American dollars).

The only thing that we could do was to divide the cash at our disposition among the priests for their maintenance. Each of them was given 20 dollars, while at the beginning the diocese had given them 50 Hong Kong dollars, about 20 of the old yuan, as a subsidy. In addition, each priest was given twenty Mass intentions of 2 yuan each. The total sum was 60 yuan a month.

In order to confront the diocese's economic crisis, I met often with all the diocesan clergy. At the end we decided to rent the episcopal residence and the Catholic Center to some outsiders. Some advised me not to leave the episcopal residence so that the people would not think that even the bishop no longer had a house. But I replied: "I must do it in order to pay the taxes and to maintain the priests."

Fortunately, it was a time in which it was difficult to find housing, so we were able to rent our properties. From there we transformed our minor seminary, St. Francis, into a provisional diocesan office and residence for the priests. It was very beautiful: there were many rooms, a parlor, a garden, and so forth. It was comfortable enough, but because of our financial straits we soon decided to rent the minor seminary, and together with Father Andrew Chan, the pastor, we transferred the provisional office and the residence of the priests to the Carmelite convent, the poor and rather shabby residence of the pastor of the cathedral. We remained there until I was arrested, on February 5, 1958. Eventually, because we could not pay the higher real-estate taxes, the idea came to us to sell all the property and to use the money to pay the taxes and to maintain the priests.

The priests, in that period, lived together and were very united, and the faithful loved us. Also at that time, we piled up a lot of old furniture in the small courtyard of the convent because we didn't know where to put it. Father Narbais took the less beautiful pieces and made firewood out of them. It was a great loss, but not having money to purchase firewood, there was nothing else we could do.

I usually worked in the garden in work pants and a short-sleeve shirt. For some of the faithful, who loved us, it was heartrending to see us so badly off.

From 1952 to 1953 the diocese was subjected to another hard blow in the area of finances. We had already used up all the diocesan funds in order to pay our real-estate taxes. We were able to survive thanks to the collection of rents from some of our houses and to the generosity of some fervent Christians. Around the cathedral there were about two hundred houses rented to Christians. The episcopal residence and two other houses were already rented for about three thousand yuan a month.

At that time (it was now 1954) I received an unexpected call from the city's Office for the Management of Real Estate, asking me to go in person to a meeting organized by the Office of Municipal Administration. The meeting in question was headed by the mayor; at least he claimed he was the mayor. I was ill and still convalescing, so I sent Father Lin and Father Yip. While they were sitting in the waiting room, a young Communist leader entered and shouted at them to get up; then he read a decree sent by the mayor, Fong Fong, which said more or less: "Since the Catholic Church is not administering its properties equitably, it is decreed that, from this day, the Catholic Church will establish, together with the Catholic Association of the Three Autonomies, a provisional commission for the management of said real estate, to be supervised by the appropriate government office that is occupied with such properties."

As soon as I learned all of this, I called a meeting of all the priests of the city to examine the question in depth. We began by making clear that according to canon law, the Church cannot permit external interference in the administration of her properties. Each one had his say, and we all agreed that the government was using this tactic to oblige the Church to unite with the Movement of the Three Autonomies. An elderly priest, Father Joseph Tam Wan-sham, exclaimed: "I prefer to go begging rather than ask for help from the Movement of the Three Autonomies."

Without a doubt the government had organized this provisional commission in order to take the Church property for itself. On our part, to place priests on that commission would have meant that we recognized its legality. We all preferred to take on new financial difficulties rather than betray the rights of the Church. Therefore, we decided not to assign anyone to the committee. As for the Office for Religious Affairs,[45] we were encouraged to meet again from time to time to discuss the question of the commission. They had assigned two places for us on that commission, and they encouraged us to send our representative, but we sent no one, and no one wished to go. Thanks to all this, the priests demonstrated their solidarity with one another.

Later, the Commission for the Management of Real Estate assigned us 1,000 yuan a month. We used that money to help the priests support themselves and for the expenses of the diocesan office. After a few months the amount was reduced to 750 yuan a month.

It was during the Chinese-Japanese conflict that the hard times had begun. The money assigned to the priests then was not sufficient to maintain them. When Monsignor Deswaziere became the apostolic administrator of the diocese, he established, as has been mentioned, that each priest would receive a subsidy of 50 Hong Kong dollars (equal to 20 yuan), for his support, along with twenty Mass offerings (at 2 yuan each), for a total of 60 yuan a month. In order to guarantee the support of my priests, I had held to this regulation.

But when I began to fulfill my duties as bishop, the financial situation of the diocese became very precarious, since we had to pay heavy taxes. In addition, we were not able to receive help from abroad. Later, during a discussion with the priests, we decided together to fix a monthly subsidy of

---

[45] The Office for Religious Affairs is the policy arm of the United Front regarding the five recognized religions (Buddhism, Taoism, Islam, Catholicism, Protestantism). It depends on the Council of State and, if necessary, is served by the support of the various entities of the police. The officials are usually atheists. Today it is called the State Administration of Religious Affairs (SARA).

just 15 yuan and an offering of fifteen Masses monthly for each priest and the bishop. Our faithful were poor: the offering for a Mass was therefore fixed at 1 yuan per Mass to say at an indeterminate time.

The rents that we were paid were controlled by the Commission for the Management of Real Estate, which left us with a total of 750 yuan a month.

I lived like the other priests. This contented everyone, and no one ever complained about anything.

The Incident of To Kam Hang

In order to attack the pope and to promote an anti-foreigner political agenda, the Communist government created the incident of To Kam Hang in order to cause greater persecution of the Catholic Church.

There were always very many poor in China, and the medical assistance had always been backward; furthermore, the people had always preferred sons to daughters. As a consequence, as in so many parts of China, each year a consistent number of baby girls were abandoned by the families and picked up by the orphanage of To Kam Hang, which was situated north of the city of Canton. That orphanage was managed by five Canadian nuns who belonged to the Congregation of the Immaculate Conception of Montreal. There were many abandoned babies; and at times they arrived at the orphanage very ill or near death, so that many of them did not survive and ended up dying there. The infant bodies were immediately buried by the person in charge of the nearby cemetery; but at times their graves were not deep enough and were dug up by stray dogs. For this reason the orphanage made a big cement pit in which they placed the little cadavers, placing lime over them for hygienic reasons.

After the "liberation," in 1950, the government began to demand a daily report on the circumstances of the deceased babies, and the nuns accepted the conditions. Later, the government inflated the number of the deceased and accused the nuns of mistreating and killing many of the babies. The nuns then decided to speak of it with me. They informed me of their problem, and I counseled them to be kind with the Communist leaders and not to display any arrogance toward them. Moreover, I told them to base everything on facts and not to accept the accusation of homicide.

Shortly after the takeover of China by the Communists, an anti-Catholic movement spread across the country, from the north to the south, and the sisters were expelled from the territory. The various educational institutions finalized their teaching, and the works of charity founded by the Church—schools, orphanages, hospitals, and so on—were confiscated. The Communists invented every type of crime and accusation in order to reach their goal of closing down the Church. The orphanage of To Kam Hang, like the other orphanages of the country, was presented as irrefutable proof of crimes perpetrated by the imperialists' invasion of China. The nuns of the orphanage were falsely accused of having killed babies. The Communist government was served by the media, which depicted the Catholic nuns, who were usually loved and respected by the Chinese population, as "imperialist assassins wearing the mantle of religion." They arrested the five Canadian nuns from the orphanage of To Kam Hang, assumed control over all the properties of the orphanage, and staged a public trial that they held in the Chung Shan Memorial Hall, the largest venue for conferences in the city. They obligated all the organizations and groups, schools and citizens to send representatives to attend the trial. They even prepared all the accusations in advance and broadcast the trial on the radio throughout the entire city.

The Jesuit priest Gerard Casey attempted to bring Communion to the nuns after their arrest, but he did not succeed. He wished not only [to perform a corporal work of mercy] but also to offer them the spiritual nourishment that would have given them the necessary strength of spirit to confront their sufferings.

The day of the nuns' trial I went to the church of Po Kong in order to avoid being forced by the government to participate. There I listened to it on the radio. Father Narbais went in person to the trial and later told us that it was a true farce. Immediately after the trial, the five nuns were put on a truck and driven around the city under close watch and escorted by some police cars. After having been treated like the worst criminals, they were then publicly exposed as further punishment. Through all of this the nuns were not permitted to wear their habits. Instead they wore black shirts and Chinese-style long pants. As they passed through the streets some spectators deliberately threw stones and garbage at them. Sister Germaine Gravel reported that she was wounded so many times that her face was a mask of blood. They were held in prison for a certain period, and then, since they were Canadians, they were expelled from China.

After the government finished with them, they ordered the people of every social level and every part of the city, from the schools and from the various organizations, to organize visits to the orphanage of To Kam Hang. They also ordered the priests to form discussion groups in order to reflect on that business together and as a group to denounce the nuns publicly, but no one came forward.

The Communist leaders would have liked the vicar general of the archdiocese, Father Andrew Chan, to denounce on the radio the crimes committed by the nuns, but he also refused to do any such thing.

After the nuns returned to Hong Kong, I wrote them a letter thanking them for having suffered so much for the diocese and for having prayed for us from prison. They responded: "It is not you who owes us gratitude; rather, we must thank you for having prayed that we would be able to survive everything unharmed."

When they returned to Canada, their bishop, Cardinal Paul Emile Léger, personally met them at the airport in order to welcome them and to accompany them to their convent.

The Legion of Mary under Surveillance

Beginning in August 1948, Father Aiden McGrath, a missionary of St. Columbine, instituted the Legion of Mary at Tianjin, Shanghai, Guilin, and in the province of Sichuan and in other localities in China. The Legion of Mary spread very rapidly at Tianjin, Peking, and Shanghai. Many young people, both male and female, enlisted. Beginning in February 1949, a total of thirteen presidiums (which is what they called their groups) were established at Canton, with a curia.

When the Communist Party took control and introduced atheism to the country, the missionaries and foreign nuns were forced to leave China, and the religious who remained were forbidden to interact with the people to spread the Faith. Meanwhile, the members of the Legion of Mary, as laypeople, were spreading out in various parishes with discreet tranquillity and were able to visit individuals and families, teaching catechism and helping the parishes in other spiritual activities. Therefore, the Legion of Mary was seen as the instrument particularly adapted to confronting the needs of the time, especially in those circumstances where it was necessary to preserve the Faith.

The State-sponsored atheism wished to destroy religion, especially the Catholic religion. The Legion of Mary exercised great influence on the Catholic Church in China; it was her powerful support; built on spiritual strength, its task was to keep the Christian life alive. Therefore, the government made it a priority to take down this organization.

Beginning in July 1951, the commissions of military control of Peking, Tianjin, Shanghai, Changsha, and other cities ordered the suppression of the "Legion of Mary, the organization that carried out counterrevolutionary activities."[46] The major newspapers of China carried out an impressive campaign discrediting the Legion of Mary, accusing it of being a repository of counterrevolutionary spies at the service of the Catholic Church.

At that point the Legion of Mary of Canton decided on its own initiative to suspend its activities.

On August 5, 1953, the Commission of Military Control of Canton declared once and for all that it would suppress the Legion of Mary. All the newspapers reported the military decree in banner headlines. All the Legion of Mary members were required immediately to report to the Office

---

[46] According to article 19 of the Constitution of 1954, to be counterrevolutionary or to carry out counterrevolutionary activity is the most serious crime possible in the People's Republic of China, punishable with death.

of Public Safety in order to register their resignations from this counter-revolutionary organization and to renounce it publicly.

Our response to these events was in line with those adopted by the other provincial dioceses. If a priest publicly registered his resignation from the Legion of Mary and admitted to its counterrevolutionary nature, then he was no longer permitted to celebrate Mass. If laymen behaved in this way, they would not be permitted to receive Communion. They would then have to repent publicly in order to have these interdictions removed. The transgressors would first have to demonstrate a public repentance; then the celebrants would be permitted to say Mass again, and the others would be permitted to receive Communion.

Later, this rule would be transformed into one of the most serious charges against me: my opposition to the decree issued by the Commission of Military Control. The government viewed it as a means of directly attacking the fundamental structures of the Church. We, on the other hand, saw it as a life-or-death situation, which obliged us to protect the Church from the enactment of those rules. Religious and laity were united in their opposition to that unjust government decree.

The battle was very difficult. Both the principal Office of Public Safety and all its branches put up enormous posters reporting: "the place for registration for the members of the Legion of Mary, the counterrevolutionary organization"; but many members showed great courage and refused to register. They had already planned in advance how they would behave in those circumstances. Later, when the government adopted repressive measures toward those members of the Legion of Mary, they were subjected to interrogations. Those who refused to register were subjected to restrictions; that is, they were deprived of their civil rights.

For example, Kung Yat-wah, of the parish of Baogang in the city, and Kwan, a young man from the cathedral, were held under surveillance for many years. Kwan Chiu-po was expelled from the university, and his sister, a nurse with the military hospital, lost her job. Kan, a young Legion of Mary member of the cathedral was beaten so severely that he suffered a broken back and was confined to bed for more than thirty years. But in spite of this enormous suffering, to which was added that of his elderly mother, he maintained his faith with great courage.[47]

The government also put pressure on parents, obliging them to order their sons and daughters to register. For example, the parents of Chan, a Catholic girl, were not Catholic. The father, who worked in customs, was given a three-day leave so that he could return home and force his daughter to go and register. The man broke their ancestral tablets[48] and reproached his daughter for her lack of filial piety and respect toward her heritage. Chan was forced to ask for refuge with relatives.

Some members of the Legion of Mary were not able to meet the challenge. Put to the test by the government, they left their job, their school, and their family and went to register at the Office of Public Safety. The directors of the Sacred Heart Middle School and the girls' middle school, and Ming Tak, together with some teachers and other members of the Legion of Mary scattered in the various parishes, left the Legion in this way. Later on, some of them repented their choice and suffered bitterly over their decision.

United in Adversity

Our Diocese of Canton was different from that of Shanghai. At Shanghai there were many priests and talented laymen, among them those who attended the Jesuits' theology school and their seminary. But in the Diocese of Canton it was difficult to find vocations. Each day we prayed to the Holy Spirit to help us to resolve our problems. I had begun to dedicate myself to the formation of the priests, and I gave them lessons in doctrine, especially during spiritual retreats, in order to elevate their moral conscience and deepen their spirituality. During the first week of every month, one day

---

[47] Kan died in a convalescent home in Canton in 2014, leaving a great example of serenity in spite of his suffering.

[48] The wooden tablets on which were written the names of the deceased members of the family are traditionally placed on a small altar at the center of the house and are the object of particular veneration.

was set aside for a gathering of all the priests in order to discuss the "moral dilemmas." Each week I held courses on canon law and moral theology to increase the theological knowledge of the priests and to help them to resolve the "moral dilemmas."

I felt that the diocese had to consider the priests as the bishops' most important collaborators. The priests of the city and the surrounding areas would have to meet in order to examine important and contingent questions, such as the taxes requested by the government for the real estate, the rent of the property of the Church in order to increase income, the offerings allotted for the priests for each Mass, the problem of the Three Autonomies, the Legion of Mary, and other important questions of a practical nature.

Everyone was encouraged to speak, to listen to the opinions of others, and to take part in the discussion. The final decision, however, was always the bishop's. In this way we opened up all the important questions to everyone. The Church belonged to the priests and to the faithful. Each one was offered the opportunity to become interested and informed of the situations in the diocese and to contribute concretely to the search for adequate solutions to its problems. United in this way, it would be easier for everyone to confront any of the pressures imposed by external forces.

"Martyrdom, the Shortcut to Paradise"

Father Francis Tam Tin-tak, was courageous and audacious, a man of strong principles and a zealous priest, both in his thought and in his action. He always encouraged Christians not to fear any difficulty, pushing them to defend the position of the Church, to preserve the Faith, and to be ready to sacrifice everything to follow Christ. His fearless spirit constituted a splendid example for both the priests and the faithful of the diocese.

In 1953 Father Tam led a group of priests and faithful from the islands of Hainan, Jiangmen, and Wuzhou, on a pilgrimage to the sanctuary of Sheshan, near Shanghai. After he arrived at the place, he began to observe how the Christians there, especially the young people, knew how to give proof of great courage in diverse and difficult faith situations. In order to safeguard their faith, they intensified and strengthened their spiritual life. In May of 1953 Father Tam organized another pilgrimage to Sheshan for more than ten priests and some of the faithful of Canton, so that they could profit from the zeal of the young Catholics of Shanghai.

Father Tam was a somber and simple man. Gentle and pure of heart, he was always content when he was able to help someone. If he managed to save a little money, he used it to help the poor. It pleased him very much to mix with the adolescents, so that he could offer them guidance on how to choose the right path. He was loved and respected by the young and the old.

Father Tam once asked a Catholic, Szeto Kwok-tsz, to design a poster with a railroad track and a train running on it and to write the following words: "Martyrdom is a shortcut to Paradise." The request was carried out, and he hung it on the notice board at the entrance of the cathedral, but Father Andrew Chan and Father Dominic Tam immediately took it down. Father Francis Tam was furious and wished to speak to me about it. Father Dominic Tam also came to me and reproached Father Francis Tam for having hung the design without first asking permission of the pastor. Fortunately, the question was resolved, and peace was restored among all the parties.

On August 5, 1953, the major dailies of Canton headlined some alarming news on their front pages: "Three imperialists sheltered by the Catholic Church—O'Meara, Egan, and Limat—must be expelled from China"; and also "Tim Tin-tak is a great counterrevolutionary given refuge in the cathedral of Canton, the bloodhound of the imperialists, the worst counterrevolutionary." After having read those notices, all the priests understood that the Communists had raised the curtain on the second act of the destruction of the Church. From the beginnings of the "liberation," it was said in the Catholic circles that the Communists would persecute the Church in three phases:

1. Attack the foreign missionaries and expel them from the country.

2. Attack the Chinese clergy, and then follow up with arrests and incarcerations.

3. Attack the Chinese Catholics, arresting them and closing the churches.

These three phases were commonly called "the drama in three acts." Initially many only partially believed this chatter.

The evening of August 4, 1953, the Jesuit priests Father John O'Meara, Father Canice Egan, and Father Edoardo Limat of the foreign missions of Paris were placed under house arrest in their priestly residence.[49] The following day everyone learned the news from the newspapers. Father Francis Tam was also expecting to be arrested within a short time.

On August 5, 1953, late at night, a knock was heard at the garden gate. Father Tam's little room was situated in front of the kitchen, on the ground floor, while my room and those of the other priests were on the first and second floor. The following morning we found the door of Father Tam's room wide open and the room in complete disorder. There was no trace of Father Tam. We suspected that he himself had opened the garden gate. He had been arrested. We were very saddened by this new loss, but his fearless spirit of sacrifice for the Lord and his good example gave great courage both to the priests and the people. Two months later, Father Tam's elderly cousin received an official request from the center for surveillance at 1 Wong Wah Street, Canton, to send him underwear and other personal articles. The woman sent them along with other basic necessities.

Father Tam was condemned to ten years of prison. At first he was sent to a labor camp near Canton in order to be reeducated. His cousin went to visit him and noted that he was wearing a hat made from newspaper that he himself had made. His morale was up, and he was cheerful: it was he who consoled the others and told them not to be displeased for him.

A short time later, Father Tam was transferred to another camp, where he was placed under a type of interrogation called a "struggle."[50] As a

---

[49] On August 8 the three were forced to leave China.

[50] The official term is a *struggle*, but it is not meant as "combat"; rather it is a type of interrogation in which a group coalesces around the victim without allowing him to defend himself.

result of this "trial," a year and a half was added to his sentence because he had made the Sign of the Cross and prayed before meals. He was then transferred to a labor camp situated in the province of Heilongjiang, where he met a Protestant from Shanghai and explained to him the difference between Catholicism and Protestantism. For this reason he was forced to submit to another "struggle," after which they condemned him to a life term and sent him back to prison. After two or three years his sentence was commuted to a year and a half. Having already served that punishment, he returned to work in the camp.

At that time he asked to return to Canton to see his family, but the permission was denied him. In 1975 he took a train on his own in order to return to Guangdong. During the trip, however, he was captured and put in prison. After two years he was again transferred to Heilongjiang to serve another ten years in prison.

In 1981, Father Tam's nephew sent a letter to the Office for the Chinese Overseas, inquiring where Tam Tin-tak was and asking the government to liberate his uncle, who had by then served thirty years in labor camps. The letter was sent to Peking through the Chinese ambassador in Washington, D.C.

In October of 1983 Father Tam was released and returned to Canton. He spent six months with a younger sister and then he returned to work at Shek Shat (the cathedral).

Shek Shat, a "Counterrevolutionary Fortress"

After my consecration as bishop, Father Andrew Chan gathered the faithful of Sacred Heart Cathedral in the dining room of the bishop's house and announced my installation. Also present were Fung Chuk-man, Kwan Pak-luk, Fong Shek-mui, and other Catholics. Someone said: "It was precisely the moment for a new bishop who could guide us during the diffusion of the Reform Movement of the Three Autonomies!"

Three days later, toward evening, Fung, Kwan, Fong, and the young Chan Chi-hung came to visit me in the dining room of the minor seminary of Saint Francis. They asked me to give in to the government of the people and to spread, like the Protestants, the Reform of the Three Autonomies. That saddened me very much, and I reproached them, saying: "We must be on the side of the Church and stand up to the other side [the Communist government]; not to take the part of the other side and go against the Church." Given my irrefutability, which left no room for objections, Chan Chi-hung let the matter go, saying: "It is late, and the bishop is very tired. It is best that we leave."

The following day Father Andrew Chan said to me: "Why did you respond with such fury last evening? Now everyone in the community knows about it."

I responded: "I did not speak with fury. I simply explained our position with clarity, which is our duty." My words did not please Father Chan very much.

When I went to Shanghai, in June 1951, I met with Monsignor Gong Pinmei and with Father Fernando Lacretelle, the apostolic prefect of Haizhou, who were enthusiastic about what I had said. The bishop Ignatius Gong was an old friend. When I was teaching at the high school at the University, he was the principal of the middle school. Every Sunday we rode our bicycles together to the Church of Santa Teresa on Datong Street for the Mass and confessions.

He was very disappointed that I had not gone to Shanghai for my consecration. Later, he wrote to me, inviting me to visit Shanghai, in order to get together with some old friends and teachers.

When I worked at Shanghai, between 1943 and 1946, I gathered a group of Cantonese Catholics, some of whom did not understand the dialect of Shanghai and were having serious difficulties in confession and in following the homilies. So I began to pray with them; and during Mass, I preached deliberately to them. I also met their families and taught them catechism. Besides these activities, on the third Sunday of each month I celebrated Mass in the Chapel of the Sacred Heart at the Women's College of Aurora University and heard confessions. I also reorganized the Aurora University Student Association for the students from the provinces of Guangdong and Guangxi. I made contact with them and invited them to enter the Church. I also helped them to resolve some personal and financial problems: at the same time I organized recreational activities for the group, such as trips, picnics, and so forth. Monsignor August Haouisée, bishop of Shanghai from 1933 to 1948, did not appreciate the idea that there was a Catholic organization for Cantonese students. He feared that divisions would arise. Later, after noticing how they were truly growing in the Faith, he began to appreciate [my approach].

Monsignor Gong, bishop of Shanghai, ordered that: (1) the faithful not be given permission to join the Communist Party, the League of Young Communists, or the Young Pioneers; (2) the members of the Legion of Mary should not go to the Office of Public Safety to register as members of a counterrevolutionary organization; and (3) those who disobeyed would not be able to receive Communion.

In 1952 we received pamphlets from the Catholic Central Office of Shanghai that spoke of the Patriotic Association. I read them on some occasions to the priests; then I made them available to them to read on their own. Beginning from this moment we formulated some rules of action.

Immediately after the "liberation," Father Andrew Chan and other priests had joined the Association of the Reform of the Three Autonomies. I told them to leave the organization. At first they feared that they would run a risk if they did not take part in their meetings, but Father Andrew Chan, who was the vicar general, demonstrated great courage and obeyed; he no longer went there. Other priests, seeing that Father Chan no longer went to the meetings, gradually began to go less often, and in the end they did not go at all. Then, when the Catholic president of the Reform of the Three Autonomies, Fong Shek-mui, and the Protestant pastor, the Reverend Hung Chan-pui came to the cathedral to invite the priests to their meetings, not one of them went.

Father Andrew Chan said: "We must make it known that we are the weak, the oppressed, those who suffer, but we have no need to use violence to oppose the Communist leaders. This is the best way to handle them, and it will receive the consensus and support of the faithful Catholics, because God is with us."

In the past, most of the priests of the cathedral lived and had meals together with their families. After I became bishop I ordered all the priests to return to Shek Shat, and we lived together.

Father Andrew Chan proposed to me a new way of keeping ahead of governmental pressures. He said: "Monsignor, the employees at the Office for Religious Affairs and that of Public Safety continue to come here to try to convince us to get together for discussions and meetings. It would be better that, in order to avoid them, all the priests spend the day with their families. In the evening we could return to the bishop's residence. If the Communist leaders come for us, seeking to stir up some problems, we could agree with the bishop and with the other priests on how to act."

I did not agree with him, however. Once separated, we would not be able to hold up under the pressures coming from the outside. Living under the same roof, we could discuss things altogether and submit to any eventuality, encouraging each other and confronting each difficulty in turn. Furthermore, we would also be able to avoid a relaxing of our discipline and other inconveniences that living separated would have caused. Therefore, I decided that we would work together, live together, and eat together. In this way, if some problem arose I would have found a way to resolve it.

Each priest was asked to hand over fifteen yuan each month for their living expenses. If the money was insufficient I would have found a way to contribute whatever was necessary. Ah Chue, Father Narbais's domestic, would cook the two principal meals each day, while each priest would have to be concerned with his own breakfast. In this way, the priests would be able to avoid the storm that was preparing itself on the outside. Later on, because of these provisions, the Communist government would define Shek Shat a "counterrevolutionary fortress."

The Causes of My Illness

The causes of my illness can be summarized as follows.

In August of 1953, the foreign missionaries Father John O'Meara, Father Canice Egan, Father Edoardo Limat, Father Pietro Narbais, and others were expelled from China. Father Francis Tam and a Catholic layman, Tsang Hing-lun, were arrested. The Legion of Mary was abolished, and all its members were ordered to go to the Office of Public Safety to denounce it as a counterrevolutionary organization and to inform the government that they had left it. Furthermore, the Office for Religious Affairs attempted to force us to join the Movement of the Reform of the Three Autonomies. Added to these worries were my responsibilities to administer the entire diocese and manage all its economic difficulties, although Father Anthony Tang helped me very much. Problems arose regarding the priests and the nuns and the other dioceses of the province of Guangdong, such as Shi-uhing. Among others, it had become ever more difficult to communicate with the dioceses of the other provinces. Moreover, each week I had to hold courses for the diocesan priests on matters of conscience, moral theology ,and other theological material, and to suggest to them how to confront questions of that type. In order to prepare for these encounters I had to read many books.

In the end my mind had accumulated so much of that pent-up exhaustion that my body began to resent it. I started to suffer from headaches and insomnia, and I lost my appetite. I was in the care of a highly esteemed doctor for six weeks, but he was not able to do anything for me. Later, the sister-in-law of Chan Chi-hung, a medical doctor and a Catholic, introduced me to a psychiatrist, Dr. Lam Ming-yan, who had been the head physician at the psychiatric hospital Fong Chuen of Canton for ten years. Dr. Lam said that I had had a serious nervous breakdown. He prescribed some injections and ordered me to sleep for an entire week. During all this time I got up solely to eat. After following his directions I gradually began to feel better. Then I moved, temporarily, to the church on Yuet Sau Pak Street to rest a little.

The Communist Government's Campaigns

In 1955 the Communist government initiated their "campaign for the elimination of the counterrevolutionaries." In September Monsignor Ignatius

Gong Pinmei and many priests and laymen were arrested at Shanghai. Then in December, at Canton, the following were arrested: Brother Adon Chau; Father Anthony Lei Ping-yan, pastor, and Vincent Wong Nim-hin of the Church of St. Ignatius, on Yuet Sau Pak Street; Father Yip, pastor of the Church of Our Lady of Fatima at Tung Shan; Rosa Yeung Kwok-yuen of the Church of Baogang; John Bosco Liu Shau-kei of the Church of Shamian; Ho Yan-yin, a member of the Legion of Mary of the Church of Gaobo; and Yip Kam-way of the cathedral.

In 1956 the government put some counterrevolutionaries on trial. Father Anthony Lei was tried by the tribunal of the people on Tsong Pin Street and was sentenced to five years in prison. Some Catholics of the church on Yuet Sau Pak Street attended the trial to observe its development.

Another priest, Joseph Chan Tsui di Beihai, was publicly tried. Father Louis Yip and I went to the tribunal to see it. The judge was sitting at the center with members of the jury on either side of him. The secretary of the tribunal was at the right, and the defense attorney was at the left. Below them, at the left was the accused, and at the right was the prosecuting attorney. Father Joachim Lau acted as defense attorney.

Father Joseph Chan was condemned to about two years in prison for having listened in secret to *Voice of America*. He had been arrested two years before, so when the sentence was issued, it was a matter of time already served. He was not released, however, and Father Dominic Tam brought him some underwear.

When Brother Adon Chau was publicly tried in 1956, some priests attended the trial. During the break, Brother Chau asked the judge for permission to speak to one of the priests. When it was granted to him, he took advantage of the moment to confess his sins.

In 1957, before the campaign against the elements of the right,[51] the government sponsored a promotion permitting the people to express their

---

[51] The campaign was dominated by the phrase "eradicate the poisonous herbs" and gave rise to one of the harshest purges against the intellectuals and public administrators who were accused of being "elements of the right."

personal criticisms. It was called the "liberal diffusion of opinions."[52] Also, in order to encourage the people to express their own points of view, the Communist Party proposed the "three nos," promising those who liberally declared what they were thinking that:

1. their words would not be written down in police records

2. their admissions of errors would not be flung back at them

3. they would not be beaten

In that period Father Andrew Chan was often called to take part in the meetings, during which he was asked either for his opinion or to make some requests of the government. Once, on returning from a meeting, he said to me that the government was hoping that the Church was formulating requests. I asked him to pass around this petition: "The priests of the diocese are few, and there is much work. I ask the government to be merciful with those priests who have already served part of their sentence and to release them. This would demonstrate that the government is interested in the Church."

Later, these words would become one of the chief charges against me: "He asked the government to liberate some counterrevolutionaries."

Assemblies of Blame and Censure: The "Struggle"

In 1957 the Communist government promoted two campaigns: for the elimination of the counterrevolutionaries and for the correction of the incorrect ways of working.

The Catholic Patriotic Association of the Three Autonomies often asked the priests and the Catholics to go to the assemblies' study group,

---

[52] It is the brief phase of liberalization promoted by Mao with the slogan: "Let us make a hundred buds blossom, and let a hundred schools debate each other." It lasted only a few months because Mao observed that too many intellectuals and public officials were taking the invitation seriously and criticizing the same communist system. In the autumn of 1957 he responded with the hard reaction against the "elements of the right."

but we priests and the Catholics, who did not belong to the Patriotic Association, did not participate. As a consequence, the Communist leaders of the Office of Public Safety and the Office for Religious Affairs frequently came to visit us in order to have discussions. From November on, it was a very dangerous period for us.

The Communist government and the Office for Religious Affairs installed a system of loudspeakers near the bishop's residence (the Carmelite convent). Each day, at full volume, they transmitted slanderous notices about me. They shouted at the top of their voices uninterruptedly: "Tang Yi-ming, repent quickly," and so on, with the intention of intimidating me and frightening me. Everywhere, on the wall of the city and even on the house, they affixed posters that said: "Tang Yi-ming, the Vatican's most faithful sleuth-dog."

The Catholics were angry, and they secretly tore them down. The leaders of the Patriotic Association asked for explanations from Chan Nai-choi. Chan responded that, although he was the guard, he also, at times, had to use the facilities, and therefore he had not seen anyone destroy those posters. Later, in order to threaten the Catholics, they hung a very large poster, about five by two meters. But the Catholics were already prepared psychologically. Often, Father Anthony Ngan would say to me, jokingly and in order to encourage me: "Many have been arrested, but we are not yet captured. We have lost the game."

In December the Office for Religious Affairs and the Patriotic Association organized a series of public meetings of censure and blame, in order to reveal my "crimes" in a public forum. Ten of these meetings were held in the Patriotic Association's locales. Before the beginning and at the end of each assembly, I went to the chapel to pray, to ask for God's protection. During the assemblies of the "struggle," I remained tranquil, with the hope of also having my part in the sufferings of the Church. Before my arrest I confessed my sins often, in order to prepare my soul for interior peace.

The first assembly of the struggle was held at the Cultural Center for the youth, on Peking Street. The members of the Patriotic Association came out in the open and accused me of not permitting the Catholics to become members of the association; of not wishing to give Communion to their members; of impeding the enrollment of the members of the Legion of Mary; et cetera. The priests and the Catholics observed an absolute silence. They felt pain on my account. After the assembly, the priests accompanied me to the bishop's residence.

The second assembly of the struggle was held at the Association of the Students Returned from America, on Man Ming Street. During the assembly of censure and of the struggle, no priest spoke, and no Catholic, except members of a small group of the Patriotic Association. A Catholic left the hall at the beginning of the assembly. The leaders were very angry because the priests protected me. From that moment on they distanced the priests from me, denying them permission to go to the reunions so I was forced to attend alone.

Once they brought me to To Kam Hang for one of the assemblies of the struggle. I saw many Catholics running to other places. Few of them, however, came to the assembly, during which only a small group spoke. Another time I was brought into the courtyard of the girls' high school for an assembly of the struggle. It was a very cold evening, so the priests asked Chan Nai-choh to send me a jacket with a padded lining, but the leader impeded him from doing so. After the meeting, upon my return to the bishop's residence, I found the priests at the entrance, waiting for me. Father Andrew Chan, the vicar general, placed a lined jacket on my shoulders. Even if my limbs were frozen, my heart was warm.

The assemblies of the struggle not only failed to break me, but they actually increased my courage. The next meeting, however, was even more crowded and was held on the second floor of the Convent School of the Immaculate Conception. There were between seven hundred and eight hundred in attendance. Many non-Catholics were also forced to attend. But I was attacked by only a small group of the Patriotic Association who faulted me with the usual accusations, as, for example, not permitting them to receive Communion. The non-Catholics lost patience and began to say: "Is it worth the trouble to have an assembly of the struggle for a little piece of bread [the consecrated host] that costs less than ten cents?" Before the

end of the assembly the leaders asked a follower of the Patriotic Association, "the lady of the Rosary, Fung Wai-fuk,"[53] to take me home, and then
he warned the Catholics not to sympathize with me.

After seeing that the atmosphere of the assemblies of the struggle was
not what they wished, the meetings that followed were held in the localities
of the Patriotic Association at Yuk Yan Fong, and only their own followers
were admitted. The accusations continued to be the same.

The assemblies took place once every two days. At Christmas they interrupted them for two days, and began them again on the third day. During
each assembly of the struggle I was very tranquil. Others were much more
agitated and fearful than I. During the last assembly, the leaders told me
to write a letter of repentance. When I asked what I should write, I was
told to write that I forbade members of the Legion of Mary to register with
the government, that I forbade the people to become part of the Patriotic
Association, and that I did not give Communion to their members. I wrote
only two lines. "The Legion of Mary is a missionary organization, and it
is not counterrevolutionary. I have not given permission to the priests to
give Communion to the members of the Patriotic Association, and this
is according to the laws of the Church. You do well to suggest to me what
to write."

Meanwhile all the priests were meeting on Pak Tsin Street in order to
study and were living there. But Father Andrew Lin returned to the cathedral to sleep, because he was ill and continued to cough. I was told that
when the priests were told to attend the assembly, the leaders showed them
the two lines that I had written and accused me of not being frank enough.

The Arrest

On February 5, 1958, I made a visit to Father Peter Chan Wai-man, who
was at the Church of St. Ignatius, on Yuet Sau Pak Street. I gave him some

---

[53] This courageous woman, whose husband made rosaries and other religious
articles, distributed those articles to Catholics in the area.

money to hold, and I took two hundred yuan. On my return I walked with Brother Chong. At the crossroad of Yat Tak Street, near the cathedral, Brother Chong returned to Yuet Sau Pak, and I headed toward home alone. When I was near the cathedral, I saw in the front yard four robust types who seemed to be expecting someone. I felt that something was about to happen. I returned to the chapel of the bishop's residence (the Carmelite convent) in order to recite five decades of the Rosary and to confess my sins to Father Anthony Ngan. During those days I confessed very often in order to prepare myself well for the moment of my arrest. Afterward I was informed that someone had come that day to ask Father Ngan if I was in the house.

I was cold, and so I wore my overcoat. Suddenly, toward eight o'clock, an official from the police station, Leung Kwok-hang, accompanied by a group of policemen, presented himself at the residence. The people called Leung the "smiling tiger." He asked Father Joachim Lau to conduct him to my room; then Father Lau went away. A policeman pointed a revolver at me and ordered me to raise my hands immediately. I was then handcuffed. Later they ordered me to sit at the desk. They took out a piece of paper and asked me to place my thumbprint there. I could not see distinctly what was written there, but it was the arrest warrant.

At that moment I was happy, because many priests and Catholics had already been arrested for having obeyed my orders. How could I not follow the same fate? They had refused to become members of the Patriotic Catholic Association and to say that the Legion of Mary was a counterrevolutionary organization. A policeman took the suitcase that I had prepared in anticipation of the event; and I had put a toothbrush and a towel in the pocket of my overcoat. I asked if I could also bring my lined jacket. The policemen took my baggage and left the room. The priests were gathered in the entrance and were sitting there in silence. When I arrived at the stairway, there was a large poster that said: "Tang Yi-ming is the reactionary Vatican's most faithful sleuth-dog!" As soon as I was led away the police searched my room.

Once we left the bishop's residence, I realized that I was in the midst of many dreadful characters; there was a notable deployment of police lining [both sides of] the lane leading from the residence as well as a sizable number in front of the nursery and elementary schools; many others, incited by curiosity, were at the windows of the second and third floor of the offices of the Sacred Heart Middle School. After being driven along the left side of the cathedral we arrived at Kau Po Tsin Street in front. I noticed two cars stopped along the side of the road. It was a strange sight in those times, since the people did not go around in automobiles. The police made me get into one of the two cars and immediately put his hands on mine, still handcuffed, and we left the area. We ended up at the detention center of the Office of Public Safety, on Wong Wah Street. The principal detention center of the Office of Public Safety of the province of Guangdong was on the other side of the street and was Canton's largest prison.

As soon as I arrived at the detention center, a policeman slipped off my bishop's ring and sequestered my rosary, my breviary, a medallion, and my belt. He also took out of my pocket the two hundred yuan, the money I had just withdrawn, plus some change that amounted to two yuan. The police kept the two hundred yuan and gave back the change. After concluding their search, they took me to the interrogation room. It was already 10 p.m. In the room where they interrogated me were three "judges"; [actually] they were officials assigned to the interrogation, which the accused had to call judges. They told me to sit in front of them on a little stool at the center of the room. A bright light was shined on my face. The first judge asked me my name, my age, and my place of birth.

Then they asked me: "Do you know what place this is?"

I responded: "It is the prison."

Then I was asked: "What crime have you committed?"

I responded: "They say that I did not give permission to certain Catholics to receive Communion."

The magistrate then asked me: "Why did you not give them permission?"

I explained the reasons to them.

In that moment in my heart there was a great peace. They also questioned me on the Patriotic Association and on the Legion of Mary. I explained to them our position and our actions and the line of conduct.

It seemed to me that they were not interested in the answers to those questions.

All of a sudden they changed the subject and asked me: "And your financial accounts?"

I responded: "I do not have any."

Then they asked me questions regarding finances. I said to them that after having paid 60,000 Hong Kong dollars (about 10,000 American dollars) in taxes on the property in 1951, our diocese had collapsed financially.

The interrogation lasted until 6 a.m. the following morning. During that time the three judges took turns resting. One of them asked me if I wished to eat something or if I would like to buy a roll. I had no desire to eat, and so I asked only for a glass of water.

The first time I asked to go to the facilities they permitted me. The second time they said that I would no longer be allowed to go. I insisted and said to them that if they impeded me from going, I would use the spittoon that was in the room. So they were forced to let me go.

A little before dawn I was extremely tired, and I asked to be able to rest, but they did not allow me. A little later, when the judges ended the interrogations, the secretary gave me a huge pile of papers to sign, and on each one I had to also put a fingerprint. I read each page. The judge yelled at me: "You just finished saying that you are tired. How is it that you still have energy to check over each page?"

After I had signed and placed my fingerprint on each page of the interrogation trial record, a guard brought me to a cell. It was a small cell about nine meters square. There were two wooden beds, a small table in the center, but no stools. In the little drawer of the table were copies of the *Regulations for the Punishment of Counterrevolutionaries* and some pamphlets for the individual reading and reflection of each detainee. That detention center was established precisely to house the recently arrested prisoners.

Around 8:00 in the morning someone opened the small wooden serving hatch in the door and gave me half a bowl of rice with some greens and a bowl of hot water. The red rice was unhusked, certainly not easy to eat. Around 4:30 I was given the second of the two daily meals. That day there was no interrogation. Toward 8:00 in the evening the jailer opened the door and brought me into the interrogation room, where I remained until dawn as on the preceding night. This happened for three consecutive nights. During the day, I tried to lie down to rest a bit, but I could not sleep because I was not accustomed to that schedule.

Two days after my arrest, the priests of the cathedral told Chan Naichoh, the cathedral's guard, a nephew of Father Andrew Chan, the vicar general, and a fervent Catholic, to bring me an old down quilt, some wool socks, a pair of shoes, a pair of slippers, and some wool clothing. When I received these things I immediately felt good, and I was extremely grateful to the Lord and to the priests of the cathedral for their solicitude and their concern for me.

In the cell with me was a well-educated gentleman, with whom I conversed often. I learned that he was a teacher who was originally from Hong Kong. His family was very poor. From time to time they did some manual labor at home in order to supplement their income. His wife and two children, who lived in great poverty, were waiting for him at home. He had been condemned for spying. In reality he had been deceived. He had not done anything [of the sort].

The First Interrogations

Ten days after my arrest the Chinese New Year was celebrated, and the jailers permitted the detainees to buy some food. I wrote a request for the restitution of part of the money that had been taken from me, in order to be able to buy something. Because my request was refused I was able to buy only a tin of soy cheese and a piece of dried pork. I shared the food with my cell companion, who did not have money to buy anything. Initially he did not wish to accept it. The authorities would not even permit his family to send him the least little thing. I also gave him a pair of trousers, because he had a great need for clothes. Then we passed the time together; I spoke to him of our doctrine. It pleased him very much, and he immediately learned the Our Father by heart. But I did not baptize him.

Ten days later I was transferred to section 3 of the principal prison of Canton. There, all the prisoners were called by numbers. My number was 2202.

After my arrest I was interrogated for three consecutive nights. Afterward, I was interrogated usually during the day, at times in the morning and at times in the evening. Each interrogation lasted about three or four hours. This schedule continued for about a month. Each day I asked the Holy Spirit to illuminate me so that I would be able to confront each interrogation wisely and to say what I should say. I believe that during those difficult trials, it was truly God, through the Holy Spirit, sustaining and guiding me.

After each interrogation the judge asked me to write my "signed confession" in the cell, reporting faithfully all the questions made during the interrogation and the subjects touched upon, including the Reform of the Three Autonomies, my opposition to the Patriotic Association, "my attitude during the campaign opposing America, helping Korea," how I received financial help from abroad, the questions on the Legion of Mary, how I obtained papal encyclicals and notices from the Information Services of the Pontifical Mission Society (*Fides*), and so on.

The first period of interrogations lasted about one month. Then, for about three months, nothing more happened. During that period I felt tranquil, and I gradually became accustomed to eating the unhulled rice. In the same prison, there were many other priests and Catholics. Seeing that they were imprisoned, I [realized that] I also had to be there. I thought that, considering the "charges" against me, I would be condemned, at the maximum, for five years in prison.

Toward June or July of 1958, the jailer once again called my number: "2202! Come forward!" I was brought into the interrogation room, and there I was interrogated, but this time by various individuals. This interrogation was substantially like the first. They added questions regarding the problems of some priests in the diocese and of some Catholics of Canton. When they asked me about Father Andrew Chan, they tried to force me to denounce him and to testify against him. This upset me very much, and I immediately burst into tears. Up to then I had not cried. Father Chan was an upright person, very faithful to the Church, kind and thoughtful in dealing with others; in short, a good priest. I will never forget that cold night, upon my return to the cathedral after the assembly of the struggle, when all the priests were sitting calmly on the second floor, except Father Chan, who, instead, had come immediately with a lined jacket to cover me. He had an iron will, and he knew how to distinguish very clearly between good and bad. What could I have said about him?

During this interrogation they posed questions to me on the following topics: the Legion of Mary and the Patriotic Association; the trip of Father Francis Tam, who had guided a group of young Catholics to Shanghai in 1953; the help given to Catholics who fled China for Hong Kong; my relationship with Father Peter Narbais in 1951; my trip to Shanghai after my episcopal consecration and my colloquial with Monsignor Ignatius Gong Pinmei and with other priests; my contacts with Father John O'Meara and with Father Renato Chevalier of Hong Kong, from whom I had received money; how I procured papal encyclicals; and so on. Then I was ordered to draft a detailed confession.

During this second series I was interrogated once a day for nearly the entire day. Some judges were very severe, while others were basically calm. At times I was interrogated by one or two persons simultaneously. At times my responses were confident, at which the judge would shout angrily and say: "Do you think that you are at Shek Shat? Do you think that you are speaking to priests?" In this second series I was interrogated uninterruptedly for two months.

Prison Life

On February 15, 1958, I was brought to the detention center on the other side of Wong Wah Street. It was known as prison Number 1 of the province of Guangdong and was subdivided into six sections. Sections 1, 3, and 5 were on the ground floor, and section 2, 4, and 6 were on the first floor, which was reached by a very long, steep stairway. I was enclosed in this section no. 1. I received my meals from a tiny wooden opening, which also served as a peephole for medical observations and to get a glance of other prisoners who were able to go out in the fresh air, one at a time, to wash their face in the morning and to empty the bucket that served as a latrine. At that time Father Anthony Ngan was in the same prison, in a cell diagonally opposite mine, as also was Brother Adon Chau, whose cell was closer to mine. On the upper floor nearly all the sections were occupied by women. The prisoners who worked in the kitchen were in front of my cell.

A Spy for a Companion

Once, a spy was placed in the cell with me. Two meals a day were brought to us, which, however, contained only half the food necessary to survive. Therefore, we truly knew what hunger was. The person in charge of the kitchen help, Chiu Tak, was very kind to me. At times, after serving the rice to the prisoners, he would come to me and give me a little of the rice that remained in the basket. Seeing that, other than rice, they gave me only half of a small piece of cheese, fermented from soy, the detainee in the cell with me teased me, saying: "Why are you so frugal?" Laughing, he would take two pieces of the soy cheese and put them on my rice.

I said, "I do not have money to buy food, for which I must be frugal."

Then he said: "In the large cell there is a Catholic [I believe that he was referring to Chan Chiu] who is very generous; he buys many things to eat and shares them with the others."

The prison regulations stipulated that all the prisoners could write home once a month to ask their relatives to send clothes and other things. But in the first few months, I was not permitted to write. During the summer I requested permission to write to Shek Shat to ask for my summer clothes, but they would not permit me. Finally, I showed the judge my heavy woolen clothing and said I did not have other clothes, and I asked for assistance from outside. Only then was I granted permission to write a letter. When the priests of the cathedral received my first letter, they told Chan Nai-choh (the custodian) to bring me a package of clothes and other things for daily use, such as soap, toilet paper, and a package of sweets from Hong Kong. The jailer yelled at me, saying: "So many sweets from Hong Kong?" I knew then that those sweets had been sent by my mother. Receiving them I was so touched that I cried. Then I shared them with the other detainees. In the following years the priests of the cathedral used my monthly subsidy of fifteen yuan to buy items for daily use and sent them to me through Chan Nai-choh.

Every time I wrote to my relatives, I asked them for cod liver oil and vitamin pills. Asking for any nutriments was not permitted except for a little sugar and a small box of food.

Usually, I was the only occupant of the cell, but sometimes I was sent a companion. These detainees, in general, were charged with espionage. The majority of them came from very poor families, and they would spy in order to earn some money. I met some condemned Trotskyites, such as a certain Lau. He was a history teacher at the middle school. Although he had not been involved in any propaganda, he was condemned to life in prison solely for the fact that he was a follower of the Marxist theory sustained by Trotsky. He was in the cell with me for three years. I also had other Trotskyites as cell companions.

In general, we got along; we did not ever speak of politics. One of them, who knew that I spoke foreign languages, asked me to teach him English and French. Given that they were younger than I, during the morning cleanup they always helped me; with great kindness, they would empty the bucket [the latrine] and carry water for me. Our cell was always very clean. The jailer and the medical doctor, a woman, always praised us and at times they would open the door of our cell so that other detainees could see it.

The Bite of Hunger

After 1959, and especially during the three years of the natural calamities,[54] they gave us two meals a day. At the beginning we were given a bowl and

---

[54] In 1958 to 1959 Mao launched the campaign for the "Great Leap Forward," revolutionizing the traditional social fabric based on village life,

a half a day. Later, the food was reduced to only one bowl, without greens or oil. During the first times, Chan Nai-choh, from the cathedral, sent me a bottle of pimento oil, saying that it would help me to combat beriberi. My knees and legs swelled from undernourishment. A prisoner who was a medical doctor visited me, and the prison's female doctor gave me an injection.

For a certain period, about a year and a half, they gave us work to do in our cells: we had to put together cardboard boxes using glue obtained from crushed lychee seeds.[55] My cellmate and I were supposed to glue more than ten dozen a day. Thus, apart from the hours spent for the interrogation and for meals, all the rest of the time was engaged gluing the boxes. If the work was not well done, we would have to glue them over again.

Although we produced much, there was no improvement in the conditions of our life. Generally, we ate rice boiled in water.[56] At times they gave us rice with sweet potatoes. The bowl seemed to be overflowing with food, but after a little while we felt famished again. For a certain period they gave us something to eat at 8:00 in the morning and then supper at 4:30 or 5:00, so that by noon we were already very hungry. Later they gave us dinner at 11:30 and supper at 5:00. After having supper, we had to wait many hours—until 11:30 the next day—to have something to eat. At each meal they gave us half the food necessary to sustain us. Thus, each day, toward 10:00 we already felt cramps from hunger. At times the hunger would cause us to have chills, and we would begin to sweat from the cold.

---

and constructed the "people's communes," where everything had to be controlled and decided centrally. Added to the people's natural resistance to this plan were a series of grave natural calamities (1959–1961). The consequences were tens of millions of deaths, especially from hunger.

[55] Lychee is a Chinese fruit with a reddish skin and white pulp and a large seed in the center.

[56] The dish was called *zhou* and consisted of overcooked rice that was eaten together with the water in which it was boiled. Normally condiments and meat were added, but evidently the *zhou* that the detainees ate was simply water and rice.

For a certain period, my body suffered very much from malnutrition and I felt very weak; I had a headache, my vision was foggy, and my pulse was irregular. I could not eat or sleep; furthermore, I also had beriberi and a hernia. Actually, I was more dead than alive.

The prison doctor did not dare cure me. One day, the prison director came to me in person and brought a military doctor to examine me. This doctor prescribed some very strong medicines: I had to take fifty to sixty pills at a time. I took this medicine several times during the day. After a few days, I felt slightly better.

Later, one of the investigators said to me: "The doctor said that you were seriously ill; fortunately we asked him to visit you in time; otherwise you would have died." Following the illness, I was given an extra half bowl of rice each day, but my cell companion took most of it. Later on, during the Cultural Revolution, I was no longer given any extra food.

Given that the rice boiled in water lacked seasoning, we bought salt for ten cents a packet. We put a little salt in the rice to give it some flavor. But most of the prisoners suffered from beriberi because of malnutrition. As a result we could no longer buy salt. It was very difficult to tolerate, but this was the life of the detainee.

Once there was a great festival. I do not remember well if it was the Chinese New Year or the national holiday. They gave each of us a thin slice of pork. Much to my surprise, my cellmate, a tall fellow, robbed my portion. I did not dare to object, because he was a born bully. I could do nothing else but swallow the words that I wished to say to him.

Then, for a limited time, they did not give us any pork, not even for the Chinese New Year or for the national feast.

At the time of my arrest, as I have related, the money I had on me was taken away from me. With much difficulty I obtained permission to get back a little of those two hundred yuan to buy something. They gave me only five yuan at a time, just enough to buy toilet paper and other basic necessities.

When the Cultural Revolution began, however, I was no longer permitted to withdraw even a penny of my money. They said that the official in charge of guarding the money did not know my case and was not sure where that money came from.

Once, during the Chinese New Year, in the prison on Wong Wah Street I had for a companion a man suspected of espionage. He was arrested by the police while he was going to visit his parents in the district of Shun Tak. He had with him in the cell packets of salted fish and roasted pork that came from Hong Kong. Salted fish was not permitted in the cell, because it was contaminated with hepatitis. He did not wish to share the roasted pork, and he finished it by himself in a few days. At the end he shared some of the oil that remained in the bowl, so that I could mix it with my rice. It was truly good. I thanked him very much, because it had been a long time since anyone had given me something.

A Year of Interrogations

The third series of interrogations took place before the Cultural Revolution (1966–1976). The content was similar to that of the previous two, but there were some novelties. It was 1964, during the campaign of the "Four Cleansings" which led the leaders to consider reexamining my case. The interrogations lasted about a year. At times they were spread out; other times they were continuous, one following the other.

During the Cultural Revolution many party officials from other provinces came to examine my case. Some came from as far as the province of Heilongjiang. They asked me questions about the problems of other dioceses, for example, those of Shanghai, Tianjin, and Peking, and about things that regard the bishops who left China, such as Monsignor Joseph Yuan Kezhi di Zhumadian, in the province of Henan, who had settled for some years at Macao, where he died. Many of those leaders came from far away just to see me. At the beginning they were very kind, perhaps because they thought that I would have given them more information. At the end, having been disappointed, they were full of anger. At first they asked me: "Who do you know?" or "Do you know a certain person called by the surname Chan?"

I was very perplexed, and so I responded: "I know many persons. If you wish to investigate the affairs of a particular person and do not tell me what it concerns, how can I tell you anything? If you wish to begin by telling me a name, then I shall be able to tell you if I know her or something about her." My response was correct and reasonable. But to the Office of Public Safety they reported that my attitude was wrong and that I did not respect them.

In order to be able to see me and to interrogate me, the leaders of the other provinces had to apply to the Office of Public Safety. Having to return shortly to their cities, they interrogated me two or three times a day. They asked me about all the priests with whom I had had a minimal rapport, what these priests had said, and so on. This type of interrogation was extremely bothersome. The detainees called me the "living dictionary."

In my twenty-two years in prison I was interrogated many times in this manner. I was questioned about the clergy of other dioceses, for example, Father Benedict Choi, Monsignor Joseph Wan Cizhang of Henyang, Archbishop Joseph Zhou Jishi of Nanchang, the Franciscan fathers of Hankou, Monsignor Ignatius Gong Pinmei, and many other priests. Regarding the laity, I was asked about the members of the Catholic youth choir of the cathedral, such as Wong Lo-Lo. They also asked me questions regarding some members of the Legion of Mary.

In a Cell with Two Crazy People

During my detention in the prison on Wong Wah Street I lived with two unbalanced persons, one after the other. The first was not bothersome, but the second had his hands and feet tied because he regularly roughed up the persons he met. Perhaps the guards put them in the cell with me because they knew that I would have put up with them, or perhaps because they thought that I would have reeducated them.

The unbalanced man who beat others was the adopted son of a party leader, the vice-director of the iron and steel works at Canton. He complained incessantly about the Communist Party, and this was probably the reason for his arrest. He was a bad subject with a very wicked nature. At times, it pleased him to talk with me, but when he was in a bad humor, he flew off the handle. Given that we were in a cell of a few square meters, we were forced to look at each other in the face. Once he suddenly came toward me and slapped me so forcefully in the face that my glasses fell to the floor. Then he said to me: "Why are you looking at me?" He had suddenly lost control of himself, and, needless to say, I did not manage to oppose him. The only thing I could do was pick up my glasses, although I felt stunned and my head was spinning.

Once, at midnight, this maniac came toward me and walked on me, frightening me to death, given that I awoke suddenly. I did not dare refer these things to the jailers, although once, speaking with one of them, I mentioned something to him. Once I heard that a prisoner had been beaten to death by a cellmate. At the time of the deed no one had dared to say a word. It was only much later that the detainees were convinced to report to the guard what had happened.

Change of Prisons

I remained in the prison on Wong Wah Street for a good ten years. Both before and after the Cultural Revolution, toward the mid-1960s, the Red Guards attacked the prisons, and both times the government transferred some of us to the prison-farm (dedicated to raising livestock) of Loh Kong, on the outskirts of Canton. Then we returned to the prison on Wong Wah. But after the second transfer to the prison-farm of Loh Kong, we were sent to the prison of Tam Kong, and we never returned to Wong Wah.

Tam Kong was a large prison situated in the periphery north of Canton, about twenty-five kilometers from the city. It rose midway up the hill of Tam Kong and had a strong military garrison. It was subdivided into two buildings. We were held prisoners in the anterior building, while the posterior building was reserved for spies and secret agents who had recently been arrested and some other particularly dangerous criminals. The prison was very well guarded, and the posterior building could not be seen from the outside. The food reserved for the prisoners in the posterior building was better than ours. In our building there were some who were already tried and condemned. Those in the neighboring cell were sent to work outside the prison.

The food was distributed by a jailer. At mealtime the wooden doors of the cells were opened, but the iron doors, the external ones, remained closed. At times I saw that the criminals who went out to work could have a second serving of vegetables, given that there were always leftovers. I also would have liked seconds. Once I asked a jailer if I could have a little more food. The guard looked at me and said: "You also want more!" He responded that way because I did not work outside the prison. Then he gave me a little more. Another time I asked the guard to give me more vegetables, but he paid no attention to what I was saying and did not give me anything. When I saw that others were able to get another serving and I did not, I became very upset.

I was incarcerated in the prison of Tam Kong twice, each time for about three months. While I was there, I was once moved to a large cell with seven or eight people, most of whom came from the province of Hong Kong. During the time I spent in that cell there was also, among the others, a paralyzed prisoner who always ate rice boiled in water. At times he could not finish everything. Each time this occurred the guard would come to take away the leftover rice. So we, his cell companions, started asking him to pass it on to us, before the guard came, because we were very hungry. Without thinking, I was satisfying my hunger eating the food from the plate of a sick person.

I was physically weak. Often my head would spin, and it made me ill. At night the prisoners slept along the walls of the cell, leaving only a small path to get to the bucket [the latrine]. Because my legs also became weak and unsteady, when trying to reach the bucket, I fell onto the prisoners, who responded by shouting at me. Afterward, when I wished to reach the bucket, I no longer dared to walk erect; rather, I began to drag myself on all fours.

While I was in the large cell, the prisoners always spoke of things that were happening outside the prison. The incarcerated from Hong Kong often spoke of their city. During those three weeks I was very cheerful: it was easy to pass the time. But I was moved again to a single cell. The jailer even asked me why I had been transferred to the large cell and which jailer had sent me there, as if it were my fault that they had moved me.

Cut Off from the World

Before the Cultural Revolution (beginning in 1966) I did not receive a single package. During the first thirteen years of prison the government gave me only two pairs of underwear. So during the summer I went around with a naked torso, while during the winter I had one suit, and above this I wore an overcoat lined with cotton. My jacket and my down quilt had been mended so much that it was not possible to distinguish which was the original material. Given that I had no trousers, I had to use the [burlap] sacks used to send various things to the detainees in the prison. In order to cut the sacks into a triangular shape, thus making some underwear, I used the cover of a little can of "tiger's balm."[57]

I asked permission to use the request form in order to write to my relatives at Canton, and, after obtaining it, I asked them to send me some basic necessities. Although I had written twenty or thirty times, I never received a response or a package. When I asked the jailers why I did not receive any news, they simply said to me: "We do not know; your requests have been sent." After a few months I filled out and sent another request form, but again I did not receive a response.

Once, before the Cultural Revolution, I was interrogated until noon. After the interrogation, on his own initiative, the judge asked me to write a letter that he himself would mail to my mother at Hong Kong. Then, full of hope, I immediately wrote my mother a few simple lines because I feared that if I wrote much, the letter would not be mailed. I simply sent her and the family my greetings, and I communicated to my mother that I was in prison on Wong Wah Street. I wrote that in prison I spent my time studying and that they should not worry about me.

---

[57] Tiger's balm is a common ointment, used in China and elsewhere, to which some particular curative qualities are attributed.

I waited month after month, year after year. Unfortunately, that letter was like a rock thrown into a great sea. It never received a response. No matter how much I thought about it, I could not manage to understand this silence. They did not even give me the right to correspond with my mother or to receive clothes and other items.

During those twenty-two years I never received any letters from my family or from my friends. Even up to a month before my release I did not receive a visitor or a piece of toilet paper or a piece of soap. I slept on a wooden bench, with the blanket that I had brought with me in prison. In spite of the change of seasons, I wore only the clothes that I had with me when I entered prison; likewise, I used only the articles for the bed that I myself had brought with me when I entered. I knew nothing about the Church outside the prison or about the condition of my relatives.

Examples of Hidden Generosity

At times in prison I encountered some youthful detainees, who, knowing that I knew English and French, would ask me to teach them the languages. In the prison of Tam Kong was a very intelligent engineer named Tam. I taught him French, which he learned with great facility. Naturally, we would cut to bits the little pieces of paper on which we wrote the foreign language and would throw them into the bucket.

The detainees whom I was teaching knew that I did not receive letters or packages from anyone. Thus, they secretly gave me some objects for daily use; for example, half a bar of soap. I was very grateful. At times, when using the bathroom, I would see flakes of soap stuck to the floor, and I would scrape them up with my fingernails in order to use them.

A few years before I exited the prison (I was at the time in the prison of Tam Kong), the jailers assigned me to cleaning, either in general or in the bathrooms. While working around the prison, I happened, by chance, to be outside the cell of Father Joseph Wong. At times, when there were no guards in sight, I opened the peephole of the door and called him. He gave me some candies and a pair of underwear. I asked him for a pair of shoes, but he told me that he did not have any. In the winter, while I was pulling weeds or cleaning the bathrooms, the people would see me going around barefoot and would say to me: "Old man, why are you not wearing shoes?" They did not know that the shoes I was wearing when I entered the prison had worn out long ago.

The Monotony That Kills

For more than twenty years my life and the atmosphere that surrounded me was very monotonous. There were no vacations. There was no type of change. When I was enclosed in isolation, life was even more monotonous. I heard only the footsteps of the prisoners who were headed toward the interrogation room and those of the person who gave me the two daily meals through the tiny opening in the door. I was always alone, and I was not able to speak with anyone, not even to say just one phrase. I had a sore throat, and my head was heavy. One day passed, another began, and the new day was exactly like the preceding day. One day repeated another; one year repeated another. One could say that life was without joy. The only thing that I could do was to become intimately united to God, inebriated with love for God.

The program scheduled for each day did not leave space for eventual changes. In the morning, after getting up, I was able to stretch my legs a little; then I cleaned my cell, did some gymnastic exercises, and so on. When these activities ended, I had to sit in an established place until dusk. At 4:00 p.m. they granted me fifteen minutes to do gymnastics, and then I had to sit down again until evening; that is, until I had to go to sleep. The daily activities were fixed by regulation. There were more than ten rules. Everything was controlled.... The jailers observed us through the opening in the door and spied on what we were doing. Evidently they had orders to check on whether I was keeping to the regulations. They tried not to attract attention when opening and closing the door of the peephole, so that I could not discover when I was being observed.

Each day I would do gymnastics. I got a little exercise in the morning and a little in the afternoon. In general, I did the exercises for my head and my neck, and I would run in place. I continued to exercise also during my illness, even while I was so weak that in order to do a few steps I had to lean on the wall with one hand. For another twenty minutes I persisted, each morning, in taking a cold bath, even during the winter. This not only invigorated my body, but it reinforced my will. The companions of my cell imitated me. My life followed an iron discipline, except during the illnesses caused by malnutrition, dropsy (an accumulation of fluids in the tissue), or hernia and the few times I had a cold or a cough.

Moreover, I suffered constantly from a headache. In my youth I had had my first migraine when I was a student in Portugal. Then at Shanghai I had a relapse. In 1954, when I was at Canton, I experienced a third attack of the migraine that lasted a year. The prison doctors who were kind enough to me gave me more pills.

While in prison, I followed the rules, and I continued to keep my cell very clean. The only thing that I objected to was the Communists' political injustice toward the Church. For the rest I kept the regulations to the letter. During the first years in prison, each morning we had to take turns going to wash our faces and empty the buckets. Later, after the restructuration of the cells, each cell was furnished with a toilet and a faucet, although the use of water was very limited. At times no water flowed from the faucet, so we had to use water from the toilet to wash our faces. From the time these services were installed in the cells, we remained locked inside twenty-four hours a day.

From the time I became the apostolic administrator of Canton, in 1951, I bore the responsibility for the entire diocese. During that time, I had also foreseen the possibility of going to prison. Sister Maria Lau Suet-fan used to always say: The vocation of bishop is the vocation of being incarcerated." And I always prayed to God to grant me the grace of this vocation.

Brainwashing

Before prison, the government often brought to the assemblies of struggle persons who were instructed on how to accuse me. After I was imprisoned, although I was detained for twenty-two years, I was never tried by an official tribunal. Consequently, I believe that one of the reasons I was imprisoned was in order that I might change my ideas and my religious faith. As a result, in prison, a part of each day was dedicated to imposing an "infusion of thought," a "brainwashing," on all the detainees. We were ordered to read *The People's Daily*. That important Communist newspaper did not report news; rather, it published articles on Marxist materialism, atheism, Leninism, and the thought of Mao Zedong. Apart from the newspapers, they would use loudspeakers for hours and hours, forcing the detainees to listen to them. These deafening noises often gave me a headache, and at times left me completely dazed. I was able to hear well only when those noises ceased to resound in my ears; but then the radio transmissions would start up again.

Besides these methods, the Communists used other means of brainwashing, such as the interrogations that lasted for days and days or all night long. At times they asked me if I had changed my mind and if they had made any progress toward this end. It was very difficult for me to take all of this.

Isolated from the Family

I was worried about my elderly mother: I did not know if she was still living or if she had died. Only a year before my incarceration, a cell companion, a doctor, said to me that he knew my older brother, Dr. Tang Yi-yin. He related some news of my family, but he did not know, at that time, that my brother had already died (he had died in 1978).

Although I was detached from the outside world, I knew that the Catholics, together with the Jesuits, supported me; that my priests and my faithful prayed for me, and that I was not refused by the people. This gave me great spiritual strength. I was faithful, I believed, and I trusted in the Lord.

My cell was very dark and gloomy. Not even a little air entered in. My eyes were extremely tired, and I feared going blind.

During the three years of the natural calamities (1959–1961), for six months of the year we ate only spinach, and for the remaining six months only cabbage. The vegetables had already flowered; the stems were very hard, and everything was cooked without oil. Consequently, my head was always spinning. Moreover, I would think: "If the Lord makes me die, I shall be very content because it will mean that I shall die for the Church." When I felt wretched, I tried to think of what martyrdom means: to sacrifice oneself for God.

During my imprisonment I did not know whether the persons I knew outside the prison were still living. Father Anthony Ngan, Brother Adon Chau, Father Andrew Chan, the vicar general, and Father Dominic Tam had sacrificed their lives for the Lord. I did not know how much longer I would be held in prison, just as I did not know whether I would be able to live another day. If I had been able to leave prison, I would have still defended the Church and the Faith.

Although I had committed sins, the Lord had granted me many graces. When, in prison, everything became exhausting and difficult to bear, I thought of the sufferings that Jesus experienced, and then I was able to bear the weight of my situation. I am weak, and so I asked the Lord to help me, to teach me how to act, and then I felt reinvigorated.

Outside the prison, the Catholics who had become members of the Patriotic Association were able to enjoy an unconditional liberty. But for these persons it was easy to give in to bad desires. Being free, they were tempted more and therefore incited to sin, into which they easily fell; and so it was that some of the priests got married.

The Power of Humility

I have already said that spiritual formation is built on the strength and exercise of the instructional period. In prison I put into practice the virtues instilled in me during the novitiate. During that period I had learned to be humble and obedient, to serve the ill, to work in the kitchen, to sweep the pavement, and to clean toilets. If I was corrected I had to remain silent and offer a beautiful smile. I thank God for having taught me so well during the novitiate.

In the minor seminary I was the vice prefect of the Marian Congregation, an association that sprang up in the Jesuit colleges. Each day I guided the prayers and meditation, and I went out to teach the doctrine to the children. When there was a religious feast, I cleaned and decorated the church. I met often with the spiritual director, and I accepted his guidance. I practiced mortification, and I did humble and spiritual works. I am convinced that the novices must build a good foundation on which to construct a spiritual life, and to cooperate incessantly with the grace to be able, in the future, to confront all of life's situations.

In prison I always asked the Lord to grant me the grace to progress in virtue; for example, in humility and obedience. I considered the authorities of the prison my superiors, and I obeyed them. Obviously I obeyed only the rules that did not contradict the principles of the Faith. I wished to be kind and polite with all the others, without resisting the mistreatment to which I was subjected. When I was controlled and trampled on, I did not complain. In prison there were many opportunities to practice virtue.

In 1982, when I went to the Philippines, I said to the novices of Novaliches: "My imprisonment was a prolonged novitiate." By that I meant that I had had to practice the virtues learned during the novitiate. If we get along well during the novitiate, we will be able to face difficulties and adversities and do God's will.

A Chinese proverb says: "Do not go to prison during your life, and do not go to hell after your death." In order to adapt to the severity and the monotony of prison life, which is full of difficulties, it is necessary to encounter great sufferings. The foundations of the faith and of the practice of the virtues were inculcated in me from my infancy. When I was a seminarian I had learned to do the will of God. Then the will of God asked me to practice the virtues in prison. This, for me, meant the love of God with respect to me.

Faith on Trial

During my long imprisonment I heard many Communist theories on Marxist atheism, and much propaganda on the theory of Darwinian evolution.

They told me that someone had gone to the moon. Even the jailer had his say on the matter: "Some people have gone to the moon to do research. Space is vast and, except for the stars, they cannot see anything else. This is science. Do you still believe in God?" At that time I was completely isolated from the external world. I was alone. Then I understood that my faith was being put to test. I thought in my heart: "Is it possible that what he is saying is true?"

In those circumstances it was not easy to believe in God. I made an act of faith, and I prayed with fervor: "God, I believe in you." When I was able, I looked out the little window to see a eucalyptus tree. In the spring I saw a sapling. In the summer it was covered with leaves. In autumn the leaves became yellow, and in winter they fell. And so the second year, the third year, and one year after another were equal. The variations of the trees, the four seasons, the stupendous sight of the sunset and the birds that were flying in the sky chirping: is all that purely chance? If there were not any God, some Creator, how would such a natural order be able to exist? All that is laid out by the Creator, and it is proof of the existence of God. Thus my faith was confirmed once again. I firmly believed. When I was attacked by materialism, by atheism, or by false scientific arguments, I immediately turned to God and prayed that surely he would give me the necessary grace to keep me firm in the Faith.

The Jesuit That Is in Me: Interior Discipline

Alongside the prison regulations and schedules, I followed my own program. Each morning, after getting up, I would recite the Apostles' Creed, offering the day to God. Then I would say the *Veni Creator* [Come, Holy Spirit], because each day so many things happened that gave me need of the light of the Holy Spirit to descend upon me. Then I would meditate for half an hour, on the life of Jesus, on his miracles, and especially on the mysteries of the holy Rosary. It pleased me, above all, to meditate on the Passion of Christ, and to recite those prayers of the Mass in Latin that I remembered. But during the last years I recalled very little. I recited the prayers of the Consecration of the Body and Blood of Christ, and then I made a spiritual Communion.

All this became a habit. Whether I was interrogated or not interrogated, I recited daily fifteen decades of the Rosary in place of the Divine Office. I recited another five decades in order to ask Our Lady to protect the Diocese of Canton. Because I did not have a rosary, I had to use my fingers to count the prayers. At times I was distracted, and it would take me an hour to say five decades of the Rosary. When I prayed I put my hands under the newspaper and pretended to read it. In general, I pronounced invocations and brief phrases such as: "Jesus, I believe in you, I love you. I pray to you. Teach me what I must do. Lord, make me ever improve in virtue." I prayed daily for the pope, the priests, the nuns, the Catholics of Donggang, Beigang, Nanhai, Shunde, Dongguan and Canton, for my parents and all my family, for the entire Church, and for all the faithful.

I prayed before and after every meal. But before and after every meal the guards would come to spy on me. If they suspected that I was praying, they would reproach me. During the meditation, either I sat tranquilly, or I stood looking out the window. If the guards saw me, they yelled at me, saying: "Are you still praying? Sit down."

My favorite prayer was the prayer of St. Ignatius of Loyola, *Suscipe Domine*:

Take, Lord, and receive all my liberty, my understanding, and my entire will, all that I have and possess. Thou hast given all to me. To Thee, O Lord, I return it. All is Thine, dispose of it wholly according to Thy will. Give me Thy love and Thy grace, for this is sufficient for me.

Besides the prayers and meditations, each day I softly sang some hymn: "Jesus, I live for you, I die for you; Jesus, I belong to you. Whether I live or I die, I am for you!" This hymn was taught to me by a Protestant detainee who was in the cell with me. At night before going to sleep, I sang: "Good night, Holy Mary, my merciful Mother ..." I would often sing "O Come, All Ye Faithful," "Silent Night," and other songs I remembered. These brief songs instilled in me a great spiritual strength.

At noon I made a brief examination of conscience, and before going to sleep each evening I made another examination of conscience, saying: "Jesus, Joseph, and Mary, I give you my heart and my soul; Jesus, Joseph, and Mary, assist me in my last agony; Jesus, Joseph, and Mary, make me able to breathe my last breath in peace with you!" And I added three Hail Marys. Then I went to sleep.

On Fridays and Sundays, besides all the usual prayers, I made the Stations of the Cross in a very simple way. Once a year I prayed the eight-day Spiritual Exercises [of St. Ignatius Loyola], with two meditations each day. Further, I interrogated myself on my relationship with God, with others, and with myself and on the three vows [chastity, poverty, and obedience]. I did the Spiritual Exercises faithfully, even during difficult times. They were a central point in my life, and the source of my renewal and correction. Where I was lacking, I tried to improve.

During the imprisonment I experienced sufferings of every kind. The pain of being alone, the interrogations to which the judges subjected me, and the admonishments I received that were able to weaken my will. I had to discipline myself to have a resolute spirit and a firm will. Each day I turned to prayer and to meditation. If I had to be interrogated, I did not forget my prayers, nor did I recite them in a negligent way; and I found a way to say them at other times. Each day I recited a certain number of prayers, and I prayed with sincerity and humility. In this way I exercised and formed my will, keeping intact my faith in the truth, in order not to lose it and not to deviate from the right path.

God Gave Me the Grace to Be Optimistic

I prayed and meditated each day and I sang hymns, so that I had no free time. This type of prayer was always the same, day after day. The practice of this exercise sustained me throughout the long years I lived in prison, and it gave me the strength to overcome both the material and spiritual difficulties; it also gave me a serene heart. God gave me the grace to be optimistic, which constantly encouraged me to look at the good side of things and only rarely the ugly. I had been imprisoned for God and for the Church; my conscience was at peace, because I had done my duty to God and the Church. If one day I died, I would die in peace. If I were released, I would have continued to serve God and the Church. These thoughts and happy sentiments, this peace that I had in the depth of my soul, sustained me during those twenty-two long winters and summers that I lived in [Mao's] prison.

The Last Interrogation

In February 1980 the head of the Office of Public Safety operated out of the Center of Surveillance at Tam Kong. With him were other high officials and leaders, such as the head of the section, Cheung, and his deputy, Lam. They lived in special quarters reserved for leaders of the party.

They interrogated me for a month, initially in the usual room, but later on in a building full of rooms for interrogations as well as at the living quarters of the high leaders of the party. The building was well maintained and the floors were carpeted. The chairs for the detainees were very comfortable, very different from the usual wooden stools. Generally there were three leaders who questioned me at the same time. Initially, they were very serious and spoke harshly. They said that for the crimes I had committed I merited nothing less than death. The topics of the interrogations regarded the same old interchanges. The judge said that I would be interrogated in the morning, while in the afternoon I would have to draw up an accurate report of what was discussed at the meeting that morning. In my cell there was no table. At times, they asked me to write everything in a hurry in the interrogation room.

Since the last uninterrupted interrogation ten years had passed. I did not know in what month or in what year they would place the word *end* on my case. And they were still interrogating me. Emotionally, I was confused enough. On the one hand, I was happy, thinking that my case would be resolved; on the other hand, during my first interrogations the judge had affirmed that my crimes were very serious. I was afraid, and I did not know how it would all end. Consequently, I was very upset.

When I finished drafting the report, as I was ordered to do by the judge, the interrogation ended.

Ever Faithful to the Pope

Then, suddenly, one day three high officials came to interrogate me; among them was the head of the Office of Public Safety, Lei. The judge asked me, as he had already asked me often in the previous interrogations: "You have been here a long time in order to be reeducated. How do you see the problems now?" And he continued: "I am the head of the Office of Public Safety. I have come to resolve your case." And then he asked me what I was thinking. I began to respond, but after a little bit he stopped me. Full of hope, I thought that this was a good sign. Then he asked me again: "As regards the Vatican, how do you see it? What do you know of it? What are your sentiments?"

In the depth of my heart, I knew that, if I did not respond according to their ideas, I would not have been able even to imagine the consequences. But I declared firmly: "There is a dogmatic, inseparable tie between us and the Vatican. If we separate ourselves from the Vatican, we would no longer be part of the Catholic Church. Without the pope, there is not a Catholic Church. For the Protestants it is different, because they do not have any pope."

On hearing that, the judge became very austere and said angrily: "You have not changed in the least." Then he added: "Well, well! Return to the cell and try to reeducate yourself." And he left the room very discontented.

I said to myself: "Things have gone very badly. I do not know what it will take to resolve my case, and I am a little afraid. But let God's will be done." While I responded to the judge, my conscience was at peace.

Two weeks later, perhaps a little more, three high officials (among the most important) interrogated me yet another time. They gave me a lot of advice and asked me some questions of minor importance. As a result, I felt more relaxed.

Once a judge named Cheung came. He seemed to be a native of San Wui. He was rather fat and, being the head of a department, was assigned to my case. He had completely changed his attitude toward me. He said: "The judge Lam has told me that you are a good man, that you have never done any harm to anyone, that you are not avaricious, that you have given your money away for public use, and that you have never had an under-standing with women."

In the depth of my heart I felt a sensation of peace. I felt that my case would soon be resolved. Later the guard sent me out into the field to pull weeds and to get a little sun. They were kinder toward me and gave me much more liberty. At that time they also gave me three meals a day and even added meat to my diet, like that of the leaders. Lai, the director of the prison of Tam Kong, came into the courtyard and asked me: "Have you never been questioned by the prosecutor? Have you never been charged?" I told him that I had never been charged, and he went away.

During this last interrogation session, when the judge questioned me, I begged him to resolve my case, because I had been in prison for twenty-two years without ever having been tried. According to the penal code, with the exception of the death penalty and life in prison, the longest sentence imposed on criminals was fifteen years. My prison term had gone well over that limit.

Toward Liberty

The Church in Hong Kong and all my relatives and friends believed that I had already been dead for a time. Many years ago (around 1970), the Jesuits of Hong Kong had even prayed that my soul rest in peace.

In 1977 Stephen Mok Kwok-ying (a Catholic from Guangdong who had studied at Aurora University of Shanghai during the Sino-Japanese War) became aware that I was still alive, in the prison of Tam Kong. So he informed my fourth cousin, at Hong Kong, that I was still alive. She immediately asked my cousin Chung Kwai-chiu, of Canton, to find out where I was. In addition, she wrote a letter to Liu Shing-chi (Liao Cheng-zhi), head of the Office for the Chinese Overseas with the Counsel of State at Peking.

Chung Kwai-chiu had been to Berlin to study engineering. After the "liberation," he began to work as the chief engineer at the Hydraulic Department of the province of Guangdong, where he had planned to construct the hydroelectric generating station on the San Fung River and the great reservoir tank at Shamchun. When Chung Kwai-chiu became ill, some high officials belonging to both the civil government and the police went to visit him at the People's Hospital No. 1 of Canton. He asked them for permission to see me: his request was granted. This occurred some months before my release.

One day an official of the prison took me to the hospital to visit him. Prior to the visit the Communist official instructed me on what I could say to my cousin. Chung Kwai-chiu asked the government if he could host me in his home after my release. The judges went to his home in order to see the place.

His wife and her younger sister came from Hong Kong and visited me. They brought me many things. Afterward, they made me new clothes to wear after my release. When I asked about my mother, the younger sister lied and told me that my mother and my younger brother were well. I was happy to be able to say to others that my mother was still alive and in good health. But in reality she had been dead for more than ten years.

The Longed-For Release

The morning of June 9, 1980, while I was going out to work as usual, the guard suddenly called me and asked me to return to my cell to gather my things. I dressed and took my miserable suitcase and followed him to the office. To my lively surprise there were photographers and journalists waiting for me. When the official in charge restored my rosary to me, the photographers immediately photographed the scene. It was the rosary that had been confiscated from me twenty-two years before, at the moment of my arrest. The official said that they would give me four yuan in compensation for my episcopal ring, which had had a ruby.

Once outside the prison gate, they took me to a large building situated on Yuet Sau Pak and Tso Pai Streets. It was a building constructed by a company managed by the Chinese Abroad. When I entered the atrium, I saw some priests and Catholics of the Patriotic Association and some Protestant ministers. The party official made me sit at the right of the president of the assembly, in view of the public. The director of the Office of Public Safety, Chiu, began by reading the document of release, in which the government declared that, with great clemency, it had decided to restore my liberty to me. In truth, given that there had not been any trial, I had never been formally charged. Then I signed the document of release.

At that point I was told to read a speech written and prepared for me for the occasion. The content, in brief, was the following:

> I admit that, in the past, I had tried to obstruct the Movement of Reform of the Three Autonomies and that I had opposed the government when it suppressed the Legion of Mary and ordered its members to register. During the agrarian reform I said to the priests: "Unless the landowners' property is sold openly, we shall not buy it." During the campaign Opposing America's help for Korea, I told the students to study; therefore, I was accused of impeding them from enrolling in the army. During the campaign of 1951–1952 against the three evils and that of 1952 against the five evils,[58] I said that the government permitted the private commercial enterprises to exist and that they achieved useful things, and therefore, it was not just to confiscate capital from capitalists. During the period of the elimination of the counterrevolutionaries, the Office for Religious Affairs asked me if I had any requests. I asked that the imprisoned priests be released; that request was interpreted as a request to release counterrevolutionaries, and so on.

---

[58] The "three evils" referred to corruption, waste and bureaucracy, and the "five evils" referred to the five sins of merchants and industrialists: corruption, fiscal evasion, appropriation of public goods, fraud on declarations of the cost of labor and materials, and theft of information on the state economy for one's own profit.

Then, I added: "The members of the Communist Party are atheistic and materialistic; they wish to destroy religion. Their ideology is opposed to ours. Actually, Communist Chinese law pursues a policy that permits the existence of religion.[59] I shall become a citizen who observes the law, and I shall administer my diocese well."

After my discourse, the chief of the Office for Religious Affairs, Liu On, said: "Tang Yi-ming is a counterrevolutionary; he has refused many times to reeducate himself; therefore, he was arrested. Now, the government, in its great clemency, has released him; but from now on he shall no longer be the bishop of Canton."

Father Louis Yip and Father Joseph Wong accompanied me to Shek Shat. During that period, the sacristy of the cathedral had become the office of the Patriotic Association. Lam Hak-oi, a woman, carried out the work. Many Catholics wished to see me, but Lam Hak-oi did not permit them.

When I arrived at Shek Shat, it was noon. After having dined and rested a little, I went into the large hall [reception room] in order to meet with the head of the Patriotic Association of Canton, Chan Chi-hung, Fung Kwok-kwog, and about ten other people. The members of the Patriotic Association said to me: "The government was benevolent toward you. From now on you must pay attention to the reeducation of your thought and your behavior."

Then Father Joseph said very seriously: "You are already no longer the bishop of Canton. Now the bishop is Father Lau Tai-tak, and I am the vicar general."

I did not change the expression on my face, because my heart was full of peace. Continuing his game, I said to Lau: "Congratulations! So now you are the bishop!"

I returned to the first floor, with a strong sense of isolation and abandonment. The encounter had lasted an hour, and then everyone went away, unsatisfied.

---

[59] According to document 19 of 1982, five religions (including Catholicism) are tolerated on the condition that they accept the supervision of the authorities.

Before Leaving the Continent

The government had mandated Tsang Mei-mei to guard us. She said that she was Catholic, but I did not ever see her receive Communion, nor did I ever see her kneel at Mass during the Consecration.

If a Catholic or a visitor ever wished to visit me, he had to go through the Office of the Patriotic Association and receive permission. When I returned to Shek Shat, many Catholics, and at times even some strangers, desired to see me, but Tsang Mei-mei did not permit it. She would lie to people; for example: "Tang Yi-ming has gone to the hospital for a checkup."

Once, some strangers wished to see me. She told them that I had gone out. By chance I saw them from the terrace. They also were aware of me; they immediately knelt on the ground and asked me to give them my blessing.

Another time a French Jesuit came to visit me. I had just gone to the house of my cousin, but this priest would not go away. He decided to wait for my return. He waited a long time. With him was a nun in civilian clothes and a laywoman. When we met, we were all very happy. The priest brought me several books. Most of them were on Vatican II and on spirituality. Tsang Mei-mei took them immediately, saying that she would hold them for me. Later I consulted the chief of the department, Wong (who was her superior, in charge of our surveillance). Wong ordered that the books be put on the public shelves and that, if I wished to read them, I would be able to request them. Wong came to Shek Shat each day, but in reality he did not understand anything about ecclesiastic affairs.

The elderly Father John Ng Yam-yu was ill, at Gaopo, Canton. I wished to visit him and to go to him for confession. So I asked Father James Lam to take me to him. But Tsang Mei-mei did not permit me to go, saying that we had meetings that we could not miss. I was so fed up that I went immediately to Wong and told him that I wished to go to confession. "Why do you not let me go? Do you also wish to control confession?" In the end he gave me permission to go.

Tsang Mei-mei would not even permit me to celebrate Mass. As an excuse she told me that my Latin was not good enough. Therefore, I would attend Mass in the midst of the faithful.

Dominic Tang, S.J.

My First Contacts with Journalists

William Sexton, a Protestant journalist for *Newsday*, a publication from Long Island (New York), resided at Peking. After receiving permission from the minister of foreign affairs at Peking and from the Office for Religious Affairs at Canton, he came to speak with me for two hours. The following day he attended Mass at 6:30. While I was kneeling in the cathedral with a group of the faithful, he took a photo of me. That photo and that conversation were published a short time later in a Hong Kong newspaper (*Hong Kong Standard*, June 28, 1980). That was the first time I had spoken to a journalist about my situation. After my arrival at Hong Kong, Sexton wished to see me again, but at that time I was in the Canossa hospital, and he was not able to meet me.

Soon after my return to Shek Shat, I had hoped to be able to travel around a bit, but circumstances did not permit me. I wished to work, but not having priests I was not able to do it. I wished to reunite the priests in the area, but all I could do was offer my help and worry about them. At that time I was ill, and Father Louis Yip often took me to the doctor. During these trips, I had the opportunity to speak privately to him, and I encouraged him to be fervent.

Up to then, since my release from prison, Father Yip had been very reserved. But then he began to open up and to speak more freely. "We also suffered much," he said. And then he told me how difficult life had been for the priests during the Cultural Revolution. They were very poor, and they had to work in the factories. They were forced by the authorities to do the heaviest work.

Father James Lam had a very big heart, and he had always worked actively for the Church, but his problem had always been a lack of courage: he was always afraid and did not understand very much about ecclesiastical affairs. I tried each day to make him aware of my concern for him in little ways so that he could feel himself surrounded by human warmth.

Before I went into the hospital, in September 1981, the Patriotic Association permitted me to celebrate Mass for the first time, but in a side chapel with the doors closed. Later, when Catholics became aware that I was celebrating the Eucharist, they rushed to participate.

DIARIES OF THE CHINESE MARTYRS

During that period, many priests from abroad, including some Jesuits, arrived at Canton. Father John Tong Hon[60] brought a group of foreigners who wished to visit me. They assured me of their support and gave me books and souvenirs.

I was enjoying a good reputation. Among my visitors were some of the leaders of the Office of Public Safety whom I had known during my travails and imprisonment. I also had friends who were engineers, doctors, and so forth who visited me in the hospital; and then there was a continuous procession of Catholics and persons from various parts of the world coming to see me.

In September, while I was in the People's Hospital No. 1 in Canton for observation, the wife of my cousin Chung Kwai-chiu and many others came often to visit me. By that time the attitude of the government toward me had changed.

After some examinations, the doctors of the hospital told me that I had a rectal tumor; fortunately it was benign and could be easily removed surgically. However, they were not agreed on the proper time to operate.

At this time my sister-in-law came to Canton. She and the wife of my cousin met with the head of the Office of Religious Affairs, Chan Tung, to ask for permission to bring me to Hong Kong for treatment. But they told her that I had never spoken of going to Hong Kong for a cure and that they would first have to ask my opinion. Therefore, I took a day's leave from the hospital to go to the Office of Religious Affairs to request permission to go to Hong Kong for medical treatment. I also told them that, since my family was at Hong Kong, my relatives had not been able to see me for more than thirty years, and that by now I was the only member of the Tang family still alive, since all my brothers and cousins had died. Therefore, I continued, if they did not permit me to go to Hong Kong for

---

[60] John Tong Hon, ordained a bishop in 1996, was installed as bishop of Hong Kong on July 15, 2009, and made a cardinal on February 18, 2012. He has been the director of the Diocesan Center of Studies on China since its foundation in 1980.

treatment, the government's reputation abroad would suffer serious damage, especially if, in the meantime, I died at Canton. They immediately took a photo and gave me the request form, which I filled out with care. My sister-in-law went to Shek Shat to get the certificate of residence and passed it and the request form on to the police. When everything was arranged I returned to the hospital and waited for the notice.

The Patriotic Association Recognizes the Bishop of Canton

One day in October the Office for Religious Affairs sent two officials to the hospital to command me without delay to return to Shek Shat, where some meetings were awaiting me. The meetings, which were prearranged by the highest authorities, were held on October 8 and 9. The first day, the head of the department and the head of the Office for Religious Affairs outlined the agenda and the procedures; then everyone took part in a discussion. The second day, there were two points of discussion: (1) Does the Diocese of Canton have need of a bishop? (2) Is Dominic Tang Yi-ming worthy of being bishop of Canton?

We discussed the two points in groups. Before the encounter, knowing that they would be discussing my case, I asked that I not participate, so that they could freely express themselves, but the leaders insisted on having me present. However, I did not offer any opinion. The participants were all priests, nuns, Catholics of the Patriotic Association, and party officials, about fifty to sixty altogether. They were divided into three or four discussion groups, each one tasked with advancing the proposals. Father Paul Ng Kau-kwong was the first to propose me as bishop of Canton. The final result was unanimous: it was necessary to give Canton a bishop and to name Tang Yi-ming bishop of Canton. After the general consensus, the head of the Office for Religious Affairs declared: "Because the participants at this meeting have unanimously settled on Tang Yi-ming as the bishop of Canton, the government declares its support." The priests immediately came to kiss the ring, while the Catholics of the Patriotic Association shook my hand to congratulate me.

At first, the delegates who were gathered there wished to celebrate a solemn Mass of thanksgiving on October 10. But I told them that I had a furlough from the hospital for just two days, and therefore, I must first return to the hospital; I would then celebrate the Mass at a later date.

The news spread everywhere like lightning. The Catholics of Canton knew about it immediately; the Vatican and Hong Kong were also informed of it. The people abroad, and especially the Holy See, took the news seriously. The foreign newspapers published it, and someone arrived immediately from Macao to acquire more detailed information. I returned to the People's Hospital No. 1 of Canton to continue treatment and to wait for permission to leave for Hong Kong. A few days later, I was informed that my request was accepted.

At the hospital, I had to undergo more tests, and I remained there about a month but without being operated on. I then returned to Shek Shat on October 24, 1980, where I would remain for more than a month. On October 26, I began to celebrate Mass and to preach. The priests wished to construct a building and a parking area in front of the cathedral. I did not give any opinions regarding their plans; I just let them do it. I now had more contact with the priests and was able to speak with them. I also had contact with some nuns who worked in private homes or clinics, and I visited their employers.

The priests of the Diocese of Jiangmen and of Zhaoqing came to visit me, and I met with the majority of the Catholics. During the great feast days I met the Catholics from the various districts, before and after Mass, and I stopped to chat with them. During this brief period I carried out much pastoral work.

My Departure

At the beginning of November of 1980 a police official informed me that I had been granted a visa for Hong Kong. After waiting some days, Wong, the chief of the department, brought me to the person in charge of the Provincial Office for Religious Affairs, who asked me: "Will you go to visit the pope?"

I responded: "I shall if the pope invites me. Our Catholic Church is very united to the Vatican." Then I asked him: "Will you permit us to establish relations with the Vatican?"

He responded: "This decision is for our superiors to make. We cannot respond to this question."

Then I added: "Given that I am the bishop of Canton and a citizen of this country, can you present my thoughts on this matter to Peking?" I did not receive a direct response to my question.

Apart from this discourse, we chatted only about my trip to Hong Kong and the treatment I needed. Then I said good-bye to him. The department head, Wong, accompanied me to Shek Shat.

A few days before crossing the border, the officials of the Office of Public Safety brought me to the neighborhood of Shek Wan di Foshan to buy some porcelain objects, vases, animals, and dolls (a dozen in all) and told me to bring them to Hong Kong as personal gifts for my relatives and friends. They also invited me to have tea at Foshan and urged me to return soon.

The visa for Hong Kong permitted me to stay for a year in order to receive the necessary medical treatment, after which I would have to return to Canton.

About three days before my departure, the Office for Religious Affairs and the Patriotic Association ordered me to pack my bags, and they told Father Louis Yip to buy me a Western-style suit. When I tried to pay the official, he declined the offer, telling me that they had decided to buy me some new clothes for my trip to Hong Kong. Given that I was the bishop of Canton, I had to be presentable.

Then I went to the local police station to cancel my ration of rice, oil, fabric, and other provisions, but I retained my proof of residence for a year.

Father Anthony Tsang Hing-lam[61] arrived at Canton from Hong Kong in order to find out the exact day of my departure, and thus come to meet me at the Shenzhen station.

---

[61] Anthony Tsang, originally from Canton, was ordained a priest at Hong Kong in 1962. He died in August 1991.

The evening before the departure, the head of the Citizen Office for Religious Affairs, Liu On, and an official of a lower rank, comrade Ma En (a member of the Hui minority), invited me to supper in a restaurant patronized by the ethnic Hui. [Profiting from the occasion,] I said clearly to Lui: "Given that I have been bishop for some time, I am familiar with the excessive bureaucracy of your system. There are so many religious problems that you do not wish to discuss with us or ask us for an opinion. You only give orders. I believe that you go too far with this line of conduct. On hearing this, Liu turned red and admitted that at times they had erred, but he criticized me for not having been close to the government.

The Patriotic Association organized a farewell reception with many sweets. The leader of the Association, Chan Chi-hung, invited all the priests of the cathedral to the gathering, and during the festivities he gave a speech, wishing me well. He said to return to Canton just as soon as I felt better and also to introduce in China the novelties and changes that have occurred in the Church, if there have been any. I responded that the state of my health would determine the date of my return. If I got better, I would return; otherwise I did not know what to say about the date of my return.

The Patriotic Association had also arranged to have some of its members present at my departure in order to say good-bye to me, but I refused because if I had been accompanied by too many people, the journalists of Canton would have known and within an hour the news would have also reached Hong Kong. Then, about the time of my arrival, many journalists would have gathered at the station to greet me, and what would I have to say to them? Certainly, I would have felt very embarrassed. Rather, I suggested that, at the most, a small group of relatives and friends should accompany me.

On November 5, the day of my departure, all the priests accompanied me to the principal gate of Shek Shat and said good-bye. The priest representative, Father Louis Yip, Lam Hak-oi of the Patriotic Association, and the wife of my cousin, Lei Chiu-ling, accompanied me to the station. Lam Hak-oi and Father Yip accompanied me to the platform and waited until I got on the train. My sister-in-law, Ruby Tang, even sent her elderly domestic,

Cheung Wai-ling, to Canton, so that she could keep me company during the trip on the train to Shenzhen. Thank God, it was a pleasant trip.

Hong Kong, At Last

When we arrived at Shenzhen, Cheung Wai-ling and I were welcomed by Father Anthony Tsang and Leung Fung Pui-chan, who were waiting for us at the station. At the border, on the Chinese side, they did not make a fuss. My travel documents and my luggage passed inspection without any problem. As soon as we arrived at the Hong Kong customs, just as we were crossing the bridge — it was dawn — two persons came to meet us. Together we crossed the bridge at Lowu. John Green, a high-ranking police officer who was at the border, came to meet me and accompanied me to a waiting room at the Lowu station, where I could rest a little. He was Irish and a good Catholic. At the station I was received by the vicar general of the Diocese of Hong Kong, Father Secondo Einaudi of the Pontifical Institute of Foreign Missions (Pime); by the provincial superior of the Jesuits of Macao and Hong Kong, Father Liam Egan; by the director of the Catholic Center of Hong Kong, Father Edward Khong; and by my nephew, Tang Szyuen. They prepared tea for all of us and three other officials. The police official said that I was the second bishop that he helped to reach Hong Kong passing through Lowu. The first was Monsignor James Walsh, of the Maryknoll missionaries of the United States. Both of us would leave China after a long period of incarceration. The Irishman noticed that I did not wear the bishop's ring and said to me: "If you had had it, I would have kneeled and kissed it."

We remained seated for a bit, while a car waited for us at the exit. The police official drove the first car, and my nephew followed him in his. Along the way, Father Einaudi pointed out all the churches that we encountered.

Around noon we arrived at the headquarters of Caritas, on Caine Street. My sister-in-law, together with my nephews and another Catholic, Poon, that I knew well, were waiting to welcome me. We immediately went to the upper floor to meet the bishop, Monsignor John Baptist Wu

DIARIES OF THE CHINESE MARTYRS

Cheng-chung. Father Renato Chevalier and other priests of the foreign missions of Paris also came to greet me. In addition, the bishop of Macao, Monsignor Arquiminio Rodrigues de Costa, and the Jesuit Father Anthony Tam Chi-tsing arrived from Macao to welcome me. We spoke for three or four hours. Monsignor Wu and Father Edward Khong informed me that there would be a press conference in the afternoon and that many journalists would be present.

At 5:00 p.m. in the Caritas reception room many journalists gathered to take part in the press conference. The English translation was done by Father Khong. Fortunately on that day presidential elections were being held in the United States, so there was not too much publicity surrounding my case.

At the end of the press conference Monsignor Wu invited me to dinner; and afterward he invited me to lodge with him. However, since the address marked for permission for the visit was that of my sister-in-law, I had to stay with her, and I remained there for two days. On the third day I entered the hospital and was not permitted to see anyone.

After a thorough medical examination, the doctors confirmed that I did have rectal cancer, for which I would have to undergo surgery. Fortunately the tumor was not yet diffuse. The hospital's nuns advised me to consult with Dr. Arthur Van Langenberg, the surgeon assigned to operate on me. The operation lasted three and a half hours: the rectum and anus were removed and a deviation was made. Then, they nourished me through an intravenous drip and so for a week I did not touch food. At the end of the week I felt truly famished. Initially the doctor permitted me to take only liquids, and only later could I progress to solids.

Given that Christmas was approaching, I asked the doctor to let me go home for the occasion.

Thanks to the attentive care of the doctors, the nuns, and the nurses, my health was gradually reestablished, in spite of the fact that I still felt very weak. I remained in the hospital another month. Initially the doctor wished me to stay even longer, but in the end he permitted me to go home. On Christmas morning, I celebrated Mass in the cathedral, and I preached a homily on peace. I remained at home for more than a month, after which I settled into the college of Wah Yan, a Jesuit school in Kowloon.

On the fiftieth anniversary of my entrance into the Company of Jesus, I celebrated the Eucharist in the chapel of the college of Wah Yan. All the Jesuits from Hong Kong attended the Mass. Father Liam Egan, the provincial superior, showed me a book that listed all the Jesuits of Macao and Hong Kong. In 1969 my name was included in the list of those who had passed away. Some had spread the news of my death and even affirmed that they had seen my cadaver carried away.

Father Egan showed me the papal bull of my nomination as bishop. In 1951, when I had become bishop, they were not able to send me the bull at Canton, and so the Jesuits had kept it with the hope of letting me see it one day.

The "Impossible" Encounter with John Paul II

When Pope John Paul II[62] went to the Philippines, he sent for me. Initially I thought of going there to meet him, but my confreres were not in agreement. Yet I truly wished to see the Holy Father, since on many occasions he had expressed a desire to meet with me. While he was in the Philippines, he often asked where I was; then, unexpectedly, he sent for me. When the newspapers of Manila reported that I had already met with the pope, the Hong Kong journalists asked me why, in fact, I had not gone. I simply responded, given that I was convalescing, the doctor would not permit me to travel.

The pope truly wished that I go to the Philippines to visit with him; and when I was unable to go, he renewed the invitation to meet him in Japan. Furthermore, Sophia University, the Catholic university directed by the Jesuits also officially invited me to Japan to meet the pope, but I did not go there either. In the end, the pope sent the Vatican secretary of

---

[62] From February 16 to 27, 1981, Pope John Paul II completed a trip to Asia, with stops in Pakistan, the Philippines, and Japan.

state, Cardinal Agostino Casaroli, to Hong Kong to meet with me and to bring me his greetings.

Peking and the "Mediator"

At 8:00 p.m. the journalists of all the most important dailies of Hong King arrived at the college of Wah Yan. Cardinal Casaroli and I each read a communiqué, after which, for more than an hour, we responded to the numerous questions that were put to us. The principal question touched on the possibility of reestablishing a rapport with Peking. Cardinal Casaroli responded that there were, of course, many means and diplomatic channels for resolving the problem of Taiwan. As for the Patriotic Association of Chinese Catholics, under certain conditions, what is now illegal could become acceptable to the Church. The journalists asked me in what way I could function as a bridge. I said that I would do all that was in my power.

The following morning the cardinal asked me to keep in contact with the government of Peking and to act as an intermediary. Before departing, he invited me on behalf of the pope to go to Rome. The Holy Father wished to see me.

The Trip to Rome and the Ad Limina Visit

When the bishops of Asia met together in Rome in 1980, I was not able to participate at the gathering because I had arrived late to Hong Kong. I went to Rome from April 30 to May 17, 1981, in order to have an audience with the pope and to make my *ad limina* visit.[63] I began the preparation more than a month before my trip to Rome, with a course of spiritual exercises.

On the evening of April 28, 1981, I took a flight for Rome with the Jesuit priest Father Franco Belfiori. Those who came to the airport to

---

[63] An *ad limina* visit (*Ad limina Apostolorum*) is a visit made by the bishops every five years to the threshold (tombs) of the apostles Saints Peter and Paul, during which each bishop must present himself to the pope and give an account of his diocese.

cheer us on were Father Secondo Einaudi, of Pime, the vicar general of Hong Kong; the Jesuit priest Father Liam Egan, the superior provincial; the Jesuit Father Francis Chan Fook-wai, the rector of the college of Wah Yan in Kowloon; the Focolari; and my relatives.

At our arrival in Rome, on April 30, the representative of the secretary of state, Monsignor Ivan Dias, the representative of the Congregation for the Evangelization of the Peoples, Monsignor Luigi Ghidoni, and the superior general of the Jesuits, Father Pedro Arrupe, were at the airport to welcome us. Four of us went to the Curia Generalizia, the Jesuit World Headquarters, on Borgo Santo Spirito (which is within Vatican City). Immediately after we arrived a message came from the Vatican saying that the pope would receive us at one o'clock. At one sharp the pope welcomed us in the audience chamber. With us were Monsignor Dias and Father Belfiori. When the pope saw me, he embraced me. Then the monsignor passed a ring to the pope, who personally slipped it on my finger. On the ring was an image of Jesus with the apostles Peter and Paul at his side. It was a souvenir of Vatican II. At that time, given that I was in prison, I was not able to participate at the council, and so the ring was saved with the intention of giving it to me later. After they took the customary photos, the others withdrew and the pope and I remained alone together; he told me that he had wished to receive me personally in order to speak with me and to tell me of his concern for me. After about half an hour, I took my leave of the pope and returned to the Jesuit World Headquarters, where I remained in expectation of a second official audience.

The pope then posed some questions to me, to which I responded. Then toward eight that evening he invited us to supper. After the meal we accompanied him to his private apartments, where he gave me numerous medallions, rosaries, and other sacred objects. Finally, we returned by car to our lodgings.

In the following days I had the opportunity to make a pilgrimage to the various Roman basilicas, including the Basilica of St. Cecilia, and I visited the catacombs of the ancient martyrs. Moreover, I celebrated Mass on the tomb of St. Peter, the head of the apostles. I also went to the offices of the

Vatican Radio, where I celebrated Mass in Chinese, and I prayed for the Church in China. The celebration was also transmitted on the Chinese continent.

Afterward I visited the Vatican Museums, some sacred places, religious houses—both male and female—and various novitiates, where I celebrated Mass and held conferences. I went, for example, to the mother houses of the Dominicans, the Franciscans, the Salesians, the Canossians, and others.

I also went to the embassy of the People's Republic of China at Rome, accompanied by Father Robert Ng Chi-fun. After I arrived at the embassy, the first thing I did was to sign my name at the entrance: "Tang Yi-ming, the bishop of Canton, desires to pay his respects to the ambassador." We waited for about half an hour in a room next to the entrance. Perhaps in the interval the members of the embassy staff were asking for instructions on how to receive us. They then led us into a room. Initially a secretary came to tell us that the ambassador had gone to Peking. Afterward a second secretary of the embassy, the press secretary, a Mr. Xie, came to receive me.

I explained the purpose of my visit to him. He seemed very content to welcome me. I asked him if he had ever gone to the Vatican, but I received a very evasive response. He said that he did not understand Church matters. I asked him if China ever had the intention of establishing some contacts with the Vatican, and he gave the usual response, which is that the Vatican must take the first step by breaking off their relationship with Taiwan; in any case, the decision was up to Peking. He asked me which other countries I intended to visit, and I responded that I would go to France, Portugal, and other countries to visit old friends. Then he suggested that when I was in Paris or Lisbon I should go to the Chinese embassies and, if necessary, I should ask for assistance.

On May 13, 1981, my birthday, the superior general of the Society of Jesus gave me a finely bound breviary in Latin. During the dinner he expressed his good wishes to me and gave a speech.

That evening, between 5:00 and 8:00, the news of the attack on the pope arrived. Later, St. Peter's Square was closed off to the public, but we could see the piazza from the terrace of our building. The unhappy news frightened and preoccupied each of us, and we prayed together for the pope. The attacker was arrested. Meanwhile many priests and faithful were gathering in St. Peter's Square to pray for the pope during the night.

At Rome I met Chinese priests and nuns at a Chinese restaurant; some were monsignors, others worked in the various Vatican congregations.

I was invited to hold a conference at Gregorian University, which is directed by the Jesuits, and then I celebrated Mass in the chapel of San Luigi Gonzaga in the Church of Sant'Ignazio. Also, at the Jesuit World Headquarters, I held an encounter on my prison experience: the superior general and all the priests showed much interest and at the end they applauded me warmly. I spoke in English, and Father Belfiore translated my comments into Italian. They also asked me some questions, and I responded willingly. In the end, we all sang *Suscipe Domine* (Take, Lord, and receive all my liberty . . .).

I left Rome for a few days and traveled through Europe and then to America to visit my relatives and friends. Before leaving, I went to the Congregation [a permanent committee of cardinals] for the Evangelization of the Peoples, whose members asked me to return to Rome for Pentecost.

From Rome I flew first to Paris, and then to London, Dublin, New York, San Francisco, Lisbon, and Madrid. I followed it with a pilgrimage to Loyola, the birthplace of Saint Ignatius, and to Javier, the place where Saint Francis Xavier was born.

The evening of June 4, 1981, I returned to Rome. The next day I was summoned to the Congregation for the Evangelization of the People, where I went with Father Michael Zhu Lide to see the prefect [the head of the congregation], Cardinal Agnelo Rossi, and the secretary, Monsignor Duraisamy Simon Lourdusamy. Cardinal Rossi informed me that the pope had decided to nominate me archbishop of the Diocese of Canton. Monsignor Lourdusamy asked me to confirm in writing that I would accept that high office. I wrote that I was not worthy but that, trusting in the help of divine grace, I would accept that appointment and would try to bear the weight of such a responsibility.

DIARIES OF THE CHINESE MARTYRS

On June 5, the vigil of Pentecost, the Vatican Radio transmitted the news of my nomination as archbishop of Canton. The following day there was a great celebration. I did not have the miter for the ceremony, however, so I had to content myself with a miter procured in a great hurry.

On June 6, the feast of Pentecost, the pope could not celebrate the Mass [of my consecration] because he was still convalescing. So the solemn Mass, concelebrated in the Basilica of St. Peter, was presided over by Cardinal Basil Hume of Westminster. The concelebrants were more than three hundred cardinals and bishops. I was immensely happy. During the celebration we listened to a recording by the pope and then, before the end of the celebration, there suddenly arose a spontaneous roar of applause; the pope had appeared at a window overlooking the St. Peter's Square and blessed the faithful who were gathered there. One could read the expressions of immense joy that the pope's appearance had stirred up in everyone's heart.

In the afternoon there was a solemn ceremony, and the bishops walked in procession with the statue of the Madonna. Some friends, on seeing me, tried to take my hand and greet me. Monsignor Matthew Kia, archbishop of Taipei, participated with me in the ceremony. During the procession a message from the pope, recorded especially for the occasion, was transmitted.

The Reactions to My Nomination

At the news of my pontifical nomination as archbishop of Canton there was an immediate reaction on the part of the media throughout the world. Most of the journalists agreed that this would facilitate the renewal of relations between the Vatican and China. The Chinese priests and nuns who resided at Rome joyously gathered together to celebrate the event with a supper. Many of them agreed that this nomination would bring advantages. But a week later Peking attacked the Vatican, accusing it of interfering in China's internal affairs and called me a traitor. The Patriotic Assembly organized numerous assemblies of accusations at Shanghai, Canton, and other places. The newspapers reported this news everywhere. At that time I was still in Rome. Also at Hong Kong many persons asked for explanations on the business; the diocese and the Society of Jesus held two meetings to decide how to confront the situation.

The "patriotic" bishop of Canton, Yip Yam-wan,[64] immediately announced that I was dismissed from the office of bishop of Canton. I received a telex from Hong Kong that informed me of the matter, given that I was still in Rome. The television stations of Hong Kong aired a film of me walking in silence in St. Peter's Square. Upon my return I met the representatives of the diocese at the college of Wah Yan; together we decided to hold a press conference the following day, in the auditorium of the Church of Saint Teresa in Kowloon. Because of this business the Diocese of Hong Kong and the Jesuits were placed under continuous pressure. Therefore, we prepared to respond to some questions from the journalists, to explain the pope's wishes, the problem of the nomination of archbishop of Canton, the Movement of the Reform and the Three Autonomies, and other questions.

On the morning of June 23, 1981, the correspondents of the various information agencies and television stations came to interview me. I released a press release to the journalists that said the following: on March 19, 1946, the Holy See announced the establishment of the Chinese ecclesiastical hierarchy; therefore, there would be Chinese bishops administering the ecclesiastical affairs in China. From that moment on, Canton became an archdiocese, and because Canton was the capital of a province, there would have to be an archbishop as the head of the Church. The first archbishop was Monsignor Antoine Fourquet, a Frenchman, who returned to France before the "liberation." When I arrived at Canton, he was already in Europe. I then became the apostolic administrator of the Archdiocese of Canton. During my imprisonment, Monsignor Fourquet died. The impossibility of making me archbishop and the subsequent attempt to find a remedy for the situation were, therefore, owed to the fact that I was in prison at the death of the archbishop and therefore, I was, in turn, not

---

[64] In 1962 Yip Yam-wan was consecrated bishop of Huiyang (province of Guangdong) but without a pontifical mandate; he was then transferred to the seat at Canton in place of Monsignor Dominic Tang.

able to become archbishop immediately. When I regained my liberty, I went to Rome where the pope nominated me archbishop, thereby restoring to me the title that was owed to me. When an archdiocese is lacking an archbishop, the Holy See nominates another. This is the Church's normal procedure. My nomination, therefore, did not challenge or violate any other diocese. Simply stated, it was an ordinary administrative appointment made for the good of the Archdiocese of Canton. It was not at all, as some Chinese Communists have said, "an interference in the internal affairs of China," nor was it a "challenge" to any political power.

The journalists questioned me about the Movement of the Reform of the Three Autonomies and about the independence from the Holy See on the part of the Church in China. I responded: "The pope is the head of the universal Church, and so there exists a necessary tie between the pope and all the Church; therefore, I do not follow the line adopted by the Patriotic Association, [which has declared its independence from the Holy See]." Later some priests came to tell me that I had said something that I should not have said. Another priest published an article in which he sustained that the pope had not been wise and that it was reckless of him to have made me archbishop of Canton.

Peking, in its turn, issued a declaration, and the Patriotic Association attacked the pope everywhere. Some had begun to worry, but I feared nothing. I thought that the Patriotic Association and the Office for Religious Affairs were none other than the poison inherited by the "Gang of Four."[65] Even before I returned to Hong Kong, without even investigating or giving me the possibility of speaking and defending myself, they decided without delay to deny me the appointment of archbishop at Canton.

---

[65] The Gang of Four—Jiang Qing, Mao's widow, his fourth and last wife; Zhang Chunqiao, Yao Wenyuan, and Wang Hongwen—are the four Communist leaders who dominated the political scene in China during the Cultural Revolution, in the shadow of Mao Zedong. They were arrested shortly after the death of Mao, which occurred on September 9, 1976, and were tried at the end of 1980.

Dominic Tang, S.J.

Attempts at Negotiation with China

On March 1, 1981, Cardinal Agostino Casaroli, the [Vatican] secretary of state, asked me to get in touch with the government of Peking, in the hope that China and the Vatican would establish diplomatic relations. With Casaroli's consent, I took Father John Tong as my assistant.

We succeeded in contacting the representative of the government of Peking at Hong Kong and presented our proposal. He responded that the opinion I expressed on China in the newspapers constituted a type of pressure, and as a result, the time was not yet ripe for a dialogue. In reality I had said that the Church is, at the same time, independent and not independent, in the sense that the local Church is, yes, independent but in communion with the universal Church. In other words, the Church in China, like the other local churches, belongs to the same Church and is in communion with the pope. This is what we understand when we say that there is only one flock and one shepherd.

Attempts to contact the government were also made through Protestant channels, but without any positive results. Father John Tong thought of offering scholarships to students as a way of facilitating the dialogue with the Chinese government (the Episcopal Conference of the Low Countries, in fact, had promised scholarships for Chinese students). Unfortunately in that moment the relations between the Vatican and China were tense; furthermore there were not good relations between China and the Low Countries (the Low Countries had sold some submarines to Taiwan).

In order to set in motion a possible dialogue with China, the Vatican would have had to prohibit all the activities of the religious congregations, which were considered disturbing by China's government. Then the Vatican would have had to demote some influential persons, such as Father Michael Zhu Lide, and conversely, promote others, favorable to China. The activities of the Catholic Church that are considered interfering by the Chinese government include the sending of money, books, or visitors to the Catholics of the clandestine Church.

The Communist government claimed that the Vatican's connection to Taiwan was a less important matter and that they hoped to present this point of view to the secretary of the Vatican State. Out of a desire for reconciliation between China and the Church I was disposed to anything. I wrote a letter to the government in which I said: "For unity between the mother country and the Church I would decline the title of archbishop." But that offer also did not produce any response on the part of the government.

In the following year, 1982, I was informed that two officials had gone to the wife of my cousin at Canton. They had asked how I was, and they said that they wished to be put in contact with me. The wife of my cousin informed me that if I desired, I could write a letter to the officials saying: "At Hong Kong everything is okay." That would mean that I intended to get in contact with them.

I wrote what was asked of me, and I sent the letter to the wife of my cousin, who showed it to the officials. They told her that the government intended to have me at Canton again; they knew that I had experience with running the schools and that I knew seven languages. They said to her: "We gave him permission to go to Hong Kong for medical treatment, but he went to Rome!"

The wife of my cousin explained: "He acted according to the laws of the Church. After some years of work, the Church requires the bishop to go to Rome to make an account of his work. He did not go to speak of your responsibilities. Did you feel that he had spoken of you?"

They responded: "No, we did not think that he was speaking of us." Then they said: "Let us leave the things of the past to the past!" They returned January 4, 1983.

I imagine that when the two officials said that they wished me back at Canton to open and run the schools, it was a trap. In reality they wished me to direct a seminary. In fact, at that time, the Chinese government was thinking of opening some seminaries at Peking and in other places.

Attempts at negotiations were also made at higher levels. In May 1984 a delegation was sent, in my name, to Peking to meet the director of the Department of the United Front; the encounter was held at the Office for Religious Affairs of the Council of State. At the end the government of Peking maintained that it was not yet opportune to establish relations with the Vatican.

In summary, they said:

1. Concerning the matter of [Mr.] Tang Yi-ming, there is nothing more to say.

2. Regarding the question of Taiwan, China does not yet intend to establish relations with the Vatican.

3. Mother Teresa may visit China; she may not come here to work.[66]

4. The writings of Ladany[67] distort the facts; they are foolishness.

A proverb says: "Man proposes; God disposes." I did all that was in my power to improve relations between China and the Vatican, but perhaps God has another plan.

The Last Thirteen Years, between Hong Kong and the World

In 1983, once I reached seventy-five years of age, I presented my resignation as archbishop of Canton to Cardinal Agnelo Rossi, Prefect of the Congregation for the Propagation of the Faith, according to what was established by the *Code of Canon Law*. The response I received was that the document *Christus Dominus* did not regard me and that I must continue to be archbishop of the Diocese of Canton.

As more time passed, it became clearer that the possibility of my return to Canton was very uncertain. I decided to remain at Hong Kong. After

[66] Mother Teresa had long wished to be able to establish her nuns on Chinese territory. At some point she seemed about to accomplish it, so that on October 4, 2005, the daily *Avvenire* published my article with the title "The Sisters of Teresa at China's Door." In it, the superior at the time explained that the Missionaries of Charity intended to open a house of charity in China [but] at the invitation of the government.

[67] As recorded in the introduction to this book, *Laszlo Ladany* (1914–1990) was a Hungarian Jesuit who published *China News Analysis*, a prestigious newsletter, containing information and opinions on what was happening in the People's Republic of China and which was very influential abroad.

the convalescence I spent at the home of Mrs. Ruby Tang, my sister-in-law, I moved to the college of Wah Yan in Kowloon, where I had an office.

After having been deprived of information on the Church for twenty-four years, one of the first things I did was to document recent developments in the Church in order to become current with the actual situation.

During these thirteen years, thanks to the help of God, I was engaged in a variety of pastoral works.

Many visitors, who were worried about my situation and desirous of having first-hand information about the Church of China, came to see me. Not only people of Hong Kong, but many religious and laity outside Hong Kong were interested in my experience. I was invited to visit them and to give an account of my life in China. Thus, I began a series of trips to various parts of the world, including Japan, Southeast Asia, Australia, Europe, the United States, and Canada.

Usually, the persons I met on these trips included the bishops and the nuncio (the papal representative) of the country, priests, religious orders (both male and female), laymen, and people of every type: from the more notable Chinese of the various places to the Chinese students abroad. Besides interviews, I was usually asked to hold conferences or to converse with various groups. The principal content of my speeches regarded the situation of the Church in China from 1949 to the present; I shared my concrete experience with them, through which I was able to clarify many points of view about the Church in China.

Catholics everywhere, but especially the Chinese abroad, gave a generous response to my appeal to support the brothers and sisters in China who are suffering for the Faith.

I did the same thing at Hong Kong. At times I preached retreats to priests and religious, and I presided over liturgical celebrations in the parishes. And wherever possible, I tried to help the priests and the Catholics of Canton.

On this, the occasion of the fiftieth anniversary of my priestly ordination and the fortieth of my episcopal ordination, I have had the joy of receiving a letter and a blessing from the Holy Father (John Paul II).

Above: Monsignor Antonio Riberi, apostolic internuncio in China from 1946 to 1959. On April 13, 1947, he consecrated Father Gaetano Pollio, a member of the Pontifical Institute for Foreign Missions (Pime), archbishop of Kaifeng.

Below: The cathedral of Kaifeng, the diocese entrusted to Monsignor Pollio. In 1948 (a year before the foundation of the People's Republic of China) Kaifeng was the first provincial capital to fall under Communist domination.

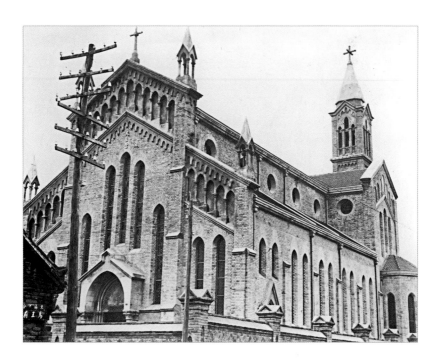

Above: Monsignor Pollio with a group of girls of the Legion of Mary, a Catholic association widely diffused throughout China and, for this reason, strongly opposed by the Communist regime.

Left: Exploiting the term *legion*, the Maoist propaganda presented the Legion of Mary with military symbolism.

From the left: Father Amelio Crotti, Monsignor Gaetano Pollio, Father Edoardo Piccinini and Brother Francesco Quartieri, all members of Pime. On Sunday, April 1, 1951, Monsignor Pollio was arrested together with Piccinini and Quartieri; the following day, Crotti, pastor of the cathedral of Kaifeng was arrested. They remained in jail until the beginning of October. During this period, Pollio was accused of at least eighty crimes. He submitted to numerous trials, always at night, each one lasting several hours.

The persecution of the Maoists toward some "counterrevolutionaries" preceded the celebration of the "peoples' trials," farcical procedures during which the victims were falsely accused of crimes that were never committed. Those charged were detained under the most precarious conditions and often mercilessly executed (facing page).

Left: Between the end of the 1940s and the beginning of the 1950s, the foreign missionaries in China, often accused of "imperialism," were expelled from the country. Some of these took refuge in Hong Kong (then a British colony); others returned to the West.

Below: Three Canadian nuns, liberated from detention and expelled from China, reenact the conditions of their imprisonment.

Above: During the sixties the portrait of Mao dominated the façade of the cathedral of Canton (today Guangzhou), a majestic construction in the neo-Gothic style. The cathedral was reopened for worship in 1979.

Below, left: Bishop Dominic Tang Yi-ming, a Jesuit, was nominated apostolic administrator of the Diocese of Canton by the pope. After being imprisoned for twenty-two years, he was liberated in 1980 and named archbishop of Canton the following year.

Below, right: Teresa, the wife of John Liao Shouji, poses next to the photo of her husband, who died July 30, 1989, and the first Italian edition of his twenty-two-year prison diary.

Maoism tries to promote the cult of the Great Helmsman (Mao) as the new religion for all the Chinese. This vignette depicts exponents of various social categories united by the same ideology. Paraphrasing from the book of Revelation, the caption that accompanies it reads: "New heavens and new lands, because the first world has disappeared."

新　天　新　地

我看見了一片新天新地，因為先前的天地已經過去了。

Father Leon Chan, a priest from Hong Kong, was active in continental China until the end of the 1950s. He managed to flee the mainland in 1962, after many years in prison, and was one of the first to bear witness to the real situation of the country under Mao's regime.

JOHN LIAO
SHOUJI

INTRODUCTION

"I recall that Jesus himself arrived at the Resurrection only after he completed the ascent of Calvary, carrying the cross on the Via Dolorosa.
Why should I, a follower of Christ, expect something different?... So
I began to transform my fears into something positive, to cultivate love
as the purpose of my life, learning to suffer with my divine Lord for the
Church in China, for the universal Church, [and] for all humanity." With
these words pronounced before five thousand Christians gathered in
Singapore, John Liao Shouji—protagonist of the story you are about to
read—summarizes the sense of his more than twenty years of detention
because of his faith.

That encounter took place a few years before his death at Macao on
July 30, 1989, during a Eucharistic celebration, which also included the
presence of his wife, Teresa. Presiding over the Mass, in the Church of St.
Francis Xavier at Coloane, was Don Mario Acquistapace, an Italian Salesian
priest who, a good thirty-three years before, at Peking, had accompanied
Liao Shouji on his journey of faith: from the Protestant Church, in which
he had been baptized, to the Catholic Church. As will then be explained,
the "conditional" baptism was administered by Don Carlo Braga, the superior of the Salesians in China.[68]

---

[68] This information was acquired by Father Mario Marazzi, a missionary
of Pime stationed at Hong Kong, who was in contact with Teresa Liao,
John's wife. Thus, she herself related the circumstances of her husband's
death: "John had read the first reading, and then with his vibrant voice
joined some others in singing some hymns. During the thanksgiving at the

DIARIES OF THE CHINESE MARTYRS

A Tormented Love Story

This testimony's exceptionality derives from the fact that it has been handed down by a layman, a rare occurrence in the history of the persecution of the Church in China. Making it unique is the fact that this prison diary narrates, in a very delicate manner, his love story with Teresa, the woman who, after a long odyssey, would become his wife. "I noticed that Teresa was very simple and very devout, a little different from the rest of her family.... But I tended to keep my distance from girls who were very pious and who seemed destined for the consecrated life." But then in 1956 this love story took on new momentum when charges were levied against Liao (John) and Teresa intervened in a completely unexpected way in the defense of her friend.

What follows was the rapid evolution of their feelings toward each other, from generic affection to more solid ties. In 1956 Liao found the courage to declare his love to Teresa, but she confessed that she had taken a vow of virginity. They then made the painful decision not to see each other. But Liao did not forget his beloved, and he decided to entrust the cause to Our Lady. John's prayer was heard: sometime later he learned that Teresa, in a discussion with her spiritual director, obtained a formal dispensation from her vow of virginity. But at that time the political situation was coming to a head. "With the specter of persecution on the horizon, it was not the right moment to plan a future together: on this Teresa and I were agreed. It was necessary to join our spiritual resources and to be ready: if God's will for me was to face another arrest and another imprisonment, I would have accepted it." Long years of persecution, physical and psychological suffering would pass before the two were able to crown their dream. (They would marry hurriedly years later, just before Teresa was able to leave China.) Meanwhile, John, who had already known prison and was suffering from

---

Communion, while he was kneeling, he suddenly fainted. The celebrant administered the sacrament of the sick. A doctor was called, but by then it was too late."

rheumatism, was sent to a laogai [a Chinese gulag][69] in an area where the climatic conditions were particularly harsh. It should have made him crazy, but Liao's faith, although tested in a thousand ways, great and small, remained firm. The pages that follow are a precise documentation of this fact.

The Beauty of Winter

Father Bernardo Cervellera, the current director of *AsiaNews* and author of the preface of this book, presents the case of John Liao as a metaphor that "challenges China's glacial air: In the frigid winter of Hubei, from branches that seem dried up and lifeless and with stems tough like stone, gray buds pop up, like wrinkled, woolly larva shells. The Chinese call them *dongmei*, 'the beauty of winter,' and they use them in various flower arrangements. The beauty of winter: There is no other way to describe the story of Liao and his twenty-two years in prison and forced labor. Like the ice flower, the style of this book is dry and harsh; poetry and sentiment are absent." This motif explains the author very well: "After twenty years of prison and labor camp and the suppression of each emotion that accompanies the experience, one nearly loses the capacity of feeling any sensation beyond that of merely bearing whatever it happens to be at that moment. One becomes insensible, nearly deprived of emotion for whatever is happening; in an already negative situation, even bad news was relative. It is the natural process of immunization that makes survival possible."

[69] The forced-labor camps were called with the euphemism *laogai* (reeducation through work). The prisoners worked in the uncultivated peripheral zones that required tilling, or in factories or mines, et cetera. Besides exploiting the condemned as manual labor at the lowest price, the authorities were set on changing their mentality by conquering their psychological resistance. An article published at Hong Kong in the magazine *Jiushi niandai* (August 1990, pp. 22–23; reproduced in *Inside Mainland China*, Taipei, September 1990) estimates that fifty million persons in China passed through the labor camps during the 1950s. See also Charles Lane, Dorina Elliot, Frank Gibney Jr., Ann McDaniel, Marcus Mabry, and Melinda Liu, "The Last Gulag," *Newsweek*, September 23, 1991, 16–21.

Father Cervellera continues:

Like the stem of the dongmei, the body of John Liao Shouji had lost flexibility: severe back pain (ankylosing spondylitis) had afflicted him from his student days. Life in the laogai accelerated the course, fusing some of the vertebrae. For the rest of his life Liao lived with severe pain in his joints and his shoulders. His spine, having been shortened by ten centimeters, was nearly immovable. But he, like the dongmei, knew how to sweeten the harsh winter: the young girl in prison with him, who became his wife, remembers his songs, the choral hymns of the cathedral of Canton (of which Liao was the director) that cheered the prisoners, especially the Christians. The guards and the doctors were stunned by his patience and goodness; his companions noted that he neither accused anyone nor spied on anyone.

Physical Fatigue and Psychological Pressure

Yet Liao was living a true hell. At a certain point he was taken to Niutoukeng to work excavating stone, an operation that was carried out entirely by hand, without any mechanical help. The bestial fatigue and constant danger was a lethal cocktail that annihilated most.

But the physical suffering, although notable, was not the worst. One reads in Liao's diary: "More oppressive than the low levels of material life were the human and psychological difficulties. In the prisons and in the labor camps were convicts of all criminal types.... One could not trust anyone. The prisoners were encouraged to foment disorder, to spy, to lie, and to do whatever they could to benefit themselves."

As a result, the prisoner John Liao Shouji was subjected to excruciating emotional leveling, a sort of human reduction; but on the same theme—in virtue of the Faith—he developed a providential capacity to adapt to the worst situations. "Because I became accustomed to every type of injustice," he observed, "I was not able to experience feelings; in similar situations one becomes incapable of reacting in a normal way; it is a type of providential safeguard that makes you capable of accepting things as they develop."

The Moral Devastation of Communism

John Liao is a direct witness of the moral devastation produced by the Communist regime's various "ideological campaigns," those launched from time to time to eliminate some of the presumed enemies of the Revolution. Emblematic is the case of his sister, who lost her job and nearly her husband for having responded positively to the question "Do you think that the Chinese farmers suffer from too much work and insufficient food?" As a result, together with the fact that her husband tried to divorce her, she was forced to seek day work as a street sweeper. "When the children are ill and there is no money in the house, you sell your blood in order to obtain what you need. These personal tragedies occurred on a national scale."

From time to time the author critiques his own experiences with Communism and its contradictions. We read, for example: "In the totalitarian regimes the party is the supreme master that hides itself behind lies, such as that of being the servant of the people, when in fact it enslaves them, reserving all powers to itself.... Under such regimes there is not much difference between life in prison, life at work in a labor camp, and life outside: all are slaves of authority, and all are manipulated by the Communist Party."

Foreign Missionaries and Chinese Priests Witness Together

In Liao's diary we find many other worthy points of interest. Very intense, for example, is a passage in which the author describes the fury of the regime against the foreign missionaries. These missionaries, he writes, "decided to remain in spite of everything and to continue to serve the Chinese people with their institutions, even if they were eventually confiscated by the state." "To serve the people" is not a casual expression: it also became, in time, one of the favorite slogans of the Maoist propaganda. Liao utilizes it in its literal sense as a gesture of gratitude toward the missionaries and their sacrifices: it is a passage that uplifts hearts.

While speaking of Liao's affection for the European missionaries, one must also mention his sincere love for Bishop Tang, whom we have already encountered in this book. Liao bestows an indelible tribute upon this courageous pastor: "In 1952 all the foreign missionaries were expelled from China, and Rome nominated Monsignor Dominic Tang bishop of the diocese. Under his strong leadership and profound spirituality, the Church of that city was pervaded by a new spirit.... Religious fervor grew, and the Church of Canton became truly united: the Catholics of every parish ... shared a lively faith and were united around their bishop as his flock and his support."

Equally infectious is the limpid example of faith and tenacity that Liao witnesses in Father Tan Tiande, a courageous priest of Canton, who spent thirty years in hard forced labor before he was liberated in 1983; he died in 2009 at the age of ninety-three. He was one of the most esteemed personalities of the Diocese of Guangzhou. Cardinal Zen said that "Father Tan was so well known and esteemed by the faithful of Hong Kong that many of them would travel to the nearby city of Canton to see him. Our faithful are continuously edified by his strength and his serenity." John Liao said: "Those are precisely the same attitudes that impressed me when I met him in 2005. Of him I recall the impassioned description that he gave us of the prison, of the terrible cold and the gnawing hunger (in order to survive he ate the bark of the trees). But, in particular I recall his mildness. He had no bitterness or hatred toward his persecutors; there was no desire for revenge. He was a man of exceptional temperament, like many of the protagonists of these and other 'diaries' of Chinese martyrs."

In closing, we must cite a moving message that Teresa Liao, John's wife, gave to Father Marazzi, informing him of the republication of her husband's diary: "As I shared the memories of his life, his friends, and his classmates, I got to know him better. The more I spoke of him, the more I admired him. In the years we spent together, John was not only the companion of my life, but also my teacher. Although more than twenty-five years have passed since his death, I am sure that he prays that my life may be filled, like his, with the love for God and for others. I do not cease thanking God for the gift that John was for me."

MY LIFE IN THE LIVING HELL OF THE CHINESE LAOGAI

A Diary of a Chinese Catholic

The Story of My Conversion

My father was a practicing Methodist, but in God's providential plan and solely through his merit, I came to know the true Church of Christ, the Catholic Church. In 1946 I was studying civil engineering at Lingnam University. Although I was only eighteen, I suffered from rheumatism contracted through the conditions of life experienced during the Sino-Japanese War, just recently over, and I was advised to seek a medical cure at Peking. My parents, although both Protestant, were close friends with Father Carlo Braga, the superior of the Salesians in China, a priest for whom my father had the greatest esteem; I recall papa speaking admiringly of the great number of conversions that this zealous priest had made in our city. When it was decided that I would conclude my studies at Peking, rather than in the province, Father Braga informed my father that his congregation had a house at Shanghai and that I could always count on the help of his confreres in that city and anywhere else on my journey to Peking.

At the time of my departure, the Sino-Japanese War had just ended, and it was difficult to organize travel; I was fortunate to have been able to count on the help of the Catholic mission of Shanghai; indeed, I was included in a party of priests who were about to leave Shanghai for Peking.

DIARIES OF THE CHINESE MARTYRS

We began our journey around December 5. It was very cold, the temperature often falling below zero. By December 8 we had nearly reached our goal, and we made our last nightly stop at Tianjin. That evening the party invited me to a feast. Making up this group were seven Italian missionaries and four or five Chinese Catholics of the province of Hunan. Although I had no idea of the purpose for this gathering, I accepted promptly in order not to offend the kindness of the priest who invited me.

Father Marcello Glustich, who was newly ordained, asked me, speaking English, to participate at the celebration of the feast of Our Lady by reciting a prayer; because, he said, "You know how to read English!" I accepted, and I recited the Hail Holy Queen in English to the great joy of those present, so that at the end they greeted me with "Bravo, bravo!" Most likely, it was on that occasion that I was given the gift of faith, and my entrance into the Catholic Church was opened to me; that entrance occurred exactly one year later on the same day.

The following morning we reached Peking, where we separated: the priests to their studies and to the practical business of opening a school in the city, and I to find a remedy for my illness. Father Marcello spoke to me of grace and prayer; he knew that, as a Protestant, I had already accepted the fundamental doctrine of the Christian faith, and he seemed to be aware that I was already receiving the necessary grace that would give me the fullness of the Faith in the Catholic Church. Two weeks later, on Christmas Eve, the superior, Father Braga, invited me, the Italian priests, and some Catholic students of Canton to participate in the celebration of midnight Mass. In the hours preceding the Mass we played bingo, and I recall that this was my rudimentary introduction to the study of Italian: after listening to the repetition of the numbers on the board, I became aware that I had nearly learned how to count to one hundred in Italian.

From 1946 to 1947 I was occupied with medical appointments, but, after a year, I discovered that there was no true remedy for my illness. I was advised to do physical exercises, get fresh air, and be attentive to my diet, but above all to maintain a positive attitude and to proceed with my studies. I wrote to my mother that it was useless for them to maintain me at Peking, and I asked her what they wished me to do. My mother gave me the liberty to remain there, suggesting that I not waste time, but begin a course of study in a reputable school. At that time, however—it was October 1947—the courses had already begun, so I went to see Father Braga and asked him if he could help me. He contacted the head of Furen University,[70] a Catholic institution, and, without consulting me, enrolled me in a course of Western languages and cultures. It was a total and unexpected change from the engineering course that I had been taking at Lingnam University; but, since I had not intended to apply myself seriously, I agreed to it; I was interested only in keeping myself occupied in doing something useful and interesting.

Each Sunday I went to the house of the priests with whom I had come to Peking, because by now they had become my friends. Nothing could have been barer than their home. When Antonio Riberi, the internuncio in China, visited that house during his trips to China, his secretary, Monsignor Giuseppe Caprio, revealed to Father Braga that, although Monsignor Riberi had traveled throughout the world and had seen religious orders in every country, he had never seen a house in such a state of poverty.

During all this time, Mary, the help of Christians, led me back to the way of the truth. Father Mario Acquistapace accompanied me on this path of preparation for baptism, which was administered to me on December 8, 1947, under conditions set by Father Braga. The baptism took place before the Mass and I made my first Communion during that same celebration. Exactly three years later Cardinal Tian, the first Chinese cardinal confirmed me.

---

[70] The University of Furen of Peking was one of the three Catholic universities of China; the other two were in Shanghai and Tianjin. Furen University was founded by the Benedictine Congregation of Montecasino of America and was inaugurated on September 26, 1927. In 1933 the management passed to the Society of the Divine Word. After the sequester by the Communists, in 1963 the university was reopened in Taipei (Taiwan) in collaboration among the secular clergy, the Jesuits, and the members of the Society of the Divine Word.

DIARIES OF THE CHINESE MARTYRS

The Situation in China at the Advent of Mao

At that time, from a political viewpoint, China was going through a period of great instability. In 1948 the People's Army of the Communist liberation occupied Manchuria and all Northeast China and by the end of the year controlled all of China. Their divisions entered China through the Great Wall and the Nationalist soldiers of Guomindang,[71] guided by Chiang Kai-shek (Jiang Jieshi) were incapable of offering a successful opposition. Tianjin was occupied by the Communist forces that then advanced toward Peking.

The general entrusted with the defense of Peking was Fu Zuoyi, a native of Inner Mongolia who was not very faithful to Chiang Kai-shek, so [in the end] he decided to negotiate with the leaders of the Red Army; and after two or three months he arrived at a peaceful agreement for the liberation of Peking. Many important officials of Guomindang decided then to leave China. At first they withdrew from the principal cities, going first to Canton, then to Hong Kong, then to Taiwan, and from there to the United States. I, along with many others and with the student population, took note of what was happening. The Chinese people, with much simplicity, hoped that whatever had taken place would bring an improvement. Two correspondents from foreign press agencies shrewdly emphasized that the Chinese people had always accepted their conquerors and their warlords. The Communists, proclaiming that theirs would be a true liberation, much different from any invasion in the past, expelled them.

In February of 1949 the People's Liberation Army entered Peking, taking "peaceful" possession of the city; Mao Zedong approached the city standing up in a motor vehicle, cheered on by the victorious forces. At the same time the Communist soldiers were taking control of the entire

---

[71] The Nationalist Party, or Zhongguo Guomindang, is the name that was given to the Revolutionary Chinese Party in 1919. It was the protagonist of the unification of China during the years 1926 to 1927, the only party governing China from 1927 to 1949, and the adversary of the Communist Chinese Party in the political-military struggle from 1946 to 1949, by which it was defeated.

country as quickly as "breaking a bamboo stick in two," because after the first cut, the bamboo breaks quickly and completely. In May the liberation army crossed the Yangtze River from the north to the south, occupying the provinces of Hubei and Hunan; in October Canton, the principal city of the south of China, was taken. Until November the Red Army was engaged in trouncing the last remnant of the forces of the Guomindang. The entire country, with the exception of Tibet in the southwest and Taiwan, fell into the hands of the Communists. China was now under the control of new masters.

In March to April of 1949 the Communists were preparing to draft a new constitution and to form a consultative assembly, replacing that of the preceding Nationalist government. Those with academic qualifications were invited to help with this work. Among them was the rector of the Catholic University of Furen at Peking, Professor Chen Yuan, a non-Catholic expert of religions, especially of the history of religions in China. He came from the province of Guangdong and had studied during the dynasty of Qing in the nineteenth century. He was an expert in the history of the monks of the Siro-Oriental church and of their arrival in China from the Middle East and Persia. In Hunan he had identified a fragment of stone with the most ancient inscriptions of Christian-Syrian symbols in China.[72]

When the People's Liberation Army approached Peking, Rector Chen was invited by a representative of the Guomindang, an ex-ambassador to the United States, to leave Peking and China along with many high officials who were fleeing. Chen refused this offer and his decision led the Communists to retain him as rector of the university. But by then he was elderly and had little influence.

---

[72] The reference is to the celebrated Stone of Xi'an. The first Christians whose arrival in China is documented were a group of monks of the Sino-Oriental Church who originated from the Middle East and were received by the emperor Taizhong in 635. After a period of liberty, during which they were able to spread out into many places in the empire, in 845 the Christians were struck with an imperial decree that prohibited foreign religions. They survived in China for some centuries and then disappeared.

DIARIES OF THE CHINESE MARTYRS

Tensions with the Communists at the University

At this point it is necessary to explain a characteristic of student life at that time: in China, unlike many other countries, the students had had a considerable influence on political life. The majority of the population, which had been deprived of academic instruction, gave great importance to those who had had this privilege. At the same time, China had not had the opportunity to evolve politically and economically like the Western countries, which had passed from the barbaric epoch to feudalism to capitalism. Furthermore, China had not yet had an industrial revolution. Therefore, the Marxist theory of the progressive advancement of society could not apply to China. In other countries, such as Poland, the workers had organized in unions and had significant influence; but in China the workers were ignorant peasants, who had no power because they had been deprived of an education.

Among the many university student organizations, the League of Young Communists had the most influence and controlled all the student activities. We had a Catholic Students Association. Each department elected two representatives who, in turn, chose a president and a vice president. It was an important association, since it was also a point of referral for the junior high and high school students, male and female: whatever position the Catholic students took, the students of the lower schools followed. I was elected a representative. Because the goal of the Young Communist League was to control all the students, the rapport between the two associations became very tense. In 1950 I was elected president of the Catholic Association. The principal objective of the Catholic Students Association was Christian formation. At the beginning of the semester there was a meeting welcoming new students; at Christmas there was a party and, at the end of the year, a farewell celebration for the graduates. Our chaplain was a Chinese priest, Father Sun.[73]

---

[73] Father Sun Jinsheng, born in 1903, entered the Society of the Divine Word and was sent to Rome to study. After he returned to China he carried out various assignments. In 1949 he was nominated the superior of the

Some of our departments, such as science and foreign languages, had superb professors and an elevated level of teaching. One of our professors was for a certain period in the same school as Mao Zedong in Hunan, at Changsha, and he knew some of the principal Communist leaders very well.

Then, toward August of 1950, the United Front[74] and the Office for Religious Affairs sent some of their own members to our university. These commissars also met with the medical doctor who looked after the health of the students. He was originally from Inner Mongolia and belonged to an old Catholic family. I received a message from him, asking me to meet with him; at his house he showed me a document that he had been asked to sign: it was a [form] that the Catholics at every level at the university (teachers, students, laboratory assistants, and other workers) had [to sign] and return to the Communist government as proof that the university was loyal to the country and to the Communist regime. The name of the above-mentioned professor and the medical doctor were already written on the document together with a certain Wang, one of the clerks in the library who belonged to an ancient Catholic family, but who was somewhat favorable to the new government.

The professor asked me to sign the document and to gather the signatures of the other Catholic students. I presented the petition to our chaplain, Father Sun, who suggested that I show it to the rector, Father Rigney, an American.[75] He read the document and copied it, including the signatures, but without making comments; he only asked me what I thought the students would think of it. I then consulted all the depart-

---

Community of the Divine Word at Peking. He was arrested in 1951 and condemned to forced labor. He died around 1975.

[74] The Department of the United Front is the organization of the Chinese Communist Party that formulates the political agenda regarding the non-Communist entities (ethnic minorities, political parties, religions, the Chinese abroad, etc.).

[75] Father Harold Rigney, a missionary of the Society of the Divine Word, was rector of the University of Furen. In 1951 he was arrested, and after a long prison term was expelled from China.

ment heads; all of them, one after the other, refused to sign and to make a similar request [of the students]. After a few days I returned the petition to the professor without a single signature.

Later, the representatives of the government discovered that I had consulted Father Rigney and that I had shown him the document, and this was one of the "crimes" with which I would be charged in 1955: that I had "worked for the imperialists," even though as president of the Catholic Students Association I was obligated to consult the administration before making decisions. At that time, however, the Office for Religious Affairs did not dare to push anyone any further or press charges against those who had refused to sign.

During the winter vacations of 1951 the Communists took formal control of our university: they said that it was no longer necessary that foreigners administer this university, since the Chinese were capable of managing their own affairs. The immediate result, however, was not what the government had hoped: the foreign missionaries, in fact, decided to remain anyway and to continue to serve the Chinese population with their teaching, even if their properties had been confiscated. Therefore, more steps were necessary: first, the period of house arrests and then the expulsion of all the foreign missionaries.

In some isolated cases single individuals were accused of presumed crimes, which were reported in the newspapers; but in the majority of the cases the missionaries were simply expelled without justifications. All the institutions dedicated to charitable activities toward the blind, the orphans, the sick, and the elderly were passed on to the government. In certain cases even very young children were used to testify against the missionaries; having been either goaded or forced to participate at the public encounters, they served to present false accusations against the foreigners.

An example is the case of Dr. Mo,[76] who was a consultant at one of the largest hospitals in Peking and at an orphanage managed by nuns.

---

[76] Mo Xingling, one of the brothers of Teresa Mo, whom we cited in the introduction.

Given that the little children were taught to lie, he told the residents of the orphanage that each one of them had a conscience to follow and that they were not free to testify to deeds that they had not seen with their own eyes. He was very courageous and upright, but he paid dearly. Two or three years later, after returning from a trip to Hong Kong, as soon as the train reached its destination, he was arrested without warning. His family did not receive any explanation or information until five or six months later, when he wrote to them from prison: he had been condemned to fifteen years for having collaborated with the religious imperialists. A few months before the end of his sentence, when the Cultural Revolution was at its height, at a gathering of prisoners he was accused publicly and ordered to bow his head in recognition of his crimes. He refused to admit any wrongdoing, and, as a consequence, a large stone was tied at his neck in order to force him to lower his head. He died several days later as a result of this torture.

The particulars of his death were discovered by one of his sons, who went from Peking to the labor camp in the province of Shanxi, where his father had been a prisoner. The authorities refused, however, to give him any information or hand over any of his personal effects. Moreover, they advised him not to associate himself with his father, who, they said, had decided to separate himself from the people. In fact, all of Dr. Mo's work for the poor was voluntary and gratis. Only after several attempts did the son manage to find a low-level official who led him to where his father was buried. A few months later, together with one of his brothers, he returned to Shanxi to bring home his father's remains.

Immediately after the Communist "liberation," all those who were at the head of an institution suffered the same type of persecution, with the same ritual. In the following thirty years this was the general policy. When the Communists believed that the moment had arrived to act against an individual or group, first and foremost, the leaders prepared a declaration of charges against the designated victim, and someone, often a child, was chosen to act as the accuser: some little children were taken, often from an orphanage, to a school or university or the like and ordered, usually under compulsion, to play a part. They recited their part well and, when the accuser was ready to discharge his task, the public trial was organized, during which the various charges were expressed. This was the political method of the "Mass Line" (the political, organizational, and leadership method developed by Mao Zedong and the Chinese Communist Party during the Chinese Revolution), in which the people seemed to be asking the questions and the government following the will of the masses. The last part of the charges always followed the same scheme: a request that the government arrest the accused on the basis of the law and inflict the appropriate penalties. The presiding judge at these popular tribunals responded to the charges and to the requests "in the name and on behalf of the government of the people, and in accordance with the will of the people"; then he punished the criminal with a sentence. For the foreigners the penalty was usually expulsion; but for the Chinese it was prison or forced labor in the camps.

Even in the labor camps these popular trials were marked by this performance. Persons such as Dr. Mo were isolated and forced to confess their "crimes" before the public, lowering their head as a sign of surrender and repentance. Those who were willing to do it passed the test, but those who refused and declared their innocence were treated brutally and tortured.

Also sixty or seventy Chinese priests from the various provinces who were completing advanced studies at the Catholic University at Peking were put under house arrest so that their activities and their influence could be monitored. Some were detained for a few months, without being able to celebrate Mass or to have any liberty of movement, and they were interrogated every day.

A last example will serve to complete the picture that became commonplace after the "liberation." At the beginning of the fall semester of 1950 our Catholic Students Association organized the usual excursion, choosing a historical place north of Peking, about ten kilometers from the city. After the visit, the meal, and the recitation of the Rosary in the church, we were visited in the late afternoon by the chief of police of that district, who asked who was responsible for our group. The vice president and I, as president, had to follow two policemen. We were told that, according to witnesses, the students had proclaimed reactionary slogans in the dining room, but no one said which slogans. After our scheduled return to Peking the police continued to interrogate us for more than an hour, and, when they permitted other students to leave, we were detained further, together with the priest who had accompanied us; the priest also worked in a parish and was the chaplain for the Legion of Mary. Until two in the morning they interrogated us on the reasons and intentions of our excursion, and then they informed us that we had to return to the city by foot since there was no means of public transportation at that hour. We arrived at dawn. The students were indignant for the treatment they had been subjected to, but we were already aware then that it was useless to complain about a representative of the Communist government. In 1955, when I was arrested the first time, this episode was held against me as one of my crimes. The Communists did not spare any effort in sifting through past history to find something that could be used against someone.

In the Legion of Mary

I was introduced to the Legion of Mary in 1949, and I joined a group that formed at our university and became president. The goal of the Legion of Mary was to spread the kingdom of God and to safeguard the purity of the Faith. It was a purely religious organization, with a spiritual goal, under the special protection of Our Lady and officially recognized by the Church. There had never been any connection with political movements, and to make this clear after the "liberation" and to distinguish it further from certain secret groups under Guomindang that combated Communism, the name was changed from the Legion of Mary to "Groups of prayer and love for Mary." This variation of names was an attempt to avoid any possibility of confusion. We used the same manual as the members of the Legion of Mary throughout the world, written by the founder of the movement, Frank Duff. We met each week for a spiritual conversation, for some prayers and for assigning tasks: visits to the sick in the hospital, to the needy, and to non-practicing Catholics, et cetera.

The Legion attracted only the most fervent Catholics, those who were prepared to dedicate all the time necessary to the works of the association. For this reason the Legion of Mary was one of the first Catholic organizations to be persecuted after the "liberation," and we were fully aware of the danger we were approaching by our participation. We expected to be the first objects of attack. Therefore, the head of our group decided that it was better temporarily to disband our group. In many cases the Legion was considered a type of political anti-Communist refuge; the government of Guomindang considered us on a par with other groups classified as reactionary and superstitious. Therefore, the Legion was declared illegal, and belonging to it was considered a crime.

Each member had to report to the Office of Public Safety to fill out a form specifying how much time he dedicated to the Legion and what type of antisocial activities he had carried out; then, voluntarily renouncing his membership, he would have to accept whatever type of penalty was imposed on him by the government. We refused to do it, and we refused to admit that the Legion was against the society of the country or that it had political or imperialist connotations. At the time of my first arrest in 1955, rather than accept these charges, I defended my membership in the Legion and defended its nonpolitical character; the personal crimes of its members, if there had been any, were one thing, but the Legion was another: it was a religious association and not an organization of foreign imperialism.

In 1953 a large-scale religious persecution was stirred up against the Legion of Mary. The campaign was organized in order to label all the members reactionaries; a demonstration was held with the objective of discrediting the Legion, and it used every form of propaganda to demonstrate its crimes: spying for foreign powers, gathering military and economic information, et cetera. It is necessary at this point to recall that, in the Communist ideology, the end justifies the means; objective truth and justice are not important: what counts is what serves the end. For example, at times, in order to expel the foreign missionaries the Communists would give them instructions to go to a place where arms and munitions had been deposited; then they would order the priests to move them. While they were working they would photograph them and subsequently publish the photos as obvious proof of the missionaries' illegal activities.

Also in 1953 the campaign against the Legion reached us. Canton had always been one of the last targets of these political programs because of the city's distance from the more important centers, such as Peking, Shanghai, and Nanking; these campaigns were, in fact, always spread from the center to the periphery. The offices of the police displayed huge posters inscribed with the locations for denouncing the military movement of the Legion of Mary: I advised all those who asked me about it not to do it, because, in good conscience, it was impossible to fulfill the requests of the Communists. At the same time pressure was also exerted on the "patriotic" Catholics to attempt to persuade any members of the Legion known to them to register with one of these offices. My response that we were not able to go against our conscience and denounce one another was reported to the Communists, and although it was not acted upon at that moment, one of the charges after my first arrest in 1955 was that of having incited others to go against the policies of the government: that is, by not denouncing ourselves and by not renouncing our membership in the Legion.

The government policy against those who are obstacles to them is, first, to gather all the possible information about them, going back thirty or forty years, or even to the period of their infancy and their grammar school days, using each detail that could construct some type of charges against them. Each government office has a section of this type, with personnel whose only task is to gather "useful" information of this kind. Those who, having been accused, confessed their faults, had a better chance of being punished in a lighter manner; and the fear of those who are subjected to interrogations is so great that often they are ready to admit to things that they have never done just to avoid a punishment.

Christian Experiences at Canton

Let us return to my story after I obtained my degree in the summer of 1951. Having completed our academic studies, we graduates were called to listen to discourses given by some Communist leaders and some generals, as well as the head of the Communist Party in that area, which included several provinces and districts. We would be assigned a job in that geographical area, but first it was necessary to receive some indoctrination, because we were considered insufficiently prepared on the topic of Communist political theory. We were therefore sent to the Revolutionary University of the People to study politics, economics, Marxism, and Leninism in order to be prepared to work for the new China according to the Communist ideology. Finally we were assigned various tasks; many of my friends were destined, along with me, for the Association of Sino-Soviet Friendship in our area.

During that epoch, because of some of my first experiences lived under Communism, I suffered from a certain nervous tension, which negatively influenced my health, including the worsening of my rheumatism. So I decided to ask for a temporary leave of absence in order to rest and to return to the doctor who had treated me during my years at school, in the hope that he would be able to continue to give me effective medical assistance. My sister was studying hygiene at the school of medicine and would come after school to visit and help me. In addition, each month some of the employees at the Organizational Office to which I had been assigned after the courses in the political and theoretical formation of Communism came by to visit me, bringing me some money. But my condition did not improve, and I was forced to sell everything I possessed, including my bicycle, in order to pay the doctor and to buy the medications.

At the end of 1951 I decided to leave Peking and return to the province of my origins. I had also decided that I did not want to work for the Communists. After some discussions, the authorities arranged for my transfer to the political office of my province, in a way that, when my health improved, I would be able to apply for work there in the provincial capital of Canton. This was the end of one period of my life—from 1946 to 1951—when I had lived in Peking and made many friends: now I had to abandon them. I remember very well the day I left Peking: more than twenty intimate friends came to a farewell dinner and then to the station. I was, understandably, very tense when I left for Canton accompanied by my sister.

I went first to my native city of Shaoguan to greet my parents. At that time the government was launching a new political campaign, the so-called three antis against the capitalists and the bourgeoisie (middle class). In the countryside it was carrying out an agrarian reform and the landowners were told to reduce their tenants' (peasants) rents, restoring part of what they had collected before the "liberation": earnings that the government was now defining as a form of oppression and exploitation. My parents were getting old, and they lived on the income from their property. The new laws obliged them to sell their possessions in order to pay what the government required as indemnification.

At the time of my return home, in the spring of 1952, there remained only a vegetable garden, which was taken from my parents in 1954, so that they were then left with literally nothing: not even a pair of shoes or other primary necessities. From then on my family and all the ex–property owners were subjected to every type of privation and mistreatment. My mother told me that both she and my father often thought of suicide, above all my father, who found this type of life unbearable, but fortunately their Christian faith and their trust in God impeded them from accomplishing such an action.

I remained with my parents at Shaoguan for about two weeks, and then I went to Canton, where my younger brothers and sisters were attending the university. My sister was studying nursing and in 1954 was assigned to the province of Shandong in order to work in the People's Hospital. When my younger brother completed his studies, he was sent to a second-ary school near Canton.

I had few relatives or friends at Canton, except for some relationships initiated through one of my old classmates, Margherita, who introduced me to her family when I was still a student. I went to the cathedral for Sunday Mass and sometimes to one of the parishes in the area east of the city, where I had a friend from school. In this way, little by little, I formed relationships with the bishop Dominic Tang, Father Francis Tan,[77] and

---

[77] Father Francis Tan Tiande, after having lived thirty years between prison and labor camps, took up his ministry again at the cathedral of Canton.

others. My siblings left Canton in 1954 for motives of work; I remained until December 1955.

In May of 1953 Father Tan and Father Ye[78] organized a pilgrimage to Shanghai to a celebrated shrine dedicated to Mary, Help of Christians. About ten of us Catholics accompanied them, with the principal objective of acquiring a direct knowledge of the situation of the Church at Shanghai and to learn as much as possible from those Catholics about their attitude toward the Communists. After the "liberation" there were cases of great heroism among the persecuted Catholics, and the most significant examples of fidelity were verified among the faithful at Shanghai.[79] We stayed there nearly fifteen days, taking in the example of the courage, faith, and strength that they demonstrated in a situation of great danger. During our sojourn at Shanghai we listened to numerous homilies spoken by Father Chen, a very well-known preacher. Many of the Catholics we met came from my province, and all were truly kind and welcoming; the entire experience was deeply moving and emotional.

We were already aware of the danger of the imminent persecution threatening the Church in Shanghai when, at our departure, many Catholics came to say good-bye to us, attracting the attention of the secret police, who followed us in a car. Half an hour after leaving Shanghai we were stopped by the police, who interrogated us one by one about the motives of our trip.

When we arrived at Canton, we immediately began to put into practice what we had learned from the Church in Shanghai. Father Tan decided that we had to share our experiences with the other parishes (there were five parishes besides the cathedral), and we began to organize prayer meetings

---

[78] Father Ye Shanting was condemned to fifteen years of imprisonment, many of them in a forced-labor camp near Xiangyand (Hubei). After he served time, he continued to remain in the camp until, in 1980, he was able to return to his diocese, where he remained until the time of the writing of this testimony.

[79] The situation of the Church in Shanghai during the 1950s is described in the book *Io prigioneiro del Signore* (Bologna: Emi, 1991).

and many other activities especially during the feast days. The Catholics of Canton were united around their bishop and one another, and they began to prepare for the persecution that, in the end, would strike their church in the same way that it had happened in Shanghai.

The Diocese of Canton was founded nearly a century before; it had a splendid cathedral and a fairly numerous but scattered Catholic community. In 1952 all the foreign missionaries were expelled, and Rome nominated Monsignor Dominic Tang bishop of the diocese. Under his strong guidance and profound spirituality, the Church was pervaded by a new spirit, especially after our visit to Shanghai and by Father Tan's zealous propagation of all that we had learned there. The love for our Faith and our religious fervor grew, and the Church of Canton became truly united: the Catholics of each parish exchanged ideas, shared a lively faith, and were united around their bishop as his flock and his support. Furthermore, we attended the sacraments in growing numbers and took part in all the religious functions. There was a sense of solidarity and brotherhood that gave birth to a great courage in the face of the threats of persecution; it was a touching demonstration of the strength of the Faith and of divine protection. Bishop Tang encouraged the priests to live a more profound spiritual life, emphasizing the importance of fidelity to the successor of Peter, who is the head of the Church, and perseverance in the Faith. In every possible way he gave strength to the faithful to oppose the pressures that were coming from the Communists.

Initially the Communists did not take these activities very seriously; unlike what had happened at Peking, Shanghai, Nanking, and other important cities in the more-Catholic north of the country. Father Tan continued to distinguish himself by his courage and zeal among the priests of Canton, by putting the faithful on guard against attacks on the Faith, and by preparing them to confront the persecutions and even death for their own faith. At the same time both the government's Office of Public Safety and the Office of Religious Affairs were making every effort to lead the Catholics to unite with the government movement for one Chinese independent Church.

Then in 1953 various priests were arrested at Shanghai. At Canton the first step was the arrest of Father Tan. Consequently, some priests and Christians were afraid and did not want more political clashes with the government. In all, however, Canton's Catholic community was ready to give testimony to Christ, to remain faithful to the teachings of the Church and the bishop, and to face any type of persecution. From 1953 on, some members of various parishes of the city met regularly in the cathedral to sing. First we met on the principal feasts: forty to fifty persons formed the choir on those occasions, which were also opportunities for reciprocal support in the faith; those gatherings were encouraged by the priests of the parishes, especially the younger ones, who demonstrated a great sense of solidarity and spiritual strength. Bishop Tang and all the priests confronted the persecution, accepting the challenges of the times and encouraging the faithful with words and example. One could say that the spiritual level of the Church of Canton was never so elevated.

The Days of the First Persecutions

After the "liberation" the Communists used every means to consolidate their control over the country. The formation of the Movement of the Triple Autonomy was one of these means; its objective was to detach the church from every foreign tie, thereby enabling it to administer itself and to expand on its own.

In general, because of the absence of principles and clear strategies, the Protestants conformed to the will of the Communists. In the south of China their churches leaned on the Movement of the Triple Autonomy and planned and joined demonstrations with the precise objective of creating one autonomous Chinese church, deprived of any "external interference." The Catholic Church, on the other hand, did not adhere to this movement.

The government, having become preoccupied with this negative attitude, organized an encounter with all the Chinese priests of Peking, including the vicar general. Prime Minister Zhou Enlai gave a three-hour discourse, in which he explained the governmental policies and invited an adequate response through the formation of the organization of the Triple Autonomy, like that which had been done by the Protestant churches. The principal objective of the government was to show the world that the Catholics were free to practice their Faith and that they wanted a national, independent church, free from foreign ties, especially the Vatican.

Even at Canton the government wished that the Catholic Church would follow the party line. The Office for Religious Affairs put pressure on Catholics to support the government's policies, but the Movement of the Triple Autonomy at Canton had very limited success. Only a minority of lukewarm Catholics, but not a single priest, were disposed to cede to the Communist pressure; such persons were well known by the local Catholics, because the Office for Religious Affairs had issued invitations to a meeting of a religious character and those who participated were looked upon with suspicion. They continued to attend the religious functions, but at times they created disorder or incited the babies to interrupt the ceremonies. If they went to the balustrade to receive Communion, the faithful Catholics signaled the priest that they had taken part in the Communist encounter and that Communion should be denied them. When Monsignor Tang was arrested, one of the charges was that he had not taken any steps to correct those priests who refused to give Communion to the members of the "patriotic" church; and the bishop admitted that he had done nothing to impede the priests.

Up until my arrest in 1955, I would usually go to Mass in the eastern part of Canton, after which I went normally to the cathedral or the seminary, where Monsignor Tang came with his priests. I worked with the bishop, helping him to translate writings of a spiritual character, such as the *The Compendium of Theological and Mystical Asceticism* by Adolphe Tanquerey, or books that explain the organization of the diocesan curia, et cetera—publications whose goal was to reinforce the spiritual life of priests and laity and to improve the pastoral care of parishes.

It may be useful at this point to list the principal political campaigns through which the Communists consolidated their power and crushed every real and potential source of opposition.

DIARIES OF THE CHINESE MARTYRS

1949–1950: Campaign to eliminate counterrevolutionary elements.

1951–1952: Agrarian reform in the countryside, persecution of the landowners and the rich peasants; campaign of the "three evils" in the cities—against corruption, waste and bureaucracy; campaign of the "five evils"—against the five sins of merchants and industrialists (corruption, fiscal evasion, appropriation of public goods, fraud on declarations of the cost of labor and materials, and theft of information on the state economy for one's own profit).

1954: Reexamination of the agrarian reform and further persecution of the landowners.

1955: Purge to eliminate completely each reactionary element in the Communist Party itself and in every organization, including the religious.

1957: Campaign against the right, to eliminate every "conservative" element.

1964: Four "cleansings": political, ideological, organizational, and economical.

1966: Cultural Revolution.

Each of these campaigns followed the same scheme: the selection of the victims, the organization of the trials, the arrests and imprisonment, and the announcement of a verdict and the completion of the sentences.

The first campaign—to eliminate the counterrevolutionaries (1949–1950)—intended to get rid of the last elements of opposition left by the Guomindang in the form of bandits, spies, secret agents, and armed groups. In 1955 a similar campaign was launched owing to a critical publication written by Hu Feng, one of the leaders of the Communist Party, a known author and vice president of the Association of Writers. He expressed his disapproval for the political control of literary works, and the publication was labeled reactionary by Mao Zedong, which initiated the campaign against all those who oppose Communism. The campaign was then extended to social groups (writers, poets, teachers, university professors) and religious organizations.

The First Arrest

In 1955 I lived in the area east of Canton with a friend, by the name of Henry. One day, at the beginning of December, Henry went to visit an exhibit that was being held in the city, but late that evening he still had not returned. Two days later there was still no news of him; his mother was very worried, but there was no way of knowing anything. I telephoned the police station near the locality of the exhibit, but they had nothing to say.

Two weeks later, early in the afternoon, I received a call from Henry, who asked me to meet him in a restaurant south of the city and to bring him some money and a change of clothes. Toward four in the afternoon I met him and, after he took a bath and had dinner, we returned home, where he had another meal. Later that evening he asked me to go out with him for a last snack before going to sleep. In less than half a day he had dined three times! Upon our return he explained his absence to me: he had been held by the police and interrogated a number of times, and he had lived for two weeks on two frugal meals a day: this was the cause of his enormous hunger. The questions they had asked him were relative to our friendship: how long he had known me, how we became acquainted, et cetera. But we had not known each other very long, and therefore he had little to say.

This system of holding a person for some weeks or even months was very common. No notice was given to the family; the person simply disappeared during the time necessary for the interrogation. I noticed, from this information, that the government was preparing an attack against Catholics.

In fact, a few days later, on December 20, after returning home rather late, I was preparing to go to bed when a police officer knocked at the door to ask if I was at home. Some minutes later he returned with the head of the office of the local police and another police officer. They came up to my room, handcuffed me, and read me the official arrest warrant—name, age, nationality, address, and then the charges: having opposed the Movement of the Triple Autonomy, having refused to register at the police department as a member of the Legion of Mary, a reactionary organization, and having others do the same. Then they asked Henry to make a bundle of some of my clothes, and I myself brought it downstairs.

A black automobile was waiting outside, and I understood that we were going to the prison attached to the police headquarters for an interrogation. I discovered later that night that there had been four Catholics [arrested]: a priest, Father Li,[80] Philip, Rosa[81]—who had recently come to Canton from Hong Kong to work as a catechist—and I.

Afterward Father Li, Philip, and I were sent to the same labor camp; Rosa was not condemned but was detained for thirteen months to be "reeducated."

We were taken to the prison under the control of the police. In China at that time (1955–1956) the procedure adopted for culpable suspects was, as I have said, to put together all the possible information about them, going back as far as their infancy and to their years at school. Then the police officers arrest the victim and transfer him to their prison so that he may be kept in custody and interrogated. Although the time varied, the procedure normally required about three months (given the elevated number of arrests, the prisons would have been overcrowded if each case had required more time); cases similar to Rosa's were very simple and quickly resolved. After the interrogation, a list summarizing the presumed crimes was sent to the prosecutor as proof of guilt; at this point he would decide whether

---

[80] In 1995 Father Anthony Li Bingyin was condemned to five years of "reeducation through work." He remained in the camp until 1969; later he was able to emigrate abroad.

[81] While at the beginning of 1950 thousands of persons fled from Communist China to find refuge at Hong Kong, the young Rosa Yang left her job as a teacher to be by the side of the Christians at Canton in the persecution that was advancing. Arrested in December 1955, she spent twenty-four years in prison and in labor camps before being able to return to Hong Kong. See Nicholas Maestrini, *My Twenty Years with the Chinese* (Avon, NJ: Magnificat Press, 1990), 126–129.

to charge the defendant. If the decision was to proceed, the defendant would be transferred to the prison of the people's tribunal to await the trial, either public or private.

I arrived at the police prison around midnight and was brought to a cell. They opened a heavy door, removed the handcuffs, and shoved me into a room about five meters square with a small window; in the cell there already were two people, who were sleeping. When I entered they awoke and helped me to set aside my belongings; then we joined the two beds to make room for three. I did not lie down; rather I remained on the edge of the bed for about half an hour, trying to adapt to the new situation and to prepare myself for whatever would happen: it was the first time in my life that I found myself imprisoned and without liberty. The prison regulations were affixed to the door. It was prohibited to speak, although this rule was not observed; those who caused disorder or spoke of their case would have gross shackles of ten or twenty kilograms [about twenty-two or forty-four pounds] applied to their calves, which they were forced to carry at all times.

After about half an hour a jailer opened the door and called me out, leading me to a room where I had to be interrogated. They asked me my name and other details about me; then they followed with questions of every type for three or four hours until five in the morning, when I was taken back to my cell, exhausted. It was not time to sleep: the new day had begun and after breakfast, at seven, I was summoned to a new interrogation.

The nightly interrogation continued during the following months in the same manner, in an empty, unheated room. The interrogator would take a break to have a meal or a hot drink, while we had to wait, tense and cold, for the process to recommence. The prisoners called this ritual a "nerve-racking bombardment." There were only two meager meals a day, consisting of rice and steamed vegetables, both flavorless. At first, I had to force myself to eat a few mouthfuls, but after a while hunger forced me to eat; the scant rations of food always left me very hungry. Even the water was rationed. They gave us about one liter a day.

The police had gathered much information on me at Peking; for example, the episode of the Catholic Students Association's trip, my refusal to sign the document as a student, the refusal to recognize the charge of being a member of the Legion of Mary, and the "reactionary" counsel that I had given to other members, whose names were listed; all these were charges held against me. In the course of the interrogation I admitted to all the facts that I recalled, but I denied political or counterrevolutionary motives; standing by my Christian faith, I emphasized the merely religious and spiritual character of my activities. I pointed out that the Church and the popes had recommended that there be a local clergy in each country; in this way the local Church would not be separated from the Holy See. I explained that I had once been Protestant together with my entire family and that I had freely converted to the Church of Peter, the rock.

I was so annoyed over the injustice of my arrest that I was not afraid of saying what I thought; I was also ready to toss back some of the same questions to my interrogators. I had abandoned all contact with my family in order to avoid creating any problems for them [so I restrained myself]. In 1956, when I left prison, I discovered that my siblings had been inter-rogated on my account and that my brother was even forced to show letters that I had written to him.

Waiting for the Trial

After about three months in the police prison, I was transferred to the prison of the tribunal of the people in expectation of the verdict and the sentence. The prison had eight sections, each with fourteen cells, that is seven cells on each side of a narrow corridor and a place to wash. The cells were about thirteen meters square and could hold about twenty persons, but we were thirty or forty in each one. The rooms were so crowded that, when dozing off on the floor, if someone changed his position, his neigh-bor would also have to do the same.

I was put in cell 808 in the eighth corridor, the section reserved for criminals considered the most dangerous: political adversaries—those whose ideology contrasted with Communism— spies, secret agents, and so forth. In fact, in our cell there were true criminals, persons who were depraved and violent. One had convinced his younger brother to shoot and kill some relatives who had refused to lend him money; later both of them killed two babies who were nearby because they were crying. Among the detainees I recognized Father Xu,[82] a priest of a nearby diocese who frequently came to Canton. We were both very passionate about music and had often played together. At first he did not recognize me, and he seemed aged and a bit absent. Out of precaution I did not let on that I knew him, but gradually I approached him and let him recognize me. We had intimate conversations for the three months that we spent together.

There was also a young Protestant who was a convinced Christian and was given to preaching the Bible; in his simplicity he understood that the Communist teaching was contrary to that of Christ. He had courageously preached the evangelical message, renting a house and displaying a poster with the schedule of his biblical meetings. He and his numerous companions were arrested. Through the Bible we found common ground, and we became friends, discovering later that we had friends in common from our school days. He also was testifying to the faith, and in the succeeding months he learned something of the Catholic doctrine and its practice.

Twice a day we received a food ration that we distributed from the large container in which it was steamed. We organized ourselves in order to take turns doing this work. The water was very scarce, even though it was spring, the rainy season. Each of us received a ladle of water from the one entrusted with the distribution in the area set aside for washing up. All the appointees were prisoners who were serving light sentences and were, from the point of view of the Communist ideology, trustworthy. Even the medical doctors who treated the criminals were serving time. One doctor would make the rounds of the cells each day to make sure that no one was ill and that there was no danger of infection because of the crowded and unhygienic conditions in the cells. The medical prescriptions were very

---

[82] Father Peter Xu Zhaofu, a Jesuit, practiced his ministry at Zhaoqing (then part of the Diocese of Macao). Having been arrested in the fifties, he was able to return to Macao in 1980. He died in 1982.

simple; at times they were limited to a slight increase in the daily ration of water. This remedy was so inviting that we would pretend to be ill in order to have a little more water. When it rained we risked shinnying up to the small window of the cell to hold out our soiled towels and dampen them as much as possible.

Before 1956 there was no precise judiciary procedure for the people's tribunals. No detainee knew when he would be tried or when his sentence would be terminated. The only indication would come through the barber, who, three months before a release, would stop shaving the prisoner's head. Only in 1956 did the Council of State promulgate the first provisional document on the legislative organization of the people's tribunals. According to the new regulation, three months of interrogations in the police prison had to be followed by three months in the prison of the people's tribunal, after which the public or private trial before a judge and two members of a jury was scheduled. Most of the political prisoners at that time were victims of the campaign against the counterrevolutionary gang of Hu Feng, which was aimed at eliminating the "reactionary" elements in the cultural and religious ambiance. In line with the Marxist philosophy of the class struggle, after the "liberation," campaigns of the masses—that is, campaigns directed toward inciting one class against another—occurred, one after the other. According to the teaching of Mao Zedong, the class struggle had to be the propulsive force of society and the basis of its progress. And if a class did not exist, it must be invented: the struggle must be kept alive for the advancement of society.

This political view was based on the theory of the three classes of men: the left, the right, and the center. It was necessary to rely on the left, to win over the center, and to isolate the right without rest, giving example to everyone. In the summer of 1956 the campaign against Hu Feng had been exhausted; it was the moment to decide whether to release or to try the many who had been arrested and to judge the success of the campaign. Some cases were managed with indulgence, and the accused were sent home with the restitution of their entire salary, especially in those provinces where the purging had nurtured suspicion and caused excessive destruction.

The situation was not without humorous notes. There was, for example, a young man of about twenty-seven who had transported munitions into combat zones during the Korean War. He had been decorated for his courage, and having returned from the war a hero, he worked for the government in the Office of Security. But in spite of being a Communist, he expressed himself with too much liberty and ease, and thus after a time he stirred up the aversion of his colleagues. He himself was aware of having become the object of criticism, and he thought of remedying the situation by personally recognizing his faults, humbling himself, and confessing before a general assembly of his group even to crimes more serious than those suspected of him.

His frankness permitted him to avoid punitive treatment, and his case was postponed in expectation of verifications. The officials of the police had to go far to verify the information he furnished, but they did not find any evidence that confirmed the veracity of what he had said. He then admitted that he had invented his crimes in order to avoid an immediate and severe punishment from the members of his group. In all, that young man was held for more than a year in prison.

In 1957 we ran into each other on the street and exchanged greetings and the latest news; he told me that when he returned to work, all his back wages were restored to him, enough to permit him to marry, something that would have been impossible with only his normal salary.

Before the People's Tribunal

One morning in April 1956, before breakfast, my number was called. Normally they called us for interrogations after the meal, not before, and it was also unusual that only one prisoner was called.

Usually they interrogated us one after another. This time I was the only one to be called. I left the cell that I shared with Father Xu and two other Christians, and I followed the jailer to a room where an armed, uniformed policeman was waiting. My hands were cuffed behind my back, and the large door of the tribunal of the prison was open: I was outside, where a rickshaw was waiting to take me to an unknown place, escorted by an armed policeman on a bicycle.

The trip lasted about fifteen minutes, during which I prayed that I would avoid the embarrassment of running into anyone I knew on the street and that the Lord and his Mother would give me the strength to face what was waiting for me. I entrusted myself to the Madonna, praying that I would die rather than betray her. When we arrived at the people's tribunal I saw on the bulletin board the trials that had been scheduled, that is, the public trials with a judge, two assistants, and the public seated behind the accused. The experimental legislative procedure was already in force at that time, and one of the rules provided that the citizens could request a ticket to participate at the public trials; it was a form of judiciary education for the people and good propaganda for the external world, because it gave the idea that China was gifted with democratic institutions. I noticed that my case had been selected to demonstrate the consequences for those, particularly the Catholics, who resist government policies regarding religion.

The guard ordered me to follow him, while he pushed his bicycle into a courtyard where a dozen people were waiting in groups. The trial was to begin at nine in the morning. I noticed that some Catholics from my parish were in attendance: Paul, Linda, Teresa, and my friend Henry. Being nearsighted and handcuffed, I did not look around, and I crossed the courtyard behind the police officer, who led me into a room to await my trial. The officer walked around while I remained crouched, but no longer handcuffed.

I then saw my friends coming as close as possible. Linda got all the way up to the door of the room. With the courage of desperation, I whispered to her to give me something to eat. For five months our nourishment was hardly above the subsistence level, and we were always hungry. In such circumstances shame and social conventions are broken: the only deterrent would have been some superior principle, but none existed that impeded me from making that request. Linda understood swiftly, and she went out into the street, returning six or seven minutes later with half a dozen rolls and some pears. Without losing a moment I began with the rolls, and not even the return of the police officer and his reproof interrupted my meal; in just a brief time I ate everything and my hunger was satisfied. For the first time I understood the phrase that mothers say to their babies: "Eat like a prisoner!" I also remembered that my friend Henry had consumed three entire meals in half a day after only fifteen days of detention; now I understood how he felt.

It was nearly time for the trial, and I was led into the courtroom. The people were taking their places behind me. The judge, with a member of the jury at his side, formally opened the process, defining my case as counterrevolutionary and listed my name, place of birth, age, profession, address, and completed studies, all of which I had to confirm as correct. Then the defendant had the right to speak directly in his own defense or to request the intervention of an attorney. It was a pure formality for propaganda purposes; there was in fact only one attorney, a government employee, and his fee was modest, around twenty yuan, but even if he were to represent me, there was nothing that he could have done, except to ask that the case be treated with clemency.

The judge asked me anyhow if I wished to assume an attorney. I said no. Did I have someone to defend me? No. Did I wish to ask someone to defend me? I shook my head. He repeated the question and at that point a voice from the public in attendance exclaimed: "I shall defend you. Tell him. Ask me to be your defender." The effect was electrifying: a profound silence fell on the room. At that point I recognized the voice of Teresa, whom I had seen in the courtyard before the trial began. The judge stared at Teresa, and then he looked at me and after a pause asked me slowly: "Do you wish to ask her to act in the capacity of your defense?" I was silent for a few seconds, and then I consented with a nod of my head and softly responded: "Yes."

In the five months during which I was in prison I did not get in touch with anyone in my family or my friends, because it would have been too dangerous for them. I remained completely alone, drawing strength from the presence of God in me and entrusting myself only to Jesus and Mary so that they would help me. An attorney seemed even useless and without sense. Far from offering help, friends and family usually preferred wisely not to get involved.

The judge was quiet for some moments, and then he affirmed that in the light of the new rules, even if the accused was able to ask someone to act as his defense, this could not occur on the same day. The tribunal had to get in contact with the defense, which in turn had to meet with the accused in order to gather information on the case. Therefore, the judge adjourned the court until the new date was determined.

The judge who was occupied with my case had worked as a clandestine Communist at Hong Kong. He had studied at that city's Catholic schools, and he knew Father Mario, the same priest who accepted me into the Church. Because of his tie with a Catholic school, he considered himself informed concerning the Church and therefore qualified to be a judge in cases like mine. After the "liberation," he was assigned to legal activities and participated in special courses for six months in order to become a judge.

After the audience was dismissed, the guard called me and we returned to the prison, passing along the same street from which we came, he on the bicycle and I, handcuffed, in the rickshaw. The meal hour had passed some time ago, but my cell companion, the young Protestant whom I have mentioned, had kept my portion of the food covered. My companions invited me to consume it immediately, but I was in no hurry to eat; indeed I had no interest in food and the even more surprising thing was that I offered to share it with them. They thought that I must have received bad news that took my appetite away completely. I told them rather that I had eaten abundantly and was not hungry; then they divided the food among themselves, and later I explained what had happened that morning.

By now it was noon, the hour for our afternoon rest, and I needed to reflect calmly on what had happened, above all on the motive that led me to accept the offer of a defense, when I had already considered it all useless. Most of the charges regarding me had occurred years ago, during the time I spent at Peking, and my connection, at that time, to the Legion of Mary, something that Teresa did not even know of; besides, she herself was not prepared for such a difficult task. I felt that I could speak much more effectively myself. But since, from the time of my arrest I did not have any correspondence with my family and, even more, because I had a great need for some indispensable items for my daily use (underwear, soap, paper, and money), having a defender would enable me to get in touch with my family and also satisfy such necessities. For this reason I decided to accept the offer.

In the course of the week Teresa and Linda came to meet with me on the basis of the normal procedure. I was brought into a room where they were already waiting for me, and I saw that they had already brought me a package of underwear and other basic items, including food, which, however, the guard did not permit me to keep. I gave them the necessary information and handed them the records that had been compiled after each of my interrogations and that I had had to sign with my name and my fingerprint. As far as I was concerned, this encounter was a simple formality. I did not expect anything from my defense, but I was content to have the possibility to inform my parents that I had not done anything wrong or unworthy of my Christian life—indeed, I was suffering for my faith. My parents would have been relieved and thus they would no longer need to be concerned about me.

After a week, the trial was reconvened, with the same judge and the same procedure. This time the audience was more formal. My crimes were listed: [spreading] propaganda of a reactionary ideology, opposition to the Movement of the Triple Autonomy and the encouragement of other persons to do the same. Then I was given a chance to defend myself. Once again I presented the same arguments against the charges, denying each political or antigovernmental activity. At times my clarifications even incited hilarity among those present. I emphasized that notwithstanding that Hu Feng, a party member, had made reactionary affirmations, it did not mean that the entire organization to which he belonged [the Communist Party] was reactionary. Likewise, the fact that some persons belonging to the Legion of Mary may have committed some political crimes, it did not mean that each member of the Legion was a criminal and that the Legion was a political organization.

It was then the turn of the defense, which was presented in a very simple, even superficial way. Anyway, the judge was embarrassed by my courage to refute publicly the charges against me: he announced the end of the session and retired with the jury in order to formulate the verdict. On his return he declared that, after the examination of the evidence and the discussion, they had found me guilty of counterrevolutionary actions and condemned me to two years of detention; if I contested the verdict I would have had to appeal it within ten days. The audience was then dismissed, and I was immediately ordered to follow the guard, and thus, handcuffed, I returned to cell 808. It took little to understand that it was useless to appeal: in some cases that recourse resulted in a much longer punishment. For me the important consideration was to maintain my faith. When, after ten days, no appeal was presented, the case was closed. All that remained for me was to prepare myself to go to the labor camp.

In the Labor Camp

At that time anything seemed preferable to life in cell 808. The crowded condition, the heat, and the scant meals made me think that any change would be an improvement. We took a bath only twice a week, and we were given only three ladles of water that also had to serve to wash our clothes. I was beginning to find these conditions intolerable, and I desired to go away at all costs. Human nature always hopes for better things: "Life begins tomorrow," says the popular Chinese maxim.

As a rule, the prison of the tribunal hosted some detainees who, like me, were already judged, together with others who were still waiting for a judgment. Several times a month some employees from the labor camps came to the prison and took away the detainees who had been assigned to their camp, like businessmen acquiring their acquisitions. We recognized these employees from their uniforms, and some of us were even able to understand which part of China they came from. First, they called each prisoner by number for a medical exam; the checkup was very simple: name, age, height, and illnesses. When it was my turn I said nothing about my rheumatism, because my only concern was to go away from there.

One afternoon, ten days later, at the beginning of June, the same numbers were called up. All my belongings had already been wrapped up. I said good-bye to Father Xu and the others, and I joined the group of thirty or forty destined for the labor camp. We climbed onto the covered lorry that headed in the direction north of Canton. The prisoners sentenced to less than ten years were not handcuffed, because those who had a lighter sentence knew that it was not worth the attempt to flee. After some time the lorry stopped at the foot of a hill, about fifteen kilometers north of Canton. Someone recognized the place: Niutoukeng, a stone cave in which the work was carried out entirely by hand, without any mechanical assistance. The manual labor was divided into various sectors. One group, each tied with a safety cable, had the task of scaling the steep side of the mountain in order to make holes in the rock and to insert the explosives, causing the rock to jump, and then another group, using hammers weighing eight or nine kilos [about seventeen to nineteen pounds], had to break the rock at the base of its veining. It was extremely dangerous work, since chips and splinters of rock scattered in every direction. Once, while I was close to one of the stonebreakers, a large piece of rock struck me in one eye; fortunately I was not wounded by the pointed end, but the accident caused the loss of 50 percent of my sight. Our feet were covered with rags to protect them from the flying chips, but in spite of this precaution accidents occurred every day. In that camp I saw many persons with only one eye: it was very easy to lose your sight doing that work.

Then another group, using a light hammer and wearing long sleeves, had to break the rock into smaller pieces; finally, others, using a hammer weighing a little more than a kilo [a little more than two pounds], would break them into pieces of various dimensions: a centimeter, two centimeters, et cetera. Father Li and Philip were in the same camp with me: the former had to serve a sentence of five years, the second three years, because they were condemned for specific offenses, while the pain of my two-year sentence was imposed principally to correct my attitude. Philip and I were in the group that used the small hammer, and Father Li was in the group employed to transport the loads of stone on their shoulders. Since the group that used the small hammer completed the final phase of the work, every two days we had to transport the finished product in baskets to the foot of the hill, where it was gathered daily by the lorries. Each person was required to do a fixed quantity of work each day: about twenty baskets of about fifty kilos [about 110 pounds] each. The smaller pieces of stone were more labor intensive, and we worked from morning until evening, literally from dawn until sunset. Our hands were covered with bloody sores and our wrists were rigid from the long hours of hammering; and very soon our hands did not open and close more than was necessary to hold the hammer.

In addition to the hard work were the even more precarious conditions of life and hygiene. The buildings in which we slept were made of bamboo and covered with straw. The interior walls, with a thickness of just a centimeter, divided the room into three dormitories that housed several hundred prisoners. The hygiene was terrible. After the work we were covered with dust, but the only places to wash were two puddles of dirty, stagnant water at the bottom of the hill: we had to immerse ourselves in that murky water, full of algae, both in the summer and in the winter. The food was better than in prison because in that year, 1956, the National Assembly of the People had met and the delegates had the task of visiting the prisons and the labor camps in order to evaluate the conditions. As a result the food was improved.

The hours of work varied according to the season. At the first light of dawn the bell rang, and ten minutes later we had to get in line with our tools, and two by two we went up the hill and began to work in our groups. During the winter the workday began at about six in the morning, and in the summer it started before dawn, when the stars were beginning to disappear and there was just enough light to see the street. At 8:30 in the morning we returned for our first meal of rice and vegetables in an area in front of the dormitory. We had about half an hour to eat, and then we returned to work until 12:30. There was no meal at noon, only a break, more or less, according to the season. On the basis of the directives from Peking, the workday in the camps was ten hours, but if necessary, it could be extended. We were like slaves at work all day long.

Although I tried to hide it, the terrible conditions in the camp worsened my health and made me suffer even more. I was slowly deteriorating and was sent to the camp doctor. He, also a prisoner, came from my province. When he learned the long story of my delicate health, he told me that I was not able to carry out the work of the camp, and he informed those responsible, who reproached me for not having informed them of my illness. They then gave me the possibility of choosing lighter work so I began to help the cook. But this task was also too heavy for me, because I had to transport water some distance, up and down the hill more than fifty times a day; two buckets of water weighed about fifty kilos [about 110 pounds]. So I returned to my previous work, doing whatever I was able; but each day life became more insufferable, and all I could do was to submit myself to the will of Providence.

Liberation

In the summer of 1956 the National Assembly of the People met at Peking. The political purge called the "campaign for the repression of the counterrevolutionaries" was reaching the end, and the Council of State tried to initiate, at least temporarily, a more moderate policy in order to mitigate the hardness of the conditions engaged in the campaign for the elimination of the reactionaries. A series of provisions that pardoned certain types of counterrevolutionaries was enacted. The tribunals then reviewed and reexamined the cases to which the new law may have applied and worked on a revision of the sentences for those serving less than five years and who were the principal providers for their families, or persons physically not able to work in the labor camps. In my case there was never any crime in the strict sense: I simply had refused to recognize some [personal] deficiencies, and that was considered an example of obstinacy and infidelity to the country.

DIARIES OF THE CHINESE MARTYRS

We had no knowledge of the new orders until they were applied in our camp. The first one to be released was a rather elderly man who had served five years for having used opium. Then there was an old peasant and me. My companion was a very simple man whose only crime was having openly expressed a criticism of the government, which got him a sentence of eight years.

The day of the liberation began in the usual way: we walked along the street to the hill by the light of the stars, and then we returned for breakfast at 8:30. At the foot of the hill, while crossing a little street on our return, I saw my friends Paolo and Henry near the camp offices.

There were fixed rules for visitors, and this was not a day for visits; dates were established at the beginning of the year, and the prisoners could request permission for one of these days, as long as they had not broken any rules and had informed the camp of the visitor's name. Every two Sundays we had a free day, and we called it the "great Sunday," in comparison with an ordinary Sunday, on which we normally worked. Those who were expecting visitors on the free day got in a line and followed the guard to the meeting place, where the visitors were also waiting in a line for their turn to sit opposite the prisoner, who was half a meter away and under the control of the camp personnel. Crying was strictly prohibited: if the prisoner cried, the visitor would be sent away, and the prisoner would not be granted other meetings. Furthermore, the "guilty one" who cried would be subjected to criticism or punishment during the gathering of the prisoners that evening. It was, therefore, essential to maintain good humor during visits, however difficult it might have been under the circumstances.

Paolo and Henry's visit aroused my suspicions. I continued in the line up to the camp where we had breakfast; immediately after, the person responsible for our political education came to me and told me to pack my belongings. Some of the long-term prisoners knew it meant that I was being liberated and going home. Many acquaintances, such as Philip, came to me and asked me to leave them my personal possessions: a bucket, a fountain pen, some stationery, et cetera. Everything was precious.

That morning I was not hungry; twenty minutes later, when a prison employee returned and called our two names, I was ready with the few things that I was taking with me. We followed them to the offices where my two friends were waiting for me. They had been informed that they were releasing me on bail because of my health. Waiting for the old man were four young people, two of whom were his children. The judicial authorities had warned his relatives that he was suffering from a grave illness, and for this reason he was being released, and they, thinking that their father was on the point of death, had prepared a stretcher on which to transport him. However, the old man was not at all ill. As for me, I was given a certificate of release to hand over to the police of Canton; and the two guards at the entrance of the camp were already informed that I was being released.

The official in charge of the camp shook my hand and told me that "the government had used clemency; therefore, in the future, I should avoid illegal activities; in other words, it was a type of "go in peace and sin no more." My two friends thought that I would not be able to walk, so they brought a bicycle. In effect I was very weak, but I managed to stay on my feet. The first objective was to find a place where I could wash up and eat something; then we took a bus back to Canton. That evening my friends celebrated my return with a festive supper in the city's best restaurant; however, I had intestinal problems and was not able to eat.

On the following day, when I went to the police station to sign the certificate for bail, I encountered Wen, the policeman who had arrested me. Seeing that I was in a bad state, he was extremely kind and counseled me to take care of myself, to rest, and to eat! I had to report to the station every three days; in addition, I had to report whenever I wished to go out for more than an hour, to attend the political classes and periodically to write a report. In the beginning I had to go to the police even to ask permission to go to the cinema, but soon the police officers grew weary of it and told me that it wasn't necessary.

Little by little I regained my liberty of movement. In order to be informed, I subscribed to two newspapers, one from Peking and one local. I went to Mass each morning, causing perplexity in Henry, who did not understand why I risked going to church. I reminded him that they arrested me for little or nothing to do with crimes; if the Communists wished to find some fault in someone, they could construct crimes even where there wasn't a trace of any. In brief, two or three months after the release, I was leading the same life as before my arrest. From Christmas of 1956 I moved about fairly freely, with the firm intention of practicing my Faith and helping the Church and the bishop.

After my return, my friends took the precautions that were necessary to visit me. The first to come, for example, were Maria and Teresa. They stopped on the opposite side of the street, and Maria came to knock at the door; she was a very courageous woman and after the persecution of 1958 suffered much because of the Faith. She invited me to follow her to a nearby café; successively other friends ventured out to visit me, given that the government's policies had moderated somewhat. On many Sundays and then at Christmas, I attended the solemn Mass in the cathedral; very often I would also go to visit the bishop. In January of 1957, on the occasion of the feast of my patron saint, I was invited to the parish of Linda and Teresa, where the bishop was presiding over the celebration and giving a dinner. A year later, when I was arrested for the second time, that encounter among Christians was used as the chief accusation against me: I was charged with plotting and carrying out illegal activities with the bishop and other Christians.

The Encounter with Teresa

While I was studying at Peking I had become a friend of Dr. Mo, who came from my province; I encountered him various times because, being retired, he came regularly to visit his son and his grandchildren, who resided in the capital city. When in my last year of studies I returned to Canton for the winter vacation, I met his daughter Teresa for the first time. She was still in high school, and I had nearly finished the eight years of the university. Having begun school at the age of four, because my mother was a teacher, I was very advanced in my studies, and I began my university studies very young. I was not particularly impressed with that schoolgirl, who was shy and not inclined to speak. At home her nickname was *lauhei*,[83] since she seemed to take life very calmly.

When I returned to Canton in 1952, after spending fifteen days with my parents at Shaoguan, as I have mentioned, I got in the habit of going to the cathedral for Sunday Mass, since I knew few Catholics. Later, however, I got to know Teresa's cousins, one of whom was my classmate at Peking, who invited me to functions in their parish. Dr. Mo was still living, and, as a courtesy, I visited him many times. Occasionally he also visited me. His wife and the other members of the family, however, were not as hospitable: there were internal conflicts in the family, a typical phenomenon in large Chinese families; the mother-in-law and the daughters-in-law were never on good terms, and Mrs. Mo knew that I had learned of it from the cousins.

The family gave the impression of modernity and haughtiness. Only Teresa's brother and sister had been baptized. From the beginning, however, I noted that Teresa was very simple and fervent, somewhat different from the rest of the family. I met her sometimes at the cathedral or at functions elsewhere, but I tended to keep my distance from girls who were noted for their prayer life and were probably interested in the consecrated life. Therefore, Teresa's intervention in my favor in 1956 came as a complete surprise. At that time I interpreted it as an expression of Christian charity, but later I took into account that it had derived from other sentiments.

When I returned from the labor camp we began to see each other. Teresa used to visit me, and we went to the cinema together or to concerts. An out-of-the-ordinary friendship developed between us: on her part there was a kind of special admiration for me, and although she did not express her feelings at that time, I was aware that our friendship was turning into a reciprocal love. One day, in late spring, I spoke to Teresa about it, but

---

[83] It is a Cantonese term that means "to lose air." It refers to something inflatable, such as a ball, that is full of air and is deflated slowly. Regarding a person, it means slow, not tempestuous.

she sadly confessed to me that she had taken a vow of virginity. That was sufficient for me to break off our relationship immediately: in such a case, there could not have been any type of prudent compromise, and I did not agree with Teresa's insistence that we continue to see each other and go out as friends. Therefore, we broke up and I handed over all my needs to the prayers of Our Lady, asking her to indicate to me what I had to do.

For the first time, I was free to consider my future; I was convinced that, if marriage was to be my vocation, my companion would have to be chosen by Our Lady herself. Teresa's vow was an unexpected obstacle to our relationship, but I referred the entire question to Mary, placing everything into her hands; I asked her to intercede for me and for Teresa, so that I could know God's will and could be illuminated as to what he wished for us.

For about two months I avoided her company, but one midsummer afternoon, Teresa came to visit me, and in all simplicity, without preamble, she showed me a letter. Reading those few lines I understood everything: she also had prayed; she also examined the problem and made a decision. Then, after consulting her spiritual guide, she went to the bishop and formally requested a dispensation from the vow she had made. I then felt a greater sense of responsibility for our relationship: it was necessary to consider the question seriously. Our characters were very different: I was accustomed to looking at things objectively, giving ample room to reason in my decisions, and this was not at all Teresa's attitude. She herself confessed to me that even her mother was well aware of the differences in our characters and for this reason she did not encourage her to marry me.

At that time—the summer of 1957—Mrs. Mo had obtained permission to go to Hong Kong, and before leaving Canton, she wished Teresa to understand clearly her point of view. Besides my delicate health, her mother believed that my strong character and decisive convictions would cause Teresa too much suffering; and therefore she felt it her duty to warn her. On the other hand, I also felt some conflicting sentiments: I was touched by Teresa's esteem and her simple and pure affection; but then I also had hopes of leaving China and going to Hong Kong and there having the opportunity to become a priest.

The thought of expatriating stayed with me up to 1952, so much so that I decided to complete an application along with the naming of two guarantors required by the law. But then the police reminded me that if I were to be charged with some criminal offense, the guarantors would be held directly responsible, so one of the two, fearing the possible consequences, backed out. However, I began to reflect on some observations that Father Tan had brought to my attention: that many of those trying to leave should remain and give witness in favor of the Mystical Body of Christ. Therefore, I decided to abandon the idea of leaving China and to steer myself in another direction, waiting for whatever God's plans were and preparing myself to give testimony to my Faith. I was resolute in my desire not to work for the Communists in any way, and I began a business activity with my friend Henry, sufficient to maintain my support.

At this point, in the autumn of 1957, the campaign against the elements of the right was beginning to develop, and although the Communists would not have placed difficulties in my path if I wished to get married, it was obviously not the moment to take a step of that kind. Besides, some officials of the Office for Religious Affairs were repeatedly coming to warn me that if I did not modify my attitude, I would be risking a more serious condemnation. I had been put on my guard numerous times about the dangers of my continuous involvement with the Church, but I entrusted myself completely to the Lord, not thinking of my future. I had intended to continue to witness to my Faith and to face whatever was reserved for me.

Anyhow, with the specter of persecution on the horizon, it was certainly not the moment to put personal matters in order: on this Teresa and I were agreed. It was necessary to join our spiritual resources and to be ready: if God's will for me was to face another arrest and another imprisonment, I would have accepted it. I entrusted myself to the hands of God. In December, however, Teresa was arrested, together with some Christians from other parishes.

DIARIES OF THE CHINESE MARTYRS

The New Persecution

Toward 1956 the Council of State, the party's central administration, began to modify its politics in order to present a more positive image to the people. From the first days of the "liberation" the population had suffered because of the oppressive measures taken to eliminate every type of opposition to the government; now they became aware of some necessary changes. In 1956 the Hungarian revolt and the Soviet Union's oppressive reaction to it alarmed the world. When the Soviet troops invaded Budapest and repressed the rebellion, Mao Zedong criticized the fact in an article in which he indicated two fundamental principles for the party: *fandui*, "to be opposed" (to insurrections), and *bupta* ("no part"), because the party had the means to deal with any type of opposition [and therefore there would be no need for the repression that had been imposed on Hungary].

This resulted in the transitory policy of clemency that brought about the cancellation of some convictions, such as mine. But it was only a tactic to ensure greater and more effective control over the people. It was not a question of principles, democratic or humanitarian: it was a policy that would change again as soon as it had reached its objective of calming the masses after a long period of turbulence.

At the beginning of 1957, at a meeting of the Central Committee of the Communist Party, Mao proposed the launching of a campaign for the revision of the policy, for the examination of the strengths and weaknesses of the party, and for the verification of eventual gaps. He invited all the persons of goodwill to contribute suggestions and criticisms that would help the party to correct eventual human errors. Besides the Communist Party there were also in China six or seven democratic parties that attracted the major part of the intelligentsia: capitalists, businessmen, and professionals; people with important ties abroad. Together with the Communists these parties had struggled against the Guomindang, and after the "liberation" Mao Zedong permitted them to continue to exist. They formed a consultative political core of intellectuals and professionals in the fields of politics, industry, education and literature, and so forth.

In the first months of 1957 they were asked by the party to give their opinions. But by June or July the trick was revealed: an editorial in the *People's Daily*, an organ of the Communist Party, attacked those who, in response to the request, had criticized the government. In a follow-up to that article, Mao called for a counterattack on the capitalists, who with their critiques were threatening the government. It was the so-called politics of the *kaimen, shuanmen*: you open the door in order to shut it again. During the second half of 1957 this campaign against the so-called elements of the right was gradually spread from district to district. Whoever did not fall in line with the party was labeled a reactionary. One observation, made just one time, was sufficient [for someone] to be faulted.

My sister, for example, was working in an office of the Ministry of Health; she and her colleagues had to respond to a questionnaire during the course of an indoctrination. To the question "Do you think that the Chinese farmers suffer because of too much work, insufficient food, et cetera?" she responded yes. Immediately the official from the Office of Public Safety began to gather information about her past and constructed such a case against her that she had to leave her job. Her husband, wishing to disassociate himself from her, filed for divorce, but the request was not accepted. Then my sister and her husband were *xiafang*, that is, they were expelled from the city and sent to the country to work in the fields. In the new place, her husband asked again for a divorce but was again refused. My sister was then forced to seek work sweeping the streets. When the babies were ill and there was no more money in the house, she sold her blood to procure what she needed.

These personal tragedies occurred on a national scale: each person's situation affected entire families, their relatives, and their friends. Whole families were broken apart and condemned to prison and labor camps; innumerable lives were destroyed. Even those who had some education were sent to work like peasants; throughout the country political persecution became savage and cruel. But Mao was satisfied: he had laid a trap, and he captured many unsuspected victims. He denied that this strategy was *yinmou*, a secret plot; to him it was, as he described it, *yangmou*, an obvious plot. It was a plan to bring the truth to light, in line with the Chinese proverbs: "Flush out the serpent from his hole"; or "Toss the bait and wait to catch a big fish." This catastrophe of human misery and suffering continued for nearly twenty years; in theory the policy was formulated by the Communist Party, but in reality it was the work of Mao Zedong, the expression of his personal supremacy.

The political purging was also felt at Canton. For many years the Communists had attempted to organize the Patriotic Association of the Chinese Catholics,[84] but they were not successful. Now they had sufficient power to put their policies into action. The first step was oppressive, that is, the removal of the obstacles that opposed their plan: bishop, priests, and devout Catholics. The bishop, Dominic Tang, was the first objective: he did not cooperate; he never followed the party line regarding questions of the Church, neither the good nor the bad. The priests and the fervent Christians, especially the members of the chorus, were also upright in their fidelity. The first weapon of the dictatorship was arrest. On December 23, 1957, a Christian from every parish was arrested, Teresa among them. The goal was to demoralize the Catholic community and to create an atmosphere of fear and terror around the Christmas feast days. For all of us it was a moment of pain and suffering. The curtain was raised on the drama of the persecution of the Catholic Faith Canton; little by little, one by one, hundreds of Christians were involved in that painful business.

I also suspected the same destiny. Not wishing to involve my friend Henry a second time, I then moved to a western district of Canton, with a close friend, a Chinese from Malaysia who had set up a dental practice and gave me lodgings. He had come to Canton with the dream of helping the country, but he was not engaged enough to understand the true situation and very soon he left the new China with his family.

---

[84] As already said, the Patriotic Association of Chinese Catholics is the structure organized by the Communist authorities in 1957 to "liberate" the church from the elements and tendencies contrary to the revolution.

All the Catholics of Canton had been strongly impressed by the arrests at Christmas and were waiting day by day for news of other priests and faithful. I was planning to return to Shaoguan for the Chinese New Year and had bought some gifts to take to my parents. But some days before the feast a friend came to visit me: we sat and spoke together. At one o'clock a police officer appeared with the excuse of obtaining medicine from the dentist, but actually to check if I was home. A few minutes later, in fact, he returned with another police officer and with the official who had interrogated me at the Office of Public Safety; when I saw him, I understood what was happening.

I was expecting to be arrested and my personal effects were already packed and ready. They went over the same procedure as the previous time, except that, when the policeman gave the "hands up," my old acquaintance from the police station intervened, explaining that it was not necessary, and I was not even handcuffed. While my room was being searched they enlisted the proprietor of the house as a useful witness for the eventual trials; then, after I gathered my baggage, we went down to the street; a black car was waiting. We were in full daylight; but the police wished the least publicity possible. We headed speedily toward the prison. I felt like an old client: I knew what awaited me.

I was shoved into a cell where there were already two other criminals, and the door was closed. What I had long foreseen was happening, but I was calm and at peace; I even felt unburdened because the wait was over. Therefore, the arrest was nearly a relief.

In Prison for a Second Time

The prison at the police station had been built by a "warlord" during the Nationalist government between 1920 and 1930, according to the same design as Stanley Prison at Hong Kong. It had been planned in such a way that each day each cell received at least a few minutes of sun through the small window. There were three buildings, each one with two rows of cells on each side of the corridor. The prison was surrounded by a high wall and heavily guarded since it housed political prisoners. This time I was led to the first floor, where all the men were in one part and all the women in the other; I learned a little later that Teresa was in the last cell in the front. But the bishop, Monsignor Tang, who had been arrested before me, was in my row, as was Paul and another friend.

I could spy across a small fissure in the door that at times the jailer did not close well; Rosa's cell was exactly in front of mine, so at times I was able to see her when the prisoners, one by one, would go out to the lavatory to get clean water for the day. The doors were of massive wood; and in the cell there was only a small window high up near the ceiling, so that normally no sound could enter. But I sang as loud as possible—the Mass in the Gregorian Chant, the hymns of the benediction of the Most Holy Sacrament, the Te Deum, and the Dies Irae—so that I could be heard by the other Catholics and establish a communion with them. A month later I was transferred to the cell directly under Teresa's; later, she told me that she could hear me sing. But if the other prisoners were able to hear, the jailers also could hear; so it was necessary to respect the many rules indicated on the door of the cell, including the prohibition of noisy disturbances.

With my next transfer to another building I was able to see Teresa's cell; so, when I would start to whistle familiar refrains, keeping to a high tonality so that the emitted sounds could pass over the walls of the division, she would risk climbing up to the little window of the cell in order to be able to see me. We managed to communicate in this extraordinary way about a dozen times, and even her cell companion risked looking out.

At times I was called to undergo interrogations. My attitude of total indifference regarding some charges, and my ability to refute them, infuriated my inquisitors.

Each day, after breakfast, the jailer made us make entries in a journal, usually over a fifteen-day period; and at the same time he collected notes from those who requested medicine or necessities of other types. At that time I shared a cell with a prisoner who had been in jail for four years (which, in itself, was not unusual). His hair had turned white; however, he still observed a disciplined and orderly life: each day he spent about fifteen minutes doing gymnastics, and then he had breakfast, followed by reading. He was a teacher, and to pass the time he was teaching himself Russian: he had acquired two copies of Lenin's *State of the Revolution*, one in Chinese and the other in Russian, and he was able to learn a great deal of the language. Since I had also studied Russian, I was able to correct his pronunciation while he taught me what he was learning. It was a profitable shared experience.

One morning, after breakfast, the small rectangular door through which we received our meals was opened unexpectedly. [It was the medical doctor.] Both of us were enjoying moderately good health and had not requested the doctor. My companion did not even consider looking up from his reading. However, I noticed the doctor signal me to come to him; and when he approached me, he asked for my wrist so that he could check my pulse and at the same time tell me softly: "Teresa sends you her best wishes." He also informed me that Teresa had been sentenced to fifteen years in prison. I asked the doctor to return the following morning; meanwhile I wrote her a letter to give to him so that he could hand it to Teresa. I encouraged her not to fear, to trust in the Lord and in Our Lady, and they would give her the courage to face everything; and I also advised her, if it was possible, to appeal her sentence.

I wrapped the note around a rosary that I had brought with me; it had been given to me ten years before by a priest who, while on a pilgrimage at Rome had had it blessed by the Holy Father. The following morning I gave the little package to the doctor so that he could bring it to Teresa. Later, she told me that she had managed to keep the rosary for two years, but then it was taken from her during her transfer to a labor camp. Indeed, before being interred in one of the camps, the designated prisoner had to present all his personal effects for inspection; such an operation would then be repeated many times during the year.

With the help of the same medical doctor, Teresa was also able to deliver a letter to Bishop Tang, and he responded to her by the same means.

For me the situation was very simple. I was familiar with the formalities of the process, and so I was able to face everything without too much concern; moreover, because the officials knew me well enough, they did not ask me too many questions; but when they asked me to explain my views and opinions, I took advantage of the occasion to defend my Faith and to criticize the government's antireligious agenda and its persecution of the Church, saying that I refused to conform myself to any of it.

I remained in prison for longer than the usual three months when I was transferred to the prison of the people's tribunal to be tried. During the transfer, I traveled in the same van with Linda and later on, in the prison, I was able to meet Father Ye and Father Tan[85] of Canton.

My trial was even simpler than the first time. The presentation was private; therefore, everything took place in a room; besides the judge there was the additional presence of two jurors, safeguarding the technical appearance of a court of justice. At that time the political campaign against the espionage of the right was at its height; anyone who was minimally considered on the right was suppressed and the sentences were severe, especially in cases like mine, when I revealed my intransigence and inflexibility during the interrogation. Indeed, with every phrase addressed to me, I did not miss the opportunity to refute the inquisitors' errors and reject their charges of political activity against the government. Even during the preliminary interrogations, from time to time, my judge ended with slamming his fist on the table, reminding me of their power to express a judgment against me: "Do you not know that we have the power to condemn you or release you?" Unperturbed, I responded: "You do not have to tell me; otherwise I would not be in prison."

In their propaganda, the Communists like to clarify their judiciary policy, which consisted in "the policy of the seventeen words." It can be summarized in a brief formula that expresses four principles:

---

[85] Father Dominic Tan Ganchao, after having studied at the University Urbaniana at Rome, became coadjutor of the cathedral of Canton. He died in the sixties in the Yingde labor camp.

1. indulgence toward those who respond with frankness and openness

2. rigor in facing those who refuse to confess and recognize their crimes

3. the prize, a sentence reduction for those who reveal information not yet in possession of the government

4. total annulment of the sentence for those who furnish an even greater amount of information

The inquisitor would always explain these principles to the accused prisoner before the interrogation. The accused was invited to say the complete truth and to furnish information that compromised other persons in order to obtain personal benefits for himself. Many fell into this trap and would release testimony and false accusations in order to obtain a reduction or annulment of their pain. Thus, the truth lost its objectivity and its value and was disregarded; and the conscience and morality of the people were corroded and corrupted.

The same tactic was adopted outside the tribunals: in the camps and in the work groups, in factories, and in every business; people were constantly urged to denounce others in order to gain personal benefits. If everyone submitted to authority in this way, the State would indeed have become an absolute dictator.

The following is one of the innumerable examples of this. Seven or eight citizens of Hong Kong were falsely accused of being spies on behalf of Taiwan. The documentation relevant to the charges was kept secret for ten years, that is, until one after the other of the accused no longer came to Canton to visit their relatives. On those occasions everyone was arrested and accused of espionage; after repeated denials and investigations, the initial accuser, who had given origin to this theory and who was still serving time in a prison camp, was again interrogated on this matter and ended up admitting that they were false and that he, at that time, had simply wished to be useful. This type of procedure caused indescribable suffering to numberless innocent people.

In any case, the authorities were well aware that neither for the activities I had carried out when I was still liberated nor for the affirmations released after my arrest would I have ever put myself at their disposal as an informer. Thus, when my case ended, the public minister emphasized my obstinacy and my reactionary principles, maintaining that while I believed that I was hiding behind a religious habit, in truth I was carrying out counterrevolutionary activities, without ever having wished to recognize the crimes that I committed or shown signs of repentance; therefore, my punishment would have to be particularly severe. I was in fact given a twenty-year sentence, with the right of appeal within ten years. I did not have any intention of seeking an appeal, and I made this clear; I was already prepared to accept whatever sentence was formulated, placing myself in the hands of the Lord.

Considering the weight of such a sentence, I accepted it nearly with indifference; however, no one, in similar circumstances, would have dared to think about his future prospects. Some, upon hearing their sentence, would have a mental breakdown, thinking about their responsibility for a wife and a family and lacking the means to provide for them. Rather, at my return to prison, we even joked about the penalty inflicted on me, perhaps as a way of reducing the tension and maintaining optimism: "How many years have they given you?" "One day," we would say, referring to Marx and Lenin's prophecy that the masses would accomplish in one day the many splendid things that take twenty years.

The New Labor Camp

After the conviction I had to wait longer than usual, until November of 1958, for the officials (the "shoppers," as we called them) to come from prison No. 2. As on previous occasions, they asked for the list, then they met with us briefly, asked us some generic questions, and within about fifteen days, they returned to pick us up along with our baggage. I said farewell to Father Ye and Father Tan: it was an emotional moment.

That day, thirty to forty handcuffed convicts, marching by twos and guarded by a large armed police escort, left the prison. It was evening when we were transported to the railroad station on two enclosed lorries and got on the train along with seven or eight guards. Because my native city was three or four hours from Canton, I knew that line well, and I knew that we found ourselves north of my city (Shaoguan) when, at ten in the evening, we were told to get off the train. After a preliminary roll call to check, we walked toward prison No. 2, still handcuffed and carrying our baggage. After months spent in prison with scant food and no physical exercise, the energy necessary to carry the baggage with one hand immobilized was extremely hard. The younger ones who had fewer belongings managed to walk in a fairly normal way; the elderly and the sick proceeded with difficulty, and the distance between the young and the old increased. Even the guards' repeated command to move faster was useless; the pace slowed even more, and at the end some asked the guards to grant a rest. Nothing doing! That march across the rice field at night seemed like a scene from Victor Hugo's novel *Les Miserables*.

At a certain point a boy of about nineteen, lame and incapable of continuing because of his weakness, knelt down before a guard and begged him to kill him rather than make him continue. It was an unexpected dilemma for the guards, who were eager to arrive at the end of the trip in order to be relieved of their responsibilities. So, after a brief consultation the soldiers called some of the younger prisoners who were at the head of the line and ordered them to carry, or rather, to drag the lame boy, one at each side. Thanks to the setback, we were able to get a two- or three-minute break; we arrived at our destination around eleven at night, having taken an hour to walk a distance that normally takes twenty minutes. Before us rose a huge complex, on which was prominently written: "Prison No. 2, City of Canton."

After the "liberation" six prisons and many labor camps were established in my native province; each district had its own camp. Those with lighter sentences served in the camps, those with heavier sentences in the prisons, which were surrounded by high walls. The work camp did not have any walls, only a line of demarcation, and there were many guards ready to shoot anyone who attempted to cross it. Prison No. 2 was particularly secure because its location, in the northern part of the province, not far from the province of Hunan, made contact with the external world difficult. Each convict's head was completely shaved, and each wore a gray uniform with two large characters depicted on the back: laogai ("reeducation through work"). During that time prison No. 2 held several thousand inmates.

The original construction was two floors and a quadrangle, with four wings that surrounded a central courtyard. Later, other buildings, laboratories, housing, shops for tailors, bath houses, and a building for women were added. At the prison they put together nineteen or twenty various work groups and camps, all forming a complex of seven or eight thousand persons. That night we were all assembled in a room to rest. The following day we were assigned a job on the basis of our physical and technical capacity; I was included in a group assigned to make shoes.

In general those in charge of the prison tried to operate it in a way that was as satisfactory as possible to the prisoners, but without violating the principles that inspired their task. There were two infractions that were taken very seriously: the formation of gangs and attempts to escape. The detainees in the internal area of the prison were condemned to the more serious charges; outside the walls were those whose sentences were near the end and were therefore less interested in fleeing. The prospect of serving long sentences or life in prison made some try to escape; many others chose an alternative way: suicide.

The organization of our day was very similar to that of my first labor camp: ten-hour days, with two hours of political studies after supper, during which we had to study documents and reports and discuss them under the direction of special officials. It was the most efficacious way of keeping the prisoners occupied and preventing disorder. We lived in groups of ten per room; we slept on one common bed as long as the room, with a mattress and mats of straw spread on the brick floor. In the summer we got up earlier, but we had a longer break at dinner; during the winter we had a brief break during the day, but we worked as long as there was light. As before, we had a "great Sunday" or free day once every fifteen days, with the same rules regarding visitors.

The visits were not permitted on official holidays: the New Year, October 1,[86] May 1, and so forth; and for an entire year from 1962 to 1963, we could not send letters or receive visitors because of the difficult political situation. One of the prisoner's daughters continued to come anyway, and she succeeded in seeing her father: she continued requesting visits and the officials, fearing that eventual complaints would be filed against them in the name of "citizens' rights," permitted her to come. During the actual visit, the prisoners and the visitors were arranged in two rooms, one in front of the other and the guards walked in the intermediate space. Gifts had to be examined by the guards; packages of food were permitted only during the "lean years" (1959, 1961, and 1962), when everyone throughout the country suffered hunger, not only the prisoners; in that era even the central authorities recognized that that national disaster was owed only partly (30 percent) to natural causes and the rest (70 percent) to human error. We called the gifts "offering for the spirits," because we were like people from an underworld who were rising up to see their dear ones for a brief time.[87]

The Imprisonment of Teresa

Teresa also was ultimately transferred from the prison of Canton to prison No. 2. I did not know it until all of a sudden, one day in 1968, I saw her in our workshop with her group and the guard about ten meters away. Naturally we would not dare show any sign of recognition. Immediately after, her work was changed, and she was transferred to the group that organized entertainment for the camp. As part of the politics of reeducation and reform, the officials were required to organize something to render

---

[86] The national holiday in remembrance of the proclamation of the People's Republic of China made at Peking by Mao Zedong on October 1, 1949.

[87] According to Chinese beliefs, the world of the spirits is like that of the bodies: in the afterlife it is impossible to live without eating. This is the basis for the custom of offering food to the souls of the deceased. This occurs particularly on the feast of the "hungry souls" (the fifteenth day of the seventh moon).

prison life more bearable, so twice a month this group organized a show, or there was a film; naturally everything was aimed at the glorification of the Communist regime. The authorities boasted that the labor camps and the prisons were schools of mental rehabilitation: not with the goal of oppressing the body, but solely with educating the mind. Every aspect of life under Communism had this goal, and it is necessary to recognize that a certain success was reached after months and years of brainwashing.

Given that Teresa belonged to the group engaged in the entertainment, I was able to see her once every month or two.

At times the entertainment was good, because some of the performers were semiprofessional artists taken from among the prisoners or others who were gifted in some way. In these cases the company was allowed to go out of the camp, under guard, in order to perform in the nearby factories, and the members even managed to earn some money. Once I saw Teresa in the theater, where I had gone to pick up some materials in the storeroom. Another time I saw her at the foot of the hill, while she was carrying two buckets of water. Once we both had visitors on the same day: I met with my mother and my cousin, and immediately after that her brother came to visit her. My mother came to visit me about twice a year, on the traditional feast days of the dead;[88] other times my nephew or a cousin would take her place.

I had a way of seeing Teresa fleetingly on various other occasions. The officials of the prison usually organized spectacles or concerts for the prisoners on the national feast days in an attempt to revive the atmosphere of everyday life and to stimulate our interest. Once I joined a group that had to organize a show, and I happened to meet Teresa in the changing room where she and her companions were preparing a show on a more professional level.

One day in 1962, the official responsible for the entire education department of the prison, a certain Li, went up to the official of our group and asked to see me. After the usual questions (name, surname, place of

---

[88] Qingming (the fifth day of the third moon) and Chongyang (the ninth day of the ninth moon).

birth, et cetera), he paused and asked me if I knew some other prisoner in the camp. At first I gave a negative response: it was necessary to play the game, waiting for their move as in a game of chess. After many questions, he asked me again if I did not know one of the women prisoners. From this question I was aware that he probably already knew of my rapport with Teresa, so I changed tactics and immediately said that I knew Teresa Mo very well, and then I told him of our relationship at Canton. He was not interested in the story, but he wished to know if we had had contact while we were in the prison. I responded that, except for the shows in which Teresa recited with her group and which I attended as a spectator, I did not have any opportunity to see her, even if I wished it. Later, I discovered that one of Teresa's companions had noted the change in her expression when her group passed near me, as did others in a courtyard that they crossed on their way to perform in one of the factories nearby. After the performance this fact was reported; Teresa had been interrogated and had admitted knowing me. There was, anyway, no action undertaken. The officials viewed any type of contact between the prisoners a potential danger.

Another time I saw Father Yan,[89] the ex-secretary of Monsignor Tang at Canton. I was walking along one of the dormitories with another prisoner, and Father Yan was seated in front of the door like a guard. The dormitory was for the elderly and the handicapped, those unable to work,

---

[89] Father Anthony Yan Degeng was a priest esteemed for his holiness by the Catholics of Canton. He was arrested together with his bishop on February 5, 1958, and was condemned to forced labor in the stone cave of Niutoukeng, north of Canton. A Catholic who was his prison companion gave this testimony: "At the cave, when I felt the bite of hunger and the rheumatic pains made me suffer terribly, I wished to die as soon as possible. But at the sight of Father Yan, who, notwithstanding his emaciated body, took upon his shoulders a load of stone that made him ooze blood and pus, and who showed among so many sufferings a serene and calm face, I felt profoundly moved, and the strength to continue to live increased in me." Another Catholic who knew him at Canton before his arrest describes him as a humble and lovable priest, sought after as a guide and a confessor. Father Yan died in the labor camp of Niutoukeng in the sixties.

so guarding them was not very demanding. Father Yan had an excellent manner; modest in demeanor, he had never broken a prison rule, for which he was trusted with taking the names of those who entered and left the dormitory. In the hope of speaking with him, I told my companion to go ahead because I had to use the bathroom. As I had hoped, Father Yan had heard what I said and followed me. For about ten minutes we were able to exchange all the news that we knew about Monsignor Tang and other Catholics who were imprisoned. Eventually, Father Yan died in that camp.

Our meals were miserable: even the peanut shells were ground up and offered as food. Moreover, I soon became aware that that food was the cause of internal hemorrhaging, and so, notwithstanding our diet was at a level of starvation, I no longer ate the peanut shells. Wild herbs and a scant quantity of rice were all the food that we had; with that nourishment we had to work ten hours a day.

One day, while I was working at my cobbler's bench, a woman came near me and, watching the work that I was doing, said in a low voice, as if she were making a comment on my work: "Are you John Liao? God bless you!" These words, "God bless you," revealed something to me. I did not know her, but when I left the work camp years later, I discovered that she was a nun, and that at the end she returned to her native city, about an hour away by train. She and another nun had been the head of an orphanage managed by her congregation; and then, when all the foreign nuns were expelled, she, along with many others, was arrested.

During the summer of 1963 I was transferred from prison No. 2 to another camp near the province of Hunan; often they transferred groups of two hundred or three hundred prisoners. This time they transferred all the ill and infirm to the labor camp that previously had hosted the many thousands of prisoners who had been employed in the coal mines. There had been eight groups of several hundred prisoners each, but by now all the coal resources were nearly completely mined, and only one group extracted coal while the others cultivated vegetables. Now the camp buildings were used as a type of infirmary for the sick, and about twelve hundred of us were from prison No. 2. The camp was in the coldest part of the province, near the mountains. We were divided into four groups, without any task, with the exception of the domestic activities of daily life; each day, however, we had to spend eight hours in classes to educate ourselves in the Communist ideology, studying politics and reading books and articles that we then had to discuss. The principal goal of the program was to keep us occupied and under control since so great a number of prisoners without work could have caused problems if all had been free to walk around and to speak. In actuality we were not free to move or to rest.

I discovered that two Catholics were part of another group several miles away, and they were tasked with cultivating all the lettuce and cabbage necessary to feed the entire camp. One of them was Peter, a member of the Legion of Mary of Canton. The second came from another part of the province; he was an electrician by the name of James, who, because of his work, had much liberty of movement. Each time there was a transfer of prisoners, the two occupied themselves searching for any Catholics among them; and although their group was rather distant from ours, there was, at times, contact among us. On "great Sundays," the officials of the camp organized basketball tournaments; the two Catholics once came to our camp for a game, and I purposely took a place near them. They gave me news of the priests and Catholics of our acquaintance, speaking so that only I was able to hear. A little later the electrician was transferred to our group, and we met fairly often. At times the employee who was occupied with our political studies had us organize some entertainment, and this allowed us to be in contact while we rehearsed or sang. James accompanied us with a harmonica and always needed to rehearse, which gave us more time to speak to one another. At the end, however, the prison guards became suspicious and interrogated us on our relationships: thanks to the spies the guards were readily informed of each and every contact among the prisoners.

Communist Reeducation: The Methods

More oppressive than the low levels of material life were the human and psychological difficulties. In the prisons and in the labor camps were convicts of all criminal types: men guilty of the most unthinkable crimes were living, working, and studying with others accused only of political crimes. One could not trust anyone. The prisoners were encouraged to foment disorder, to spy, to lie, and to do whatever they could to benefit themselves. A person might seem very open and sincere, but he would not hesitate to betray anyone to obtain an advantage.

Consciences were corrupted, the bad became worse, and the prisoners looked for every opportunity to deceive and to create disorder through tricks and cunning. The Communist propaganda asserted that in China there were no prisons, only places for reform and reeducation tasked with eradicating all the bad elements and of transforming the people from ghosts to real men. The Communists claimed that they would transform man and the world, but even in the party the lie was an accepted principle: the truth, as such, did not have value. The party officials, on every level, were in competition with one another, and it did not exclude coming to blows in order to obtain power and personal benefits. From this aspect even the leaders provided an example: Liu Shaoqi, the president of the People's Republic, had been a personal friend and companion of Mao Zedong for more than thirty years, but Mao had no scruples about eliminating him in the struggle for power. The Communist political theory offered a great illusion to the people of the world: the practical application of that theory, which is based on a lie, can only be called diabolical. And the longer the prisoners stayed in the "schools" and labor camps, the more depraved and expert they became in each type of tactic.

On the basis of Stalin's theory, the Communists had to be better than average in terms of quality, because they had the special task of transforming the world, both from the human and the material point of view. The Communist ideology is aggressive, not passive, and it has the goal of transforming everyone, especially the criminal subjects (including property owners, capitalists, and the middle class), into new men, the bad into the new, on the basis of the Communist view of "good" and "bad." Not only the individual, but the entire social, economic, and political structure had to be changed, so that the old order and all its evil could be eliminated.

The committed Communist makes a special vow to dedicate himself to spreading the Communist ideology and its practical application in society.

The Communist policy of reform through work had two aspects: the transformation of the mentality of the individual and the participation in work as the means of reforming the world. According to Engels, it is man who created the world: at the beginning man was a type of animal that used his hands and feet in order to move himself and that gradually acquired the capacity to use his hands more appropriately and to develop himself and the surrounding world through the means of work. In this sense man has created the universe. According to the Communist ideology, work is the fundamental instrument for the continuation of that process of transformation, especially in the case of the bad elements of the society: according to a saying of Mao Zedong: "Every crime and every evil begins with laziness; evils begin when man has nothing to do."

As a starting point the person must acquire a specialization and must train in order to carry out a productive occupation that permits him to earn a living. On the basis of the theory that work itself corrects and modifies, the criminals, on their release, will become reformed individuals. But during their imprisonment they must maintain themselves through agricultural or industrial work and ought not to expect to be maintained by the State. Incidentally, the prisoners' manpower generates wealth that is handed over gratuitously to the State.

The policy of reform through work has the goal of transforming each nonproletariat constituent into a lover of Communist ideology and the new China. Mao Zedong went even further, criticizing the members of the party who apply this Communist theory to others while retaining a type of bourgeois life for themselves. He reminded them to reform themselves. One simple formula summarizes this ideological transformation: *poli*, "destroy and construct"—that is, destroy the old world and rebuild the new, Communist world.

Each year the politics of the Communist Party had to be explained and propagandized in specially designed programs. Articles, documents, and commentaries considered useful for the prisoners were gathered and presented for discussion as part of a course of study that lasted several months. All this material was presented and read to us during class lessons, and we then discussed it in our respective groups. Particular officials, different from those who supervised the work program, were responsible for these courses of study. It was their assignment to organize the entire course and to coordinate the discussion groups, listening to all the speeches and trying, as much as possible, to grasp the points of view and the mental attitudes of the prisoners. These discussions were an effective instrument for acquiring information on the mentality of individuals, especially when they provoked discussions and debates.

Each labor group or organization throughout the country had its courses of study in "the political science" of Communism; businesses, factories, and farms all followed the same model: listening to the report, studying the documents, taking part in discussions, and expressing opinions. The important thing is that everyone have the same way of thinking regarding the national and international events, that there exist only one outlook in the entire country, the Communist outlook. The party line, as indicated in *The People's Daily* or *The Red Flag*, and in the publications of the Communist Central Committee, gave us who were in prison and in the labor camps all the information that was considered useful or convenient from the point of view of the government. National or international affairs and political changes (as, for example, the improvement of relations with the United States) were presented in such a way as to support the policies of the government, past and present, and to eliminate all points of view that differed from those of the party. Their objective was to convince those of us in prison or in the labor camps that the policies of the government were the secure guide to an authentic Communism.

This imposition of propaganda and indoctrination is of primary importance to a totalitarian regime. The minister of propaganda was responsible for the entire system of reeducation and had the task of eliminating any type of reactionary trend. Whoever, for example, considered it possible that Taiwan would one day be able to take back political control of the country was considered a dangerous reactionary. (The Nationalist Party in

Taiwan had, in effect, sent many secret agents to the mainland to gather information about China.) Although they considered a role for Taiwan in China's future, the Communists never accepted the possibility of Taiwan taking political control of the mainland or of the United States helping them to regain power.

The sessions of political study followed a workday of at least ten hours, and all the participants were required to be actively involved during the lesson; each participant was expected to express his points of view in the form of self-criticism and criticism of others. Criticism was the principal form of ideological formation. At times the encounters were held solely with the goal of "helping" a prisoner to correct his ideas and of reeducating him. These individuals were obligated to stand up in order to recognize their faults and to accept the criticisms of the assembly; the more frank and complete the admission, the more likely the prisoner would receive clemency.

For example, a person could say that he had been deceived about the importance of the United States and that he was now able to recognize this deception; that he was aware that the Chinese people were sufficiently strong; and that China could expect to become a potential world power and thus part of the United Nations. This politics of self-incrimination, followed by reciprocal "help" and criticism, was the teaching and learning method used for all the materials that made up the program of study in politics.

Then the living targets, those who became the objects of the lesson during the evening political sessions, were selected. It was very easy to become one of these tools: a comment would be sufficient to transform a criminal into a recipient of every type of criticism and public insult. In addition the "revisions of life" took place regularly, at least once a month. The revisions were a type of public examination of conscience; each participant reviewed his life beginning from the preceding examination of conscience and publicly confessed his own faults and deficiencies. There were many rules to observe in prison and in the labor camps, so it was not difficult to find something to confess: having been lazy, not having been fully attentive during the lessons on politics, speaking of one's own crime or sentence with others, et cetera.

Every omission was noted by others and reported: one could not omit anything. Consequently, we were all hyperaware of the regulations, even the minimal, and we paid close attention not to break them or at least not to let them see that we did not respect them. All that was said during these encounters was annotated and regularly reviewed every three, six, and twelve months, when the final accounting was examined and the group chose the prisoner who had completed the most significant improvement. The prizes consisted of the most desired articles: a towel, a cup, et cetera. In addition, each year some acknowledgments resulted in a minor reduction of the sentence or in some treasured item, such as a pair of shoes or a fountain pen. Before the Cultural Revolution, now and then, a prisoner would be given money, which permitted him to buy things considered a luxury, such as cigarettes or sweets, things that represented great encouragement in these situations.

The application of these methods, being psychological in nature, encouraged the prisoners to respect the law and to behave, thereby making it easier for the authorities to control them. The two types of encounters, the open and the revision of life, were completed in succession and evaluated. Even the party officials followed the same system. The head of the labor camp formed a group, and their discussions and criticisms were carried out according to rules appropriate to their life and responsibilities. The same procedure was followed at each level, even among the highest members of the party. Zhou Enlai was noted for his strict observance of this organizational system: he always consulted the members of his group, which included secretaries and bodyguards, and asked for the authorization to do whatever was diverse from what was written by the rules of the party.

The method of formation through reciprocal criticism was very efficacious for controlling errors and for creating an atmosphere of diffidence, fear, and suspicion among the prisoners. It was dangerous to have a friend or a confidant or even to make a critical comment regarding authorities or the government. Sooner or later indiscreet confidences would be divulged, and conversations spoken in the past would be revealed.

Thus, the politics of the struggle, what Marxists considered the principle of progress, was developed. To attack and trample others was also a way of improving one's own position, a way of acquiring merits and at times even a reduced sentence for one's zeal. Those who did not criticize others were considered passive elements who could not sustain the Communist ideal. In reality, rather than improve the mentality of the prisoners, this type of coercion and oppression augmented their shrewdness and their bad faith; everyone learned to play along with the authorities, showing humility and submission exteriorly, but in fact hiding things more important than those they acknowledged. It is not possible to change man with the power of fear, but only with the help of God and free will.

Again Farther North

In late autumn of 1964 several officials came to our camp, and there was the usual convocation that preceded the transfers as well as a more detailed medical examination. We noted that there was something different from a normal transfer in the atmosphere. James informed me that, while he was doing a repair in the house of one of the prison officials, he learned from some documents that this transfer would be outside the province, in the province of Hubei, a location even farther north. He urged me to keep this information secret, so I kept it to myself.

Transfers occurred regularly in the camps in other parts of China, in Heilongjiang, near the border with Siberia, in Qinghai, in Inner Mongolia, and in other remote localities of the north. In 1964 the political situation was very tense, and ours was part of a massive transfer of several thousand prisoners; even our group infirmary was moved during the winter months in various stages. The last of the transfers arrived in Hubei in midwinter. A series of trains was available for this operation: each convoy was composed of twenty cars of the type used to transfer livestock, each car able to hold fifty to sixty prisoners. Therefore, each convoy included more than a thousand prisoners. The cars were well adapted to this end, having only four small windows in the upper part for ventilation, and the access door was securely closed externally. Because we were in the most northern part of the province, when we climbed on, the train was already completely full; each province had several prisons and each district various labor camps, so that those who had to be transferred were already on the train heading north.

Although we knew that the transfer was imminent, no one knew of the destination, and the prison officials were careful to avoid leaking any information. A transfer farther north would not have been well received, as it would have meant even greater adversity, above all because of the climate in places where the temperature registered under zero. The prospect generated the fear that we could not ever survive in such conditions and that we would be dead before having served our entire sentence. Among the prisoners, then, there was an aura of depression and anxiety that encouraged attempts to flee and suicides; therefore, the officials, who were doing everything they could to keep secret our destination, attempted to raise the prisoners' morale with more material care, procuring for them better food and some type of entertainment.

Since I already had a certain idea of our future destination, I gave a dear friend in the camp some of my best books. But even this gesture was reported, and I was therefore interrogated and commanded not to encourage the general worry by disposing of my things in this way. It was necessary for everyone to back up the jailers' game: pretending that all was proceeding normally and that nothing special was happening.

Before our group of six hundred left the camp, we were gathered together to spend three days in psychological preparation for the transfer. The "course" consisted in administering a series of encounters, discussions, and pastimes, intended to create a more positive attitude in the prisoners. It was necessary that the doubts and anxiety come out into the open so that they could be dissipated and so that the baselessness of each fear could be demonstrated. To this end they even dished out extra spending: one of the better-than-usual films was rented; the diet was improved, and even meat was added. In short, everything was done to render those three days a time of rest and reassurance.

On the morning of the third day of this special treatment, we were called very early; we had breakfast, and then we got on the lorries that would take us from the camp to the station. Armed guards checked us before we all got on the train; the presence of closed cars clearly indicated that the train was already full of prisoners and that we were the last group to join the convoy. The train departed: it traveled slowly, stopping for some time at each station in order to allow regular trains and expresses to pass. Under normal conditions and onboard an express, the trip, which for us lasted two days, would have taken twenty-four hours. At Wuhan a group of prisoners left the train and were directed to a porcelain factory, which constituted one of three work groups at prison No. 3 in the province of Hubei, an area that was "blessed" with six immense prisons. Immediately after, the train deviated toward the northeast; the pace was even slower, because at that point the line was newly constructed and the work had not yet been completed. The following morning the train was stopped and, after a new roll call, several hundred prisoners left the convoy to be transported to a farm.

At the end, it was around eight in the morning when the remaining prisoners were ordered to collect their baggage and get off the train. Fifteen lorries were waiting to transport seven to eight hundred of us; the first and last lorries carried the armed guards who were directing the operations and keeping the situation under control with portable radios. During the journey we crossed three districts and several cities, covering a distance of about four hundred kilometers [about 249 miles]. All along the way, at intervals of seventy to eighty meters, guards were in position: the local military of each commune[90] had received the order to prevent flight using every possible means. In fact, it did not involve a normal transfer; rather,

---

[90] The popular communes (agricultural) represented an attempt to realize the collectivization of every aspect of the life of the Chinese peasants: economic, cultural, administrative, military.

it was a massive operation directly organized by the central government of Peking. The importance that this event assumed in the eyes of the military was made plain by the fact that at each station they opened each car in order to verify whether some prisoners had need of medical treatment; indeed they were being held directly responsible for each prisoner.

We arrived at Xiangyang between the fifteenth and the sixteenth but without any stop; the convoy continued north for fifteen to eighteen kilometers toward our destination, a labor camp placed under the jurisdiction of prison No. 6 of the province of Hubei. This camp produced bricks and tiles; it was very large and comprised many sections specializing in works of diverse types: machinery, repairs, farming, and so on. Our section was a factory, famous in the province for its products and extremely profitable for the government, since it annually earned more than a million dollars. I would remain there until the end of my sentence.

My New Labor Camp

In my new labor camp the work was exhausting. Mechanization was scarce, and most of the labor was manual. Being so far north, the cold was very intense; in the winter the temperature dropped below zero, and the chill reigned. Thus, the winter months were utilized for repairing and overhauling the factory and extracting the raw materials necessary for the production of the bricks and tiles. The major part of the hand labor was engaged in extracting the clay and bringing it to a place near the establishment. The clay had to be extracted from holes always covered with water. About fifteen hundred prisoners were employed in this work during the winter; only later were machines substituted.

The production of our factory garnered nearly 100 percent profit: the primary material was furnished by nature, the labor force was gratis, the tools were simple, and the costs of production were minimal; therefore the profit was elevated. One could estimate that the cost per brick was about one-hundredth of a yuan and that the sale price was five cents or more. During the last period of my stay in the camp, in order to increase production, more machinery was introduced. Tractors replaced manpower, at least in part, relieving the prisoners of the heavy work that made them so tired they could not even manage to eat. During this period the factory produced four hundred thousand bricks a day; the annual production between 1976 and 1978 surpassed a billion pieces.

Each day the bricks and tiles were loaded onto lorries. Notwithstanding the great profits (our factory was only one of the many labor camps), the country continued to decline economically; the greater the production, the greater the waste. Later on, even the general secretary of the party, Zhao Ziyang, recognized that the most serious problem of the country was the waste of resources, because the bureaucratic system absorbed all the profit; the officials took everything and gave back nothing.

The Communist policy for all the prisons and labor camps was that the prisoners' food rations must not exceed those of the inhabitants of the area; indeed, they had to be less. It was not taken into consideration that those who were free could procure something in more diverse ways.

At the beginning I became part of the manual labor that extracted the clay. But the severe climate and the heavy labor in the water was disastrous for my rheumatism, which progressively worsened until after a few months I woke up one morning incapable of moving. Apart from the pain, my knees were too weak to move or to permit me to stand up, and they had to carry me on shoulders to the ambulance. Until then I had managed to drag myself around but now I could no longer do it.

I remained in the camp infirmary seven months, incapable even of eating during the first month. For four or five months I had to remain in bed; then I tried to walk with crutches. I tried to do it several times a day, encouraged by the guards who admired my efforts and perseverance. The medical doctors tried to use remedies that had been effective in cases like mine, but the medicines turned out to be useless.

Then there was the rule that, after a month's stay in the infirmary, the food rations for the in-patients would be reduced, since the sick were not working; for the first month, I was not able to eat, and when I began to improve the ration was reduced. Thus, the guards encouraged me to return to my group, where I would have at least benefited from the entire food ration; formally I would have had to return to work, but in reality I would have done only what I was able. Then my work assignment was changed, and I was transferred to a group assigned to cultivate vegetables for all fifteen prisoners.

There were forty acres of vegetable gardens, which produced fifteen hundred tons of vegetables a year. The work was not easy or less tiring, but I was able to work according to my capacity and to transport only what I was able; for example, I was permitted to carry the sacks of dung filled only halfway. The prison employees were supportive in their own way, and they advised me to return to my former work in order to obtain a little more food, emphasizing that their objective was not to destroy the prisoners physically, but only to change their mentality. As for the work, I would be required to do only what was possible for me.

The Communist practice in the matter of work is a typical example of the policy followed in each sector of the Communist State. According to such an ideology, work is the effective remedy for correcting each vice or crime against society: the use of instruments for developing the brain and work can create a new man and a new world. This materialism is, in effect, an anti-theory, a trick that leads to an illusion; work is certainly part of the law of life, a command given by God to man through Adam; but it should be only a part of the life of man. Work is in itself good and necessary; but to elevate it to the role of the universal remedy is a perversion of the truth. Work can stimulate the exercise of the faculties of a person, develop his capacities, provide the means of sustenance, and be corrective or punitive, but it should not be enslaving.

In totalitarian regimes the party is the supreme master, hiding itself behind lies such as that of being at the service of the people, when actually it enslaves them, reserving all powers for itself. Where before there was the exploitation of some, now all have become instruments directed toward producing wealth for an egoistic single-party system and their self-interests. Under such regimes there is not much difference between life in prison or in a labor camp and life outside: all are slaves of the authority, manipulated by the Communist Party. It is true, there is more liberty outside the prison, but the condition of life is still essentially slavish. The same can be said for the Soviet Union, Vietnam, North Korea, Cuba, and other totalitarian regimes: the people are exploited and enslaved, the salaries are low, and the profits end up with the party. This is the essence of Communism. On the basis of the principle that the level of life of the prisoners must be on a par with that of the local peasants, the conditions of the detainees varied according to the location of the prison or the labor camp: those in a more prosperous locality fared better, and those who were in a village or in a mountainous area or in the countryside fared worse. In fact, the entire country was in a state of poverty, with the exception of the cities near the railroad that were better connected. In the south and the southeast there was greater prosperity; toward the north the conditions of life became gradually worse. In Hubei we had three meals a day: with only two it would have been impossible to carry out that heavy work. There was a fixed ration of rice, determined by the tenor of the local life, but the quantity of vegetables could be augmented whenever the supplies increased. The officials were aware of the importance of an adequate diet to maintain or to increase the production and to avoid discontent in the camp: if we produced more vegetables, we would be able to have better meals.

In Hubei we discovered the low level of existence in the northern provinces, and the harsh conditions of the local life made us more content with ours. The inhabitants of the zone were so poor that many prisoners saved a little of the money that was given them (a small sum, one or two yuan a month, to permit us to buy things such as soap, paper, toothbrushes, and so forth) to send to their families, so that they could improve their situation a little; at Canton we were not aware of the existence of such poor conditions because we had never experienced them. In some cases a prisoner, father or son, represented the principal source of earnings for his family, and therefore he saved everything that he could in order to send it to his family for their basic necessities: salt, oil for the lamps, and so on. The officials of the prison encouraged this practice.

DIARIES OF THE CHINESE MARTYRS

The Years of the Laogai

After the "liberation" many soldiers and officials were transferred from the military to the civil sector. Those who had special gifts or qualifications followed a course of formation and became magistrates. These men had demonstrated their fidelity during their military service; and they had worked long enough to prove their obedience to the party. Some were members of the party, others were not, but all had to be completely reliable regarding the Communist ideology; that is, they had to have a strong sense of the importance of the class struggle; otherwise they would not have been qualified to apply the party's policies.

The officials of every level followed a more intensive program of political studies than the prisoners because it was up to them to explain it to us and to promote it. The guards also formed their own study group; led by the head of the camp and an official responsible for propaganda, they followed the same procedure of listening to the reports, studying, and discussing. Whatever their rank, it was necessary to study and absorb the policies of the central government so as to be able to apply them to the daily life at every level.

The officials also met to choose the prisoners who had acquired the greatest merit through observation of the rules, a spirit of criticism, and a positive zeal in sustaining the policies of the party. This was the way to obtain advancement and—ironically—to enjoy some privileges reserved to those high up. The Communists boasted of being completely disinterested and of working exclusively for the ideals of the party, of being one society without classes in which all are equal, unlike what happens in the Western capitalist system. In reality Communism did not reach this ideal, because human nature retains all its ambition, its imperfections, and its individualism.

History speaks for itself. What are the real conditions of the life of the people in the Soviet Union after seventy years of Communism, in China, in Cuba, and in other socialist countries? What has changed? And why do the people try to leave these countries, employing every means, asking for political asylum in the free, noncommunist world? Human nature and noble aspirations cannot be suppressed. The conscience cannot ever be completely suffocated. Even after so many years of pressure directed at suppressing the conscience and substituting the truth with political convenience the prisoners, in various ways, continued to manifest that the conscience remained alive.

Even the party members did not always succeed in suppressing reactions and behavior that proceeded from their own human nature. During the Cultural Revolution, for example, when cruelty and materialism were very common, some officials did not allow the victims to be tortured, maintaining that no one could be converted through force. In effect the ignorant masses were the only ones to believe in the Communist propaganda and to seek the Communist paradise on earth. They leaned on the revolution and worked for the government in expectation of the rising of the new era, but in the end they had to wake up from this dream; little by little, the years passed and their state of slavery remained the same. Even those entirely dedicated to the Communist ideology and who conformed to it for many years were, at times, moved by their consciences, which were still alive in them, rather than by a thought inculcated in them throughout their lives. According to the Communist theory, responsibility is in the hands of a minority: the heads at the top. The masses are not able to discern the true from the false and should let themselves be guided by those who make beautiful promises, which, however, do not ever become reality.

In the camp, at times, I would happen to see a familiar face. Father Ye, who had been with me in the prison of the tribunal, and later transferred, was in the end in the camp of Hubei during the same massive transfer that also brought me there. He was in the same brick and tile factory, but not in my group. At first both of us transported the clay; then Father Ye was assigned to transport the material with a small locomotive to the factory about ten kilometers away. First the clay had to be broken up with explosives; then we loaded heaps of it on the railroad cars for transport. Another priest, Father Su,[91] was also working with Father Ye; only a couple

---

[91] Father Su was originally from Hubei.

of months before the end of his detention, in 1972, Father Su was killed by a load of clay that fell on his head after an explosion. Two other persons lost their lives in that accident.

In 1972 Father Ye completed his sentence and was transferred to a farm where there was more liberty, in the category defined "occupations for criminals following their release." I encountered him once, some months after his transfer, when we were sent to that farm to help harvest the peanuts. After that I had no news of him until six years later; having left prison, I went to Canton, where I met his nephew, who worked in the government hospital. He told me that Father Ye wished to ask for a vacation, but that he did not wish to be liberated from the camp: it was difficult to find work, and those who had served time in prison were always discriminated against, so he preferred to remain where he was.

In that brick and tile factory I knew another priest, Father Chen,[92] who was originally from my province. I considered it unwise to show that I recognized him, and he also seemed not to know me. As already mentioned, Father Xu had also pretended not to recognize me when we found ourselves in the same cell at Canton in 1956. In that state the mind suffers from the pressures and the physical deprivations and becomes nervous and absent. Father Xu had found a pastime during the long hours he spent in his cell with nothing to do: because he had only wooden clogs and shoes without laces that made walking difficult (the laces had been confiscated), he fabricated a pair of shoes out of an old book and some glue that he made from a paste of water and rice flour (made from some rice saved from his meal). The shoes were solid enough, because he kept them away from water.

Meanwhile, for two years Teresa had remained in the police prison at Canton; after her appeal, her sentence of fifteen years was changed to life in prison. The life in prison was imposed because she had not admitted

---

[92] Father Chen Shigao belonged to the Diocese of Shantou (Guangdong). He studied at Rome and was a docent at the University of Furen at Peking. After a period of forced labor at the beginning of the eighties he was liberated and able to return to his diocese.

to her crimes! Afterward, in 1963, her sentence was again changed to fifteen years of seclusion; by this time the wave of political persecutions had abated and the officials of the city of Canton, in reviewing some of the cases, decided that the sentences seemed too severe. Teresa was also transferred to a farm where the released criminals worked, and here she met up with Rosa and Linda. All three remained on the farm until 1977. The conditions of life in these agricultural colonies were halfway between prison life and liberty. The regulations there were different from those of the labor camps, but there was also the same work and study program as in the other types of detention. Moreover, among the prisoners there was the same reciprocal mistrust, denunciation, and struggle. There was, however, also a limited liberty: during the "great Sunday," for example, one could request permission to go out to shop in the nearby village or city, where better food and underwear could be found. Once or twice a year one could ask permission to go visit relatives for two or even three weeks (journey included, if the distance was notable); the government paid the expenses of the first visit. But the political prisoners who were on the farm were able to request this permission only once every two years: "Wearing the hat,"[93] they were deprived of all the rights of citizens. An irony of the regime permitted other criminals "without a hat," even if they were assassins, to ask for permission once a year and at the same time enjoyed their full rights.

The factory pay was about twenty-five or thirty yuan a month, a little lower than the usual salary for that type of work. In fact government policy considered agricultural work inferior to industrial work, which gave greater profit. The prisoners were encouraged to save money and to send it home in order to help the families that were often living in poverty.

From 1972, after being transferred to this farm, Teresa enjoyed greater liberty and resources. By now ten years had passed since the last time we met, and she wished to learn whether I was still alive and, if so, where I was.

---

[93] The phrase refers to the practice of forcing a "criminal" to walk through the streets crying out his faults and wearing a high, pointed paper hat (like a dunce cap) on his head.

DIARIES OF THE CHINESE MARTYRS

Thus, in 1974, during a leave, returning to her family at Canton, Teresa went to my younger brother, who lived a short distance from the city, to ask for news of me. Neither he nor any other member of my family was in contact with me, with the exception of my mother; for years it was dangerous to be in contact with a "counterrevolutionary" relative. My brother then wrote to my mother to get my address, which he sent to Teresa at Canton through my nephew.

Although I had contact with my mother, it was impossible for her to visit me, given the enormous distance between us. Once, while I was in the infirmary and was unable to move, my nephew came to see me from Canton, traveling thousands of miles to visit with me for just half an hour. I could not think of the future; and only as long as my mother was living would I have been able to have news of my family. So the arrival of a letter from Teresa, in April of 1975, caused me some agitation: knowing that the guards at the prison would have read the letter before handing it over to me, she told me briefly of her transfer to the farm and asked about me. She also sent me ten yuan and various coupons for cotton, which was rationed: each one had the right to twenty-five, thirty, or thirty-five centimeters.

For several days I remained shaken by this unexpected letter: I had abandoned the hope of ever seeing my family and my friends, and of resuming a normal life, and I looked to my life in paradise as my only possible future; now I did not know how to respond to Teresa's letter. After thinking about it for a few days, I wrote to her, telling her to be realistic and not to have illusions about the future. She was by now over forty years old, and therefore she should not lose time and should plan her future: she should find someone with whom she could be happy. I wished her every good. But two months later I received her response, in which she wrote that we had been intimate friends before and that we would be able to be so again, that she would not think of marrying another man, and that she hoped that I would get back in condition so that I could be released as soon as possible. All these letters were read by the authorities, for which reason they had to be simple and clear, in order to avoid problems. In those years Teresa was under pressure, and she suffered much, like all those theoretically "released from prison." All were eager to marry and to have a house and a family; marriage, in fact, permitted one to have a room of one's own, rather than having to live in a dormitory commune on the farm. Therefore, many individuals married each other simply for this reason and then ended up divorcing after a few months together.

Teresa was criticized because she sent a letter to a work camp and she was thinking of marrying an inmate. The official who was the head of her group wished to help her find another companion and, when the packages that she sent me were returned to sender, they put her on guard, saying that I must be uninterested and obstinate if I was not even allowed to receive her gifts. The politics of the work camps wished to discourage the sending of packages to the detainees, also because of the inconveniences to the family who sent them. They thought that the detainee should help his family. Besides, the packages caused jealousy and resentment among the detainees and induced them to steal; if someone was robbed, it was the one robbed who was criticized for having created the problems! This, however, was not my manner of doing things. I preferred to trust in Providence: if a letter arrived, I would have responded; otherwise I would not have done anything.

In Expectation of My Release

During the usual political campaign that took place various times during the year, each evening, after the lesson on politics, there was a mass encounter: each one had to make a contribution, denouncing or giving information in order to follow the Communist policies; the "struggle"[94] was always necessary in order for a person to advance, and criticism was considered a way of "helping" others.

I did not ever actively participate at these meetings, and I was criticized for my passivity. I was asked to take a copy of Mao's *Little Red Book*, to open it to a certain page, and to read a passage that spoke of "antiliberalism,"

[94] See page 125, note 50.

which referred to those who did not give any importance to the struggle, but only to their own affairs. Furthermore, I was reminded that I should put into practice the study of Mao's doctrine, that the struggle was a principle of progress, and that I myself was helped by the struggle that was sustained by others; for this reason, I also ought to make a contribution and be ready to intervene and criticize. At the next meeting I was obliged to say something, but I did it with great moderation, not as those in charge would have wished; they told me that my responses were superficial and lacked substance; they were not content, although they did not add anything else.

In some periods of intense political activity and persecutions, these mass gatherings were held every evening. Then, when the campaigns failed, they became less frequent, although they were an integral part of the system of political reeducation of each work group. Within certain limits the officials understood me: they recognized that I was conscientious and honest, that notwithstanding my fragile physical conditions, I did not ever try to absent myself from work. They praised my spirit of public service and my sense of duty, and they entrusted me with responsibilities, such as checking the storerooms and keeping everything secure and in good order.

Three months before the end of my sentence, the official responsible for our group told me that the managers of the camp had the task of notifying the local police office of every criminal who was to be released, in order to know whether, once he was released, he could return to the province of his origin. If the office gave its consent, they had to find a piece of land to cultivate, a place where he could live, and some work instruments; otherwise the released prisoner who returned home without a means of support would create problems, increasing the risk that he would rob and commit other crimes. The official then told me that they had discussed my case and sent a letter to the office of Public Safety of Shaoguan, notifying them of the end of my sentence.

On the basis of the policy of the central government, that is, of the Office of Public Safety, there were generally three types of release at the end of a detention:

- *Liu* (to remain) was the rarest and consisted in remaining in the same camp, but with conditions analogous to those in force for whoever was released: a small salary, liberty to go out twice a month for the "great Sunday," et cetera. Usually that meant that at the camp there was need of the prisoner until someone could take his place as a technician, a tractor driver, or some other skilled worker.

- *Diao* (to transfer) was the normal case, consisting in the transfer from the labor camp to a farm or to a factory.

- *Fung* (to release) was ultimately a total release and return home. It was not very common, especially if the prisoner came from one of the border provinces. This total liberty was granted only when there was a certainty that the prisoner would not create problems or commit crimes. But if one were not a criminal and had behaved well during the detention, there was no objection to letting him go completely free; the prison officials knew very well that those who had been arrested and condemned during the wave of political persecutions were less dangerous from the criminal point of view.

The head of our group told me that he had informed my family at Shaoguan and the Office of Public Safety that as soon as they received their response approving my return, he himself would look for work for me that was appropriate for someone in my physical condition, for example, bookkeeping or accounting. He wished to do as much as he could for me, because he knew that I was trustworthy and that I had behaved in a trustworthy manner during my imprisonment. In January 1978 I received a letter from my mother, in which she wrote that an official had recently gone to see her to ask her some questions about me; she did not understand the sense of such questions and was perplexed. I then discovered that it concerned an inquiry that preceded the notification of my release.

My father came only once to see me during my imprisonment. He was already elderly, and the officials criticized me for having asked him to come, given his age and the uncomfortable conditions of the journey. In reality I had not asked him to come; rather, it was he who wished to see me at least once and probably for the last time. Later, my mother told me how all the family had suffered because of the political discrimination toward those who belonged to the class of former landowners. Between 1957 and 1964 my parents were living with my younger brother when they were obligated to return to their native city under surveillance during the campaign of the four "purges." Everyone avoided them, and they suffered great poverty. They had to provide for themselves and procure water from the well that was two hundred meters from where they lived. In 1972 my father, who was over eighty years old, fell while transporting two buckets of water and broke a leg; he was not able to move, but no one dared give him a hand and help him because he belonged to a class branded by the regime.

My mother was forced to work in the fields every day, and she found out what had happened to my father only three-quarters of an hour after the accident, when an elderly woman, who had seen my father on the ground, went secretly to tell her to hurry. But my mother didn't have enough strength to lift him up, and it took her a long time to find someone who had the courage to help her transport him to the hut where they lived. My father could not move his leg, and he suffered very much. Finally my mother brought him to the hospital, but the doctors did not wish to treat him; they told him to go home because he was too old to endure the medical treatment.

From that moment my father was not able to move. My mother wrote to me and informed me of all that had happened. The guard who read the letter first asked me about my family situation: the principal concern of the prison authorities is that bad news from home could upset the prisoners and disturb the others. In November 1977 my mother sent me a brief note that my father had died on October 30. When this news arrived, once again the guard took me aside and interrogated me about my family before handing me the letter. But I had foreseen this moment for some time, and the official was satisfied with my tranquil reaction; he interpreted it as a demonstration of success on the part of their reeducation program and was somewhat sympathetic; he invited me to write to my mother to console her and to remind her that I would be liberated soon and free to return home.

John Liao Shouji

In fact, after twenty years of prison and labor camp and the suppression of each emotion that accompanies the experience, one nearly loses the capacity of feeling any sensation beyond that of merely bearing whatever it happens to be at that moment. One becomes insensible, nearly deprived of emotion for whatever is happening; in an already negative situation, even bad news was relative. It is the natural process of immunization that makes survival possible.

The date of my release arrived, but there was no response from the authorities of my native city. The prison authorities were not able to do anything until the arrival of that response, so that night I left the premises of the prison and was transferred to another dormitory with others who had completed their sentences. After two months of not having yet received a response from Shaoguan, I asked permission to visit my mother, now that I had expiated my sentence; she was already old, and I could have received news of an illness or her death at any moment. But in spite of the fact that the officials were aware of the situation and were understanding enough, the normal procedure would have to take its course even in my case; it was impossible to permit me to return to my native city without the consent of the authorities of that city. Toward the end of April there was still no response, so I was transferred, with others awaiting the second type of release (diao), to a camp not far away, in a suburb only a few miles from the city. It was a cave of stone where the work was carried out mechanically. All year long several furnaces, twenty to thirty meters high, worked full time: the extracted stone was brought there, and the lower layers were flushed, transforming them into a lime powder and calcium oxide. Other businesses working at the same cave produced calcium carbonate, bricks, and tiles. There were many lucrative activities at this camp: our group of about 130 persons procured a net profit of around five hundred thousand yuan a year. We were paid very little, about twenty-five yuan a month: while there, I often thought of the Jews who had worked as slaves for the Egyptians before the Exodus, making bricks and pulling carts.

The task was greater than my strength, however. Already in 1956 this labor was too difficult for me, and after twenty-three years of scant nutrition and mental stress, it was even more so. The heads of the operation wished to help me, but they were not able to do anything because they had to respect the rules. The difficulty of the labor was apparent: there was no limit to the alcohol permitted, and meat was served twice a week, as were eggs and other nutritious foods, yet those in charge of the factory noticed that I was losing considerable weight. They encouraged me to eat everything I could, and they obtained medications for my rheumatism but without any results. They were struck by the fact that I did not demand to be exonerated from the work, and they cited me as an example to the others who were trying to avoid the work even if they were better off than I. At times, in order to give me some relief, they made me teach the others to sing, granting me half a day to rest to prepare the lesson.

Return to Shaoguan

I had had no news of my mother since January of 1978; in April I was still waiting to know something from the authorities at Shaoguan. I did not expect any happiness in this life; I accepted the suffering and the daily work as God's will for me, for his glory and for the love of the Body of Christ, the Church. For me it was enough.

Finally the response arrived. The head of our group came to bring me the letter. The refusal was motivated for two reasons: I did not have a residence at Shaoguan, and it was not possible to give me any land to cultivate, because the urban and industrial development of Shaoguan had exceeded the limits of the surrounding areas and the authorities were short of land for cultivation. Although it was their duty to provide tools and the means of support for whoever returned from prison or from the labor camp, they did not have the means to do so.

The response was completely unexpected; I was especially stunned that they had taken six months to inform me that they could not permit me to return home. Even those in charge of the prison could not understand their motives, and they encouraged me to try again and to convince my relatives to speak on my behalf. Meanwhile my mother wrote to me again, enclosing a letter from Teresa, the first in a year. The guard wished to know about Teresa and was amazed that that girl was still trying to keep in contact with me after twenty years; he then urged me to try with every means to obtain permission to return home, particularly because of the advanced age of my mother and her needs for assistance; and to ask my beloved to use her influence to help me. It seemed to me that the only way of resolving the matter was for me to go to Shaoguan to deal personally with the authorities. But although the heads of the prison were favorable, they could not violate regulations: given my position as a political prisoner, I had the right to go home only after two years, and my sentence had terminated just two months before. They were not able, therefore, to make any special concession.

On June 30 I received a telegram that resolved the case. A friend, having encountered my mother, who was anxiously waiting my return, took the initiative to send me a telegram: "Mother gravely ill, return immediately." The telegram was given to me at seven in the evening after I returned from work; even if I had suspected that it was a ploy to help me, I did not imagine that it could have worked. The official at the head of my group had already seen the telegram; he also thought that it was only a way to permit me to return home, but he used it anyway to help me. He immediately accompanied me to the Office of Permits, even though it was after hours. For the office to release a document after hours was something exceptional, but the insistence of the official won out over the reluctance of the worker, and I was able to leave that day.

It was cold, and the journey took three days. When I arrived at Shaoguan I understood the situation: my parents, who had belonged to the property class, bore, for all of us, the loss of citizenship, social status, and property—the loss of everything. To facilitate the confiscation of all our goods, our social status was lowered to that of a peasant belonging to a commune. My mother now lived in a small hut, twelve by thirteen square meters; it was dirty, dark, and without windows; it was a hovel not worthy of a hobo. I asked what it had been used for previously, and they told me that it was a pigpen. In the summer it was like a furnace, and in the winter it was freezing and the rain came inside. My parents had lived in these conditions for many years.

The health of my mother seemed pretty good, as well as her sight and her hearing; she feared that the telegram might have stirred up some problems with the authorities. I reassured her that everyone knew this system of resolving a problem and the law had been respected.

My relatives, however, did not favor my return to Shaoguan, and they were opposed to my becoming a member of that commune. They advised me to return to the labor camp and to attempt another way of returning to Shaoguan or to Canton. Moreover, they informed me, once placed in an agricultural commune it was more or less impossible to transfer to a city; besides, beyond the lack of land, the work was too heavy for me and the systems of labor were beyond primitive. They advised me to reflect well before deciding.

When I began to understand the situation, I decided to go to Canton to look for Teresa and other friends, in order to see what could be done. Three days later I telephoned my nephew, who accompanied me to Canton, to see one of my best friends.

I discovered immediately why Teresa had not written to me for more than a year: she had ended up under surveillance, in the category of those who "wear the hat." "Wearing the hat" signified a total lack of civil rights, including having to attend various classes on politics during the week, having to participate in services benefiting the community, such as sweeping the streets, and having to notify the police when leaving the house. My nephew and my friend were aware of the situation and helped me. The contact with Teresa was accomplished through an acquaintance who agreed to go to the Mo family with the excuse of visiting Teresa's brother but in reality to inform her that I was in Canton.

She came to see me at noon, after having said that she was going to the hospital. When she saw me all skin and bones and the signs of the hard labor of all those years, she held back the tears with difficulty. Although the prison official had suggested that I ask for her help with my quest to return home, it was clear that she would not be able to do anything; she herself was not free, and her family was not cooperating. For her it was dangerous even to visit me, so after two days I decided to return to Shaoguan.

It was clear that there were no hopes for the future. My friends advised me not to be in a hurry, to wait until Teresa had "lost the hat" and reacquired her citizenship and then see if she could go abroad and try to join her. That may have taken five to eight years. While I was with Teresa I availed myself of the opportunity to tell her what I was thinking. I said that it made no sense for us to think of a future, that my prospects were too uncertain and that the best thing for her was to be realistic in this matter. Meanwhile, her mother and her brother had applied for authorization to permit her to leave the country; it seemed to be what God had in reserve for her and for her future, rather than having her cling to an idea that could never be realized.

When I decided to return to Shaoguan, Teresa wished to risk accompanying me to the station to see me depart; so, with my friend Dominic, she walked on the opposite side of the street to avoid the danger of being seen in the company of an undesirable person. Having seen Teresa's situation, I was not able to think of asking her to help me to return to Canton; on the contrary, I repeated to her that she should not wait for me and that she should go abroad if she had the opportunity.

A sense of desolation filled our farewells: so many years away from Canton and still it was not possible to speak or to move freely, nor were there any prospects for the future. Then the train departed.

Free Again

As soon as I returned to Shaoguan I sent a letter, special delivery, to my younger sister, who was living in the province of Guangxi. Having known of my return home, she made the long trip to see me, in spite of the heat and her poor health. She had suffered much during the political persecution, and even her husband had gone against her, attempting to divorce her several times. But not even my sister knew how to advise me about the best course to take. My leave was about to expire, and I requested the help of a son of one of my cousins; it seemed to me that the best thing was to leave the work camp and take care of my mother. There was no future for me at Shaoguan, much less in the province of Hubei. But in any case I had to return to the camp.

The officials were eager to know what I managed to accomplish and were not pleased to learn that I had no prospects for the future. I had to find an excuse for the lack of success with Teresa: I did not intend to reveal that she was not able to do anything because she was classified as a counterrevolutionary. They were aware that physically I could not be a farm laborer, and they were anxious about my liberation, so they passed on any suggestions that might help me to go home.

Toward the end of July I decided to chance returning to Shaoguan, whatever the risks for changing my future status from peasant to citizen; if nothing else, I would be home and able to find a way to resolve the problem. Therefore, I wrote to my cousin and to his daughter, asking them to help me. I also wrote to the authorities of Shaoguan, telling them that I was not asking for their intervention to procure money, materials, or instruments for work or a piece of land; I wished only to occupy myself with my mother, who was alone, and that my siblings had promised to maintain me. In August I sent this letter to my relatives so that they could hand it over to the proper authorities on my account, and within a month, I received permission to return home. At camp the formalities were rushed and in the fall, one evening toward nine, after the political studies, the official produced a paper, saying that it was a list of the names of those who were going home; there were five of us.

At the time, I had a bit of a fever, and I had to wait a few days before leaving Hubei. As on the occasion of my previous release, my companions asked me to leave them what I had that would be useful to them; my relatives and Teresa had given me a little stove and some kerosene and a few other objects that I left them. For this reason, and because I was not able to transport heavy items, my baggage was rather light.

I took the train to Xiangyang at eleven in the evening, after having sent a telegram to my sister in Hubei, to inform her that I would be passing by Wuhan during my journey home and to ask if she would be able to meet me. By chance her husband was working nearby, so she asked him to meet my train and to look for me; she wished me to go to her house with her husband and to stay there for a few days, rather than our seeing each other for just a few hours at the station. I accepted her invitation and with my brother-in-law I traveled on the train about 450 kilometers. After remaining at their house for a day, I spent all the forty yuan they had given me on my departure from the camp, all that would have served to pay for tools and everything else that would have helped me to earn something for my own maintenance.

My brother-in-law had been a businessman and had traveled much on ships before meeting my sister in a naval hospital. He was young and naïve, and when the Communists appealed to all the Chinese abroad to return to build the new China, he returned to the country and was assigned a good job. But already in 1957 he understood the reality; I met him when he came to Canton with my sister to meet my parents and already on that occasion, even though we had just met, he perceived that my way of thinking was very dangerous. He put me on my guard, saying that if I did not change my opinions and my way of seeing things, sooner or later I would find myself in trouble. Later, during the Cultural Revolution, he also suffered: all those who had returned home from abroad were suspected of crimes and political disloyalty. He was banished to a village to be "reeducated" by the workers. Fortunately he was given office work as a bookkeeper, and later he and my sister were permitted to return to their city. This brother-in-law was kind toward my sister and also to my family, unlike my other brother-in-law, who lived at Peking—the one who turned his back on his wife because she belonged to the landowner class and, as such, was considered an element of the right. My sister told me that as a nurse assigned to the population control of that area, it happened that she was sent to Xiangyang for an entire day and therefore was near the camp where I had been interred for fifteen years. It was impossible, however, for her to get in contact with me without her office discovering that she had a brother who was a "counterrevolutionary," something that would have had disastrous consequences for her.

After spending a few days with them, I returned to Wuhan, and after traveling for an entire night, I arrived at Shaoguan the following day; my sentiments were completely different from those that I had felt when I was on leave from the camp.

Now I was free.

Life as an Ex-Prisoner

The government policies regarding prisoners and liberated prisoners have never been publicized; they are a well-kept secret, but after many years spent at the camp we discovered facts and methods that otherwise would have remained unknown.

Normally those who completed their sentence but were still considered a threat did not return home, particularly if their place of residence was near the border: the government believed that the released criminals would try to leave the country at all cost. This is the supreme irony: those who in their propaganda boasted of reeducating these individuals, transforming them from "ghosts into men" (and this was the goal of the sentences), are precisely those who clearly prove that the reeducation is an illusion. The only prisoners the government sends home are those who are ill and elderly, on the basis of the principle that those who can no longer work or create wealth for the government or the society are a burden. The government policies consist in obtaining the maximum in work and production; therefore, the government looks with interest at those who are able to produce, but if it is evident that a prisoner cannot work and is an invalid, the secret government policy is to liberate itself from such a burden.

After returning to Shaoguan, I lived with my mother, and I was considered part of the farm population. Given that the work was very heavy, the daily food ration was greater than that given to those who lived in the city. Once I encountered the official responsible for the agricultural commune; he told me that it was he who had opposed my return home, because there were no means for the provision of my support. I belonged to the category of those who "wore the hat," that is, those who were deprived of political rights and who had to perform useful public services, such as cleaning the streets. In fact, in my case, this discrimination remained only on paper, because I was never asked to do anything, and I was barely controlled at all. However, on certain occasions, usually before the Communist holidays, I had to attend the encounters that studied policies.

The local government official who came to see me had compassion on me when he discovered that he had to remain outside the door in order to speak with me, given that the ambience was extremely narrow and the entrance too low to enter without bowing down. He admitted that the arrangement was inadequate for me and my mother and that he was displeased; but I did not want anything from the Communists, other than being left in peace. Our home was unworthy of human beings; since 1964 my parents were forced to change residences five times. Initially they had lived in an old temple, a rather large construction, but they were eventually thrown out of it and ended up going from one place to another. During the Cultural Revolution the policy toward the adversaries (such as my parents, who were former landowners) was that of being: (1) found lacking ("grabbing the pigtail"), (2) "inflicting a blow" and (3) "wearing the hat"; and my parents were victims of that policy.

At the beginning of 1979 we were gathered together to listen to an important press announcement. During the preceding winter, an assembly was held at Peking on the activities of the Office of Public Security throughout the country, and the party's Central Committee decided to take some steps to remove "the hat" from four of the categories on which it had been imposed: (1) former landowners, (2) rich peasants, (3) reactionaries, and (4) counterrevolutionaries, as well as various bad elements. This was the plan of Deng Xiaoping and other leaders. They knew that that initiative would promote the stability and cohesion of the Chinese people and that this act of clemency would affect not only the interested persons, but also the broad circle of their families and their friends. At that time the slogan of the party was to wake up the national conscience and consciously to promote the proper attitudes for the realization of the four modernizations: industrial, agricultural, scientific-technological, and defense. With this move Deng and his followers hoped to encourage everyone to join in one common effort, but the exponents of the left were opposed and criticized the new policy because it corresponded to "permitting the demons to circulate freely."

The program was carried out on a national scale, and the same model was followed everywhere. A meeting was planned, a report presented, and a debated followed, during which everyone was expected to take part. This tactic had a twofold end: it was above all important that each one have the correct attitude toward the party's policy and understood the objective of what was being proposed, so that the government's line would be firmly followed; further, this "Mass Line" would resolve the problem of putting into effect an unpopular policy imposed from the top. In fact, through this method of general discussion, it was possible to see if there were serious oppositions and how they could be overcome. After the debate, the result of the discussion was entrusted to the secretary of the party, and the leaders would decide. This system was followed in each work group, establishment, or industry of China, even for lightweight decisions, such as the increase of a person's pension. Each proposal would be submitted for debate, and each one was invited to say what he thought, whether favorable or contrary, on the basis of personal experience and the usual way of doing things.

This unifying policy had begun to operate at the end of the preceding year, first at Peking, then in the large cities, and finally in the small cities. Not long before, I had heard from Teresa that Canton had begun to put this new policy into play, and she herself had been among the citizens rehabilitated. A list was posted near the local post office with the names of those from whom "the hat was taken": even before, on the basis of the policy of the seventeen words, those who were well behaved were remunerated. But in fact very few were liberated, because the party had fixed a maximum of 5 percent. Both my parents had observed the regulations for many years, however, and they would have had the right to request the restoration of their citizenship if the proportion of those admitted to the rehabilitation had not been so low.

On March 5, 1979, my mother was called to an encounter during which personal documents were distributed. Her citizenship was restored to her, but some forms of discrimination remained, and we had to continue to observe some rules. In reality I had to follow only some of these, given that the local officials did not pay too much attention to them, except when there was some political campaign in action. Now I could leave Shaoguan for a day, I could go to Canton, even if I had to ask for official permission to travel; before, the local official would not have granted the permission, because he was responsible for those considered political delinquents.

Teresa

Although it had become easier to write to each other after I returned to Shaoguan, Teresa was not able to receive my letters at home, nor could she tell her family of her friendship with me. I sent the letters to my nephew at Canton, and Teresa went to get them, inventing some excuse to give her family so that she could go out.

From the day of my release Teresa had continued to believe that we would be able to build a future together, notwithstanding my attempt to dissuade her. In my letters I encouraged her to accept the first opportunity to leave the country in order to make a future for herself alone; I told her clearly to renounce the plans of twenty years ago. I wrote of my uncertainty about the future and so on, to the point that my niece and her husband told me that Teresa was depressed after reading my letters and that when they asked her the motive, she responded that in each letter I invited her to renounce the idea of building a future together, and it saddened her very much. Both my niece and her husband wrote to me, criticizing me harshly for my attitude, and so did my brother. From then on I avoided the topic.

From March 1979, after having reacquired citizenship, I could go to Canton with a different mood from that of the previous year. Even when I went to Wen, the policeman who had arrested me, his attitude regarding me was completely different. Before he had looked at me with a certain contempt; after my release he became more respectful, calling me Old Liao, as if I were an older person. Now he called me Uncle Liao. I told him that I had come to schedule an eye examination and to procure some prescription glasses. He helped me, saying that he would write the necessary permission immediately.

This was the first time that I met my niece's husband; during the preceding visit to Canton, in 1978, I did not indeed dare to meet them. All the released political criminals, those of my category, were avoided like lepers; it was dangerous to have contacts with such persons; in any case I had not wished to cause them problems.

I also was able to meet Teresa secretly, avoiding her brother's discovery of my visit. Just at that time, Carlo, Teresa's brother, had arrived from abroad for work and also with the intention of seeing the officials at the Ministry of Foreign Affairs in order to try to obtain permission for Teresa to leave the country. Teresa had also asked him to help me to emigrate, but she received a dry refusal from her family: their mother was waiting for Teresa and for permission for one of her brothers to emigrate so that all three could live together. If I left the country Teresa would have followed me, and all her mother's plans would have vanished. Her brother then warned Teresa of the danger of marrying someone that, as soon as she left the country, might then leave her and marry another, a younger, prettier woman. In the Chinese tradition it is very important to have a family with some children; but by now Teresa was too advanced in years to have children and this, according to him, was another motive for which the husband would have abandoned her once she left China. In brief, Teresa's brother concluded that she should not have done anything to help me leave the country. I personally considered it unwise for Teresa to pursue her brother's help again, and I asked her not to do it.

It was only the second time that Teresa and I had a chance to meet in twenty years, and I wished that she would have assumed a more realistic view of the future, even if I understood that it was very improbable that she would change her way of seeing things. Although I tried again to persuade her, I recall her saying that, if she had the opportunity to go away, she would do everything possible to help me join her; and if she did not succeed, she would return to China to be with me.

There were many reasons for which it was opportune to dissuade her from marrying me. Although citizenship had been restored to me, I still belonged to the country, and it was rare for the party to go against their policy and permit transfers from the rural areas to the city. On the other hand, it was impossible to ask Teresa to come live in the poverty that characterized life in the rural areas. So as things stood, I would have never had a tranquil conscience if I had married her in my situation, thereby denying her the opportunity to leave the country immediately in order to build a happy future elsewhere. Besides, her health was not good; she had a long history of tuberculosis that required regular checkups.

There were also the problems of my health; my rheumatism, for which there was no cure, had worsened after twenty years of prison and labor camps. It was not possible to confront all the problems that these facts implicated for daily life; for myself, I was able to accept suffering and bitterness, but, as I saw it, my duty toward others was to bring them happiness and goodwill. I could not inflict my suffering on others. I insisted on my point of view, but it did not make an impression on Teresa; my reasoning did not have any influence on her at all.

When my brother, my niece, and her husband supported Teresa's point of view, I began to consider what possibility there was for me to leave the country in order to build a better future with her. Since her brother had no intention of helping me, I decided to contact my older brother in Hong Kong, asking for a letter from him inviting me to visit him after a long thirty-year separation and to seek medical help for my health problems at Hong Kong. It would have been even better if he had written from Macao than from Hong Kong.

After some days at Canton, I returned to Shaoguan, in order to take care of my mother. There I found myself in a difficult situation: the local government officials called me several times, asking me to teach English, because they had an urgent need for English teachers. During the Cultural Revolution every type of teaching was suspended for ten years, and now the shortage of qualified teachers was being felt. I was expected to render this service to society in order to "repay" how much it had done for me. It was comical when they had to come to the hovel that we were assigned as a house to ask me to render them this service.

But in 1950 I had decided never to work for the Communists, and even now I would not have given my consent freely to work for them. I excused myself, saying that my health was not yet good and that I had the responsibility of my mother. They agreed to wait until I had gotten my brother and one of my sisters to occupy themselves with my mother; then, after a period of rest, I would be strong enough to take on the teaching assignment.

Meanwhile I did not lose time contacting my brother in Hong Kong. He was ill with cancer and this, besides his age, made his request to visit me reasonable, especially because my mother and I were the beneficiaries of his will. I also asked for a letter from a lawyer to use as support for my request to leave the country. And when my friend Dominic had to leave for the United States from Hong Kong, I asked him to see my brother and to explain the situation to him. But at the end of May, it was officially established that all the requests to leave all the provinces would be suspended.

Once again there was nothing else to do but wait. Although I was doing everything I could to leave the country, I also had to consider the possibility of finding a job to support myself until I departed. Teresa had expressed her intention to return if I was not able to join her abroad, so I had to be realistic and consider what type of work I could do. My relatives advised me against taking on a teaching career; during the Cultural Revolution the teachers had been treated very badly, and the effects were still visible in their low salaries and in the lack of respect students demonstrated toward them. I was also aware that my health would not permit me to work for too many years.

Marriage and Teresa's Departure

In July I brought my mother to my brother's house, about forty-five kilometers from Canton. At this time the wife of my older brother arrived at Canton from Hong Kong to visit the family, and we went to see her. It was in this critical moment that Teresa was notified that her request to expatriate had been accepted.

Normally the prospect of leaving the country for the free world would have given anyone great joy, but for Teresa there was a complication: she was anxious and insecure about our future, whether we would still be able to meet or whether I would have married another woman on the mainland. She expressed all her sadness and all her anxiety very openly, and since Rosa and Linda were at Canton in those days on leave for a medical visit, they and my friend Paul discussed the matter, and they agreed that this was the right moment for Teresa and me to get married.

It also happened that Father Ye and Father Li were at Canton, the former on leave from his labor camp in the province of Hubei and the second on leave from his village for a medical appointment. So it was established that we would get married immediately, in Paul's house. After confession, the marriage was celebrated by Father Li, who was Teresa's pastor, in the presence of Father Ye, Paul, Rosa, and Linda. For Teresa this meant everything; for me it confirmed the faith that I had placed in Our Lady, whom I had asked to choose a companion for me twenty years before.

Paul advised that, although we were now really married before God, it would have also been useful to have a marriage certificate from the State, in case I was presented with the possibility of leaving the country. I could not risk, however, asking for it at Canton, out of fear that Teresa's two brothers would come to know about it; so Paul suggested going in secret to Shaoguan to ask there.

Teresa had to invent an excuse to go visit some relatives. My nephew accompanied us to Shaoguan, where at first the authorities refused us any type of certificate until the end of September. According to the law, no man could marry before reaching twenty-four to twenty-six years and no woman before the age of twenty-three; early marriages were discouraged. But when they checked the forms and saw that our age was fifty-one years, the officials were stunned that we had postponed marriage so long and they were a little suspicious. Only on August 15, the feast of the Assumption, did we receive the necessary certificate.

I immediately bought two tickets for Peking: we had to go to the embassy of a foreign country to prepare the papers for Teresa. We traveled third-class in order to save money and spent two days and two nights seated, arriving at Peking exhausted. There were many formalities to complete: a visit to the Office of Hygiene, vaccinations, et cetera, so we did not have time for anything other than going from one office to another. We remained at Peking about a week. We also met Teresa's sister-in-law while we were there, and she suspected the truth; so Teresa told her everything. She already knew me as a friend of her husband and godfather to her youngest child, and she promised Teresa that she would help, although she knew that she would be going against the will of Teresa's mother and her brothers. Meanwhile Carlo, Teresa's brother, was traveling through China with the young wife he had recently married; they left Peking for Shanghai the same day we arrived, but when he returned to Canton and was told that Teresa was at Shaoguan to visit relatives and then at Peking, he immediately guessed that his sister had gone to Shaoguan to get in contact with me. Finally his nephew from Peking gave him the news that Teresa and I were married.

When Teresa returned to Canton, after an absence of nearly fifteen days, Carlo did not scold her; he warned her that when their mother heard the news, she would not be content.

We returned from Peking to Canton on August 27, and the following day we visited my mother, who was living with my brother in one of the suburbs of Canton. When Teresa returned home, in the late afternoon, she found a message telling her to report as soon as possible to the local police station. That evening Teresa informed me of the situation and that she had decided the best thing to do was to conform to the request.

The following morning Teresa went to the police and was interrogated by two officials of the Public Security Department, who asked her to collaborate with them on an inquiry concerning a certain priest. After a long interrogation, during which Teresa for the most part was silent, the policemen let her go but specified that they may have need of her again when "her mind was clearer" and she was "more disposed to cooperate." They were referring to her permission to go abroad, and they made her understand that it could be revoked if she did not give them the information they needed. Teresa had reattained her citizenship; therefore, their approach had to be more prudent and moderate; but in reality nothing would have stopped them from attaining their goals.

That night my niece and her husband invited some friends to celebrate our marriage. But the atmosphere was spoiled by this new frightening threat; Teresa and many of our friends were crying. I had to keep my nerves firm and decide on which plan to follow. It seemed essential that Teresa go away as soon as possible in order to prevent further interrogations and delays that would bar her from expatriating. So that same evening we reserved a ticket for her on the first train leaving Canton the next day; there was naturally some risk, but it was worth the trouble to confront it. It was also possible that the officials would discover that Teresa had left Canton and that they could telephone the police at the border of Hong Kong and request that they hold her.

All our friends said good-bye to her, crying, and she went home to prepare the few things that she would take with her: two changes of clothes and a little money in case she was held at the border. I accepted the event without emotion, accustomed by now to every type of frustration and failure. But for Teresa it was different: she was very upset. I reminded her that the first thing she must do when she arrived at Hong Kong was to send a telegram to her brother and to me.

Teresa departed. We were waiting to receive the telegram at 4:00 in the afternoon, but at 8:30 there was not yet any news; I advised our friends, who had come to ask about Teresa, to return home: we had only to have faith in Divine Providence and in the protection of Mary. A quarter of an hour later, in fact, a telegram was delivered to us from Teresa: thank God she was safe in Hong Kong and, as it happened, just in time. That day the officials from the Department of Public Security had been to her house twice before noon, asking about her and telling her brother that they would return in the afternoon and that Teresa should expect them. Her brother was truly frightened, but he was able to say sincerely that Teresa had gone to visit relatives and that he really did not know when she would return.

DIARIES OF THE CHINESE MARTYRS

Good-Bye to China

Now that Teresa was in a safe place I was free to occupy myself with my mother. She had lived with my younger brother and his family for scarcely two months, but by now the situation had become impossible: my sister-in-law no longer wished to have my mother living with them, and the day after Teresa's departure she asked my niece to take her to Canton, where I was. It was useless to oppose her; my mother herself was very sad and offended, after having desired so much to live with her son and daughter-in-law. Even my nephew found it impossible to understand the unnatural attitude of his mother, knowing that she herself was expecting to live in the care of her children during her old age.

I decided in the end to return to Shaoguan alone, to try to make our hut more habitable, recleaning it, repairing the stove, and putting clean newspapers where the walls were rotted. Meanwhile, my mother remained with my cousin for fifteen days.

There was no more news about exit permits, but at the end of September the police officer Wen told me in confidence that the government had begun again to grant emigration permits, and perhaps I could try once again. At first I was rather hopeful of succeeding in my intent, but at the beginning of 1980 I understood the situation was worsening and that my possibilities were extremely scarce; there were restrictions for entrance into Hong Kong, and thousands of persons had to wait years. At Shaoguan some friends had asked a high-ranking official to obtain the necessary permit for me. But, after having agreed to help me, the official read the details of my record and commented that it was nearly impossible to do such a favor, given my having been a counterrevolutionary.

Toward March or April I was aware that no human help could resolve my problem; it could only be put in the hands of the Lord. Friends at Hong Kong and at Macao wrote to me to say that they were praying for my future. Thus in May, the month dedicated to Our Lady, I decided to ask her to help me and, if it was for my spiritual good, to make my expatriation possible. I put myself completely in her hands, asking her to speak for me to her Divine Son and to obtain for me this request.

On May 29 I went personally to the Office of Public Safety of Shaoguan to see the head of the department who was occupied with the approval of visas and passports. It was not the common procedure; usually one had to pass through minor officials, who in turn sent the request for information to their superior. But I avoided the normal channels, and I went directly to the head of the department to ask for the passport. He was surprised, and he reminded me that I had to wait my turn for the necessary quota at Shaoguan.

I knew by now that the prospects were without hope; the accord of the government of Hong Kong with Peking permitted about 3,500 émigrés a month from all of China, about 100 or 130 a day. Although my province had the benefit of a majority of these permits, I knew that few of these permits were assigned to Shaoguan by the provincial administration. One could calculate a wait of sixty to seventy years, since there were six thousand to seven thousand requests per hundred visas. In any case, I knew that the five permits assigned to Shaoguan were utilized by officials at their discretion; the power to give or take was in their hands, and a gift of some importance was necessary: such as a television or something of similar value, such as a gold necklace or bracelet. Therefore, the only hope seemed to me to go to the head official and to trust in the help of Our Lady.

The chief of the Office of Public Safety was surprised at my new request: "I wish to change my request from Hong Kong to Macao." Why do I wish to make this change? I explained that it did not matter to me whether it was Macao or Hong Kong; I simply wished to be free to go abroad. I spoke very frankly of my situation: my mother was very old, I had poor health, my brother at Hong Kong would have been able to find medical help for me and a means of support in order to maintain me and my wife, who was also at Hong Kong. Using their own propaganda I reminded the official that the government was promising to work for the people.

The official did not expect such frankness: "I see that you are very loyal," he observed, and having nodded with understanding when I said that I wished simply to leave the country, he advised me to write to my relatives in Hong Kong or Macao telling them to send me letter at Shaoguan stating their desire to help me. Then I would be able to bring this declaration to the Office of Public Safety. That same evening I wrote to Teresa, asking her to go to Macao and to write to someone from there so that she could do what the official at Shaoguan had advised. Teresa received the letter on June 7 and responded immediately, very concerned about the change of my request from Hong Kong to Macao.

Meanwhile I had to do whatever was in my power to improve the conditions in the little hut for my mother during the hot summer months. I wrote to Paul, asking him to find me an electric ventilator, and I decided to go to Canton to get it, leaving my mother in the care of a neighbor. I stayed at Canton three days, until a telegram arrived from Shaoguan, in the name of my mother, asking me to return immediately. I took the freight train, and after a trip of eight hours I reached Shaoguan at three in the morning; an express train would normally arrive in three or four hours.

When I opened the door of our hut, I did not know what was waiting for me; the woman who was with my mother was illiterate and did not know how to give me a clear explanation of the telegram. But I understood from her words that Our Lady had given me this grace: my passport had been granted on June 5, the news had reached the local official on the seventh, and my acquaintance sent the telegram on the eighth. Without even resting, I went directly to the Municipal Office of Public Safety to complete all the formalities. The official was smiling, giving me the forms to fill out. He asked me when I would depart, but I told him that first I had to make arrangements for my mother and to see my nephew, my younger brother, and other relatives. He was surprised that I did not wish to leave without delay, but in the end we established the moment for departure: I would leave within a brief period; otherwise my permit would expire.

When my mother was forced to leave the house of my younger brother, it was explicitly agreed that, if I ever obtained permission to leave the country, he would take her back with him; so I went to Canton to discuss the matter with him. But he said to me privately that his wife would not ever permit my mother to live with them, although she did not have any reasons for refusing. His wife did not even wish to discuss the business with me, so my brother had to go back and forth between the room where I was and the room where his wife was to try to reach an accommodation.

His wife was inflexible, and she threatened to leave the house if my mother entered it. My brother was very upset, but there was nothing that could be done. I went to other relatives to discuss the matter, and we got in contact with a Protestant lady whom we had known many years before and who was now living alone and was looking to gather other Protestants in her house on Sunday for a religious service. She was very devout and pious and agreed to occupy herself with my mother, promising that she would care for her as if she were her own mother.

On my return to Shaoguan, the government official asked me again when I would depart, and he urged me not to wait. He did not see any reason for risking the loss of my exit permit solely because of my mother, and he offered to find her a temporary situation; then they would officially inform my younger brother that he would have to receive his mother into his home. I knew, however, that such an action would have created an impossible situation: if my sister-in-law would not take her of her own free will, it would be an intolerable situation for my mother: she was not furniture to be moved around; she had feelings. I told the official that I was looking for a situation, and I was making plans to say good-bye to my family and my relatives.

I wrote to my sisters, giving them news of the permit. My sister in Peking responded that she had read my letter with tears of joy, because I was free to go away, and with tears of sorrow because we did not know when we would see each other again. I begged her not to come to Canton, because the trip was too exhausting in the summer heat, yet she came to say good-bye anyway after traveling three days by train. She did not even ask for permission at work so as not to lose time: she simply left a note saying that she was called for an emergency. Also my other sister from Wuhan came to Canton to see me and to say good-bye. It was our first family reunion in thirty years. My sisters had made a great sacrifice for the trip, apart from the cost, which was equivalent to two months' wages. My brother and his wife came from Hong Kong; it was their first visit in thirty years. Our mother was also present. The only member of the family missing was the closest, our youngest brother, whose wife would not let him come.

My sisters were very sad at the thought that our mother was forced to live with a stranger, although she had many children, and she had hoped to live with one of them in her old age. My sister-in-law returned to Hong Kong alone, letting my older brother come to Macao with me and then from there to Hong Kong; he had been ill with intestinal cancer for eight years and, since we had not seen each other in thirty years, we were happy to make the journey by train to Macao together. Once again I experienced the truth of the proverb: "In life and in death we must separate," suffering the pains of separation from those that are nearest and dearest to us.

The distance from Canton to Macao was not much, about 150 kilometers, but on the road there were four grade crossings—and each one took about half an hour—as well as a stop for fuel and an additional half an hour for a meal; it was about one in the afternoon when we arrived at the frontier. I was searched and interrogated by the military police. They went into detail, giving the impression that they were ready to continue to speak for some time, so I took out a cigarette. This gesture ended the conversation: smoking was prohibited, and the interrogation was concluded. There were, by then, only about one hundred meters to make before crossing the border, where Teresa and my family were waiting for me. What had been a dream less than a month before was now a reality.

The Good Battle

My story began on the feast of the Immaculate Conception of 1946. From my entrance into the Catholic Church and from my first invocation to Mary, the Mother of the Church, with the Hail Holy Queen, the faith took root in me, and it grew and matured.

From my baptism, a year later, to my two arrests in 1955 and 1958, I spent about ten years of regular Catholic life in the Church of Peking and Canton and twenty-three years in prison, having lived by the grace of God in the mystical Body of Christ. Two other years followed my release from the labor camp.

Now I was free again to live my Faith in the company of the visible Church.

In all these facts I have seen the clear manifestation of the mercy of God, through the maternal protection of the Blessed Virgin Mary. In the first place, just being alive to tell my story is in itself an extraordinary fact, considering my poor health at the beginning of the twenty-year sentence, the insufficient food, the heavy and dangerous work from which a loss of life or a wound were not unusual. I found myself near death in some occasions: once a tractor loaded with bricks skimmed over my back before I could save myself.

But more miraculous was the fact that I survived from these pressures —physical, mental, and moral—with my faith intact; indeed, it was even more profoundly rooted in God because of the dangers from which he had preserved me, especially of never giving in to the Communists out of weakness or fear. It was not unusual to succumb to the pressures imposed on Catholics during the succession of purges and persecutions that meant the loss of everything held dear. I thank God that he did not ever permit me to betray him; I fought the good battle and maintained the faith, thanks to his mercy.

Praise to you, Lord Jesus Christ!

LEON CHAN

INTRODUCTION

The Historic Value of This Documentation

As we arrive at this point, we might ask ourselves: what could Leon Chan, a priest of the Diocese of Hong Kong, possibly add to what we have already read in the preceding pages. Father Chan fled China in 1962 after having lived thirteen years in a Communist prison.

We find the first response to this question in the introduction of the priest's testimony, which was originally an interview, but for editorial purposes was transformed into an account given in the first person, simply by eliminating questions of the interviewer (Father Piero Gheddo). We read: "[Father Chan's] is the first direct testimony by a Catholic that comes from China during recent times.... However, it regards not only the situation in the Church, but also the principal aspects of life of the Chinese people during this period."[95] [Thus, apart from the valor of his own personal testimony, Leon Chan offers the reader his valuable insights on the failure of China's Communist system.]

Since the publication of these memoirs, other documents and books have been published confirming all that is contained in Father Chan's testimony. But the fact remains that, in responding to Father Gheddo's questions, the priest has, in effect, painted a fresco of the Chinese Church and society under Communism that is so vivid and detailed that it stuns

---

[95] Father Chan was liberated in May of 1962; the following month he went to Italy, accompanied by the bishop of Hong Kong, Monsignor Lorenzo Bianchi of Pime, and was received in a private audience by Pope John XXIII and by the cardinal prefect of the Congregation for the Propagation of the Faith.

even the protagonist himself. For example, in describing the daily life of the communes, Father Chan arrives at the point of exclaiming: "I know that I am relating nearly incredible things, but this is the absolute truth." His testimony alone would have become a book if Father Chan had not been so reluctant to recall all this suffering so soon afterward.

Communism Seen from Within

There are, also, in my opinion, two particular aspects that render his contribution current, even today. The first concerns his reading of Communism as an ideology that distorts human nature and, as a result, is destined to fail. "While I was in prison, the atmosphere in China totally changed; absolute terror reigned, and the people refrained from speaking out of fear of being reported. By then everyone had learned to distrust one another, even members of their own families. For this reason, the Christians never questioned me about what happened to me; [anyhow,] they already knew, and there was no need to speak of it."

Regarding the agricultural failure, Father Chan analyzed the Chinese situation from the anthropological point of view, even before the economic or political: "The principal cause of the agricultural failure was the lack of trust in the people; it quickly ruined everything: why, indeed, work with goodwill," he wrote (and his words are cutting), "when there is no hope of improving one's own personal condition?" Once again, we find confirmed here the intrinsic structural weakness of the Maoist revolution that lasted for decades: contrary to all the propaganda that our country [Italy] made us believe for so long, it was a movement with an inhuman face, one of the worst "social experiences" ever, causing millions of deaths and an infinite number of personal and collective tragedies.

The Origin of the Fracture within the Catholic Church

Also of notable interest in Father Chan's testimony is the extremely delicate theme of the relationship between the two "souls" of the Catholic Church in China: the "unofficial" or clandestine (in harmony with Rome) and the "official," erroneously defined as "patriotic" (forced to follow the dictates of the Patriotic Association of Chinese Catholics, controlled by the government). It is often though—even among Western Catholics attentive to the Christian reality in China—that clearly defined lines of demarcation exist between the two communities or, worse, that all the true believers belong to the "unofficial" community. It is also often assumed that all those who accept the norms imposed by the regime on the public expression of their faith are pro-government, and, in the last analysis, inferior Catholics.

On this topic Father Chan's testimony is particularly illuminating. Here he refers to the historic period of 1958 to 1960, which generated the fracture between the two communities (the Church with ties to Rome and the "official" church). That era was considered very promising: "There was much work to do," the author observed, "but for the Church in China after the war, hopes were very high, because it had truly acquired a notable influence in all the country, even though the converts were still a minimal part of the Chinese population. If only the Communists had not come ..." In his narrative, Father Leon Chan clearly explains how, in the confused reality of the time, the Catholics happened to make clearly diverse choices, each one seeking to work out, in good faith, which option better preserved their faith and membership in the Church.

In another testimony Father Chan describes how the penetration of the regime and the acquisition of popular consent throughout the country was an underhanded, diffused, and gradual operation; he himself affirms that initially he had shown an interest in the "new masters" of China: "Although I knew very well that Communism was and is the enemy of the Church and of religion, at first I nearly let myself be convinced of the good intentions of the Communists and even of the utility of their victory for the well-being of China and the Chinese people. Indeed, order reigned everywhere in an exemplary way.... Thus, for nearly a year we got along, respecting one another."

But then the Communist regime will attempt to give life to a Church that is autonomous and separate from Rome. "In 1958 I was invited repeatedly to attend the meetings of the 'Patriotic church,'" relates Father Chan. "I went only once, when they told me that if I did not go 'freely,' I would have to go as a prisoner, by force. In fact, at a conference that was held at Canton in the spring of 1958, more than a hundred priests were in attendance, and several came only under the threat of coercion."

Many priests, having been threatened with heavy limitations of their personal liberties, found themselves forced to participate at gatherings of that type. Furthermore, the regime had the astuteness and perfidy to conclude those meetings with a true and proper infringement on the rights of the Church, that is, as Father Chan relates, "with the 'election' of the bishops." "There were some who refused to elect them, but the majority of us voted because we thought of it as a farce that would permit us to exercise our ministry a bit. Anyway, it was only an 'election': we, in other words, were thinking only of electing our own superiors, given that those who were legitimate were either in prison or had been expelled. The ugly fact was that then some of these 'elected' bishops were consecrated."

This business of the first illicit episcopal nominations would be the snowball that becomes an avalanche. In simple terms, the division that continues to the present day between the official church community and the unofficial Church community hinges on which bishops the members are obedient to: those who were ordained illicitly or those who were ordained validly, according to canon law.

The range of personal attitudes with which the various bishops accepted or did not accept the illicit ordinations was (and still is) vast: some have been opportunistic and dreamed of "careers," some have submitted unwillingly, and some have publicly taken positions opposing such a solution and then paid the price of such a courageous decision. This is not the place to sink our teeth into this crucial problem of the Chinese church; however, it is a wound that still bleeds.[96]

---

[96] On the genesis of the fracture between the "clandestine" community and the "official" community see E. Giunipero, *Chiesa Cattolica e Cina comunista. Dalla revoluzione del 1949 al ConciioVaticano II* (Brescia: Morcelliana, 2007).

Let us return to the text of Father Chan's narrative. Very moving is the case of Monsignor Yip, a priest who finds himself swept away by events and ends, against his will, submitting to the commands of the regime; but in his heart he remains faithful to the true Church and to the pope. Also, Father Chan relates:

> Even Father Yip had himself consecrated a bishop in Manchuria by a legitimate bishop; therefore I think that the consecration, although illicit, was valid. Father Yip, however, did not consecrate other bishops or priests; he was a good rural pastor, and when we were among ourselves we never called him bishop, nor did he request us to do so.... He was a good priest, elderly, very ill and very timid. Initially, when he returned after his consecration, the authorities prepared a triumphal welcome for him, and several Christians were forced to participate. On that occasion Yip was dressed like a true bishop.... But after that occasion I no longer heard of him dressing like a bishop, indeed he himself did not wish to: it was enough for him to dress like a simple priest. He continued to exercise his ministry and the faithful went to him because they understood that he had not betrayed the faith.

The good faith of the bishop was so evident to those around him that when Father Leon decided to go to Hong Kong, he tried to convince Father Yip to go with him: "I went to Father Yip,... and I proposed to him to flee with me; but ... he was very shy and elderly, and he feared he was being strictly watched, so he did not come."

In Father Chan's text, an explicit referral is made to this type of person:

> Of the Chinese priests, I must say that, at first, very few compromised with Communism, but for those who did, they could not turn back: they had to stay with the Patriotic Church; otherwise

---

On the current situation, M. Nicolini-Zani, *I nostril fratelli cinesi* (Magnano: Edizioni Qiqajon-Monastero di Bose, 2009).

there would have been trouble for them. But they are the few, and in general they repented the errors that they committed in the past, many of which were forced on them through physical and moral torture. However, the vast majority of the Chinese clergy remained faithful to their own legitimate bishops and to the pope and were not snapped up by the Patriotic Church; the same must also be said for the Chinese faithful; and it is with profound joy and pride that I offer this testimony to my confreres and to our faithful. It is not to our credit: the grace of God has helped us.

The final words of this citation are extremely precious, because they help one to understand how to overcome the division between the "official" and the "unofficial" Church, a means that was also invoked by Pope Benedict XVI in his beautiful *Letter to Chinese Catholics* of 2007: "Such a way calls for a profound reciprocal respect, a common feeling of belonging to the Church and the firm wish for reconciliation." In this way, a person who has submitted to trials and persecutions is able to say: "It is not to our merit: the grace of God has helped us."

I FLED FROM RED CHINA

At the beginning of our conversations Father Leon Chan would speak with some circumspection. It displeased him that we were recording everything; if he was saying something important, he would lower his voice and speak so softly that we could not hear him and we had to plead with him to respond in a normal tone of voice. Begging our pardon and smiling, he would say: "Please understand . . . it is a habit!" When he became accustomed to speaking freely, he would indeed go in the opposite direction, speaking liberally and openly, and then no one could stop him! Evidently, after many years of obligatory silence, to be able to speak about his experiences without fear of the consequences was for Father Chan nearly an invitation to the wedding feast; and he would go on for hours, demonstrating that when one truly has something to say, it is less tiring to speak than to listen!

Thirteen Years in the "Red Paradise"

I was born into a Catholic family in 1911 in the small village of Hoifung, near Hong Kong. My grandfather was a close friend of Monsignor Henry Valtorta, of Pime, bishop of Hong Kong: he was one of the first Christians from the zone evangelized by the bishop. After having studied at the small parochial school, I went on to the minor seminary of Hong Kong and then to the major seminary. I was ordained a priest in 1937 with three other priests of the diocese, two of whom died under Communism: one was killed with Father Emilio Teruzzi in 1940,[97] when bands of red partisans

---

[97] The actual date of the death of Father Teruzzi was November 26, 1942.

infested our area; the other, Father James Wong, died in 1958 in a forced labor camp.

Immediately after my ordination, the bishop assigned me to go to the Catholic University of Peking, but I could not get to the capital because in that year, 1937, China was invaded by the Japanese and moving around became difficult and aroused suspicion. So I began to work with Father Alessandro Cometti, then with Father Ambrogio Poletti,[98] and finally in other districts by myself. There was much work to do, but for the Church in China after the war, hopes were very high, because it had truly acquired a notable influence in all the country, even though the converts were still a minimal part of the Chinese population. If only the Communists had not come ...

In my area, October 1949, the last Nationalist troops abandoned our villages, and, soon after, the Communist troops arrived; they were, however, stopped at the border of Hong Kong [which was then a British colony]. I was, at that time, in Chinese territory, in the district of Huiyang.

Initially the Communists acted like friends; they invited me to dinner and to their patriotic celebrations, and they also asked me to give speeches. Indeed, I must say that, although I knew very well that Communism was and is the enemy of the Church and of religion, at first I nearly let myself

---

[98] One reads a description of Father Poletti by a confrere of Pime: "With windblown hair, cowboy hat, neck scarf, full beard blowing to the four winds, rushing here and there on his motorcycle, he truly became legendary in the New Territories. At the time of the 'Exodus' of the refugees from China in 1950, Father Poletti was called par excellence 'the gatekeeper of China.' His guarantee was enough for any expelled bishop, priest, nun, or Christian who arrived at the border without travel documents (or a passport) to be welcomed and accepted in the Colony of Hong Kong without many formalities. The government had immense faith in Father Poletti and never doubted his honesty. How many bishops, including our own Monsignor Bianchi (a bishop of Pime), and how many missionaries were welcomed by him, clothed, fed, and comforted. I have read letters written by him from every part of the world, expressing gratitude and affection toward him, 'the good Samaritan.' And this also honors Pime."

be convinced of the good intentions of the Communists and even of the utility of their victory for the well-being of China and the Chinese people. Indeed, order reigned everywhere in an exemplary way: if someone robbed or did something contrary to the law, an armed Communist soldier would immediately arrive and take him away.

As to religion, they told me that we could find agreement, that they had nothing against religion; that a religious problem did not exist, unless the Church went against the people ... I responded that I had nothing against them, unless they were to go against the Church and limit our freedom of religion, which we had enjoyed even under the Japanese and the Nationalists.

Thus, for nearly a year we got along, respecting one another; for me it was easy enough to maintain this position of neutrality toward the Communists, because effectively, up to the summer of 1950, when they truly had control of China, they did nothing against the Church, at least not in my area, or, in general, against the people and their personal liberties. However, when enforcing martial law, they did kill too readily.

The First Incident

The first incident exploded in the summer of 1950. Having gone to Hong Kong for a spiritual retreat, I was away for twenty days; when I returned, I became aware at once that something had changed. I immediately visited all the Christian communities in my district, something I did each month, and, when I returned home, I was informed that the police had come various times looking for me during my absence. I went straight to the police headquarters, and they asked me what I had gone to do in the villages.

"I went to see my Christians, as always," I responded.

"You went to spread religious propaganda!" they said to me. "Understand that if it is true that there is religious liberty, it is also true that there is liberty to combat religious propaganda!" This phrase impressed me very much, because I understood that after so much serenity, the ugly times were beginning.

I limited myself to replying that liberty of religion was permitted by the government and the constitution.

"Yes," they answered me, "but we who are atheists are free to act against God, just as you act in favor of God."

"Okay," I said, "but let the game be evenly matched."

"What are you saying?"

"I am saying that I shall limit my preaching on the existence of God as long as you are disposed to do the same; you shall not preach that God does not exist, and we shall see which of us pleases the people."

They responded: "You are a priest and you preach; we are the police and we must use our means: meanwhile you shall not go further than twelve kilometers from the city."

Some days later I went again to visit the Christians in the villages. Upon my return, I ran into the police, and I said that I had not gone beyond twelve kilometers.

"No," the police chief said to me, "even if you do not distance yourself more than twelve kilometers, you must always inform us every time you leave the city; without our permission you shall no longer be able to leave the city or visit the Christians."

This was how I became confined to my residence and separated from the Christians, although I continued to see them from time to time, because they came to visit me. From that day, however, I began to experience precisely what Communism was and how blind fanaticism animated its supporters.

I was able to go around my little city, but I could not visit the Christians in the surrounding villages; I tried with some subterfuge to go out of the city, but I very soon saw that I was strictly watched, and it was not worth challenging the situation. Meanwhile the police began to go to the villages that I had visited, making enquiries about my activities. But they did not discover anything blameworthy, simply because I limited myself to accomplishing my priestly duties. The Christians still came to visit in my residence, and they participated whenever they could at the sacred functions; I, however, had to be very cautious in my relationships with everybody, because I knew that my every action and my every comment was being observed. The people, even non-Catholics, were always very cordial with me. They asked if they could do small tasks for me, and they came to ask for advice; indeed, the heads of the little city wished to elect me their representative with the authorities, they even wished to make me the mayor, but naturally I did not accept.

The Path to Prison

At a certain point it became clear to me that they were seeking a way to imprison me. I continued to direct the mission (we also had an elementary and a middle school), and with the help of some women, I worked in the medical dispensary gratis because, thanks to the medicines they sent me from Hong Kong, I could still keep it open.

The first serious incident happened one Sunday in December 1950. I was celebrating Mass with the Church filled to capacity when a police officer entered and, from the back, began speaking loudly against the Vatican and the pope, which he called "servants of American imperialism." I responded confidently to the officer, who went away, impressed also by the reaction of the Christians who had given him a severe lesson. It was a real provocation, but at that moment nothing happened.

Two months later, after having spread negative gossip about me and my residence, they called me to the police station: it was February 21 or 22, 1951. I was made to sit down and submit to an interrogation that lasted the entire day: they were trying to obtain a general confession of all my crimes, in particular those against the government and the people.

After seeing that they could get nothing from me, they asked me: "How come you still keep the dispensary open?" (They had in the meantime already commandeered the schools.)

"Because," I responded, "I did not ever feel that it was prohibited to do good by curing the people gratis; my dispensary is the only one in the area, and many people make use of it."

"Okay, but we now have need of your dispensary, and you must donate it to the government," they said to me.

"And why?" I responded. "The government already has many hospitals and dispensaries and so many means to construct others. I am continuing to do some good to the people, and you are no longer permitting me; so now I must close the dispensary?"

Then I was put in prison, without any precise charge. I remained there for twelve days in a cell four meters by four meters, together with about ten others condemned of political and other various crimes. Among them were, without a doubt, diverse spies for the police, who were attempting to broach some incriminating subjects, but I never responded to their questions. A week after my arrest they came to arrest my catechist, who was helping me and two women who assisted me at the dispensary, specifically to assist women in labor. I thought that they wished to accuse me of having given the wrong medicine to the people, something that could have mistakenly happened, but I learned later that I was accused of sending some young people to put poison into the wells of the city.

Evidently they had arrested my assistants in order to get them to confirm the accusation. That same night I heard their shouts and cries of desperation for a very long time: they were beating them to force them to admit to that absurdity. Finally they found a youth not fully in possession of his mental faculties, whom they convinced to accuse me of having sent him to toss poison into the wells!

The following day we were brought to the central prisons of Huizhou; along with me were my catechist and the two poor women who had so generously helped me in the dispensary. We were all tied together with our hands behind our backs and with a tie connected to our necks; in this way we were not able to move at all. But the best part is that they charged me for the expense of transporting us by train and for all the meals during the period that we remained in prison before the trial, and we had to pay them.

Condemned to Three Years in Prison

After we arrived at the prisons of Huizhou, we were placed in different parts of the prison so that we could not see each other; then they interrogated us separately. I was questioned several times during the day. Each time I was asked to give a full confession of my crime, but I always responded that I never committed or made anyone else commit what I was accused of.

"If you wish," I said, "go ahead and kill me. Condemn me to forced labor if you wish, but do not make me confess something that I have never had in my mind to do."

But they continued unperturbed: "Tell us only where you bought the poison to put into the wells; if you will confess, perhaps the jury will be lenient toward you."

Several months passed, and on August 1, 1951, I was told that the jury had decided to condemn me to three years in prison. It was the feast day of St. Peter in Chains, and I was a little consoled. Considering the months that I had already spent in prison, I thought, perhaps there remained only two and a half years to serve. I wished to know for which crime I was being condemned, but I was never told, nor was it ever published in the sentence of condemnation (this also occurred to many other priests and Christians who were condemned simply as generic "enemies of the people"). I protested strongly with the directorship of the prison, and I also decided to demonstrate that they had not given me a real trial, but then they told me that the judges were very good with me, that if I had had a public trial I would have received a life sentence or many more years in prison, and so I convinced myself that it was better to accept that "mild" condemnation rather than to look for other troubles.

From the Prisons to Forced Labor

I was condemned to three years, but I remained inside from February 21, 1951, to June 3, 1955. Initially I was in the prison of Huizhou, a small city of sixty thousand inhabitants; then I was sent to the forced-labor camps in the surrounding countryside; finally I spent six more months in prison before I was liberated.

Life in prison was hard. At first I did not work because I always had to be at the disposition of the interrogators. I was in a cell with many other prisoners, sometimes ten or fifteen or even twenty. The jailers took from me whatever I possessed: I asked to keep the holy rosary with me, but not even this was permitted.

At the beginning, during the period of the interrogations, we were not permitted to have anything from the external world, no contacts and no gifts. In the following years I could receive something from the Christians and from relatives, but I was not permitted to see anyone or to speak with anyone.

During the interrogations physical violence was never used, except for some hard slaps or something of that kind; but being tied during the interrogations was already a torment. The poor Christians who were arrested with me submitted to torture and truly unheard-of violence, but toward the priests they did not dare to do it; perhaps because they hoped to pull us toward their side, or perhaps because we were too well known. The Christians killed in prison disappeared without any stories, while we priests were too well known in our areas and our disappearance would have embittered the people.

In prison, undoubtedly, there were other priests, nuns, and simple laypeople, but I was never permitted to see them or to speak with them. We were deliberately separated from one another. I knew, however, that the two women arrested with me were liberated after a few months in prison, while my catechist, after spending more than two years in prison, was sent home because he was seriously ill. For all that time he had remained tied with three chains: at his hands, at his feet, and at his neck.

In the period of forced labors along with others, I cultivated the lands of the State; in reality, they were lands taken from the large property owners. In those times there were no communes, the collectivization of the lands was in the process of being set up: the government demanded very high taxes from the private landowners, and those not able to pay had to cede their lands to the government.

At the forced labor camp we ate better than in the prison, and there was also more liberty; usually there were two meals a day, but in the times of more work a third meal was added.

Overall the forced labor was better than prison, at least the work of the fields, to which I was assigned. If I had been forced to dig dams or canals or work on the railroad, I would have preferred prison, because I heard that in those camps the discipline was terrible: the work practically never ended, and the prisoners died like flies. For us, there was also the forced indoctrination, on Marxism, on the philosophy of atheism, and on the thought of Mao Zedong. We patiently listened, content that for half a day we were seated instead of going out to work.... At other times we were gathered together for conferences on the current political scene, usually concerning the opposition to America, the victory of our soldiers in Korea, or news of diverse party deliberations, et cetera. There was no discussion, and we were carefully observed; we sat passively in order to rest ourselves, often not even listening to what the various lecturers were saying.

The Return Home

Nearly six months before my release (around January 1955), I was sent back to prison, this time to Shantou, for other interrogations and because they wished to see if the long period in prison had changed me. They imposed long written confessions on me: I had to respond, always in writing, to hundreds of questions on how the Church is organized, on the pope and his bishops, on the offerings from the faithful and where they end up, on the foreign missionaries I knew, on my past life, and so forth. Perhaps they thought that, being forced to write for entire days, I would say something compromising. I responded to all the questions truthfully, but I avoided furnishing information that could be used to compromise someone. My goal was to demonstrate that I was changed, ready to collaborate with the government, so that they would let me go home; I could not therefore truly write what I thought, or say everything good about the Church; otherwise I would have had to remain in prison. I did not say anything bad about the priests and some of the Christians who remained in China; otherwise they would have gone to get them and we would have been pitted against one another, so I related some of the character defects of the diverse Italian missionaries who were at Hong Kong: this one was too severe, another one was too nervous and treated others badly, et cetera. The police told me, "Bravo," and that finally I was disposed to do good for the people and other things of the kind. Then they asked me to say everything bad that I possibly could about my bishop and the pope; but then I had to disappoint them, saying that the pope and the bishop had never done anything bad to me.

They thought, evidently, that I was not yet ripe for liberty, so they proposed that I remain incarcerated as the prison doctor. I accepted very willingly. Although it was a compulsory assignment, it was better than working the land; it permitted me to have a privileged position in prison and to be liberated from the control of the authorities for many hours of the day. I was not able to visit all the prisoners, but only those they presented to me; obviously they wished to keep me from the other priests and the Christians. Also, each day a police officer would come to me for a discussion, always telling me that a smart man like me should have made a career in the party, that for the good of the people it was best that all the brightest become Communists and other things of the sort. I told him that I wished the people well, but that I was also able to obtain the same thing as a private citizen, by giving a good example and by working and showing enthusiasm for my ministry.

After some months in prison and after having many discussions, that officer asked me expressly if, when I returned to my home, I would collaborate with the government and with the party. I responded that I would cooperate voluntarily for the good of the people and for my country, as long as they did not ask me to go against the principles of my Faith. He said that I had nothing to fear on this point. On June 3, 1955, they liberated me, warning me not to say anything to anyone about where I had been or that I had been imprisoned. Then they said that they considered me a collaborator of the government and that, if I saw any acts of sabotage, I should report them. I assured them that I would do as much as possible, and I returned home.

While I was in prison, the atmosphere in China was totally changed; absolute terror reigned everywhere, the fear of speaking, the fear of spies, and so forth. By now everyone had learned that they could not trust anyone, not even the members of their own families. The Christians, therefore, never asked me what had happened to me; anyhow, they already knew, and there was no need to speak of it to me. They welcomed me as if I had returned from a long journey; only after a period of time did some of the more courageous ask me about my imprisonment.

After prison, I returned to live at Huizhou, to the only mission remaining in our district. Now and then the police came to see me "for a friendly chat," or better, to ask me if I had someone to denounce; but I always responded that I did not know of any sabotage, mainly because I never left the house.

For some time I continued to remain confined at home. I did not dare go out of the city, and I almost never put my nose outside the door; I feared that they had liberated me simply to have further excuses and a pretext to put me away again. I wrote, however, to the bishop of Hong Kong, Monsignor Lorenzo Bianchi of Pime,[99] in order to tell him that I was associated with the Church at Huizhou (without telling him that I had been in prison, but he already understood this on his own) and that I had need of his economic help. The bishop sent me some money that permitted me to maintain myself without working for the State. However, after 1958 I was not able to receive any help from Hong Kong, and I had to work all day for the government, that is, in my local commune.

Before 1958 I worked at home, doing odd jobs, and therefore the major part of my time was given to the faithful who came to me, and with great courage because everyone knew that I was under strict surveillance and that once a week I had to present myself to the police for inspection.

I worked as a plumber and as a mechanic, or I was assigned to practice medicine. In brief: I managed to support myself. The Christians would

[99] The last European bishop of Hong Kong. Born at Corteno (Brescia) in 1899, ordained a priest in 1922, he left for China in 1923. Destined for the Diocese of Hong Kong, he was instead assigned to the mission of Hoifung, inside China. In 1925 he was arrested by the Communists and later liberated.

have helped me, but I never permitted it because they were already too poor and the times were very difficult for anyone with a family. Although I was working, I was able to dedicate a good part of my time to the ministry. I taught catechism, privately, to anyone who came to me; I visited the sick near my house with the excuse of bringing medicine, but especially in order to give them the sacrament of the sick. I consoled those who were afflicted (and so many came to me who were not Catholic!). In addition I celebrated Mass every day, especially on Sunday; and the Christians came, some from far away, making me get up even at two or three in the morning in order to hear their confessions and to give them Communion; then, concealing themselves as best they could, they returned home in secret. But others—because they were more courageous or because they did not have families—remained for the Mass that I celebrated in the morning and then went to work. On the Communist holidays, when there was no work (usually every fifteen or twenty days on average), I spent the entire day receiving visits from the Christians, even those from places very far away from Huizhou: because they would go where no one knew them.

No one ever told me to remain closed up in my house, but I knew that if I had begun to go around to the villages, as I had normally done, and as I would have wished, I would have immediately ended up in prison on the usual pretext. Having seen that I served the Christians well even from home, I continued to carry on in this way. However, during the last months before fleeing, the discipline was so relaxed in everything that I could begin again to go around to the villages and to visit the ill, even those at some distance, and no one said anything to me.

But up to 1959 (that is, up to the failure of the communes) the discipline was extremely strict. Suffice it to say that it was necessary to ask permission even to listen to Communist radio.

I had a radio at home, but in order not to stir up suspicions I never listened to it. During the periodic searches I always kept it well in view because I did not want them to think that I was hiding it; otherwise there would have been problems. I would have listened very willingly to the radio from Hong Kong, but I did not wish to end up in prison out of a simple curiosity. Thus I kept the radio, but without using it; the police may have thought that it did not work.

Hunger and Desperation in China's Communes

During all these years, with the exception of the period spent in prison, I lived the normal life of the Chinese people. I worked as everyone else did, and, therefore, I think I am qualified to give a faithful enough picture of the situation in the country, naturally always in relation to my particular area; but I think that, more or less, what I say of the district of Hoifung is valid also for all the rest of China.

We can begin by saying that when the Communists conquered China, they were well received by the people. In general there was a great and sincere enthusiasm. The Communists presented themselves as benefactors, conquerors of all the injustices, people who loved order and equity; and above all they promised great things. China was exiting a long war with Japan (1937–1945), and it was tired of brigands, guerillas, the changing of currency, the Nationalists, and the corrupt generals. Chiang Kai-shek had enjoyed immense prestige in all of China from 1925 to 1940, but then the long war ruined him, the best troops deserted him, and he was left with the sharks, the profiteers, and the usual gangs of adventurers. The people accepted the Communists as true liberators, not because they were Communists, but simply because they promised peace, order, and justice. Their first acts corresponded to what they promised.

The people's enthusiasm for the Communists lasted as long as the illusions lasted, as long as the people were not put in contact with the extremely hard reality of the Communist dictatorship. Today, except for some young fanatics in the State schools, the people no longer believe in the well-being that Communism promised. The majority began to be fed up with the people's trials; they doubted, then they secretly criticized, then they were silent, out of fear of spies, and finally they began to hate. But now it is too late; the regime is solidified. However, the hate is so strong that, if tomorrow the police apparatus were to collapse, we would have a chain of bloody vendettas against the Communists that I hope I shall never have to see.

What first caused the vacillating faith in the Communists were the people's trials, which began during the agrarian reform in 1950 and lasted throughout 1951. They were so terrible that they even stunned the fanatics. The property owners were led to a stage at the center of a village and were made to confront a session of a "people's trial." Also subjected to these trials were the enemies of the regime, in general all those who for some motive bothered them; either personally or for various absurd accusations, et cetera.

These poor devils were beaten publicly for entire days and exposed to the derision of everyone; anyone who was able could go up to them, hit them, and spit at them. The Communists favored these personal vendettas because they divided the people and made them easier to dominate.

But most of the people were moved to pity and did not accuse anyone; I myself saw several of them cry, even robust men, after having been forced to assist at similar "people's trials." In some parts of China many missionaries, priests, and even the faithful were subjected to these trials.

These public trials lasted two or three years at most, and then the Communist leaders saw that they were doing harm to themselves and that the people were rebelling: today the public trials are very rare. However, these were the first deeds that opened the eyes of the Chinese people: everyone began to think that the Communists were worse than the Japanese: crueler and more fanatic. I think, without a doubt, that those public trials were a colossal mistake on the part of the government; if the leaders thought they were frightening people, they succeeded there, meanwhile they lost a good part of their good reputation and made the bitterest of enemies: all the children, the relatives, and the friends of those who were tried became enemies of the Communists.

The Failure of the Commune Model

As to the organization of life in the communes of China, we must distinguish between different periods. At first, one breathed a certain liberty, but little by little with the continuous control placed over all personal activities, it disappeared. Especially after 1958, with the beginning of the experimental communes, personal liberty became a mere dream; little by little the leaders became aware that they had lost the people's favor, but they stiffened discipline even more, until, in the last four years, it became unsupportable. Only after a few months, perhaps a year, of not having anything to eat and fearing an open rebellion, was this discipline relaxed — I think more spontaneously than voluntarily.

With the communes life had been collectivized in every aspect: everyone worked in common, amused themselves in common, and ate in common. Each village, each neighborhood in a city, had its refectory (dining hall for communal meals) and its kitchen. The children had to be educated by the State in the nursery schools and the grammar schools because the parents were busy with production; they could not see their children during the evening, only on holidays and in case of illness. I know that I am relating nearly incredible things, but this is the absolute truth.

From 1958 private property no longer existed, neither farmland nor houses: everything became the property of the State, and everyone worked for the State. The same was also true for individual transfers: no one could go from one city to another or from one region to another without written permission from the police.

A person could receive letters from Hong Kong or from abroad and respond to them, but they were always suspect, and all the mail was censored. I was able to communicate with the bishop of Hong Kong through other means, of which I cannot speak; but I lived right on the border of Hong Kong, and it was easy for me to have some clandestine communication.

The results of the commune experiment were disastrous for the Chinese economy, as well as for the liberty of the people, so much so that the government had to take steps backward. Today the government does not insist on meals in common; they still exist, but one is free enough to participate or not participate. Small plots of land for private, family cultivation are also permitted, and these succeed very well while the common fields yield very little. It's enough to say that as a result of this program China went through a terrible agricultural crisis. Zhou Enlai, the leader at that time, in his official discourse to the Congress of the People in April 1962, admitted to a "vertical decline in the production of agriculture" and he exhorted the Congress to give first place to the State's agricultural concerns, even above those of industry.

The agricultural failure was caused by the institution of the communes, which nationalized all the farmlands, all the means of production, all the businesses, and even the private lives of the Chinese people. This created such a state of rebellion that practically everyone became a potential saboteur; there was no longer anyone in charge of the instruments of work and the success of the labor; when people are not supervised, they cease working or they destroy what they have already done a moment before. For example, if a peasant had a hoe or a plow of his own, he would take care not to ruin it so that it would last several years; today there must be a special caretaker to supervise the use of these tools, because after a few months they are unusable, either from carelessness or from deliberate misuse.

Everyone thinks only of himself; there is no longer a spirit of working for the State or for the common good with the enthusiasm of the early times of the Communist occupation. One thinks of succeeding sooner or later with the breakup of the regime and its police state, and thus the restoration of each one's personal liberty. [But first things have to get worse before they get better; as the people like to say: "So much the worse, so much the better."]

But there are other causes of the agricultural failure; for example, the inexperience of the supervisors of the communes and the agricultural works. At the head of the agricultural works were Communist or military officials who perhaps had never seen cultivated fields and as a result would give absurd orders; or a leader would supervise peasants from the north of China, where the farming and the situations were different; but since no one was able to speak, they fulfilled the tasks with the mistaken orders they were given, compromising the entire harvest. Then there was the national campaign for the destruction of the birds: apart from the insensitivity, by killing the birds, insects, pests and worms multiplied excessively, and so today they are promoting a campaign to protect the birds. The peasants who initially tried to convince the leaders that certain orders were mistaken and harmful were accused of sabotage and imperialism, so that at a certain point everyone remained silent.

Another cause of the failure of agriculture is that the field hand works less than in previous times, even if he is engaged for more hours. In times of major necessity, a Chinese peasant would get up before daylight, even at two or three in the morning, because, when the sun scorches, the work renders less. Today, instead, everything is organized: in summer and in winter the peasants get up at about six, then there are gymnastics in common, an hour of Marxist indoctrination, breakfast, and finally the call to forced labor and the work schedule for that day.... When one truly begins to work in the fields, the sun is already high, and everyone works very little. Formerly, certain jobs that a peasant would have accomplished in a few days, "killing himself," today require weeks and end up badly; and little jobs that could have been done in a few minutes are dragged out for entire days. While at one time, during the "dead season," the peasant slept or made handcrafts or engaged in some other small commercial activity, today he goes to work in the fields and does nothing, just military exercises. In the evening, when he returns from the fields, there is a roll call, then political conferences, and other foolishness that tires the people.

A third cause for the failure of Chinese agriculture is that China tried to industrialize in too much of a hurry. A great part of the agricultural earnings were eaten for years by industry and by aiding countries abroad, such as the African, Asian, and South American countries, and Albania.

But, I insist, more than all of the above, the principal cause of the agricultural failure is the people's lack of trust in the system; they did not work as much as they possibly could, and as a result they ruined everything; why, indeed, work with goodwill, when there is no hope of bettering your own personal condition?

Among the causes some cite for the failure of the collectivized agriculture are the natural calamities. But I lived in the Chinese countryside all my life, and it seems to me that in recent times there have not been particularly negative atmospheric conditions, at least in the region where I was living. I read in the Chinese newspapers that the center and the north of the country had undergone the most serious flooding of this century; this could be true, but then of what value are the famous dams that according to Mao had definitively resolved the problem of the waters?

As a consequence of this agricultural failure, the people ate worse than in the previous years: the Communist leaders also admit this; however, they say it concerned temporary atmospheric conditions. From the second half of 1961 the situation, at least in our parts, had become unsustainable, and many complained openly, even though the police had more power and the capacity to intervene [and make arrests].

Today in China the purchase of all the basic necessities is limited; everything is bought with a ration card. It can be said that one is free to buy only the objects that cost too much for the common people: cameras, radios, motorcycles, some automobiles ... Everything else is rationed: food, clothing, shoes, fabric, and other common items.

Those who have money can also buy these things freely on the black market, which is sustained in our area because of its close vicinity to the free port of Hong Kong. I do not know the situation in other areas of China; probably it is not possible to find anything other than rationed goods. But even in our region, who has money? Working for the State earns so little that after purchasing necessities, there is nothing left to spend on the black market.... Only those who had put something aside before, gold or silver, for example, or perhaps the party officials, could permit themselves these luxuries. The fortunate have always existed. At one time they were called mandarins and landowners; today they are called the stewards of the people, directors of the communes, officials of the police or police officers, party theorists or ideologues, and so forth. If it were not for those who were a little better off than the general population, the Communist system would not hold up a single day longer.

Rice is the principal nourishment of the population. In the city of Huizhou, where I lived, each one had the right to acquire twenty-two pounds of rice per month; plus half an ounce of oil (provisions are always given once a month), about a pound of salt, one pound of salted fish, and three or four ounces of sugar. The vegetables were not rationed but were distributed according to the local harvest. Meat was seen only a few times a year, always during the Communist holidays or for the great feast at the beginning of the Chinese New Year; on the same occasions, other foods not found at any other time, such as eggs, pastries, spicy sauces, and other delicacies, were put on sale.

Certainly before Communism the people ate more and better: I have no doubt. At least in our area (since I do not know the rest of China), we never had anyone die from hunger, and the people bought what they wished at moderate prices. Naturally there were also periods of famine and the people had to emigrate for a time, but during normal periods of daily life, people ate more and much better than now.

I have already outlined the motives for this situation: today the fields produce much less than when they were cultivated privately. Let me just say that in recent times the government had to give some small plots of land to private individuals to help the people provide for the family's basic needs, because the government itself could not think of everything. These small fields and vegetable gardens were cultivated with great care compared with those of the communes; so much so that the heads of the communes were always inciting the peasants to work with the same intensity for the State as they worked for themselves! But in order to cultivate his garden, the peasant had to remain on his feet all night; then he would sleep during the day while at work for the commune.

An Evaluation of Communism in China

When I ask myself what could have saved us from the Communist experience in China, I respond that without a doubt a government that has dominated all of China, unopposed, for over thirteen years must have done the country some good. Even Hitler brought German science to the forefront and built the first highway system in the country. But let us return to China. The positive aspects of the Communist domination, from the material or economic point of view, are the following: above all the unification of this immense country under one government, universal education, the struggle against illiteracy, industrialization, the construction of the railroads, bridges, dams, and canals, et cetera.

One can make at least three observations concerning the Communists' accomplishments in China: first, that if China had enjoyed an internal and external peace during this long period, it would have progressed under any government, indeed, perhaps the progress would have been even more stable and more general. For example, if we look at India, which also started out very disadvantaged, it had—with respect to China—a greater population density, fewer natural resources, and a more backward economy (since China already had vast industrial areas such as Manchuria, inherited from Japan), yet its industrial progress was not less than China's, even with regard to public works.

The second observation is this: regarding Chinese progress, too little is known with certainty to be able to evaluate it overall. The statistics are not certain and are often denied after a few months or a year by the same sources that released them; then, various aspects of the progress that had been flaunted are revealed to be fictitious; for example, the canals and the dams that were built with dirt floors that collapsed with the first serious floods, and the iron and steel fused in the "village ovens" that remained unutilized because of their inadequacy and that now have been completely abandoned. Another example: the railroad from Canton toward Vietnam, built in record time and often boasted of during the early years of the regime, is today, piece by piece, under reconstruction, after serious accidents occurred due to the collapse of bridges and roadbeds. Examples of this type, although only among those of my experience, are many. Not to speak of agriculture, which, as I have said, has seen a serious regression, such that all the harvests for all of China today are inferior to those before Communism and during the first years of the regime.

The third fundamental observation that one could make on the effects brought about by Communism in China is that the cost to the Chinese people was exorbitant. Only when it collapses will we know the depth of its nefarious deeds: the massacres, the deportations, and the tortures it has carried out. Likewise it was not possible to take into account all the wickedness of Nazism until Hitler's regime fell: at first few believed, even with documentation, what was said about it; their deeds seemed impossible, but then everyone had to open their eyes. Today it is the same with Communism in China; indeed, I am sure that the Communist experience is for the Chinese people much worse than the Hitlerian experience was for the Germans. It is difficult to make this comparison, but I do not believe that the Hilterian regime was as spiteful toward the Germans as the Communist regime was toward the Chinese.

At the beginning, as I was saying, Communism had many enthusiastic followers — perhaps the vast majority of the young people — who were excited by the promises that the Communist leaders were making. Then the fervor of the masses diminished, and today very few demonstrate any support for the regime; there are still some, especially among the young and the very young who have been educated from their infancy with only one idea and only one fanaticism. One can never know, however, if this enthusiasm is sincere or simulated. Many, for example, are enthusiastic in public: they shout during the parades; they clap their hands for the Communist orators; they are the first to listen to the indoctrinations; they stir up others over the saboteurs and the spies; they complete solemn oaths to serve the cause to the end; and other similar things. But are they sincere or not? They have everything to gain by being enthusiastic, and indeed they are better off: in general they do not work; they supervise others; they have, in brief, a privileged position in the Communist society.

We can admit that some of them are sincerely convinced, fanatically convinced; but we can also note that, in recent times, those who show enthusiasm in public are a very small minority; and if we subtract from them those who are pretending, then indeed we may properly conclude that, by now, only a very low percentage of the population has any enthusiasm for Communism, whereas the vast majority, if it could, would immediately decree an end to the regime.

Today in China, there are frequent open rebellions, and even if they are immediately put down, it is because there is no coordination among the various opposing groups. The number of groups opposing the regime grows continuously; without a doubt they are the great majority of the Chinese people: one sees it by the many unmistakable signs. Certainly no one has been committed to an open rebellion; these happened only in certain extreme cases of desperation when they explode: for example, at times workers of some "commune" have rebelled because they want improvements, or in the morning one sees posters against the government tacked onto the city walls, and so forth.

But it seems to me that unfortunately, for the time being, it is not possible for the people to oppose the regime. Yet I cannot understand how the world can turn their back on the prolonged torment of an immense people like the Chinese without doing something to help it.

The "Church of Silence" in China

As I have already said, at first the Communists were presented as friends of everybody, respectful of personal liberty and religion, defenders of the poor and the weak ... Although the ecclesiastical authorities had spoken clearly from the beginning about the danger implicit in Communism, in its materialist theories and dictatorial practices, many Christians (and not a few priests) were slow to understand the Communist reality in China. Initially it was thought that Chinese Communism was different from Russian Communism, more humane, that it did not question atheism; but then we became aware that it was much worse.

The persecution did not begin with a precise action; it is not as if one fine morning we got up and on the city walls we read a poster that said: "Today the persecutions begin." Little by little, the Communists began to feel secure in their possession of the entire country and of the irreversible defeat of Chiang Kai-shek. They then began to tighten the reins, impose limitations, and provoke this or that priest and this or that Christian. They immediately imprisoned the most inflexible, and then they continued on this path, sowing terror, spying, and so forth.

First, they got rid of all the foreign missionaries: all they needed was three to four years to eliminate or expel the five thousand missionaries who were in the country before Communism; then it was the turn of the Chinese priests and the most notable Christians.

While I was in prison no one spoke of the "Patriotic Church," only the "Movement of the Three Autonomies" and of the "Patriotic Catholics." Everything was diffused through special comic books that they gave to all the prisoners; the stories were ridiculous, so that no one with a minimum of good sense and good faith would have been able to digest them (for example, they claimed that the nuns killed babies in the hospitals, that the priests were all enemy spies, that Americans, before coming to China, took courses on espionage, and tales of that type). On the other hand, they had also condemned me for throwing poison into the wells of the city.

In prison they said that only the best among us could enroll in the patriotic Christian associations; then the insistence became stronger, until after 1958, they applied moral and physical pressures to force us to declare that we wished to separate ourselves from Rome.

During the first years, there were many Christians, especially young people, who truly possessed the courage of lions: they said clearly and firmly that they would never condemn the pope and the bishops, and many of them were incarcerated. When it came to eliminating the foreign missionaries (1951–1954), the government searched for Christians who would accuse them of imaginary crimes, incarcerate them, and beat them, but in spite of the suffering, rarely did someone give in. At times they had already prepared the written document with the charge: it was enough to sign it, and one was liberated from every nuisance. Yet, even so, very few gave in; a large part ended up doing forced labor and either died or were dismissed when their health was ruined forever. Only in heaven will we be able to admire the heroism of so many Chinese Christians who were true martyrs for their faith.

I think the worst years were 1955 and 1958. In 1955, after sending the foreign missionaries abroad, the regime attempted to get the Chinese priests and Christians to cooperate with the government; in that year there was a true persecution directed at separating the bishops and the Christian communities from Rome. The culmination was when Monsignor Ignatius

Gong Pinmei, the heroic bishop of Shanghai, was incarcerated with hundreds of his priests and faithful. Then in 1958 they changed tactics and asked that everyone become members of the "Patriotic Church."

A Congress of the "Patriotic Church"

In 1958 I was invited repeatedly to participate at the encounters of the "Patriotic Church." I went only once, when they told me that if I did not go "freely," I would have to go as a prisoner, by force. In fact, at the conference that was held at Canton in the spring of 1958, there were more than a hundred priests, and several came only under the threat of arms. We were all priests of Guangdong, because it was a reunion of the "Patriotic Church" of our region.

The conference lasted a little more than two months (April to May 1958). During that time one meeting after another was held, in order to weaken our resistance. They told us always the same things for hours and hours: they wanted our written confessions; they wanted us to declare the Church in China independent from Rome, and other things of the kind.

There was no freedom of speech, obviously: it was necessary only to applaud; we were able to speak only what they invited us to say. A priest presided over the sessions, and there were some double-dealing Christians who guided the discussions and were assigned to look at the reactions of the priests in order to pick out those who resisted the most. I pitied them; I thought that perhaps they had arrived at that point after submitting to torture or in order to save their families. The police did not take part in the discussions, but they guided them from a distance.

At the beginning of the gatherings they immediately posed the question of the imperialism of the Vatican. They had everyone write a response to the question "What do you think of the imperialism of the Vatican?" But immediately a Chinese Jesuit got up to speak, naturally without having been invited. He said that he preferred to respond orally, and he affirmed that the pope had always acted for the good of all the peoples on earth and that he loved the Chinese people very much. The Christians and the police wished to interrupt him, but he continued to shout that the Vatican had never done anything against China. Then there was an uproar, because all of us got up in defense of the Jesuit. When everything had calmed, I asked to speak and they permitted me, perhaps hoping that I would say pleasing things. I said that it was necessary to understand the significance of "imperialist." If they wished to say that the Vatican was against Communism, then I said we priests in that hall were also imperialists; if rather they wished to say that the Vatican was against the people, then no one of us, and not even the pope, was an imperialist.

They accused me of being a servant of America, because America is imperialist, and I responded that America was against Communism also, but not against the Chinese people. Then a Christian said to me: "You are against the Chinese people who have chosen Communism and also against God, because in Latin it is said: "*Vox populi vox Dei.*"

I responded that that proverb was not the teaching of the Church. I said that at Jerusalem the people acclaimed, "Hosanna to the Son of David" and then, a few days after, they cried out, "Crucify him! Crucify him!" I posed this question: "What is the voice of the people, the first or the second?"

He said he didn't know any of these stories invented by the priests.

"Okay, then, tell me if it was the voice of the people when the Chinese were crying out, 'Long live Chiang Kai-shek!' or now that they cry out, 'Long live Mao Zedong!'"

Then they stopped speaking to me and cried out that I was a servant of the imperialist Americans. After me other priests spoke; throughout the days of the conference all the priests who spoke expressed their support for the pope and their opposition to Communism. Later, they prohibited us from speaking, making us express everything in writing instead.

The Jesuit who had spoken first and had used violent terminology was immediately arrested: we did not see him at the sessions during the rest of the conferences. Other eminent personalities were also arrested: vicar generals, superiors of religious orders, and professors at the seminary. I also feared being arrested, but they saw that I was not a known personality. And then they thought that the years I had already spent in prison would have kept me in my place. Finally the Patriotic bishop of my region, Joseph Yip,[100] who was my good friend, told the authorities that I was not a dangerous type for the State and that they could let me go home.

At the end of those gatherings, an election of bishops was held. There were some who refused to elect them, but the majority of us voted because we thought of it as a farce that would permit us to exercise our ministry a bit. Anyway, it was only an "election": we, in other words, were thinking only of electing our own superiors, given that those who were legitimate were either in prison or had been expelled. The ugly fact was that then some of these "elected" bishops were consecrated.

Even Father Yip had himself consecrated a bishop in Manchuria by a legitimate bishop; therefore I think that the consecration, although illicit, was valid. Father Yip, however, did not consecrate other bishops or priests; he was a good rural pastor, and when we were among ourselves we never called him bishop, nor did he request us to do so. He was a good priest, elderly, very ill and very timid. Initially, when he returned after his consecration, the authorities prepared a triumphal welcome for him, and several Christians were forced to participate. On that occasion Yip was dressed like a true bishop (at least that is what they said to me because I was absent, having left the city a few days earlier so that I would not be forced to participate in the festivities). But after that occasion I no longer heard of him dressing like a bishop, indeed he himself did not wish to: it was enough for him to dress like a simple priest. He continued to exercise his ministry and the faithful went to him because they understood that he had not betrayed the faith.

---

[100] Joseph Yip was ordained a priest for the Diocese of Hong Kong in 1934. After the Communist occupation he continued to work in the district of Huiyang in continental China. Ordained a bishop without the sanction of the Holy See, he was destined by the authorities for the seat of Canton in place of Dominic Tang, in prison first and then a resident of Hong Kong. Father Yip died in 1990.

Leon Chan

How the Church Lives in China

With the passing of time, about 1958, the pressure on the Church let up
a little. In China there had been a significant relaxation of all the discipline. The motives, I believe, were principally two: above all, the failure of
the communes had created an enormous sense of discontent that, from
time to time, exploded into open acts of rebellion, sabotage, and strikes;
things that had never been seen prior to then. Even the Church was left
somewhat in peace, in order not to irritate the people exceedingly. The
second decisive motive was the failure of the "Patriotic Church." They
understood that they were not able to lead the priests and the faithful
en masse to this new phenomenon; therefore, they contented themselves
by controlling our ministry and imprisoning those who bothered them
most; others were considered heedless (for criticizing the government, for
example) or simply ignorant of what was good for them. I have to say that
this was the situation in my area, in the south of China; perhaps it was
very different in other areas; for us it was certain that a latent popular rebellion, brought about by the scarcity of food, had, in general, relaxed the
discipline and also the pressures on the Church. For example, the Marxist
indoctrination was no longer obligatory as before; theoretically everyone
was required to attend the evening conferences on Marxism, but even if
some did not, nothing happened, while in the past the absentees would
have ended in prison.

Of the Chinese priests, I must say that, at first, very few compromised
with Communism, but for those who did, they could not turn back: they
had to stay with the Patriotic Church; otherwise there would have been
trouble for them. But they are the few, and in general they repented the
errors that they committed in the past, many of which were forced on
them through physical and moral torture. However, the vast majority of
the Chinese clergy remained faithful to their own legitimate bishops and
to the pope and were not snapped up by the Patriotic Church; the same
must also be said for the Chinese faithful; and it is with profound joy and
pride that I offer this testimony to my confreres and to our faithful. It is
not to our credit: the grace of God has helped us.

Many priests died in the prisons and in the forced-labor camps; I know several of those who died in the camps of Manchuria, Tibet, and Xinjiang. Many of those who were sent into the regions on China's borders had to build roads or railroads or bridges or dams and are still in prison today; others died a natural death or are living at home with their families, but without having a church where they can officiate. In total, if one takes into account that from 1950 there were no more ordinations of new priests, the priests who exercise the ministry and remain faithful to the Church are not very many.

In my area there are three of us, but the other two priests carry out the ministry in private. I met with some priests when I went to Canton, two or three times during the year. With the excuse of going to visit relatives, I visited these priests in order to exchange ideas and to confess myself and to hear their confessions.

I had to ask permission to go to Canton. Even later, when the discipline was very relaxed, if I had gone outside my city without permission, I would have ended up in prison. I also had to obtain the proper coupons in order to be able to eat in Canton, because the ration ticket that I had was valid only for the common meal or for some State stores near my house. To go to any other places in China, I (as well as any other Chinese) had to ask permission from the police of my city; then I would have to present myself to the police at the city or village where I was going and ask for the coupons that I needed in order to eat there.

As for the nuns, they went back to their homes and lived with their families dressed like all the other women. At Huizhou there were several nuns at the hospital. At first the Communists sent them home to their families; then they wanted them back in order to care for the sick, but I did not give them permission to return out of fear that it was some type of trap.

Initially the Communists pressured the nuns to marry, but then they did not dare to do it anymore, because in China, the people are very reserved and these matters are considered too personal and above any type of interference. Today the nuns still go out every day to work in the fields or in the state offices. There were, however, some nuns who were imprisoned as "American spies," because the officials found them more annoying than the others or because they strongly resisted various situations. For example, I remember the case of the nuns of the Immaculate Conception in Canton, who were imprisoned at the times of the persecution of 1951 because they would not accuse the bishop and the priests of foul deeds. I do not know if they survived; but they never returned home.

As to the faithful laity, those who were able married in Church, but if they were too distant, sooner or later, they would ask the priest to bless their marriage. I married many of them, even without publishing the bans, with dispensations from the bishop of Hong Kong. I also married several Catholics whose spouses were non-Christian or were pagans. I recall that while I was in prison a Communist official came to me secretly and told me that he was a Catholic and that he wished to marry a girl at the place who was not Christian. I did not believe him, and I thought that it was a trap; I asked him various questions, and he responded well, but I knew that the Communists are masters of deceit. Then I told him that if he wished to marry, he had to get the proper credentials from his priest. That poor devil was desperate because his town was in the north of China. But I held to my positions; so after a few months, the official presented me with a letter from his priest, written in Latin, undoubtedly authentic! I married him secretly, and I was never bothered over it for this reason: evidently he truly was a Catholic.

Unlike in other years in the past, today we can have prayer books and catechisms at home and receive them in the mail, secretly, from Hong Kong. Since things went badly in China, they no longer dare come to search homes, but at the time of the violent persecutions, woe to you if a book or newspaper that was not Communist was found in your home. Right after I left prison, in 1955, the police came once and for three consecutive days they searched my residence, looking even in the stuffing of the chairs, in between the walls that seemed hollow, and peeling away the wallpaper. What trouble there would have been for me if they had discovered a Catholic book or catechism or newspaper, even if it were old: I would have ended up in prison again. Later, I learned the motive behind these searches: someone had reported that I had a storage space for Catholic books in the house!

The situation ultimately changed, at least in our parts (in the south of China). We were permitted to have some catechisms, and we literally unearthed old books that were hidden and no one said anything. Again, however, the area in which I lived, which is on the border with Hong Kong, was very different from other zones in China: there one breathed the air of the free territory of Hong Kong; there was commercial activity, visits exchanged between families and relatives, et cetera. In other areas of China, without a doubt the Catholics were much worse off; there was no possibility for them to have any contact with the outside world.

As to the churches and other Catholic institutions, they were all searched, even in our area. The churches became warehouses or cinemas or barracks or public offices. In 1955, when I was liberated from prison, there was a little ramshackle church at Huizhou where I celebrated the holy Mass, and then they closed even that.

Inevitably, in the presence of a context so problematical, even the ordinary pastoral activity was deeply resented. There were very few new conversions, it is true. I baptized four or five entire families and a few isolated individuals. Others exhorted me to keep their name in mind, so that, when the Communist dictatorship was finished, they would be able to be baptized. I never pushed anyone to convert, knowing well the danger that they would encounter; I would tell them to pray to God, to flee evil, and to do good.

There would have been vocations to the priesthood if the climate had permitted it. But from 1955 none of the seminaries were operating, and there were no new priests; several seminarians had been forced to flee to Hong Kong, and all are now completing the requirements for their ordination. Still today there are young Christian men who come to ask for instruction in order to become priests, but it is not possible to train priests with a single, private tutor.

Hopes for the Church's Future

My hope for the future of the Church in China is that it changes for the better. Never before has the Church been known in China in such a favorable light by all the people—and to think that this service has been performed by the very Communists who wished to destroy the Church.

Before Communism the Church represented one of the many religions in China, and certainly it was one of the least known. There were then also the Protestants, whom everyone confused with us Catholics. The Church was the principal obstacle to Communism, while all the other religions, including the Protestants, were emphatically and slavishly reduced to venerate the dictatorship. I do not wish to say, with that, that there were not some Protestant pastors who had not suffered for their faith. There were, but very few; the vast majority, if they were foreign missionaries, fled from China before the arrival of the Communists, or they accepted Communism without any opposition. Those who resisted were the exception, while among the Catholics the exceptions were those who gave in.

The Catholic Church was known by all the Chinese people as the principal adversary of Communism; all the newspapers spoke of it, and by now everyone knew that the pope of Rome was the number-one opponent of the Communist doctrine and dictatorship; up to 1958 or 1959, all the trials against the Chinese missionaries or priests or against simple Catholics were flaunted by the press and by the radio, and this was optimal propaganda for the Church, because the people were asking what was this Catholic Church, which was very rarely ever mentioned, that dared to resist Communism with so much strength?

The admiration for the Church and for the Catholics came directly from this. The same Communist policemen, when they were in a mood for sharing, confessed to me several times, that they admired us and that they could not succeed to explain to themselves how we were able to suffer prison for an idea and for fidelity to the pope who lived so far away. Once one of them said to me: "Look, the pope will never know that you accused him." The patience and the calm of the Catholics and the priests condemned unjustly was something that the people, including the Communists, could not explain. The other prisoners would cry, would suffer desperation and at times would commit suicide. But we, generally, remained calm and tranquil. At various times I heard people who came to the prison praise the attitude of the Catholics and the priests, saying that they were helping everyone by giving good example and not cursing.

One day, when I was at forced labor, I was asked by another condemned man if I was Catholic.

"Why do you ask?" I replied.

"I don't know," he said to me: "you do everything differently from the rest of us."

Therefore, I think that the persecution will bear good fruit for the Church. I am truly convinced of it. By now in China everyone knows the Church for what it is; that is, a society formed, in general, by good people who help others, who are ready to die as witnesses to their Faith; everyone knows that the Church has been opposed to Communism from the beginning, that it has been a difficult problem for the dictatorship, a tough nut to crack, et cetera. I think that when communism disappears many will come to us to ask for solutions to life's problems. This has already been confirmed, in my view, because even in these times of persecution, many have said to me that if they could they would become Catholic and others have asked me for a little religious instruction in order to help them, to give them the strength to better support the burdens of these years.

The Approach to Hong Kong—Opening the Border

At a certain point in China the food situation became unbearable; in our area the scant supplies obtained with the ration ticket were not distributed with regularity, and the common meals were served only when there was something to cook. Then the people's anger reached a point at which it could no longer be contained, and the authorities, who in the past would have shot the grumblers as a way of forcing the people to suffer in silence, realized that, this time, they could not run the risk of being disobeyed by the soldiers.

One day, in our villages and in the city near the border with Hong Kong, it was rumored that the border was not guarded: one could freely cross it. Then all those who were able fled, forming endless columns of refugees. It seemed like the time of the Communist conquest of China, when, from the north, long columns of refugees, who had already experienced Communism for long periods, escaped to Hong Kong.

The Communist soldiers were standing guard, but there was not much discipline among them either, and in fact some soldiers were joining the flight. At times soldiers would try to push back the refugees, but the infuriated crowd hit back, and the path was opened up; in other cases the soldiers told the refugees to tie their hands and their feet so that the authorities would see that the soldiers had attempted to hold back the tide.

After a few days, the English soldiers, having become aware that the Chinese border was no longer guarded, began to repel the refugees. They arrested them, brought them to a camp where they were able to eat and to sleep, and then gave them clothes and sent them back to the border.

In twenty days, in spite of the surveillance by the English soldiers, seventy to eighty thousand persons passed the border into Hong Kong! Entire populations of the towns bordering Hong Kong were depopulated; however, the refugees also came from long distances, even from Canton and then all the rest of the region of Guangdong. The Christian world should have taken care of these refugees; they should have opened up the world's various ports, welcoming them like brothers; instead, no one wished to know, and the government of Hong Kong was not able to do what it had to do to save the colony.

Hunger was the primary cause for the mass flight. Some may have also fled for ideological motives, but the great mass of people fled because of hunger; out of desperation, they thought that they would find in Hong Kong all the abundance of which they had heard spoken. This was the initial motive of the flight; naturally, when this escape then became an eruption, everyone fled without even asking themselves why.

They ran with the clothes they were wearing, carrying just the cash that they had; they were people of every social condition and especially the young, who had the capacity to walk; they ran, they pushed each other in agricultural carts, and they rode bicycles and beasts of burden. Some even took the train from Canton or Shantou.

DIARIES OF THE CHINESE MARTYRS

As for me, the bishop of Hong Kong, Monsignor Bianchi, wrote to me several times telling me to flee, as soon as the opportunity presented itself. Given the bishop's insistence and also because I had had enough of it all, when I heard that the border was open, I immediately prepared myself for the flight; indeed, a Christian came to me from a village near the border and invited me to flee with him and with a Christian woman from his village. We waited a few days to study the situation well; I celebrated Mass in the morning, and then I consumed all the Eucharistic hosts in order to be ready to flee immediately. We decided to leave on May 13 [the feast of Our Lady of Fatima]: I presented myself to my foreman, and then at the police station I asked permission to visit a sick friend who lived in a village nearby. We left on bicycles and we truly went to that priest, because I considered bringing him with me to Hong Kong, but he was too ill and too timid and he did not wish to come. I then went to Father Yip, the illicitly consecrated bishop of whom I have spoken, and I proposed to him to come with me; but he also was very shy and elderly, and he feared he was being strictly watched, so he did not come.

We slept that night, and in the afternoon of May 14 we were in sight of the border; there was not a solitary Communist soldier guarding it in places where, a few days before, there had been dozens; all along the border fence there were hundreds of poor Chinese, others were scattered in the forests and in the fields waiting until dark to climb over the barbed-wire fence that separated China from Hong Kong. We went to a small wooded area; then the three of us climbed over the fence. As soon as I was over the border I took out my priestly clothes and collar, and after dressing myself completely, we headed toward the nearest police station. But some English soldiers had already seen us and came running toward us with their rifles leveled. We were then led to the police, and an official interrogated us.

Fortunately the official was an Irish-Catholic. "Are you a Catholic priest?" he asked me.

"Yes, and I wish to speak to the bishop of Hong Kong."

"Well, tell me how the holy Mass begins."

I responded: "*Introibo ad altare Dei.... Ad Deum qui laetificat juventutem meam ...*"

I did not have time to finish, when the official emotionally embraced me and led me to Father Poletti, of Pime, who was always near the police station in order to assist the refugees. Father Poletti recognized me immediately and embraced me in tears.

I do not even know what I felt at that moment. I seemed to be dreaming, I thought it was a miracle of the Lord, and I thanked him with all my heart. I had lived for thirteen years in a true hell, only a few kilometers from liberty.

As soon as I arrived in Hong Kong I immediately wrote to my foreman and to the police of Huizhou, saying that I alone was responsible for my escape, as indeed it is true. I said that I wished to visit my bishop, Monsignor Lorenzo Bianchi, at Hong Kong. I hoped that no one would have to suffer for my flight.

Last June I was given an immense honor by the pope: together with Monsignor Bianchi, I was received in a private audience at the Vatican. Pope St. John XXIII was interested in the situation of the Chinese Church, and he said that all the world prays for China; I was, therefore, truly consoled for everything that I had suffered throughout these years, and I fervently hoped that the pope was right: that all the Catholics will remember to pray each day for the bishops, the priests, and the Chinese faithful that still live behind the bamboo curtain.

ACKNOWLEDGMENTS

Among the readers, some, knowing my height, will smile. But it is the pure truth: never, as in the work on this book, have I ever felt like a dwarf on the shoulders of giants.

This book is the result not only of my effort but of that of various persons who, in diverse capacities, have supported and collaborated with me, offering me precious suggestions, corrections, and, above all, encouragement.

I wish to thank in a special way Father Mario Marazzi, a missionary of Pime at Hong Kong, for his Carthusian patience (the patience of Job) and discretion, but also for his concrete support on this and multiple other occasions. Without him I would have undoubtedly committed errors of which, fortunately, the reader will be spared.

A sincere word of gratitude goes to three other missionaries of Pime. The priests, Angelo Lazzarotto and John Criveller—the first from Milan, the second from Hong Kong—who have followed this project with passion and competence, verifying names, dates, writings, place names, and so forth. As for Father Bernardo Cervellera, the director of *AsiaNews*, who accepted with pleasure the assignment of writing the preface: to him, I am deeply grateful.

In the proofreading and organization of the texts I had the helpful assistance and collaboration of a colleague and friend, Ilaria Nava, to whom I offer my gratitude for her passion and commitment.

Thanks also to the editor of Emi, Giuseppe Romano, who demonstrated patience and competence in his work.

DIARIES OF THE CHINESE MARTYRS

At the Pime center of Milan, once again, I found valid collaboration from Rosalba Ravelli, in the library, and among the photographic archives, Mauro Moret. I thank them both from my heart.

—G.F.

Sophia Institute

Sophia Institute is a nonprofit institution that seeks to nurture the spiritual, moral, and cultural life of souls and to spread the Gospel of Christ in conformity with the authentic teachings of the Roman Catholic Church.

Sophia Institute Press fulfills this mission by offering translations, reprints, and new publications that afford readers a rich source of the enduring wisdom of mankind.

Sophia Institute also operates two popular online Catholic resources: CrisisMagazine.com and CatholicExchange.com.

Crisis Magazine provides insightful cultural analysis that arms readers with the arguments necessary for navigating the ideological and theological minefields of the day. *Catholic Exchange* provides world news from a Catholic perspective as well as daily devotionals and articles that will help you to grow in holiness and live a life consistent with the teachings of the Church.

In 2013, Sophia Institute launched Sophia Institute for Teachers to renew and rebuild Catholic culture through service to Catholic education. With the goal of nurturing the spiritual, moral, and cultural life of souls, and an abiding respect for the role and work of teachers, we strive to provide materials and programs that are at once enlightening to the mind and ennobling to the heart; faithful and complete, as well as useful and practical.

Sophia Institute gratefully recognizes the Solidarity Association for preserving and encouraging the growth of our apostolate over the course of many years. Without their generous and timely support, this book would not be in your hands.

www.SophiaInstitute.com
www.CatholicExchange.com
www.CrisisMagazine.com
www.SophiaInstituteforTeachers.org

Sophia Institute Press® is a registered trademark of Sophia Institute.
Sophia Institute is a tax-exempt institution as defined by the
Internal Revenue Code, Section 501(c)(3). Tax I.D. 22-2548708.